Penelope's Renown

Penelope's Renown

MEANING AND INDETERMINACY IN THE *ODYSSEY*

Marylin A. Katz

PRINCETON UNIVERSITY PRESS
PRINCETON, NEW JERSEY

Copyright © 1991 by Princeton University Press
Published by Princeton University Press, 41 William Street,
Princeton, New Jersey 08540
In the United Kingdom: Princeton University Press, Oxford

All Rights Reserved

Library of Congress Cataloging-in-Publication Data

Katz, Marylin A., 1942–
Penelope's renown : meaning and indeterminacy in
the Odyssey / Marylin A. Katz.
p.   cm.
Includes bibliographical references and index.
1. Homer. Odyssey. 2. Homer—Characters—Penelope.
3. Penelope (Greek mythology) in literature. I. Title.
PA4170.P46K38   1991   883'.01—dc20   90-24444 CIP

ISBN 0-691-06796-1 (alk. paper)

This book has been composed in Linotron Galliard

Princeton University Press books are printed on acid-free paper,
and meet the guidelines for permanence and durability of the
Committee on Production Guidelines for book Longevity of the
Council on Library Resources

Printed in the United States of America by Princeton University Press,
Princeton, New Jersey

1 3 5 7 9 10 8 6 4 2

For Jay

εἰ μὲν δὴ γῆράς γε θεοὶ τελέουσιν ἄρειον,

ἐλπωρή τοι ἔπειτα κακῶν ὑπάλυξιν ἔσεσθαι.

CONTENTS

Preface	ix
Glossary of Greek Terms	xi

CHAPTER ONE
Indeterminacy and Interpretation ... 3
   Indeterminacy and Narrative Construction ... 6
   The Odyssey *and Its Readers* ... 12

CHAPTER TWO
The Construction of Absence (Books 1–4, 11) ... 20
   Kleos in the Odyssey ... 20
   The House of Atreus Story and Penelope's Kyrieia *(Books 1–4)* ... 29
   Penelope and Clytemnestra: The First Nekyia *(Book 11)* ... 48

CHAPTER THREE
Coming Home/Going Home (Books 13, 15, 16) ... 54
   Warnings about Penelope (Books 13, 15) ... 55
   Telemachus's Kleos ... 63
   From Nostos *to* Xenia *(Book 16)* ... 72

CHAPTER FOUR
What Does Penelope Want? (Books 18, 19) ... 77
   The Appearance before the Suitors (Book 18) ... 78
   The Character of Penelope's Character (Book 19) ... 93

CHAPTER FIVE
The Construction of Presence (Books 17–21) ... 114
   Narrative Disjunction and Textual Disguise (Books 18–19) ... 115
   Telemachus: Maturity and Misrepresentation ... 120
   Penelope: Return, Remarriage, and Xenia *(Book 19)* ... 128
   Dream and Toxou *Thesis* ... 145
   Summary and Conclusion ... 153

CHAPTER SIX
Duplicity, Indeterminacy, and the Ideology of Exclusivity (Book 23) ... 155
   Duplicity, Disguise, and Indeterminacy ... 155
   Duplicity and Complementarity ... 160

The Wedding Digression (23.117–73)   166
Homophrosynē, Anagnōrismos, and the Ideology of Exclusivity   170
Duplicity, Complementarity, and the Example of Helen   182

CONCLUSION
Indeterminacy in the *Odyssey*   192

Bibliography   197

Index Locorum   209

General Index   217

PREFACE

THE CORE idea from which this manuscript developed first took shape a very long time ago, in 1971, as a set of musings to which my mind wandered while writing my Ph.D. dissertation. For a long time after it was a class lecture for those early interdisciplinary courses in Women's Studies where many of us first embarked on a kind of scholarship for which graduate school had—if I may be permitted the distinction—prepared but not trained us. In 1980, Joy King invited me to participate with Sandra Gilbert in an Interdisciplinary Faculty Seminar at the University of Colorado at Boulder, and I first presented there an early version of what was to become Chapter Five. The stimulating discussions I shared with Joy and Sandra on that occasion encouraged me to pursue my work further, and I am grateful to Joy for that early opportunity to explore my ideas in an interdisciplinary framework. A later version of Chapter Five was part of a panel organized by Adrienne Munich on "Power and Gender in the Western Epic" at the 1984 Modern Language Association annual meeting in Houston; Adrienne too was unflaggingly enthusiastic about this project, and I thank her for this and several other opportunities that she took to foster my work. I am grateful also to Anthony Long and to an anonymous reader for *California Studies in Classical Antiquity* for helpful comments on another draft of this same chapter, which gave me some needed direction at an important moment. I tried out versions of Chapter Two at Dartmouth College in 1987, at the invitation of James Tatum, and at Princeton University and Hebrew University in Jerusalem in 1988, thanks to Froma Zeitlin and Ilana Klutstein, respectively. I am grateful to these colleagues for the opportunity to test in a public forum some of the ideas out of which this manuscript eventually grew. My many discussions and conversations over the years with my friend Froma Zeitlin have sustained and nourished me in countless ways, and have constituted as well the single most important influence on my own intellectual development. I hope that this work bears the stamp of that powerful influence, and that Froma will find it a welcome tribute to our friendship.

Among the other friends and colleagues who were patient enough to hear or read some part of the manuscript, and generous enough to offer comments on it, I would like to thank Molly Meyerowitz Levine, Hannah Roisman, and Jack Winkler. And I owe a special debt of gratitude to my Wesleyan colleague James O'Hara and my husband Jay Katz, who were kind enough to give their meticulous attention to the entire final draft. Their sensitive and insightful suggestions for revision led to the composition of another entire draft of the manuscript, and to their ruthless insistence on clarity and availability I owe whatever of those qualities this book now possesses.

Wesleyan University has been kind enough to support my work on this book though the generous award of a research grant in 1988–89 for translations from the German and Italian. The resulting renditions in the text of citations in German are the work of John Lawless at Brown University; the Italian citations have been translated into English by Luciano di Pietro at Yale, with the exception of the quotations from Russo 1985, which have been cited by the permission of the author from his own forthcoming translation. The final copy was patiently checked by Eisha Lee at Yale University.

The *Odyssey* is a poem whose affective center touches upon the most intimate and tender of human emotions, and it invites readers and critics alike to project onto its great figures the small particularities of their own lives. I began work on this manuscript at a time when my own experience of marriage was, like Penelope's, lived out among grown children as a memory of a former life become forfeit to the contingencies of human existence. I have brought it to completion during the first year of composing also the harmonies of a new marriage. And so I have dedicated this book to my new and newfound husband.

GLOSSARY OF GREEK TERMS

THESE TERMS appear frequently in my discussion, and are glossed on first occurrence. They refer either to well-known episodes in the *Odyssey*, or to personal and social characteristics that are specific to Greek culture and that are hence best left untranslated.

anagnōrismos — recognition, recognition scene
basileus (pl. *basileis*) — king, but not in the sense of monarch; rather, "man of preeminence"
basileus amumōn — "excellent king," referring to a simile that Odysseus applies to Penelope in 19.109–14, describing the prosperity that flourishes under his reign. (On the translation of *amūmōn* as "excellent" rather than, as it used to be interpreted, "blameless," see Russo 1985:244 ad 19.332; West 1988:77 ad 1.29)
dolos (pl. *doloi*) — a contrivance, trick, or strategem; trickiness
gamos — marriage, as an institution, involving the exchange of gifts
geras — power, privilege, especially that of being king on Ithaca
homilia — the meeting and conversation between Penelope and Odysseus in Book 19
homophrosynē — like-mindedness
kleos — glory, renown, reputation, rumor; what is heard or reported about someone
kyrieia — guardianship; entailing especially the responsibility for the welfare of a daughter, sister, mother, or wife, and including the obligation to arrange her marriage or remarriage
kyrios — lord and master, (male) head of household
lokhos — ambush, referring in the *Odyssey* both to the murder of Agamemnon upon his return from the Trojan War, and to the suitors' plot against Telemachus's life
megaron — great hall (of the palace); by metonymy, the palace itself
mētis — crafty intelligence, resourcefulness
mnēstērophonia — the slaughter of the suitors in Book 22
mythos — story, plot
nekyia — scenes in the underworld in Books 11 and 24
nostos — homecoming, return, specifically from the Trojan War
oikos — household, including the house itself, its land, and all persons associated with it (husband, wife, child, slaves, etc.)
parainesis — the advice offered to Telemachus by Athena in Books 1 and

sēma (pl. *sēmata*) — signs enabling the recognition of a person, usually consisting in clothing or a mark on the body

telos — the logical end of a poetic composition, in the sense of the goal toward which the action of its plot is aiming

tisis — revenge, scene of revenge, esp. the *mnēstērophonia* of Book 22

toxou thesis — the setting of the bow-trial in Book 21

xeinēion — gift of guest-friendship

xeinodokos — one who receives a stranger, host

xeinos — stranger, both guest and host

xenia — hospitality, the offering and accepting of hospitality; the establishment of a permanent and inheritable relationship between men and their descendants on the basis of an instance of *xenia*

Penelope's Renown

Chapter One

INDETERMINACY AND INTERPRETATION

TOWARD THE END of the *Odyssey*, in the second of the underworld scenes, the shades of the suitors slain by Odysseus and his son encounter those of the Trojan War heroes. Agamemnon is in the midst of explaining to Achilles how he came to be cheated of both his homecoming (*nostos*) and his renown (*kleos*), when the arrival of the suitors' shades interrupts his narrative. The suitor Amphimedon explains the suitors' collective fate, and includes an account of Penelope's weaving and the contest of the bow. Whereupon Agamemnon, overcome with admiration, addresses a congratulatory apostrophe to Odysseus, his living counterpart:

ὄλβιε Λαέρταο πάϊ, πολυμήχαν' Ὀδυσσεῦ,
ἦ ἄρα σὺν μεγάλῃ ἀρετῇ ἐκτήσω ἄκοιτιν·
ὡς ἀγαθαὶ φρένες ἦσαν ἀμύμονι Πηνελοπείῃ,
κούρῃ Ἰκαρίου, ὡς εὖ μέμνητ' Ὀδυσῆος,
ἀνδρὸς κουριδίου. τῶ οἱ κλέος οὔ ποτ' ὀλεῖται
ἧς ἀρετῆς, τεύξουσι δ' ἐπιχθονίοισιν ἀοιδὴν
ἀθάνατοι χαρίεσσαν ἐχέφρονι Πηνελοπείῃ,
οὐχ ὡς Τυνδαρέου κούρη κακὰ μήσατο ἔργα,
κουρίδιον κτείνασα πόσιν, στυγερὴ δέ τ' ἀοιδὴ
ἔσσετ' ἐπ' ἀνθρώπους, χαλεπὴν δέ τε φῆμιν ὀπάσσει
θηλυτέρῃσι γυναιξί, καὶ ἥ κ' εὐεργὸς ἔῃσιν.

(O fortunate son of Laertes, Odysseus of many devices,
indeed you got yourself a wife with great virtue.
How noble were the thoughts of excellent Penelope,
Icarius's daughter, and how well she remembered Odysseus,
her wedded husband. And so the renown (*kleos*) of her virtue
will not die, but the immortals will fashion a song
for people upon the earth, a lovely one of mindful Penelope.
Not like the daughter of Tyndareus, who devised evil deeds,
killing her wedded lord, and she will be a hateful song
among men; and she will make evil the reputation
of female women, even for the one who acts well.)

(24.192–202)[1]

---

[1] The *Odyssey* is cited from the text newly edited by West, Hainsworth, Heubeck, Hoekstra, Russo, and Fernández-Galiano (1981–86) and referenced in the Bibliography under *Odissea*.

Agamemnon appears to attribute *kleos* to Penelope here, and to base it upon her "noble thoughts" (ἀγαθαὶ φρένες), her "excellence" (ἀμύμονι), and her constancy (ὡς εὖ μέμνητ' Ὀδυσῆος). As we shall see below, however, not only are the meaning and interpretation of the passage disputed, but what is more, the particulars of Agamemnon's comparison assign to Clytemnestra one of the principal features by which Penelope's *kleos* in the *Odyssey* is defined. For Clytemnestra indisputably "devised evil deeds" (κακὰ μήσατο ἔργα), and the etymology of one form of her name makes explicit her reputation for "deviousness": *Klutai-mēstrē* "connotes that she is renowned for what she devised," since *mēstrē* is derived from the same verb *mēdomai* that appears in 24.199 (Nagy 1974:260; cf. Nagy 1979:37–38). It is equally the case, however, that Penelope's *kleos* is associated with her *mētis*, with a different but related capacity for devisings and artifice. She herself uses *mētis* to describe the weaving trick in her discourse with the disguised Odysseus in Book 19.158, and when *kleos* is first attributed to Penelope in the poem, it is in connection with this device.

In the assembly in Book 2, Antinous attributes to Penelope the traditional feminine virtues: "to know the working of fine fabrics and [to have] noble thoughts" (ἔργα τ' ἐπίστασθαι περικαλλέα καὶ φρένας ἐσθλὰς, 2.117). This same formulaic line characterizes, for example, the women of Phaeacia (7.111 = 2.117). But Antinous adds to this line the phrase "and crafty contrivances" (κέρδεά θ', 2.118) at the beginning of the next one. He goes on to describe the weaving trick, and he concludes by explaining that Penelope's *noēmata* ("scheming") distinguishes her from the traditional line of Greek heroines: "Of these [heroines], none was acquainted with *noēmata* like Penelope" (τάων οὔ τις ὁμοῖα νοήματα Πηνελοπείη / ᾔδη, 2.121–22). As a result, he explains to Telemachus, Penelope "is fashioning great glory (*kleos*) for herself, but for you [she is bringing about] a great dearth of livelihood" (μέγα μὲν κλέος αὐτῇ / ποιεῖτ', αὐτὰρ σοί γε ποθὴν πολέος βιότοιο, 2.125–26).

Penelope discusses her own *kleos* in Books 18 and 19, first when addressing the suitor Eurymachus in 18.251ff., and then when speaking with the disguised Odysseus in 19.124ff. She employs the same statement in both instances (18.251–56 = 19.124–29), and in both she repudiates the attribution of *kleos* to herself, asserting that when Odysseus went off to Troy, "the immortals destroyed my nobility and form and shape" (ἤ τοι ἐμὴν ἀρετὴν εἶδός τε δέμας τε / ὤλεσαν ἀθάνατοι, 18.251–52 = 19.124–25), and claiming that only upon his return "would my *kleos* be greater and so would it be better" (μεῖζόν κε κλέος εἴη ἐμὸν καὶ κάλλιον οὕτω, 18.255 = 19.128). Eurymachus does not use the term *kleos* when he addresses Penelope, but Odysseus had invoked it in connection with the famous simile of the *basileus amumōn* ("excellent king," 19.107ff.).

On the first occasion when the lines appear, Penelope's remarks are specifically attuned to Eurymachus's compliment, which attributes to her the combination of qualities that traditionally distinguish female excellence in the heroic world: "... Since you surpass [other] women in form and shape and sound mind within" (ἐπεὶ περίεσσι γυναικῶν / εἶδός τε μέγεθός τε ἰδὲ φρένας ἔνδον ἐίσας, 18.248–49; 18.249 = 11.337, of Odysseus). We can compare, for example, the characterization of the daughters of Pandareus in the *Odyssey:* "And Hera gave to them, beyond all women, form and understanding, and chaste Artemis endowed them with stature and Athena taught them the knowledge of renowned handiwork" ("Ἥρη δ' αὐτῇσιν περὶ πασέων δῶκε γυναικῶν / εἶδος καὶ πινυτήν, μῆκος δ' ἔπορ' Ἄρτεμις ἁγνή, / ἔργα δ' Ἀθηναίη δέδαε κλυτὰ ἐργάζεσθαι, 20.70–72).

In the second instance, in her conversation with the disguised Odysseus, Penelope goes on to describe the weaving trick, and so she provides an advertisement, as it were, of her *kleos*, at the very moment when she appears to repudiate it. Thus, even when she herself addresses it, Penelope's *kleos* comprises both constancy and cleverness. It includes both the beauty, probity, and skill that make her an exemplar of her sex, and the cleverness otherwise associated with the "evil doings" of women like Clytemnestra.

Traditionally, however, including in the ancient tradition, the understanding of Penelope's *kleos* is characteristically restricted to what we might call the simple or denotative meaning, to the level, that is, at which it is identical with her capacity for endurance and her faithfulness to Odysseus.[2] Aristophanes, for example, refers to Penelope as a γυνὴ σώφρων ("woman of discretion," "chaste woman"), an exception among womankind (*Thesmo.* 546–50). And the Latin elegiac poets of the first century B.C. canonized a Penelope who was the ideal of Roman chastity (e.g., *pia Penelope*, who together with *fida Evadne* is contrasted to the present-day *genus infidum nuptarum* in Propertius 3.13.24, and is adduced against the examples of faithless wives in Ovid, *Ars Amatoria* 3.15ff.). In Cavafy's poem "Ithaka," the specificity of Penelope's endurance is generalized into the figuration of the hero's goal as static, fixed, and purely referential:

> Ithaka gave you the marvelous journey.
> Without her you wouldn't have set out.
> She hasn't anything else to give.[3]

Critics, too, are inclined to underplay the complexity of Penelope's *kleos* in the *Odyssey*, and either to align themselves with Agamemnon in restricting it to her constancy, or to assimilate her craftiness to it. Beye, for ex-

---

[2] There are, to be sure, traces of a very different evaluation of Penelope in antiquity, which I discuss briefly at the beginning of Chapter Four; a fuller account is available in Jacobson 1974 and Mactoux 1975.

[3] From *C. P. Cavafy. Selected Poems*, trans. E. Keeley and P. Sherrard (Princeton: Princeton University Press, 1972). Cited by permission.

ample, says of Penelope; "Like the marriage bed rooted to the earth, she is the all encompassing stability at the end of man's adventuresome travels outside the home" (1974:98). A. T. Edwards explains, "Penelope's κλέος will be that she remained faithful to her husband in the face of the suitors, and through her μῆτις put them off until he returned" (1985:81); and Russo likewise, in characterizing Penelope as "renowned throughout Greece for her loyalty and cleverness," identifies this as her *kleos* (1982:9). Penelope's *kleos* in this system of meaning, then, is identical with her constancy, and it is equivalent to her identity with herself, as it were, which functions as a stable and unchanging reference point for the adventures of Odysseus.

But Penelope's *kleos*, properly speaking, must include everything reported about her in the *Odyssey*. I allude here to the etymology of *kleos*, according to which the word means "that which is heard," with specific reference to the poetic tradition (Nagy 1974:244–55). From this point of view Penelope is a far more ambiguous figure than tradition allows. This ambiguity appears especially in Books 18 and 19, where questions arise concerning the conscious (and unconscious) intentions behind Penelope's words and actions. These have generated an extensive debate in the scholarly literature. As the example of Antinous's speech in the assembly shows, however, this ambiguity is present in the text from a very early point.

In the study that follows, I focus on this double aspect of Penelope's renown, and in particular upon the implications of a *mētis* that entails the appearance of her yielding to the suitors' importunities while in actuality remaining faithful to Odysseus. For although on the denotative level of meaning Penelope's *kleos* is identical with her faithfulness, I argue that Penelope's *kleos* understood connotatively and from within an explicitly interpretive framework is itself a problematic concept, and that it is also one in which some of the poem's central narrative features are inscribed. I argue that there is a slippage between these two levels of meaning in the *Odyssey*, a disparity whereby the second, more inclusive understanding of Penelope's *kleos* destabilizes the narrower and simpler meaning, although without ever displacing it.

INDETERMINACY AND NARRATIVE CONSTRUCTION

I begin in Chapter Two by discussing the Odyssean revision of Iliadic *kleos*, and by examining the relation of this redefinition to the juxtaposition in the text of Penelope's *kleos* and Clytemnestra's renown. I argue that the House of Atreus story, in which Clytemnestra's *kleos* is embodied, is the governing paradigm for the development of the plot of the *Odyssey* as a whole and that the poem, from this point of view, can be read as the construction of an alternative to it.[4] In my view, then, the *Odyssey* is configured as a text, not only against the *Iliad*, and in an intertextual relationship with it, but intratextually with reference to traditions about the Trojan War (and in particular, the stories of Helen and Clytemnestra) that the narrative itself constructs.

The story of Agamemnon's *nostos* ("return") is represented in the poem as a fixed element in the tradition, and this endows it with a certain prestige.[5] In Book 1, Phemius is singing the "sad song" (ἀοιδὴ λυγρή, 1.340–41) of the "wretched homecoming" (νόστος λυγρός, 1.326–27) of the Greek heroes, and this story is given further shape in Book 3 as the history of Agamemnon's return (3.132ff.), and its culmination in a "wretched death" (λυγρὸς ὄλεθρος, 3.194; cf. 24.96) brought about by the woman who "preeminently cherished bitter wretchedness in her mind" (ἡ δ' ἔξοχα λυγρὰ ἰδυῖα, 11.432). Furthermore, this story intersects with the plot of *Odyssey* itself, since its *kleos* is not just a reference point in the past, like the κλέα ἀνδρῶν that Achilles sings in *Iliad* 9.189, or a hope for the future, like Hector's expectations regarding his own death (*Iliad* 22.304–5). Rather, the *kleos* of this story is being sung, and is thus entering the tradition, as the *Odyssey* is going on. And as I try to demonstrate in Chapter Two, there is a strong sense developed in the *Odyssey* that its narrative is drawn toward this tradition, and that its plot is ever veering in that direction.

I discuss the particulars of Penelope's marital status in Chapter Two, and I argue that the situation in which Penelope finds herself is a state of sociological indeterminacy constituted within the poem that is analogous to what we might call the geographical uncertainty associated with Odysseus (cf. Suerbaum 1968:176) and to the chronological indeterminacy of Telemachus's status. For the *Odyssey* as a narrative is premised explicitly on the uncertainty of Odysseus's whereabouts, and implicitly on the question of Telemachus's coming of age. These two open questions in turn combine to open the question of Penelope's status.

The plot of the *Odyssey*, then, is organized as a narrative complement to the state of radical indeterminacy around which its *mise-en-scène* is formulated. For Penelope, as Telemachus says early in the poem, "neither refuses the hateful marriage nor does she bring matters to a *teleutēn* [to an end]" (ἡ δ' οὔτ' ἀρνεῖται στυγερὸν γάμον οὔτε τελευτὴν / ποιῆσαι δύναται, 1.249–50 [= 16.126–27; cf. 24.126]). Likewise, the *telos* of the plot, the point toward which its action is aiming, is endowed with indeterminacy

---

[4] I am not referring here to the kind of alternative that West discusses, that is, to the possibility of a different tradition of Odysseus's wanderings that has been suppresssed in our present text (West 1981).

[5] Cf. Murnaghan 1987:125: "The *Odyssey*'s sense of its own story as extraordinary is expressed throughout in its use of the Agamemnon story, not just as a foil to the story of Odysseus, but as a norm from which the story of Odysseus departs."

from the beginning by the incorporation into the narrative of the House of Atreus story as a "master plot." In this respect, the indeterminacy of the poem is not represented as a state of directionlessness, as an absence of aim, but as an alternate plot toward which the action of the narrative is drawn.

This particular way of configuring indeterminacy is tied to the trope of disguise, and thus provides the mechanism for converting the problem of Odysseus's *nostos* into one of identity. For in order that Odysseus's return not replicate the established story of *nostos*, it must be disguised as something else, and I argue in Chapter Three that in the middle section of the poem the question of Odysseus's return is redefined as one of *xenia* ("hospitality"). Thus, the paradigm of the violation of *xenia* associated with the beginning of the Trojan War displaces the motif of the violation of *nostos* represented by the House of Atreus story, and the question of Penelope's fidelity is reformulated against the model represented by Helen. A reference to Helen and Clytemnestra together appears only once in the *Odyssey*, at approximately the midpoint of the poem (11.438–39), and this is correlated, in my view, with the shift in narrative direction.

At this point, then, the perspective of the poem is shifted from the outside world to the inside one, and from the end of the Trojan War to its beginning. By the same token, Odysseus's interaction with Telemachus in the middle section of the poem is played out as a conflation of the "truth" of *nostos* with the fiction of *xenia*. Unwilling at first to assume the role of *xeinodokos* ("host"), and then hesitant to accept his claim of paternity, Telemachus does finally recognize Odysseus as his father. This *anagnōrismos* ("recognition") effects the first stage of Odysseus's *nostos*, but immediately thereafter Telemachus and Odysseus conspire to disguise the plot of *nostos* as a scenario of *xenia*.

Disguise in the *Odyssey* is characterized especially by its close relation to "truth," and by the quality that it thus acquires of being something like a second-order representation of reality. This is preeminently so in the case of Odysseus's lying-tales, in which Odysseus's fictional self-representation represents a "true" characterization of who he is (Erbse 1972:154–57; Walcot 1977; Block 1985; Pucci 1987:98–109); and in Book 19 the account he gives to Penelope is characterized specifically as "fiction similar to truth" (ψεύδεα . . . ἐτύμοισιν ὁμοῖα, 19.203; see Pucci 1987:98 n. 1). Likewise, in disguising himself as a beggar, Odysseus exposes himself to sufferings and indignities that he had experienced as Odysseus, and that are part of his heroic character as Odysseus *polutlas* and as the man "who suffered much grief in his heart" (πολλὰ . . . πάθεν ἄλγεα ὃν κατὰ θυμόν, 1.4, 13.90; compare the reference to "my suffering," πάσχοντος ἐμεῖο, in the instructions to Telemachus at 16.275). Disguised as a stranger, a *xeinos*, on Ithaca, Odysseus replicates the role he had played as Odysseus on Scheria and elsewhere.

If, then, the *Odyssey* as a whole, as Pucci has said, "displays semblances as momentary ways of disguising an immutable self" (Pucci 1987:82), then it is also true that the poem develops a close relation between "semblance" and "being." Thus, both Telemachus and Penelope are conscripted in the second half of the poem into roles that resemble disguises,[6] and I argue in Chapter Five that these roles bear a specific and complex relation to the notion of "truth."

In Telemachus's case, the biological "fact" of his birth anchors his identity and provides the reference point for his assumption of the role of Odysseus's replacement, the role of his "double," as it were. Thus, Telemachus is specifically invited by Odysseus to play a part in which his capacity for duplicity will reveal the truth of his "blood": "If you are truly mine and [born] of our blood . . ." (εἰ ἐτεόν γ' ἐμός ἐσσι καὶ αἵματος ἡμετέροιο, 16.300; cf. 4.611). Odysseus authorizes Telemachus's enactment of this disguise, and this complicity ensures its ultimate status as semblance rather than truth.

The case of Penelope is more complex, since she is bound to Odysseus by no biological tie, and since the ambiguity of her sociological status calls into question her very relationship to him. The conjunction in the plot of mutually exclusive claims to her guardianship provides the mechanism for Penelope to acquire her own autonomy. And this accident of circumstances renders her free of subjection to male authority in a system that did not ordinarily countenance such a situation, precisely because she is now, in an important sense, outside the system. She is in a temporary state of liminality that nonetheless defines the poem's narrative limits.

I suggest in Chapter Five that Telemachus's accession to maturity has specific consequences for Penelope's status. His eligibility to assume the role of her *kyrios* ("guardian") provides the occasion for Penelope to resume her own role as mistress of the household. In this function she proffers *xenia* and thereby brings into being a relationship with Odysseus that is in important respects analogous to that of marriage. Yet Telemachus's coming of age also authorizes Penelope to take steps toward remarriage, and thus to dissociate herself from Odysseus, to resume her own state of unknownness to him and to become once again a stranger to him.

In Books 18–21, therefore, Penelope enacts both the role of the one who "stays beside her son and keeps everything secure" (μένει παρὰ παιδὶ καὶ ἔμπεδα πάντα φυλάσσει, 11.178 [= 19.525]; cf. 16.33, 16.74), and the role of the one who "follows after whoever is the best of the Achaeans

---

[6] See below, in Chapter Five, for a clarification of the difference between my argument and Murnaghan's claim that Laertes, Telemachus, Eumaeus, and Penelope experience a "disjunction between their nominal identities [as Odysseus's father, son, loyal servant, and wife] and the places they ought to occupy in the social world . . . which is represented . . . as a kind of disguise" (1987:25).

at wooing her in the halls, and who offers the most [bride-gifts]" (ἢ ἤδη ἅμ' ἕπηται, Ἀχαιῶν ὅς τις ἄριστος / μνᾶται ἐνὶ μεγάροισιν ἀνὴρ καὶ πλεῖστα πόρῃσιν, 16.76–77; cf. 11.179, 16.33–34, 19.528–29). Through the use of various devices, the text assimilates this situation to that of Odysseus and Telemachus, and hence invites us to interpret the relation between Penelope's two roles on the analogy of the relation between disguise and truth. Such phrases as "but her mind has other intentions" (νόος δέ οἱ ἄλλα μενοινᾷ, 2.92 [= 13.381; cf. 18.283]), along with references to Penelope's *mētis, kerdea* ("cunning"), and *dolos* ("trickiness"), as well as the thrice-repeated account itself of her weaving, combine with the profusion of narrative disjunctions in the text to endow her actions with the appearance of duplicity.

My interpretation of Penelope in the *Odyssey* requires that this aspect of the text be left unresolved. Thus, I do not argue that Penelope is consciously part of Odysseus's plot, in the manner of Harsh or Winkler; nor do I think that she is part of it all unawares, like Murnaghan and the unitarian interpretation in general; and I do not agree that she self-consciously designs for herself a multiplicity of plots, as in the feminist readings represented by Marquardt and Felson-Rubin.[7] Rather, I argue that the interpretive issue in the poem is constituted by the disjunction between the two conflicting directions of narrative action, and that this discordance itself should be regarded as meaningful. It operates in my view as the means for thematizing the relation between disguise and truth, and thus for calling into question, as it were, the reality of reality—including, to be sure, narrative reality itself.

This is an aspect of the *Odyssey* to which Pucci especially has drawn attention recently, and he has shown how the poem evidences throughout a self-consciousness about the nature of its own fictionality, which is construed as a "disguise of truth" (Pucci 1987:98). In my reading, it is Penelope who particularly embodies this aspect of the narrative, though not directly through the representation of her character.[8] From the point of view of character, Proteus might be the text's best embodiment, as Ferrucci recently has suggested: "[Proteus] epitomizes the spirit of the whole work. . . . The *Odyssey* is assuredly one of the works in which the problem of identity is most acutely and profoundly perceived. A doubt is often voiced by its characters: And what if I am not what I am? . . . The spirit of Proteus runs through the entire poem" (Ferrucci 1980:34, 37).

I argue in Chapters Four and Five that it is especially in the case of Penelope that there exists a dissonance in the text between the denotative and

---

[7] For presentation and discussion of these interpretive positions, see Chapter Four.
[8] Besslich remarks that at many points in the text "Penelope virtually 'personifies' the uncertainty and ambivalence of the situation on Ithaca" (1966:20).

connotative levels of meaning, or between what is said and what is implied. This indeterminacy is peculiar to the *Odyssey*, and it is incorporated into its narrative structure as its defining quality. It is particularly evident at the end of the poem, where it appears as a refusal of closure in the form of Teiresias's famous prophecy (Peradotto 1985), but it is manifested also as the liminal, temporary, "as if" or "almost" quality that characterizes both the settings and the figures of the narrative:[9] the divine assembly in Book 1 from which Poseidon is temporarily absent; the employment of disguise in divine epiphanies;[10] Calypso's retention of Odysseus on her island; Nausicaa on the verge of marriage in Book 6; the semi-divinity of the Phaeacians; Laertes' consignment to the outskirts of the property and his life on the threshold of death; the faithful dog Argus who waits to expire until his master's return; and so forth. Furthermore, the device of withholding or deferral, which is exemplified principally by Penelope,[11] operates as the master strategy of the text.[12] Thus, the thrust of my argument overall is to suggest that the longstanding problem of Penelope's character is better addressed from the perspective of narrative function than from that of psychological verisimilitude.

I conclude in Chapter Six with a treatment of the end of the *Odyssey* (principally Book 23), and with the discussion of the resolution of indeterminacy. I take up the conversion, through Penelope's recognition of Odysseus, of duplicity into *homophrosynē* ("like-mindedness"), and the conflation of the scene of *anagnōrismos* with the scene of *xenia*. I go on to argue that these recognized features of the text, and in particular the representation of *homophrosynē*, require further interrogation. For the reunion between Penelope and Odysseus is unquestionably the high point of the poem, and the *telos* toward which its narrative development tends. And this romantic aspect of the poem's dénouement has formed the basis of its interpretation from antiquity until the present time: the scholia report that

---

[9] Vester discusses the operation of an "as if" form of composition in both the *Iliad* and the *Odyssey*, which keeps before hearers possibility that action will go otherwise. Although Vester regards this as an "Homeric" form of composition, he abjures insistence on the identity of the poets of the *Iliad* and *Odyssey* (1968:433, 434).

[10] Reinhardt 1960b:43–44 and others have noted this feature of the poem; for a detailed examination of its implications for the poetics of the *Odyssey*, see Pucci 1986 and Murnaghan 1987:11–16.

[11] Withholding or deferral otherwise appears especially as the reluctance to reveal one's identity. On the apotropaic gesture involved in withholding the name, see Austin 1972; cf. also Fenik (1974:5–60), who discusses this strategy as one feature characterizing "scenes of secrecy and incognito" (p. 40), Bergren (1983), who discusses deferral, return, and narrative structure in the central books of the *Odyssey*, and Murnaghan, who discusses similarities between scenes of self-disclosure and scenes of divine epiphany (1987:12-19; cf. also Kearns 1982).

[12] Peradotto discusses briefly the analogy between Penelope's "evasive strategies" and their relation to "the poet's strategy" (1985:443, 451–53).

Aristophanes and Aristarchus located the "end" or "limit" (*telos* or *peras*) of the *Odyssey* at the point where Odysseus and Penelope make love, or, in the words of the text, "arrive welcome at the ritual of their bed of long standing" (οἱ μὲν ἔπειτα / ἀσπάσιοι λέκτροιο παλαιοῦ θεσμὸν ἵκοντο, 23.295–96).

I argue in the final chapter that these aspects of the text should be interpreted as constituting what I call the *Odyssey*'s ideology of exclusivity, and that this aspect of the poem accords primacy to the constructed or fictional aspects of human experience and social life. This outlook is partially consolidated in the poem through the idiosyncratic configuration of Penelope's recognition of Odysseus, and I examine this in detail, focusing in particular upon Penelope's refusal to countenance the simple substitution of "reality" for disguise, of Odysseus for the stranger.

This aspect of the poem also calls attention to the fiction of truth with which we endow our own constructions, and I conclude my discussion of the poem with a treatment of certain indications in Book 23 of the *Odyssey*'s self-consciousness about the fictionality of its own truth. In her recognition speech to Odysseus, Penelope instances the example of Helen as the story that might have been her own. Thus, she simultaneously consolidates her *kleos* by differentiating herself from Helen, and undermines the fixity of its meaning. Finally, the stories that Penelope and Odysseus relate to one another once they have been reunited in lovemaking are constructed so that they merge into the narrative action itself. In this way, the boundary between the two levels of representation—the narrative action and the narrative of the action—are blurred in the end. Penelope's *kleos*, then, as Agamemnon's speech in Book 24 suggests, remains in the *Odyssey* conditioned by an indeterminacy concerning its ultimate status that contradicts the superficial authority of its paradigmatic force.

The *Odyssey* and Its Readers

An adequate confrontation with the aspects of the text that I emphasize often involves attention to small details of the narrative structure, whose implications for the *gestalt* of the poem become clear only when an attempt is made to bring them into alignment with other details of the narrative. This means that I am interested in aspects of the *Odyssey* that become evident principally in the course of engagement in the interpretive enterprise, and that might therefore be considered a function of it. Consequently, in Chapter Four, where I discuss issues having to do with the representation of Penelope in Books 18 and 19, I include an extensive discussion of the interpretive history of the question. This is not intended as a comprehensive statement, but is designed rather as a representative selection of viewpoints indicating the principal trends in the scholarship, and as an opportunity to identify the interpretive premises underlying the various perspectives.

My own concern with indeterminacy in the text involves a bias of interest toward analytic, neoanalytic, and neounitarian interpretations of Homeric poetry, and away from the unitarian point of view as traditionally conceived. These approaches, which I define more fully below, are useful ones for me because they are concerned, as I am, with inconsistencies and discrepancies in the narrative, and with the dissonances that compose the *Odyssey*'s rough music. The unitarian reading, by contrast, is generally concerned to resolve discrepancies in the text, and often proceeds by making inferences about the actual or potential thought-processes of the characters. This not only obscures the constructed nature of the text by conscripting into the interpretive process an identity of character with person, but it also often blurs the line between what is in the text and what is in the world, including in the social world of the critic. Thus, for example, Thornton explains a discrepancy in the early part of the narrative between Athena's report to Telemachus that "cruel wild men are keeping [Odysseus] prisoner" and the narrative representation of Odysseus as a virtual prisoner on Calypso's island as a tactful adjustment of the truth in order to spare Telemachus doubts about his father's loyalty to his mother (Thornton 1970:106). Such an interpretation not only imports into the poem our own squeamish disapproval of the double standard, but also disregards the narrative construction of an equation between Calypso and "cruel wild men."

Neoanalysis is a "research trend" (Heubeck 1978:1) applied to the *Iliad* that has risen into prominence among German-speaking scholars since the postwar period, and that analyzes epic composition as an individual and even idiosyncratic adaptation of themes and motifs drawn from the epic cycle. It focuses upon the unique rather than traditional aspect of the relation of the poem to its sources, and in this, as well as in its emphasis on the deliberate and probably written rather than improvisational form of composition, it differs from the oral-formulaic theory of the Parry/Lord school. "The task of the neoanalyst," as Clark describes it, "is to clarify motifs" (1986:387), and as Kullmann explains further: "It was the original intention of neoanalysts to bridge the gap between unitarianism and (old) analysis. They believed that they could explain a great many of the irregularities observed by the analysts . . . by assuming that motifs of other epic contexts have been adopted to the plot of the *Iliad*" (Kullmann 1984:311).[13]

The *Odyssey* has not been subjected to a comprehensive examination from the neoanalytic point of view, despite the fact that, in the view of one

[13] For review and discussion of the theory, see Fenik 1968:229–40; Heubeck 1978; Kullmann 1981, 1984; and Clark 1986.

of the school's leading exponents, "the *Odyssey* is more strongly marked by the style of written composition than is the *Iliad*" (Kullmann 1981:35).[14] Nevertheless, a number of individual studies address problems in the *Odyssey* from this point of view, or from one that is closely related to it, namely the neounitarian perspective.

Kullmann's discussion of the three accounts of the weaving trick, "a classic *zetema* [interpretive issue] of ancient analysis," as he says (1981:35),[15] exemplifies the neoanalytic approach to the *Odyssey*. Kullmann isolates linguistic irregularities that show up differently in each of the three accounts, and he concludes: "The origin of this difficulty is clear. Because the weaving trick lies in the past, and also because it is consciously driven into the background of the *Odyssey*—apparently on account of its naiveté—Penelope must rush from deception to deception. The earlier weaving trick is only one deception among many.... Yet from what source did the poet of the *Odyssey* take these verses? Apparently from an old, shorter epic narrative in which the discovery of the weaving trick probably led directly to the preparations for the wedding, as the passage in Book 24 seems to indicate clearly" (Kullmann 1981:37).[16] Reinhardt discusses the weaving trick under the heading of "incidental stories . . . which by their nature do not enter into the form of the great epos."[17]

This example makes clear the continuity between neoanalysis and the older analytic perspective. And the analytic view, at least so far as the concentration on inconsistencies is concerned, itself derives from that of the Alexandrian scholiasts. Indeed, as Wilamowitz points out, the difference is principally one of final causes: "The idea of analytic criticism, i.e., seeking the explanation of the present text in its origins, never occurred to anyone in antiquity" (Wilamowitz 1927:48).[18]

---

[14] Although it would be possible to construe Schadewaldt's group of major articles taken together as an analysis of the poem from this perspective (Schadewaldt 1970b–g). For a critical evaluation of Schadewaldt's interpretation, see Eisenberger 1973:1-12.

[15] They are narrated at 2.93ff. by Antinous in the assembly; at 19.138ff. by Penelope in the interview with the disguised Odysseus; and at 24.127ff. by the shade of Amphimedon speaking with Agamemnon.

[16] "Die Entstehung dieses Anstosses ist klar. Da die Weblist zurückliegt und offensichtlich wegen ihrer Naivität in der Odyssee bewusst in den Hintergrund gedrängt wird, muss Penelope von List zu List eilen. Die vergangene Weblist ist nur eine List unter anderen. . . . Woher nahm aber der Odysseedichter diese Verse? Offenbar aus einer alten, kürzeren epischen Erzählung, wo wahrscheinlich die Entdeckung der Weblist sofort zu den Hochzeitsvorbereitungen führte, wie das an der 24-Stelle noch deutlich zu sein scheint."

[17] Thus, Penelope becomes "the 'clever' and 'understanding' one" in the epic "in a completely different, higher, nobler sense"—namely, in the manner demonstrated in Book 18: "Where the story teller needs weaving stool, work at night, and treachery, the epic poet in the Homeric style needs intimacy and spiritual contrast and the hidden ambiguity of words spoken and heard" (Reinhardt 1960a:20).

[18] "Der Gedanke an analytische Kritik, dass heisst, die Erklärung des Gegenwärtigen in seiner Entstehung zu suchen, ist niemandem im Altertum gekommen."

Neoanalysis, to be sure, adopts a unitarian perspective, but its interpretive method, like the analytic one, precludes accounting for the unity of the text. As Kullmann himself puts it: "Neoanalysis gives rise to a fundamental methodological problem. Does not the admission of absurdities and inconsistencies in the *Iliad*, through which one attempts to show this sort of adoption of motifs, entail the confession that the *Iliad* is a poetically defective work?" (Kullmann 1981:13).[19] And as Clay remarks of the analytic and neoanalytic points of view taken together: "All these views have a common foundation: discrepancies in the Homeric epics arise from the historical evolution of the poems. Internal contradictions can be explained by the incorporation of diverse materials at diverse periods without any attempt to bring about a synthesis" (Clay 1983:5).

I am generally interested in the same sets of discrepancies that are brought forward for treatment in analytic and neoanalytic readings, and I focus much of my discussion on the repetition of lines or of themes and motifs. Like the analysts, neoanalysts, and neounitarians, I am concerned to identify the fissures in the text, and to discuss how they condition its meaning, rather than, as in the unitarian approach, how they might be reconciled. I interpret these discrepancies differently, however, and I am in the end concerned to discover not so much a synthetic unity in the text as the basis on which the text establishes its narrative coherence.

A synthetic perspective in the more traditional sense has been provided from the researches of scholars concerned to specify what Uvo Hölscher designates as the *Odyssey*'s "transformation of folk-tale into epic" (Hölscher 1967b, 1978).[20] This orientation shares certain features with the separatist distinction between "the fairy-tale world of Greek sea sagas, and . . . the novella, which has not lost its character because it is connected with a hero's name and in the final analysis wears heroic dress" (Wilamowitz 1927:177).[21] In contrast to the analytic view, however, this "neounitarian" perspective is concerned neither with the genesis of the epic narrative nor with the reconstruction of its stages of development, but rather with the transition from what Hölscher calls "fact" ("the simple story is pragmatic, it consists of a series of facts" [1978:60]) into what, borrowing the term

[19] "Es stellt sich bei der Neoanalyse ein grundsätzliches methodisches Problem. Bedeutet das Zugeben von Ungereimtheiten und Brüchen in der Ilias, durch die man derartige Motivübernahmen zu beweisen sucht, nicht das Eingeständnis, dass die Ilias ein poetisch mangelhaftes Werk ist?"

[20] For a comprehensive review of scholarship on the folktale element in Homer from Radermacher and Kakridis to the present, see Petersmann 1981.

[21] "In der Odyssee sind wir in einer anderen Welt, genauer in zwei Welten, in der Märchenwelt der griechischen Schiffersagen, und in der Novelle, die darum ihren Charakter nicht verloren hat, dass sie an einen heroischen Namen geknüpft ist und in dem Endkampfe heroische Farben aufträgt, ähnlich wie es die Telemachie tut, namentlich in den Erzählungen, die doch nur noch zum Teil wirkliche Heldensagen geben."

from Reinhardt, he designates as "situation" ("the situation is existence in time, existence in which a person's circumstances, a psychological element, an internal relation are expressed" [ibid.:60–61; cf. Reinhardt 1960c:47–53, esp. 50]).

This transformation is generally regarded as having imparted to the material of saga a "new ethical aspect" (Petersmann 1981:59), and this has certain elements in common with that "tragic" vision of life which has come to be identified with "true humanity" itself in the western tradition.[22] Similarly, though from a less sentimental point of view, Peradotto has proposed the thesis that the narrative idiosyncrasies of the *Odyssey* should be understood as mediations of two contradictory forms of narrative structure oriented toward two opposite forms of outcome: myth eventuating in loss and even death, and *Märchen* resulting in the achievement of desire, especially sexual desire (Peradotto 1985).

I myself am interested less in questions of genesis or outcome, and more in how the poem's internal contradictions affect—and even more, effect—its overall meaning. In this respect my own project is similar to Peradotto's, with the exception that I do not identify the colliding elements with generic outlooks. And it has in common with the neounitarian perspective (and in particular that of Reinhardt) an interest in redefining the relation, in the representations of Penelope, between the facts of the matter, as it were, and the notion of interiority that is developed in the poem.

My understanding of the *Odyssey* has also been influenced by that extension of oral-formulaic theory which analyzes "themes," "motifs," "typical scenes," and other repeated patterns and elements in the Homeric poems, and shows how they function as compositional units. This interpretive approach originates, properly speaking, from Arend's *Die typischen Scenen bei Homer* (1933), which was a purely literary analysis; Arend's findings were adapted to oral theory by Lord, who proposed an extension of the principle governing Parry's definition of the "formula" to include the "theme." A formula, in Parry's classic formulation, is "a group of words which is regularly employed under the same metrical conditions to express a given essential idea" (Lord 1951:71); the theme, as Lord defined it, is "a recurrent element of narration or description in traditional oral poetry" (ibid.:73).[23]

---

[22] E.g., Petersmann remarks concerning divine intervention in Homeric poetry: "the intervention of the gods . . . usually extends only to their assistance in battle and crisis, where they inspire the heroes with courage, cleverness, and strength; they do not thereby spare them personal distress and grief. Yet it is exactly through this that they open up for the Homeric heroes, in contrast to the heroes of folktales, avenues to true humanity. To this has Homer, for the first time in the history of western man, erected in his epic poetry a shining monument" (1981:68).

[23] For discussion and illustration of this approach, see Lord 1951, 1960; Gunn 1971; and

This approach has itself been amplified and extended in a number of different directions (e.g., Nagler 1974), of which the most relevant for my purposes is Fenik's treatment of recurrent narrative patterns in the *Odyssey*. In *Studies in the Odyssey* (1974) Fenik attempts to isolate and identify typical situations such as that of "the nameless stranger" who lands on foreign shores and encounters a local inhabitant who aids him (Fenik 1974:153).[24] This pattern recurs in Books 6 and 13, when Odysseus arrives in Scheria and Ithaca, respectively, but its fullest extension and elaboration is represented by the *homilia* (the conversation between Penelope and Odysseus) of Book 19, which includes what Fenik calls "the standardized format for recognition and name-giving" (ibid.:47).[25] I discuss these same scenes in Chapters Four and Five, and I there address resonances with earlier, similarly constructed episodes in the text. By contrast with the interpretations of Fenik and other scholars who adopt similar critical perspectives, however, my analysis is not oriented toward problems of compositional technique. Thus I do not, in the end, regard the generation of "irony" (Fenik 1974:39–47) as an explanatory or interpretive principle that is sufficient to define either the meaning or the function of thematic and structural parallels.

In the end, I want to offer to the reader a new kind of unitarian interpretation of the *Odyssey*—or rather, of a large segment of it—that does not conceptualize the notion of unity in the traditional way, that is, as a unity of either plot or character defined with reference to the intention of the author. Nor, on the other hand, do I have in mind the kind of unity that is constructed in the mind of the reader or listener and is the subject of that school of criticism concerned with audience response.[26] Rather, my discussion proceeds from the unity of the *Odyssey* as we have it, and is concerned to discover what might be called the text's strategies of meaning, and to define the basis on which the text is experienced as having narrative coherence.

For as readers or hearers of the *Odyssey* we characteristically experience the poem as a seamless whole, like Penelope's web itself; and as a narrative the *Odyssey* possesses a compelling and irresistible quality that has often made it the centerpiece of contemporary narratological analyses. But a dif-

---

M. Edwards 1975; for a considered critique, see Tsagarakis 1979. See also Thornton 1984:73–109 on the "motif-sequence," and also Gaisser 1969.

[24] For other examples of analyses that focus on narrative patterns rather than typical scenes, see Fenik 1968, Gaisser 1969, and Hansen 1972.

[25] For analysis of the elements making up recognition scenes as a "motif-sequence," see Emlyn-Jones 1984; see also Murnaghan 1987.

[26] For a discussion of how this critical approach might be useful in the ancient context, see Pedrick and Rabinowitz 1986. In the discussion that follows, I make no assumptions about the so-called "original" form of the poem, or about its "originally" oral or written character.

ferent sense of the poem emerges when it is examined more closely, and when it is treated with the kind of contentious engagement with particular words and lines that scholars characteristically bring to bear. Then, the coherence of the text begins to disintegrate, unwoven like Penelope's web at night. My approach to the *Odyssey* is located at the juncture of these two points—in the evening or early morning boundary between the integrity of the composition as a whole and the discontinuity among its parts. I first try to show how it is scholarly analysis of the poem that has in fact discovered the units and elements of the *Odyssey*'s structure. I then try to understand, and to explain, how I think that overall structure of the poem brings about the effect of unity and coherence.[27]

Thus, my analysis focuses on the narrative logic of the *Odyssey*, and on the conditions by which the text establishes its meaning. For example, I am interested in understanding how the House of Atreus story functions in the poem as a dynamic force that gives direction to its plot, rather than as a static reference point: in how the narrative suggests at various points that that "other" story might become its own, might overwhelm the direction of its own narrative development. Likewise, in the case of the inconsistencies having to do with the presentation of Penelope in Books 18–21, I abjure equally the attempt to discover "what Penelope wanted" and the attempt to define what the poet intended. I focus instead on defining the meaning of the text as we have it, and on thematizing Penelope's inscrutability as the logic of narrative truth. In the end, I argue that we, as readers, occupy the position of Telemachus in Book 1, who, when asked for exact and precise information about his identity (ἀλλ' ἄγε μοι τόδε εἰπὲ καὶ ἀτρεκέως κατάλεξον, 1.206), replies:

> τοιγὰρ ἐγώ τοι, ξεῖνε, μάλ' ἀτρεκέως ἀγορεύσω
> μήτηρ μέν τέ μέ φησι τοῦ ἔμμεναι, αὐτὰρ ἐγώ γε
> οὐκ οἶδ'· οὐ γάρ πώ τις ἑὸν γόνον αὐτὸς ἀνέγνω.

> (Therefore I will speak openly to you, stranger, and precisely.
> My mother says that I am his [son], but I myself
> do not know. For no one ever knows his own begetting.)
>
> (1.213–15)

Similarly, the source of truth in narrative is inevitably opaque, its referentiality forever open to question. In the *Odyssey*, it is the figure of Penel-

---

[27] In this last respect, my approach to the *Odyssey* is similar to that of Sternberg to the Bible, in that it emphasizes "discourse" over "source": "As interpreters of the Bible, our only concern is with 'embodied' or 'objectified' intention. . . . Intention no longer figures as a psychological state consciously or unconsciously translated into words. Rather, it is a shorthand for the structure of meaning and effect supported by the conventions that the text appeals to or devises: for the sense that the language makes in terms of the communicative context as a whole" (Sternberg 1985:9).

ope through whom this indeterminacy is encoded into the text. Telemachus, as we shall see, is eventually required to accept his father with no sign given, on the basis of paternal authority alone (16.190ff.). And the burden of my argument overall is to establish the basis on which we, too, must ultimately yield to the authority of a text that will not, in the end, vouchsafe us a sure sign of its truth.

Chapter Two

THE CONSTRUCTION OF ABSENCE (BOOKS 1–4, 11)

THE ODYSSEY OPENS with an announcement that its subject is the man Odysseus and his homecoming, but Odysseus himself does not appear as a character in the narrative until Book 5. This absence from the text is not simply a nonpresence, a not being there; it is endowed in the first four books of the poem with a particular shape and form, centering, as I shall argue in this chapter, on the House of Atreus story. It is this story which initiates the action proper in the poem, for this is the *mythos* that Zeus takes up when he begins to speak to the gods (τοῖσι δὲ μύθων ἦρχε πατὴρ ἀνδρῶν τε θεῶν τε, 1.28). Zeus brings to mind, and thus to the foreground of the narrative, the story of Aegisthus, who seduced his cousin Agamemnon's wife and murdered Agamemnon when he returned home from the Trojan War; Aegisthus was himself killed in turn by Agamemnon's son Orestes. The details of the story appear in the narrative in a particular and, as I shall argue, significant order, and they construct an authoritative account of *nostos* toward which the story of Odysseus's return is drawn in the ensuing books of the poem.

When Penelope first appears, in Book 1, she attempts to stop the bard Phemius from singing the νόστος λυγρός ("wretched return") of the Achaeans (1.326–27), which she calls a "wretched song" (ἀοιδῆς λυγρῆς, 1.340–41), implying that it is inconsistent with the *kleos* of Odysseus, for whom she longs (1.344). Telemachus, with the brash authority of a character who speaks for the poet, overrides this subtext and asserts boldly the compatibility of the subject of *nostos* (1.354–55) with celebration in song (1.351). In the first part of this chapter I shall address myself to this association between *nostos* and *kleos*, and to the particularity of the Odyssean view of *kleos*. I shall turn then to the House of Atreus story, and to a discussion of how this particular *nostos* is constructed in the first four books as an alternative plot for the *Odyssey*'s narrative. I conclude with a treatment of the first *nekyia* (underworld scene), in Book 11, where the House of Atreus story is explicitly brought into association with Odysseus's own return.

KLEOS IN THE ODYSSEY

Agememnon, in the passage cited at the beginning of the first chapter, attributes *kleos* to Penelope, if lines 24.196–97 are translated as they are ordinarily understood: "And so the renown of her virtue will not die" (τῷ οἱ κλέος οὔ ποτ' ὀλεῖται / ἧς ἀρετῆς). Nagy, however, translates "the *kleos* of his *aretē* [virtue]" in line 196, referring to Odysseus, and explains with reference to line 193 that "it is his [Odysseus's] *aretē* 'merit' to have won a Penelope (rather than a Clytemnestra)": ἦ ἄρα σὺν μεγάλῃ ἀρετῇ ἐκτήσω ἄκοιτιν ("indeed, you got yourself a wife with great virtue"; Nagy 1979:37–38); A. T. Edwards adds that "σύν phrases are always adverbial in Homer, and never adjectival" (1985:88),[1] and so σὺν μεγάλῃ ἀρετῇ ("with great virtue") in line 193 must refer to the manner in which Odysseus "acquired" (ἐκτήσω) his wife, rather than to her personal characteristics. Segal adopts the traditional reading (1988:31), which is also defended by Untersteiner on the grounds that σὺν μεγάλῃ ἀρετῇ is equivalent to ἀρίστην (1968:59 ad 193).[2] And Heubeck reflects what is now the general opinion, in insisting that "the sense requires that σὺν μεγάλῃ ἀρετῇ be read with ἄκοιτιν, not with ἐκτήσω: it is an unusual construction" (1986:357 ad 193).

Edwards attempts to preserve the ambiguity by arguing that the speech awards *kleos* to both Penelope and Odysseus, and thus instantiates what he interprets as the interdependence of the *kleos* of husband and wife throughout the poem (Edwards 1985:73, 75, 79–83). Similarly, Pucci, with reference to this passage, says that "the text attributes *kleos*, 'glory,' 'reputation,' to Penelope and only through its ambivalent syntax also to Odysseus; but the grounds for his *kleos* remains Penelope's good and honest behavior" (Pucci 1987:217). Clay avoids the problem in these lines by incorporating an interpretation into her translation of 24.196–98: "And the gods themselves will make a pleasing song about them [Odysseus and Penelope] for mortals" (Clay 1983:111–12).

Penelope's *kleos* here, then, is awarded through "an unusual construction," and this is in keeping with its unusual content, which, as we have seen, includes an aspect of female renown more commonly associated with disrepute. For Penelope's *dolos* ("trickiness") and *mētis* ("wiliness"), like those of Odysseus, contribute to her *kleos*, and this represents a revision of the notion of *kleos* as we find it in the *Iliad* and as it is generally understood in the tradition.

Several recent studies in the intertextual relationship of the *Iliad* and *Odyssey* have dealt with specifying the Odyssean revision of Iliadic *kleos*, though none regards the application of the term to Penelope as particularly

---

[1] Citing Chantraine, *Gram.* II:136 (sect. 198), who reports that "σύν n'est accompagné que du seul datif (instrumental)" (ibid. II:134 [sect. 197]).

[2] Cf. also Ameis-Hentze-Cauer 1964, 2(2):164 ad 24.193, who translates "a wife with great virtue," and explains: "This is perhaps the way to translate ἀρετή here"; and Thalmann 1984:233 n. 20: "It seems more natural to understand the *kleos* and *aretē* as belonging to Penelope. . . ."

significant (Nagy 1979; Segal 1983; Edwards 1985; Pucci 1987). At the same time, in a number of recent studies of Penelope in the *Odyssey* influenced by feminist and anthropological/sociological theory, the passages referring to Penelope's *kleos*, when they are instanced, are not regarded as standing in need of interpretation (Emlyn-Jones 1984; Marquardt 1985; Murnaghan 1986, 1987; Felson-Rubin 1988; Winkler 1990).

Agamemnon's encomium is part of a larger statement in which he contrasts Achilles' *kleos* (24.94) with the λυγρὸς ὄλεθρος ("pitiful death") that he himself suffered ἐν νόστῳ, "upon his homecoming" (24.96); and indeed it is a feature of *kleos* in the *Odyssey*, like *olbia* ("prosperity") in Herodotus's famous saying,[3] that it can be abrogated by an untimely death: "just as a hero's death can enhance and preserve κλέος, so a wretched, unworthy death can destroy it" (A. T. Edwards 1985:74). In the *Iliad*, by contrast, the right kind of death confirms *kleos* (see Vernant 1982; Loraux 1982). Thus, Hector determines in Book 22 to remain outside the walls and face Achilles, "so that I might not die without a struggle and ingloriously (*akleiōs*), but having accomplished a great deed for even men hereafter to hear about" (μὴ μὰν ἀσπουδί γε καὶ ἀκλειῶς ἀπολοίμην, / ἀλλὰ μέγα ῥέξας τι καὶ ἐσσομένοισι πυθέσθαι, *Iliad* 22.304–5). And Achilles, in a well-known speech in Book 9, balances *nostos* and a long life against death and the achievement of *kleos* (*Iliad* 9.412–16). *Nostos* in the *Iliad* is the spatial equivalent of cowardice, and thus *nostos* destroys *kleos* in that poem. For example, when Agamemnon reports to the assembly in Book 2 of the *Iliad* that Zeus has advised returning home, he regrets that "this will be a disgraceful thing for even men hereafter to hear about" (αἰσχρὸν γὰρ τόδε γ' ἐστὶ καὶ ἐσσομένοισι πυθέσθαι, 2.119; compare "for even men hereafter to hear about" in 22.305 cited just above).

Thus, the first aspect of the *Odyssey*'s revision of *kleos* is not actually a revision of *kleos*, but of *nostos*, or rather, of the relation between *kleos* and *nostos*. In the *Odyssey*, a successful *nostos* confirms *kleos*, and a disastrous one destroys it. And so, as Nagy argues, "we see in the *Second Nekuia* a triadic assignment of *kléos* to Agamemnon, Achilles, and Odysseus. Odysseus gets the best *kléos*, through his wife. Through Penelope, he has a genuine *nóstos*, while Agamemnon gets a false one and Achilles, none at all"; consequently, Odysseus is the "best of the Achaeans" in that "he has won both *kléos* and *nóstos*" (Nagy 1979:38, 39). Similarly, A. T. Edwards argues that "the ultimate implication" of the presentation of *kleos* in the *Odyssey* "is that Odysseus has won a *kleos* surpassing even that of Achilles" (1985:89). And Rüter regards the *kleos* of Odysseus as equivalent to that of Achilles: "What remained unresolved in the earlier Hades scene now has become fully clear:

---

[3] Solon, reflecting on Croesus's fortune, warns him not to regard a man as prosperous, but rather to call him fortunate, until he reaches the end of his life (πρὶν δ' ἂν τελευτήσῃ, ἐπισχεῖν μηδὲ καλέειν κω ὄλβιον, ἀλλ' εὐτυχέα, 1.32.7–8).

Odysseus has won his fame and his return and can for that reason be put on the same level with Achilles. Achilles' fame is not diminished, but the fame of Odysseus is at least equal to his" (Rüter 1969:253).[4]

As Segal points out, however, this superiority of Odyssean *kleos* must also be considered ironic, in view of its definition through *dolos* ("trickery"), specifically, the *dolos* of the encounter with Polyphemus in Book 9: "I am Odysseus the son of Laertes, who am a concern to men [because of] all my *doloi*, and my *kleos* reaches to the heavens" (εἴμ' Ὀδυσεὺς Λαερτιάδης, ὃς πᾶσι δόλοισιν / ἀνθρώποισι μέλω, καί μευ κλέος οὐρανὸν ἵκει, 9.19–20; Segal 1983:26–32). Similarly, Edwards says that "Odysseus' κλέος will be the revenge he was able to exact against all odds by relying upon his μῆτις" (1985:81). Pucci, however, restricts *kleos* derived from the exercise of *dolos* and *mētis* to Odysseus's exploits in the *Iliad* and in connection with the capture of Troy (1987:216–17), and it may be a *kleos* of this kind to which Penelope refers in Book 4, when she speaks of Odysseus as a man "preeminent in every kind of virtue (*pantoiēisi aretēisi*) among the Greeks, a noble man, whose *kleos* is widespread throughout Hellas and the middle of Argos" (παντοίησ' ἀρετῇσι κεκασμένον ἐν Δαναοῖσιν, / ἐσθλόν, τοῦ κλέος εὐρὺ καθ' Ἑλλάδα καὶ μέσον Ἄργος, 4.725–26 = 815–16).

In view of the restriction of the phrase *pantoiēisi aretēisi* ("every kind of virtue") to association with Odysseus (cf. 18.204–5, where Penelope describes herself as "longing for the *pantoiēn aretēn* ["various virtue"] of my dear husband"), and the usage otherwise whereby *pantoioi* ("every kind of") and *pantes* ("all") qualify *dolos/doloi* (Pucci 1987:61–62), perhaps *pantoiēisi aretēisi/pantoiēn aretēn* should be interpreted as instances either of textual self-reflexivity or of Penelope's awareness of her husband's outstanding qualities. Telemachus, when he is first reunited with his father, indicates that he has heard about Odysseus's "great *kleos*" as both a spearsman and a shrewd councillor (ὦ πάτερ, ἤ τοι σεῖο μέγα κλέος αἰὲν ἄκουον, / χείράς τ' αἰχμητὴν ἔμεναι καὶ ἐπίφρονα βουλήν, 16.241–42), and it may be that Penelope too alludes to some such combination of qualities.[5] In any case, the association between *kleos* and *dolos* that Odysseus makes in his boast to Polyphemus reflects the characterization through which he is principally represented in the *Odyssey*, and for which he is known also in the *Iliad*.[6]

[4] "Was in der früheren Hadesszene noch hatte offenbleiben müssen, ist jetzt völlig deutlich geworden: Odysseus hat seinen Ruhm und seine Heimkehr gewonnen und kann darum mit Achill auf eine Stufe gestellt werden. Der Ruhm Achills wird nicht verkleinert, aber der des Odysseus ist ihm mindestens ebenbürtig."

[5] Thalmann argues, on the basis of the representation of Odysseus as poet *and* warrior, that it is he, and not Achilles, who "fulfills the [Iliadic, i.e. 9.443] ideal of the epic hero" (1984:170–84; citation p. 182).

[6] For a discussion of Odysseus's *dolos* and *mētis* from a sociological point of view, see Farron 1979–80. On *pantoiēn aretēn*, see also 13.38ff.

Penelope's *kleos*, too, participates in the ambiguity of an association both with traditional female excellence and with *dolos* and *mētis*. And the *Odyssey*'s own self-consciousness as a text about the ambiguity of the *kleos* that it celebrates is indicated by the unqualified positive valence that it assigns such characteristics by associating them with Athena ("and I among all the gods have *kleos* for my *mētis* and crafty contrivances," ἐγὼ δ' ἐν πᾶσι θεοῖσι / μήτι τε κλέομαι καὶ κέρδεσιν, 13.298–9), along with the unqualified negative representation of these same characteristics where (and only where) they are associated with Aegisthus and Clytemnestra: the adjective *dolomētis* ("tricky-crafty") occurs six times in the poem, five in connection with Aegisthus (1.300 [= 3.198,308]; 3.250; 4.525), and one with Clytemnestra (11.422). In addition, the murder of Agamemnon is described by both Menelaus and Odysseus as a *dolos* of Clytemnestra (4.92; 11.439). The *kleos* of both Odysseus and Penelope, then, is defined both through *dolos* and *mētis* and through the virtues traditionally associated with male and female excellence. The ambiguity of the former qualities, however, opens the pathway through which the *kleos* of Odysseus and Penelope might become their ἀκλεία ("lack of renown") or δύσκλεια ("ill-repute"): Agamemnon's λυγρὸς ὄλεθρος ("pitiful death"), of which Odysseus stands at risk at several points in the narrative, not all of them having to do with Penelope;[7] and the στυγερὴ ἀοιδή ("hateful song") of Clytemnestra that Agamemnon assigns to her in Book 24.

There are other dimensions to Odyssean *kleos*, and these will be taken up in succeeding chapters. For the moment, let us return to Agamemnon's encomium, and to implications of the χαρίεσσα ἀοιδή ("lovely song") that he claims the immortals will compose on Penelope's behalf. As Redfield explains in his excellent brief essay on the subject, *kleos* is a form of "social identity": "A man has a history.... His story is in a certain sense himself ... and from one point of view the most real version of himself.... In Homer a man may be conceived of as a narrative, may conceive himself as a narrative" (Redfield 1975:34).

This aspect of *kleos* is especially prominent in the *Odyssey*, which self-consciously reflects upon *kleos* as a creation of the poetic tradition (Nagy 1974:244–55; Segal 1962:23–24, 1983:27) and as "that which is heard," not only in common discourse but with specific reference to repetition in song.[8] Thus, in the *Iliad* Hector refers to his own *kleos* (ἐμὸν κλέος, 7.87–91; 6.446; cf. 22.304–5), and he thereby expresses a certain self-consciousness about the implications of his achievements on the battlefield (Segal 1983:25–26). In the *Odyssey*, however, as Segal points out, Odysseus not

---

[7] E.g., when he is in danger of perishing in the shipwreck of Book 5 (line 311); cf. also 1.240, 14.371.

[8] Cf. Pucci's discussion of the relationship between κλέος as repetition ("hearsay") and as fame (1980:163–86).

only undergoes the experiences that are the subject of *kleos*; he also assumes the role of singer and recounts his own adventures, in that long central section of the narrative composed as what Reinhardt calls an "Ich-Erzählung" ("first-person narrative," Reinhardt 1960c:58–62; Segal 1983:26; cf. also Suerbaum 1968).

The same is true for Penelope, who likewise becomes the celebrator of her own *kleos*, but without explicitly appropriating this role for herself. For at the opening of the *homilia* in Book 19, just after repudiating the *kleos* of the *basileus amūmōn* ("excellent king") that Odysseus wants to attribute to her, she describes the weaving trick. It is this *dolos/mētis*, in particular, through which Penelope remains faithful to Odysseus while appearing to do otherwise, that makes up Penelope's *kleos*. And this device, as we have seen, is described in the poem three times, and with a lack of variation that has seemed to editors and commentators to call for explanation.[9]

It is significant that this story is related first in a public venue, and indeed on the only occasion when such a world on Ithaca is represented in the poem—in the first assembly (2.7ff.). There are allusions to other public assemblies in the poem (e.g., 17.52, 72; 20.146), but none is represented; at 16.376–77 the suitors are concerned that Telemachus might call an assembly and reveal publicly their attempt on his life. The assemblies in which the suitors devise their plans are all private, for obvious reasons: the second assembly, in which the suitors plot Telemachus's ambush, transpires "in front of the palace of Odysseus" (πάροιθεν Ὀδυσσῆος μεγάροιο, 4.625); the third similarly takes place in the courtyard (αὐτοῦ δὲ προπάροιθε θυράων ἑδριόωντο, 16.344); and the last, from which the youth and elders are excluded, occurs on the seashore (οἱ δ' ἀνστάντες ἔβαν ἐπὶ θῖνα θαλάσσης, 16.358; cf. 361–62).[10] This first repetition, then, of the account of Penelope's *dolos* in the poem's only public assembly makes it a *kleos* in the etymological sense (i.e., *kleos* from *kluō*, "that which is heard [publicly]"). Its second repetition, in Book 19, makes it *kleos* as "glory" or "fame"; and with the third account of it in Book 24, as Agamemnon makes clear, it enters the realm of heroic song. This threefold repetition, in three different contexts, illustrates the process of formation of *kleos*, and it is significant in this respect that Penelope, unlike Odysseus, has no *kleos* outside the *Odyssey*, as Pucci points out: "The *Odyssey* and its tradition must be at the origin of [Penelope's] *kleos* [in Book 19], for in the *Iliad* Penelope has no *kleos* at all, since she is never mentioned" (1987:219 n. 12).[11]

[9] The immense bibliography on this subject, which extends to take in the discrepancy in the account of the bow-trial, need not concern us here; for a comprehensive discussion and analysis of the principal issues, see Bona 1966:107–22; for further discussion, see Kullmann 1981:37 n. 86.

[10] For the typical elements of the *Odyssey*'s assembly scenes, see Arend 1975:120–21.

[11] Cf. the remarks of Mackail: "There is an instinctive tendency to wonder how the story

The account of the story that Penelope gives to Odysseus in the *homilia* is a complex act, taking place as it does under the sign of *kleos*, a discussion of which, as I remarked, precedes the narrative. Beyond this, Penelope's story is given in place of Odysseus's own tale. For to him as guest, and not to her as host, belongs, by the conventions of etiquette that govern such scenes of *xenia*, the role of accounting for oneself (see below, Chapter Five, for further discussion). It is only when Odysseus demurs at providing an account of himself that Penelope's own intervenes. She, too, then becomes the author of an *Ich-Erzählung*, and in her case, as in his, the transformation from the third to the first person makes a difference that enables the narration to become a form of self-characterization.[12]

The last of the accounts of Penelope's *dolos* takes place in the underworld, in the *nekyia* of Book 24, and it is this account which fixes it as *kleos*. That is should transpire in the world of the dead is perhaps the poet's own pun on the notion of κλέος ἄφθιτον ("undying fame"),[13] but more important is the fact that through this account Penelope's *kleos* is inserted into the world of Iliadic heroism. For the rest of Book 24 is also much concerned with accommodating the world of the *Odyssey* to the heroic standards of the *Iliad*, and the narrative of the battle with the suitors draws freely on Iliadic themes and motifs (on this section of the narrative as an *Iliasimitatio*, see Müller 1966:161–64).

Agamemnon's encomium opens by invoking Odysseus, and congratulates him heartily, but critics have found it troublesome that he then goes on to celebrate the *kleos* of Penelope. As Finley remarks, "That comes near making our *Odysseia* a *Penelopeia*" (1978:3). And as we saw above, it is generally assumed that Odysseus's *kleos* is included in hers here, but even this interpretation is unsatisfactory from the point of view of Odysseus. Pucci, for example, regards Agamemnon's statement in Book 24 as consistent with what he identifies as the general tendency in the *Odyssey* to deprecate Odysseus's *kleos*, particularly in contrast with that of Achilles: "Such a limited concession [of *kleos*] to Penelope's husband is set against the preceding celebration of Achilles' *kleos* in its Iliadic splendor.... The contrast

---

went on . . . the more so, the more that one appreciates the vivid reality of Penelope's figure. . . . Even now, after so many centuries, [Penelope] makes us try to get beyond the picture, as though it went on behind the frame. . . . It is difficult to realize that, out of the *Odyssey*, the Penelope of the *Odyssey* does not exist at all" (1916:19).

[12] Cf. Reinhardt's remark on this feature as it concerns Odysseus: "Self-characterization, inasmuch as more and more emphasis is transferred from adventures to the enduring self, is already something very developed" (1960c:58 n. 1).

[13] This small but highly significant Homeric *hapax legomenon* has been the focus of a very large debate in recent years; Floyd (1980), disputing Nagy's interpretation of the phrase κλέος ἄφθιτον, argues that celebration in song is not germane to the meaning of the phrase; he is answered by Nagy (1981); and cf. A. T. Edwards 1985:78 n. 18. See also Martin 1989:182–85. On ἄφθιτον, see also Clay 1981–82 and Finkelberg 1986.

is striking: Odysseus's *kleos* is debased to a generic reputation for his share and merits in Penelope's domestic virtues" (Pucci 1987:217).

Unquestionably, Penelope's *kleos* is given prominence here. Despite what Agamemnon says, however, this *kleos* should not be understood as a celebration of domestic harmony.[14] For Agamemnon's statement must be interpreted as part of a complex scene of interrupted discourse[15] that formulates the final intersection of the House of Atreus story with the *mythos* of the *Odyssey*. As Book 24 opens, Hermes is conducting the shades of the slaughtered suitors to Hades. At the point when these new arrivals come upon the heroes of the past, a discourse between Achilles and Agamemnon is in process, a device through which the epic tradition of *nostos*[16] encounters the *Iliad*—for in response to Achilles' surprise to find him in Hades, Agamemnon summarizes the epic tradition from the point of Achilles' death to that of his own (24.35–97).

As Agamemnon is on the point of narrating to the shade of Achilles the particulars of the fate he met "at the hands of Aegisthus and my deadly wife" (24.97), the heroes are joined by the suitors. At this point, then, Agamemnon's own story is interrupted by Amphimedon's account of Penelope's *dolos* and of the *mnēstērophonia* ("slaughter of the suitors;" 24.121–90). This narrative displaces and so substitutes for the story in the first *nekyia*, in which Agamemnon had detailed for Odysseus the murder that "Aegisthus devis[ed] together with my deadly wife" (11.409–34).[17] But this attempt to complete the formation of the epic tradition by displacing Agamemnon's *nostos* with that of Odysseus is only partially successful. For Agamemnon responds to Amphimedon's story with the apostrophe to Odysseus that we have discussed, and so this account concludes with the same "moral" that closed the narrative in the first *nekyia*: "[Cly-

---

[14] Or, indeed, sentimentalized in the manner of, e.g., Wender: "[Homer's point in Book 11 as in 24 is that] life itself is the most important thing; a glorious funeral is less to be desired than a fine son; Odysseus' human domesticity and self-preservation are better in the end than Achilles' divinity and glorious death. It is not, perhaps, a very noble point of view—but it is a lucid and sensible one" (1978:41–43; citation p. 43).

[15] Fenik discusses the structure of the scene in detail and responds to analytic criticism of the scene (1974:78–80); he remarks also: "The contrast between the two wives (and the comparisions of Telemachos-Orestes and Odysseus-Agamemnon) begins early in the poem and reaches its climax in 24" (ibid.:79).

[16] On the word *nostos* as the title of an epic tradition that related the homecoming of the Achaeans, see Nagy 1979:97 n. 6.2; see also Heubeck 1988:53 n. 10, and Frame 1978.

[17] Another sign of the narrative equivalence of the two accounts, by which the second story inverts the first, is the relationship between Agememnon's description in 11.412ff. of his comrades slaughtered like swine at a wealthy man's marriage-feast, and the suitors' report that their bodies are lying still in Odysseus's halls (24.186ff.), where the fictive marriage-feast has just taken place (23.130ff.). D'Arms and Hulley comment on this "similarity of setting," which they think "Homer intentionally used . . . to heighten the contrast in the outcome of the action" (1946:213). Cf. Segal 1983:46 n. 46.

temnestra has poured shame upon/made evil the reputation for] all women, even she whose behavior is virtuous" (θηλυτέρῃσι γυναιξί, καὶ ἥ κ' εὐεργὸς ἔῃσιν, 11.434 = 24.202).

This narrative equivalence of the stories of Clytemnestra and Penelope is the final manifestation in the poem of the well-known theme of the House of Atreus introduced in the epic's opening segment (1.32ff.) and operative throughout the *Odyssey* as a paradigm for the household of Odysseus (Kunst 1924–25; Lesky 1967; Hölscher 1967a; Matsumoto 1981). Here, as elsewhere, the polarity appears to be a clear one. Agamemnon awards a χαρίεσσα ἀοιδή ("lovely song") to Penelope, and a στυγερὴ ἀοιδή ("hateful song") to Clytemnestra, and this accords with tradition—perhaps even, as Nagy has suggested, with a "formal tradition of praise poetry centering on the theme of Penelope . . . [and] blame poetry about Clytemnestra" (1979:36 n. 1). About στυγερὴ ἀοιδή Nagy remarks, "We have here one of the clearest instances of blame as blame poetry" (ibid.:255 n. 1).

As we have seen, however, Agamemnon's judgment in Book 24 is only superficially conclusive. For the example of Clytemnestra is advanced as the general type, and displaces that of Penelope in the end. Commentators are all too quick to dismiss Agamemnon's final sentiments as the justifiable bitterness of a husband betrayed, or as a typical expression of Greek misogyny. Stanford, for example, explains: "Generalizing from his personal experience . . . as men are apt to do, he condemns the whole sex in words that are the first in a long series of anti-feminist gibes in Greek literature" (Stanford 1978; 1:396–97 ad 441ff.). Similarly, Eisenberger says that "for Agamemnon the shameful betrayal by his wife naturally stands in the foreground: he wants to stigmatize her faithlessness" (Eisenberger 1973:181–82).[18] And Wender too regards Agamemnon's views as self-explanatory: "Agamemnon is . . . (understandably) a considerable misogynist, who in the eleventh book had called woman an untrustworthy lot . . ." (Wender 1978:38).

Agememnon's words, however, are not merely a reflection of his personal experience; they are also a second-order means of refusing closure to one of the principal questions in the poem, that having to do with Penelope's faithfulness and its paradigmatic force. As Murnaghan's more subtle reading of the situation makes clear, "While the *Odyssey*'s portrait of Penelope is one of the most sympathetic treatments of a female character in Greek literature, that portrait is also placed in a wider context of misogyny through the presentation of Penelope as an exception to the general rule. The poem self-consciously depicts the formation and authorization of a

---

[18] "Für Agamemnon . . . steht ganz natürlich der schändliche Verrat seiner Gattin im Vordergrund, ihre Treulosigkeit will er brandmarken."

tradition of misogyny even as it places a counterexample at the center of its story" (Murnaghan 1987:124).

Thus the *kleos* operative in Agamemnon's speech only superficially refers just to Penelope. It includes not only the *kleos* of Odysseus, but also the *kleos* of the whole of the poem, which, as I argue, is worked out intratextually as a controversy with the "other" myth of return. Therefore, this final example in the poem of *kleos* meaning "fame," "glory," "renown," should be understood as an instance of the poem's reflection upon its own strategies for generating *kleos* in the sense of "glorious song." This, certainly, is the burden of Agamemnon's reference in lines 197–98 to a χαρίεσσα ἀοιδή and of his assignment of its composition to the gods from whom the bard traditionally "hears" the very song that he recites (cf. Nagy 1979:16). And so, as Heubeck puts it, "By means of song Penelope's κλέος will become immortal. It is significant of the poet's conception that here the gods are the ones who shall 'compose' the song for Penelope: they are the ones who put the song into the poet's mouth. On the other hand, the poet is fully aware of his lofty performance: together with Penelope's κλέος, his own κλέος will become immortal" (1986:357–58 ad 197–98).[19]

The House of Atreus Story and Penelope's *Kyrieia* (Books 1–4)

The House of Atreus story appears first in the poem without any suggestion of Clytemnestra's fault (1.35–43), and last as a condemnation of her alone (24.199–202): we can compare "Aegisthus killed him upon his homecoming" ([Αἴγισθος] τὸν δ' ἔκτανε νοστήσαντα) in 1.36 with "[she,] having killed her wedded husband" (κουρίδιον κτείνασα πόσιν) in 24.200. This internal rewriting of one of the poem's central motifs can be partially explained from the neounitarian point of view as a function of genre redefinition, and thus as resulting from the adaptation of folktale motifs to the epic context. Thus, in Hölscher's view, the House of Atreus story constructs within the poem "drei Heldenschicksale" (three [types of] heroic fate), which together make up a unity of possible outcomes for the hero—that of Aegisthus, that of Orestes, or that of Agamemnon. Odysseus's uniqueness is defined in part as his avoidance of conformity to these traditional narrative options; instead, he exemplifies a new pattern formulated on a conjunction of the "happy ending" with the just and righteous king (Hölscher 1967a:12).[20] Hölscher also remarks that the version of the

---

[19] "Per mezzo del canto il κλέος di Penelope diverrà immortale. È significativo della concezione del poeta che siano qui gli dei coloro che 'comporranno' il canto per Penelope: sono essi che pongono il canto in bocca al poeta. D'altra parte il poeta è cosciente della sua alta prestazione: con il κλέος di Penelope diverrà immortale anche il suo proprio κλέος."

[20] On the narrative implications of the "happy ending," see Peradotto's remarks on folktale and myth in the *Odyssey* (1986:450); and cf. Hölscher 1978 and Petersmann 1981.

House of Atreus story lacking the *Gattenmord* ("husband-murder") and *Muttermord* ("mother-murder") appears only in the *Odyssey*. The lyric and tragic genres, by contrast, know Orestes only as a "Muttermörder" (1967a:2). Pope's translation of Agamemnon's words reflects the paradigmatic force of the tragic representation of the myth: "her [Clytemnestra] shall the Muse to infamy prolong, / Example dread! and theme of tragic song! / The gen'ral sex shall suffer in her shame, / And ev'n the best that bears a Woman's name."

From this same point of view, the House of Atreus story is generally understood as providing a "foil" for the development of Penelope's character; as Hölscher remarks concerning the "bad wife" theme, "The story is developed toward providing a foil for Penelope" (1967a:6).[21] By this reading, however, the development of Penelope's character in the poem is entirely subordinated to that of Odysseus's and is reduced in fact to being a function of it: "Because Odysseus must be the cautious one, the shadow of unreliability must fall on Penelope" (1967a:7).[22] In what follows, I argue that the *Odyssey*'s representation of the House of Atreus story is a far more complex and dynamic matter, and that the story operates throughout as an alternative plot that threatens to attract the *Odyssey* into its orbit. Its elements are spelled out early in the poem and come to the foreground at critical junctures throughout it. The clearest example of this dynamic is the conjunction of the ambush of Agamemnon with the suitors' plan to kill Telemachus, which occurs in Book 4 when the scene of narrative action shifts from Sparta to Ithaca. The ambush of Agamemnon is related only in Book 4, and thus only just prior to this transition. The effect of this conjunction is to suggest that the story of Telemachus is being brought into conformity with that of Agememnon.

The House of Atreus story is first introduced in the poem in connection with a well-known statement regarding moral responsibility, in which Zeus both condemns mortals for "their own foolishness" (σφῆσιν ἀτασ-θαλίῃσιν, 1.34) and insists on the capacity for free choice—the right, as it were, to write one's own story, to select one's own plot.[23] This moral aspect of the story is sometimes identified with its function in the poem; D'Arms and Hulley, for example, regard the principal function of what they call "the Oresteia-motif" to be its use "to state the theme of man's responsiblity for his own troubles" (1946:211), and this perspective has generally dominated discussion of the story (see below, Chapter Six).

---

[21] "So läuft die Geschichte darauf hinaus, eine Folie abzugeben für Penelope."
[22] "Weil Odysseus der Vorsichtige sein muss, muss auf Penelope der Schatten der Unzuverlässigkeit fallen."
[23] On the relationship between ἀτασθαλίαι in line 34 and in line 7, see Allione 1963:39–48; Clay 1983:34–38; Fenik 1974:209–19; Eisenberger 1973:1–6; and West 1988:77 ad 1.32ff.

The content of Zeus's pronouncement, however, is also correlated with the narrative situation of the opening scenes of the poem, which presents indecision amidst a set of competing options for action and suggests an indeterminacy of narrative direction:

> τόσσοι μητέρ' ἐμὴν μνῶνται, τρύχουσι δὲ οἶκον.
> ἡ δ' οὔτ' ἀρνεῖται στυγερὸν γάμον οὔτε τελευτὴν
> ποιῆσαι δύναται·
>
> (So many [suitors] court my mother, and wear down the house.
> And she neither refuses the hateful marriage nor is she able
> to bring things to a conclusion.)
>
> (1.248–50)

The statement is repeated at the end of the poem in a slightly revised form, when Amphimedon interprets this ambiguity, along with much else, as a deliberate maneuver on Penelope's part: "She neither refused the hateful marriage nor brought things to a conclusion" (ἡ δ' οὔτ' ἠρνεῖτο στυγερὸν γάμον οὔτε τελεύτα, 24.126). In Book 1, however, the statement instantiates a correlation between narrative direction and moral choice, which is developed initially with reference to Telemachus, and explicitly against the House of Atreus paradigm.

Telemachus's prominence in this first part of the *Odyssey* has led to the designation of Books 1–4 as the "Telemachy" and to a long history of discussion of the relation of this segment to the rest of the poem. From the analytic point of view, the Telemachy is regarded as a separable (and originally separate) unit (e.g., Kirchhoff 1879:238–74 [Excurs I]), but even from this perspective distinctions are often made between the scenes on Ithaca and those in Pylos and Sparta. Merkelbach distinguishes between Books 2 and parts of Book 4, which he assigns to an older *Rachegedicht* (R), and Books 3 and 4, which he thinks formed part of a Kleinepos (T or *Telemach-Reise*; 1969:15–57).[24] But even from the analytic viewpoint it is sometimes conceded that the various threads of separate narratives that have been woven together cannot now be completely disentangled (Page 1955:52–81, 165–82). And this, generally speaking, is also what Eisenberger identifies as "a moderately unitarian standpoint" (1973:x). Eisenberger attempts to demonstrate through a structural analysis that "the Telemachy in its totality stands, as much on the basis of its content as its plan, in the closest connection with both of the other main parts of the epic [*nostos* and revenge]; it leads to them and is conjoined with them" (ibid.:100–106; citation p. 100).[25]

---

[24] For a systematic refutation of the analytic interpretation of the Telemachy, see Klingner 1964.
[25] "Die Telemachie in ihrer Gesamtheit steht nun sowohl hinsichtlich ihres Inhalts wie ihrer

But what is especially prominent in interpretive discussion of Books 1–4, whether from an analytic or a unitarian standpoint, is attention to what is regarded as the ethical element introduced into the poem through the medium of the Telemachy. Reinhardt, in claiming that the Telemachy is an integral part of the *Odyssey* and that it "captivates less through the forcefulness of the episodes than through its whole course," argues also that "only in its totality does there appear the relationship between god and man that is unique to its poet" (Reinhardt 1960b:43).[26] The most influential of such readings is Schadewaldt's argument that the Telemachy is a revision and amplification, by a slightly later poet ("B") of sophisticated religious outlook, of an eighth-century "Homeric" core *Odyssey* made up of Odysseus's *nostos*, reunion with Telemachus, and revenge against the suitors (Schadewaldt 1970b, 1970f, 1970g).[27] Moreover, in Schadewaldt's view, it is to the "Nebenlinie" (secondary theme) or "Telemachos-Linie" running alongside the "Hauptlinie des Odysseus-Geschehens" (main theme of Odysseus's exploits) throughout the poem that "Zeus's first speech is connected, the speech through which those ideas about men's own guilt achieve expression, on the example of Aegisthus and his subsequent murder by Orestes" (Schadewaldt 1970b:45).[28] Allione takes up some of these same issues from a unitarian point of view; she argues that in this first section of the poem the ethical issues of the poem are organized around a contrast between the combination of ἀτασθαλίαι ("recklessness") and suffering ὑπὲρ μόρον ("beyond what was fated")[29] on the one hand, as embodied in the person of Aegisthus, and that of being δύσμορος ("ill-fated") and δαΐφρων ("knowledgeable," "skilled") on the other, as represented by Odysseus. The House of Atreus story and the moral judgments associated with it, then, have "the effect of giving greater prominence to the figure

---

Anlage in engster Beziehung zu den beiden anderen Hauptteilen des Epos [*nostos* and revenge], führt auf sie hin, ist mit ihnen verbunden."

[26] ". . . Jedenfalls ist die Telemachie ein Teil der Odyssee, der weniger durch die Eindringlichkeit der Episoden als durch den Verlauf im ganzen fesselt. Erst im Ganzen zeigt sich das Verhältnis zwischen Gott und Mensch, das ihrem Dichter eigen ist."

[27] Eisenberger 1973 constitutes an extended counterargument to Schadewaldt's reading of the poem; see esp. viii–ix, 13–31.

[28] Schadewaldt summarizes the "momentous" revisions of his poet "B" as follows: "The poet of B has not only expanded this original *Odyssey* in a manner that is consonant with its form, but in connection with this he has added expanse and range, has opened up [the poem's] temporal perspective, has taken into consideration both ordinary realities and those of greater moment (having to do with community, court, and state), and has also above all taken account of the spiritual and personal element, and has arranged much of what his predecessor observed and expressed with a simple susceptibility to only its factual essence, so that it could represent also the sense of an era which would from now on in matters of law and religion become a more and more progressive one in Greece" (1970b:58).

[29] On the interpretation of this problematic phrase, see also Fenik 1974:210–11, 215; and Clay 1983:215ff., 217 n. 3.

and vicissitudes of Odysseus, rather than to the figure and vicissitudes of Telemachus," and make of Telemachus an altogether secondary figure with respect to the development in the poem of an ethico-juridical point of view (Allione 1963:38–48; citation p. 40).[30]

I take up the question of the ethical outlook of the *Odyssey* in my concluding chapter, but I discuss it there under the rubric of the relationship of narrative form to the ideology of exclusivity. Correlatively, the discussion below of the House of Atreus story is concerned more with how the story functions in the narrative as part of an internal polemic, and with how it operates to establish the characters of the poem and relationships among them, than with how (or even whether) it embodies the moral content of the poem.

In his initial conversation with the goddess Athena in the guise of Mentes, Telemachus attributes his father's absence and the suitors' presence to divine malevolence; he refers to "the gods who are devising evil [for us]" (θεοὶ κακὰ μητιόωντες, 1.234) and complains that "the gods have fashioned other evil cares for me" (μοι ἄλλα θεοὶ κακὰ κήδε' ἔτευξαν, 1.244). Athena repudiates the notion that divine determinism forecloses action, however, and insists that Odysseus's ultimate fate is irrelevant to Telemachus's possibilities for action.[31]

> ἀλλ' ἦ τοι μὲν ταῦτα θεῶν ἐν γούνασι κεῖται,
> ἦ κεν νοστήσας ἀποτείσεται, ἦε καὶ οὐκί,
> οἷσιν ἐνὶ μεγάροισι· σὲ δὲ φράζεσθαι ἄνωγα,
> ὅππως κε μνηστῆρας ἀπώσεαι ἐκ μεγάροιο.

(But, to be sure, these things are lying on the knees of the gods,
whether he will come home again and take his revenge, or whether he will not,
in his great halls. But as for you, come now and think through
how you will expel the suitors from the great hall.)

(1.267–70)

Athena offers Telemachus advice and sets before him two different courses of action.[32] First, beginning at 1.272, she tells him to convene an assembly and, with the authority of public opinion and the oaths of the gods behind him (1.273), to thrust the suitors out, and to let Penelope return to her

---

[30] For further discussion of the Telemachy that treats it from the point of view of compositional technique, see Hansen 1972:34–57.

[31] Clay comments in this connection, "one is led to wonder whether the accusation with which the poem opens—that the gods are to blame for mortal ills—does not originate from Ithaca. It is the complaint of the good and innocent who feel oppressed and powerless" (1983:232).

[32] For a discussion of the critical problems presented by the double advice in Athena's *parainesis*, and its relationship to the programme announced in the prologue (1.88–95), see Klingner 1964:47–54; Eisenberger 1973:37–42.

father's house and be married from there (1.275–78). As a second opinion ("but to you yourself I will propose this shrewd counsel," σοὶ δ' αὐτῷ πυκινῶς ὑποθήσομαι, 1.279), Athena suggests that Telemachus undertake a journey, and, if he should discover that his father is dead, that he pile up a tomb in his memory, "give your mother to a husband" (καὶ ἀνέρι μητέρα δοῦναι, 1.292), and devise a plan for killing the suitors "either by stealth or openly" (ἠὲ δόλῳ ἢ ἀμφαδόν, 1.296). In concluding her speech, Athena invokes the example of Orestes:

> ἢ οὐκ ἀίεις οἷον κλέος ἔλλαβε δῖος Ὀρέστης
> πάντας ἐπ' ἀνθρώπους, ἐπεὶ ἔκτανε πατροφονῆα,
> Αἴγισθον δολόμητιν, ὅ οἱ πατέρα κλυτὸν ἔκτα;
>
> (Or perhaps you haven't heard what *kleos* godlike Orestes acquired
> among all men, when he killed the murderer of his father,
> crafty-minded Aegisthus, who killed his famous father.)
>
> (1.298–300)

As Austin and others remark, the parallel is not an exact one: "For Orestes the situation was unambiguous. . . . Telemachus' situation is, in contrast, highly ambiguous" (Austin 1969:47). And consequently, comment on Athena's *parainesis* (advice) is forced to focus on the overall situation of choice and opportunity for action that now lies open to Telemachus: "Thus Telemachus receives from his visitor various directives that are not logically developed from one another, although each of them is emphatically and compellingly formulated. Their logical coherence remains hidden to him; however, he now sees various ways and possibilities for ending his unendurable situation" (Eisenberger 1973:42).[33] Similarly, discussion of the alternatives generally concentrates exclusively on the opposition between assembly and voyage (Allione 1963:13 n. 6; Eisenberger 1973:41–42; Klingner 1964:47–54).

The example of Orestes is more immediately relevant, however, if it is understood to apply to the second element in each of Athena's alternatives, that is, to the private correlate to each of Telemachus's public actions, his assumption of control over what he has already plaintively referred to as "my household" (οἶκον ἐμόν, 1.251; cf. οἶκος ἐμός, 2.64). Indeed, Klingner refers to "the prosperous house" as a "chief theme" (*Leitgedanke*) of Telemachus's speech to Athena in Book 1 (Klingner 1964:61–62; and cf. Bader 1976 on the relationship between *nostos* and *oikos*). Thus, both of the

---

[33] "So vernimmt Telemach von seinem Besucher verschiedene, nicht logisch auseinander entwickelte, aber jeweils nachdrücklich, eindringlich formulierte Weisungen. Ihr Sinnzusammenhang bleibt ihm verborgen; doch sieht er nun mehrere Wege und Möglichkeiten, seiner unerträglichen Lage ein Ende zu machen. . . ."

alternatives proposed by Athena entail Telemachus's displacement of his father as head of the household, but in accordance with two different patterns of *kyrieia* ("guardianship").

I have used the terms *kyrios* ("guardian") and *kyrieia* ("guardianship") in my discussion because, although they are not themselves Homeric, the concept that they represent is (Finley 1955; Lacey 1966; Vernant 1980a; Mossé 1981). As in the classical period, a woman in the Homeric poems was overseen and protected by her father, brother, husband, or the individual appointed in his stead; a woman's *kyrios* ordinarily arranged for her marriage and had the capacity otherwise to "ratify" her own actions, i.e., to make them socially or legally efficacious (*kuroō*).[34] Athena's first proposal, that Telemachus expel the suitors and send Penelope back to Icarius, represents a reversion to the situation before the marriage between Penelope and Odysseus, and a return to its original circumstances; in this case, Icarius's *kyrieia* over Penelope is understood to be still in force. The second alternative, whereby Telemachus, upon returning from his voyage, gives his mother in marriage, entails his replacement of his father as *kyrios* of the household, including his personal assumption of *kyrieia* over Penelope.

Both options proposed by Athena envision Penelope's eventual departure from the house, and thus the eradication of the marriage of Penelope and Odysseus as a socially meaningful reality. And in both cases it is clear that Penelope's continued presence in the house is inconsistent with Telemachus's accession to fully adult status. Thus, the option whereby Penelope might pass under Telemachus's *kyrieia* but remain as a widow in the house, does not appear at this point in the narrative. In the classical period, it appears to have functioned regularly as a third option for a widow who has produced an heir: "If [a widow] had had sons by her dead husband she probably had the choice between remaining in his house or returning to her father's. If she remained she was under the tutelage of her sons, if they were of age; of their κύριοι ["guardians"], if they were minors" (Harrison 1968:38). At a later point in the poem, this same possibility provides the basis for Telemachus's participation in the bow-contest with the suitors:

> καὶ δέ κεν αὐτὸς ἐγὼ τοῦ τόξου πειρησαίμην·
> εἰ δέ κεν ἐντανύσω διοϊστεύσω τε σιδήρου,
> οὔ κέ μοι ἀχνυμένῳ τάδε δώματα πότνια μήτηρ
> λείποι ἅμ' ἄλλῳ ἰοῦσ', ὅτ' ἐγὼ κατόπισθε λιποίμην
> οἷός τ' ἤδη πατρὸς ἄεθλια κάλ' ἀνελέσθαι.

---

[34] Although it has been held that Penelope's marriage situation cannot reflect an historically and socially coherent set of practices (Snodgrass 1974; cf. West 1988:57–60, 109–11, 133–34; Naerebout 1987), the supporting argument is based on a methodologically incorrect use of ethnological parallels and can be easily rebutted (see Qviller 1981:114; cf. Finley 1978:89; Vernant 1980a; Mossé 1981).

(And I would myself make trial of the bow;
if I should string it and shoot an arrow through the iron,
then my mother would not to my sorrow leave this house
and go off with another man, since I would have been left behind
as one able to take up my father's fine prizes.)

(21.113–17)

This alternative, however, requires a demonstration of Telemachus's maturity, and this has not yet taken place, since it is in part the function of Athena's visit to provoke it. Indeed, in the scene immediately following Athena's *parainesis*, Telemachus surprises Penelope by asserting his authority in the house; he employs a traditional formulation that in the *Iliad* designates the separation of spheres between husband and wife (cf. *Iliad* 6.490–93; *Odyssey* 21.350–53, 11.352–53):

ἀλλ' εἰς οἶκον ἰοῦσα τὰ σ' αὐτῆς ἔργα κόμιζε,
ἱστόν τ' ἠλακάτην τε, καὶ ἀμφιπόλοισι κέλευε
ἔργον ἐποίχεσθαι· μῦθος δ' ἄνδρεσσι μελήσει
πᾶσι, μάλιστα δ' ἐμοί· τοῦ γὰρ κράτος ἔστ' ἐνὶ οἴκῳ.

(But go inside the house and take up your own work,
the weaving and the spindle, and order the serving-maids
to busy themselves with it. But storytelling will be the concern of all the men,
and especially of me, for mine is the authority in the household.)

(1.356–59)

In this way, Telemachus signals his readiness to take on the role of *kyrios* of Odysseus's household. As Allione sees it, this is the entire burden of the passage: "The fact that Telemachus's words are partially similar to those uttered by Hector to Andromache is irrelevant; . . . here, in their context, they reveal how for the first time Telemachus declares himself lord of his household. . . . The assertion of authority by Telemachus . . . constitutes the principle raison d'être of this whole scene" (1963:16).[35]

Athena's use of Orestes as exemplar, then, and her reference to his *kleos*, should be interpreted not narrowly, but with reference to all of the elements in her *parainesis*. We should note also that the force of the House of Atreus paradigm has distorted the form of Athena's advice to Telemachus, since, in the second of the alternatives she sets before him, she tells him to give his mother out in marriage and then plan the *mnēstērophonia*: "Reflect . . . then . . . how you might kill the suitors in your halls" (φράζεσθαι . . . ἔπειτα . . . ὅππως κε μνηστῆρας ἐνὶ μεγάροισι τεοῖσι κτείνῃς, 1.294–96). But as critics observe, Penelope's marriage would presumably render the

---

[35] "Non importa che le parole di Telemaco siano in parte simili a quelle che Ettore dice ad Andromaca; . . . qui, nel loro contesto, esse rivelano come per la prima volta egli si dichiari padrone della sua casa. . . . L'affermazione d'autorità di Telemaco . . . costituisce la principale ragion d'essere di tutta questa scena."

issue of the suitors moot, and thus obviate the need for their slaughter (see Allione 1963:14 n. 6).

Athena's *parainesis*, then, appeals to Telemachus's desire to make the household his own in the manner of Orestes, from whom, as Zeus had predicted to Aegisthus, "there would be vengeance whenever he came of age and longed for his own land" (ὁππότ᾽ ἂν ἡβήσῃ τε καὶ ἧς ἱμείρεται αἴης, 1.41). For Telemachus, this entails a two-step process, only one stage of which concerns the suitors, and the other of which has to do with Penelope. Athena's *parainesis*, however, suppresses any reference to Clytemnestra; we can compare Zeus's description of Aegisthus's crime ("he married his [Agamemnon's] wedded wife, and killed him upon his homecoming," γῆμ᾽ ἄλοχον μνηστήν, τὸν δ᾽ ἔκτανε νοστήσαντα, 1.36) with that of Athena, who identifies Aegisthus simply as the man "who killed his [Orestes'] glorious father" (ὃ οἱ πατέρα κλυτὸν ἔκτα, 1.300). This enables Athena to suggest a morally uncomplicated analogy and to imply that Telemachus's dilemma is a matter only of men and manhood. Critics who imagine that Telemachus's choice concerns assembly and voyage alone, or that the paradigmatic force of the House of Atreus story applies only to Telemachus in this section of the poem, have fallen under the spell of the goddess's rhetoric. As the discussion in the assembly shows, Penelope is from the beginning of the narrative a problem for Telemachus. His efforts to follow Athena's advice by implementing the first option founder on the matter of Penelope, and thus his attempt to pursue his own *kleos* encounters immediately the obstacle of hers.

In the assembly in Book 2, as a correlate to his claims that his father has died ("I have lost a noble father," πατέρ᾽ ἐσθλὸν ἀπώλεσα, 2.46) and that Odysseus's *oikos* is now consequently his (2.45; cf. 2.64), Telemachus suggests that the proper course of action for the suitors is to court Penelope from Icarius's house (2.52–54). We should note that Telemachus's right to his *oikos* had been established earlier, in the conversation with Eurymachus at the end of Book 1 (lines 397–404), and is clearly not a matter of dispute. Telemachus's *kyrieia* over Penelope, however, is. The basis of Telemachus's claim is that his mother, like he, is oppressed by the suitors' presence: "Suitors beset my mother, though she is unwilling" (μητέρι μοι μνηστῆρες ἐπέχραον οὐκ ἐθελούσῃ, 2.50).

Antinous, however, objects vehemently to this formulation, and assigns full responsibility to Penelope:

> σοὶ δ᾽ οὔ τι μνηστῆρες Ἀχαιῶν αἴτιοί εἰσιν,
> ἀλλὰ φίλη μήτηρ, ἥ τοι περὶ κέρδεα οἶδεν.
> ἤδη γὰρ τρίτον ἐστὶν ἔτος, τάχα δ᾽ εἶσι τέταρτον,
> ἐξ οὗ ἀτέμβει θυμὸν ἐνὶ στήθεσσιν Ἀχαιῶν.
> πάντας μὲν ἔλπει, καὶ ὑπίσχεται ἀνδρὶ ἑκάστῳ,
> ἀγγελίας προϊεῖσα· νόος δέ οἱ ἄλλα μενοινᾷ.

> (You know, it is not at all the Achaean suitors who are to blame,
> but your own dear mother, who is exceedingly crafty.
> For already now it is the third year, and soon it will be the fourth,
> since she has been deceiving the desires of the Achaeans.
> For she holds out hope to all, and makes promises to each man,
> sending them messages, but her mind yearns for other things.)
>
> (2.87–92)

Antinous goes on to relate the device of Penelope's web, the suitors' discovery of her stratagem, and her continued delays. He then advises Telemachus to send Penelope back to Icarius (2.113–14), and this plan is later seconded by Eurymachus (2.195–97). It is the same advice that Athena had offered earlier as the first option. On this and other accounts Page and others regard these suggestions as anomalous, indications of textual intrusion from a background of alternative versions: "Who would believe, if he had any choice in the matter, that our poet would break the most elementary laws of his craft, making *the Suitors* repeat verbatim a proposal made by *Athene* to Telemachus, and then making Telemachus reject that proposal? But this is what happens" (Page 1955:57; emphasis in the original; cf. Kirk 1962:229–32). There are certain crucial shifts in language and meaning in these passages, however, which indicate that a simple replication of Athena's original advice is not at issue.

Athena in Book 1 had not hesitated to advise Telemachus to throw the suitors out ("to think how to throw them out," φράζεσθαι . . . ὅππως κε . . . ἀπώσεαι, 1.269–70), but she had shifted to the more polite, less confrontational third-person imperative when discussing Penelope ("let her go back," ἂψ ἴτω, 1.276)[36] and had conditioned her advice upon Penelope's free choice in the matter ("if her heart urges her to be married," εἴ οἱ θυμὸς ἐφορμᾶται γαμέεσθαι, 1.275). Telemachus's appeal to the suitors, phrased as a mild expression of outrage that they do not follow the proper course of behavior ("[you] who shrink from going to her father Icarius's house!" οἳ πατρὸς μὲν ἐς οἶκον ἀπερρίγασι νέεσθαι / Ἰκαρίου, 2.52–53), similarly envisions the simple resumption of *kyrieia* by Icarius: "So that he himself might dower his daughter, and might give her to whomever he wants and who is pleasing to her as well" (ὅς κ' αὐτὸς ἐεδνώσαιτο θύγατρα, / δοίη δ' ᾧ κ' ἐθέλοι καί οἱ κεχαρισμένος ἔλθοι, 2.53–54).

The suitors, by contrast, urge Telemachus to take decisive and authoritative action that would amount to the equivalent of divorce: "Send your mother back and compel her to be married" (μητέρα σὴν ἀπόπεμψον,

---

[36] Not, however, without introducing an anomaly in construction; see West's comment: "it would be hard to find a Homeric parallel for the abrupt change of construction in 275–6 (μητέρα δ' . . . ἂψ ἴτω), corresponding to the straightforward μητέρ' ἐὴν ἐς πατρὸς ἀνωγέτω ἀπονέεσθαι of Eurymachus' speech . . ." (1988:110 ad 275–78).

ἄνωχθι δέ μιν γαμέεσθαι, 2.113); "let him compel his mother to return to her father's" (μητέρα ἣν ἐς πατρὸς ἀνωγέτω ἀπονέεσθαι, 2.195). The verb that Antinous employs, ἀποπέμπω ("send out," "send back"), is in the later period a technical term for "divorce" (Harrison 1968:40). And Telemachus's reply appears to indicate that he has understood the implications of Antinous's suggestion: "If I willingly send my mother back . . ." (αἴ κ' αὐτὸς ἑκὼν ἀπὸ μητέρα πέμψω, 2.133). Antinous's suggestion entails a challenge to Telemachus to take upon himself the full authority over the household to which he claims entitlement. But Telemachus demurs; Penelope's father, her own furies, and public resentment of this kind of arrogance inhibit him (2.132–37). As he says, her wishes ("it is not possible to thrust her out of the house unwilling," οὔ πως ἔστι δόμων ἀέκουσαν ἀπῶσαι, 2.130) condition the exercise of his own volition ("if I myself of my own volition," αἴ κ' αὐτὸς ἑκὼν . . . , 2.133).[37]

Antinous's speech concludes with a pointed antithesis: "She is fashioning great glory (*kleos*) for herself, but for you [she is bringing about] a great dearth of livelihood" (μέγα μὲν κλέος αὐτῇ / ποιεῖτ', αὐτὰρ σοί γε ποθὴν πολέος βιότοιο, 2.125–26). And Antinous is partially echoing and thereby mocking Telemachus's earlier complaint: ". . . destroy all of my livelihood" (. . . βίοτον δ' ἀπὸ πάμπαν ὀλέσσει, 2.49). The discourse in the assembly explores fully the implications of Antinous's antithesis. Thus, Telemachus's unwillingness at this point in the narrative to lay claim to the *kyrieia* over Penelope that he is later willing to assume scuttles his first plan. One commentator even argues concerning this matter that "it is surely clear that in the view of the *Odyssey* the right of giving Penelope in marriage rested entirely with him [Telemachus]. The Levirate [*sic*] is not in question. . . . Telemachus may refuse to exercise the right, but he claims it . . . and the suitors admit it"(Monro 1901:302 n. 22). Once he has elected not to take charge of Penelope, Telemachus turns to the second option advanced by Athena, a voyage to inquire about his father; following the news of Odysseus's death, he intends to commemorate his father and "give my mother to a husband" (2.212ff.; esp. 221–23).

The matter of Penelope's *kyrios*, then, has been raised but left indeterminate, and the effect has been to subvert the claims of various males to her control. The comments of Aristotle on Helen's abduction by Paris are relevant here: "[It is a fallacy to argue that] Alexandros took Helen off rightly, since the choice [of a husband] had been given her by her father. For this [did not apply] for all time, but only on the first occasion; for the father is *kyrios* up to that point" (οἷον ὅτι δικαίως Ἀλέξανδρος ἔλαβε τὴν Ἑλένην· αἵρεσις γὰρ αὐτῇ ἐδόθη παρὰ τοῦ πατρός. οὐ γὰρ ἀεὶ ἴσως, ἀλλὰ

---

[37] Büchner's remark on this situation is perhaps somewhat tendentious: "The widow's lack of rights is alleviated through . . . piety" (1940:138 n. 1).

τὸ πρῶτον· καὶ γὰρ ὁ πατὴρ μέχρι τούτου κύριος, *Rhet.* 2.24, 1401b35–1402a1). In Aristotle's view, Helen's right to the choice of a husband resulted from her father's willingness to relinquish his own *kyrieia* over her; once married, her husband's *kyrieia* is in force, and her father's wishes for her no longer apply. Penelope, by contrast, has been rendered temporarily free from any *kyrieia* only because there is no mechanism for deciding among the claims of the various *kyrioi* who are theoretically eligible. Penelope has thus become a morally free agent to the extent possible in a social order that envisioned lifetime tutelage for all women. What is more, Penelope's situation here in the *Odyssey* contrasts markedly with the analogous one of Helen in the *Iliad* (on which see Groten 1968, and Zagagi 1985).

Helen in the *Iliad* is not regarded as responsible either by Menelaus or by any of the other heroes for her commission of adultery with Paris. Consequently, Menelaus in *Iliad* 3 seeks vengeance from Paris, for the crime against *xenia* (3.351–54). Helen, to be sure, regards matters differently, and she rebukes herself in both the *Iliad* and the *Odyssey*: identifying Agamemnon for the Trojan leaders in the *teikhoskopia*, she calls him "the brother-in-law of bitch-faced me, if these things ever were" (δαὴρ αὖτ' ἐμὸς ἔσκε κυνώπιδος, εἴ ποτ' ἔην γε, *Iliad* 3.180); she addresses Hector as "brother-in-law of me, whom am an evil-devising, sharp-tongued bitch" (δᾶερ ἐμεῖο, κυνὸς κακομηχάνου ὀκρυοέσσης, 6.344; cf. 3.410ff.); in the *Odyssey* she recalls the time "when you Achaeans went beneath Troy for the sake of bitch-faced me" (ὅτ' ἐμεῖο κυνώπιδος εἵνεκ' Ἀχαιοὶ / ἤλθεθ' ὑπὸ Τροίην, 4.145–46), and her words here too are spoken with regret (4.260–64). Nevertheless, in the *Iliad* Helen's own actions and intentions are morally irrelevant, since she is not, from the point of view of the heroic code, a morally free agent (Arthur 1973:16–17). In the *Odyssey*, by contrast, Helen is herself regarded as a moral agent (see below, Chapters Three and Five; cf. also Groten 1968). By the same token, the narrative focus on the issue of Penelope's *kyrieia* has the effect of establishing and legitimizing the exercise of free will for Penelope (see further in Chapter Five).

By the end of the second book then, the moral implications of Zeus's initial statements about Aegisthus have broadened to encompass Penelope's situation as well as that of Telemachus, and so Penelope is left free to choose among options unsupervised by any of the males in her life. It should not pass unremarked that the category of males in Penelope's life includes Mentor as well, into whose hands Odysseus had entrusted his household when he departed for Troy ("and when he went upon the ships he turned over his whole household," καί οἱ ἰὼν ἐν νηυσὶν ἐπέτρεπεν οἶκον ἅπαντα, 2.226),[38] and in whose guise Athena accompanies Telema-

---

[38] Bassett interprets *oikos* in 2.226 too narrowly when he claims that "even Mentor, who has been made guardian of the estate under Laertes, received no instructions to watch over Pe-

chus on his journey. Mentor had in any case shown himself unable to oppose the suitors in the assembly (2.229ff.).

Furthermore, the relevance within the narrative of the specific content of the House of Atreus story has now been established. Its exemplary function applies explicitly to Telemachus alone, but its paradigmatic force attracts Penelope's actions within its orbit and destabilizes their meaning on the surface of the text. Thus, Penelope's indecision and her strategy of evasion, together with her freedom from male supervision, are neither static nor neutral elements within the poem. Their inhibiting effect on the development of Telemachus's *kleos* is explored in the opening section of the poem. And the further development of the House of Atreus story conditions their meaning by providing a paradigm for their negative outcome.

Let us also distinguish in this connection between the public and private meanings of Penelope's remarriage. The House of Atreus paradigm applies to the private meaning as an act of betrayal of Odysseus, even though Penelope's remarriage may have public consequences as well. These consequences are difficult to assess on the available evidence. M. I. Finley certainly overstates the case when he claims that "the prerogative [of bestowing rule in Ithaca] mysteriously belonged to Penelope" (1978:91).[39] There are, however, several passages in the text that suggest that marriage to Penelope brings with it lordship over Ithaca: e.g., "to marry my mother and to acquire the *geras* of Odysseus" (μητέρ' ἐμὴν γαμέειν καὶ 'Οδυσσῆος γέρας ἕξειν, 15.522).[40] And we can compare here the implications of the question that Odysseus addresses to his mother in the underworld: "But tell me about my father and my son, whom I left behind, whether my *geras* remains with them still, or whether some other man has acquired it, and they say that I am never going to return" (εἰπὲ δέ μοι πατρός τε καὶ υἱέος, ὃν κατέλειπον, / ἢ ἔτι πὰρ κείνοισιν ἐμὸν γέρας, ἦέ τις ἤδη / ἀνδρῶν ἄλλος ἔχει, ἐμὲ δ' οὐκέτι φασὶ νέεσθαι, 11.174–76). Odysseus goes on to ask about his wife and property, which are regarded as a separate matter. West's judgment seems the right one: "Potentially there is also a political aspect to Penelope's remarriage. . . . But generally the threat to Odysseus' house represented by the suitors is treated as a purely private problem" (West 1988:59–60).

It is against the background of uncertainty on Ithaca, along with the consequence of that indeterminacy—Penelope's moral freedom—that the House of Atreus story rises into prominence in the narrative and under-

---

nelope" (1918:525), and he disregards also the implications of Odysseus's instructions to "keep everything safe and secure" (καὶ ἔμπεδα πάντα φυλάσσειν, 2.227; cf. 11.178).

[39] See the critique of Finley's argument by Thornton (1970:108–14).

[40] See also Thornton's discussion of 21.249ff. and of the relationship between the bow-contest and the kingship (1970:112–13). See also the discussions in Vernant 1980a:63–66 and Mossé 1981:152–56.

goes development and expansion. Book 3 represents the fullest elaboration of the story, which appears in Book 4 as well, but then not again until Book 11, in the first *nekyia*. Beyond this, there are only two further references to it, in Books 13 and 24, which together bracket the Ithacan segment of the poem.

In Pylos, when Nestor has completed his account of the Trojan War and the homecomings of the various heroes, he appends a brief account of Agamemnon's fate:

> Ἀτρείδην δὲ καὶ αὐτοὶ ἀκούετε νόσφιν ἐόντες,
> ὥς τ' ἦλθ' ὥς τ' Αἴγισθος ἐμήσατο λυγρὸν ὄλεθρον.
> ἀλλ' ἦ τοι κεῖνος μὲν ἐπισμυγερῶς ἀπέτεισεν.
> ὡς ἀγαθὸν καὶ παῖδα καταφθιμένοιο λιπέσθαι
> ἀνδρός, ἐπεὶ καὶ κεῖνος ἐτείσατο πατροφονῆα,
> Αἴγισθον δολόμητιν, ὅ οἱ πατέρα κλυτὸν ἔκτα.

(and you yourselves have heard of Atreides, though you live far off,
how he came, and how Aegisthus devised wretched destruction.
But indeed, that one [Aegisthus] paid the price for it terribly;
so it is a good thing for a man when he perishes to leave behind a son,
since this one took vengeance on his father's slayer,
the treacherous Aegisthus, because he had killed his glorious father.)
(3.193–98)

This account replicates in its details, its language (3.197–98 = 1.299–300), and its implications, the earlier one of Athena. In both the focus is on the Agamemnon-Aegisthus-Orestes triad and its analogue, Odysseus-Suitors-Telemachus, and in both the most important issue is the object-lesson for Telemachus.[41]

At this point Nestor goes on to hope for Odysseus's return, but to suggest as well the possibility of Telemachus's assumption of the role of the household's defender. In a manner similar to that of Athena earlier, Nestor regards Odysseus's return as an unpredictable matter: "Who knows if someday he might come and avenge these men's violent deeds?" (τίς δ' οἶδ' εἴ κέ ποτέ σφι βίας ἀποτείσεται ἐλθών, 3.216). Note also that Nestor insists on Telemachus's free will as a factor in his plight: he asks Telemachus if he is indeed oppressed by the suitors "against your will" (ἀέκητι σέθεν, 3.213), as rumor has it, "or are you willingly beaten down?" (ἦε ἑκὼν ὑποδάμνασαι, 3.214). If only Athena would take Telemachus under her protection, Nestor continues, "then some of those men might well forget about marriage." Telemachus recoils before this incitement to action, but

---

[41] Contra Eisenberger, "The warning to Telemachus is not a parainesis to revenge" (1973:67). This motif is introduced, according to Eisenberger, only in the next section of the discourse (4.218–24).

he is then brought up short by his companion Mentor, who is the goddess Athena is disguise. She affects disbelief, and affirms:

> βουλοίμην δ' ἂν ἐγώ γε καὶ ἄλγεα πολλὰ μογήσας
> οἴκαδέ τ' ἐλθέμεναι καὶ νόστιμον ἦμαρ ἰδέσθαι,
> ἢ ἐλθὼν ἀπολέσθαι ἐφέστιος, ὡς Ἀγαμέμνων
> ὤλεθ' ὑπ' Αἰγίσθοιο δόλῳ καὶ ἧς ἀλόχοιο.

> (I myself would choose to endure even many painful struggles, and
> then come home and look upon the day of my homecoming,
> rather than coming, be killed at my own hearth, as Agamemnon
> was killed, by the trickery of Aegisthus, and of his own wife.)
>
> (3.232–35)

This is the first suggestion in the poem that Clytemnestra bears any of the responsibility for Agamemnon's murder, and the combined effect of this new piece of information and Mentor's rebuke is to incite Telemachus to ask Nestor for further details of the incident. Telemachus's interest is significant, not least because his question does not take the most obvious form. He asks how Agamemnon died, and why Menelaus was not available to help his brother.[42] Austin regards this as a bit of *polymechania* ("cunning intelligence") on Telemachus's part, and a sign of his growing eligibility to be characterized by his father's most prominent epithet, *polymechanos* ("[man of] many tricks, much devising"). "His real question," Austin insists, "is the unspoken one: How did Orestes kill Aegisthos?" (Austin 1969:55). This is to attribute to Telemachus, however, an eagerness that does not appear in the text; his reluctance to take on Orestes' role continues until the point of the *anagnōrismos* ("recognition") of Odysseus in Book 16, and this is indicated explicitly in the narrative. In 3.225–28 Telemachus rejects Nestor's suggestion that he take on the suitors alone with Athena's help, claiming, "What you suggest is too great. Amazement [at it] grips me" (λίην γὰρ μέγα εἶπες· ἄγη μ' ἔχει, 3.227). When Athena prods him further, Telemachus insists that Odysseus's death has rendered the issue irrelevant: "For that one there will no longer be a homecoming in truth, but already for him the immortals have devised death and black fate" (κείνῳ δ' οὐκέτι νόστος ἐτήτυμος, ἀλλά οἱ ἤδη / φράσσαντ' ἀθάνατοι θάνατον καὶ κῆρα μέλαιναν, 3.241–42).

Similarly, in Book 16 the disguised Odysseus repeats the questions that Nestor puts to Telemachus here (16.95–96 = 3.214–15), along with the suggestion that Telemachus take on the suitors himself. Odysseus goes so

---

[42] Compare the question that the disguised Odysseus addresses to Telemachus in Book 16: "Do you indeed have some fault to find with your brothers? For these are the ones in whom a man trusts, and they fight alongside him even if a great strife arises" (ἦ τι κασιγνήτοις ἐπιμέμφεαι, οἷσί περ ἀνὴρ / μαρναμένοισι πέποιθε, καὶ εἰ μέγα νεῖκος ὄρηται; 16.97–98).

far as to wish that "either a son of excellent Odysseus were here, or he himself would return from his wandering" (ἢ παῖς ἐξ Ὀδυσῆος ἀμύμονος ἠὲ καὶ αὐτὸς / ἔλθοι ἀλητεύων, 16.100–101) and to add that if it were not for his age he would take on the suitors alone.

Telemachus's interest in Book 3 in Agamemnon's murder is genuine, then, and reflects the forthcoming narrative development, in which the role of Agamemnon—the man returning home who was ambushed and slaughtered—opens up before him instead of that of Orestes. Thus, in response to Telemachus's inquiry, Nestor gives a full account, one that focuses on Clytemnestra's seduction by Aegisthus. He reports that Clytemnestra was at first unwilling, but eventually submitted after Aegisthus had disposed of the bard (ἀοιδὸς ἀνήρ) left to watch over her.[43] Then, she went with him willingly: "And he willing led her away willing to his house" (τὴν δ' ἐθέλων ἐθέλουσαν ἀνήγαγεν ὅνδε δόμονδε, 3.272).[44] Of Orestes, Nestor reports:

> τῷ δέ οἱ ὀγδοάτῳ κακὸν ἤλυθε δῖος Ὀρέστης
> ἄψ ἀπ' Ἀθηνάων, κατὰ δ' ἔκτανε πατροφονῆα,
> [Αἴγισθον δολόμητιν, ὅ οἱ πατέρα κλυτὸν ἔκτα.]
> ἦ τοι ὁ τὸν κτείνας δαίνυ τάφον Ἀργείοισι
> μητρός τε στυγερῆς καὶ ἀνάλκιδος Αἰγίσθοιο.

(But in the eighth year as his [Aegisthus's] bane, godlike Orestes came back from Athens, and he cut down the one who killed his father, the treacherous Aegisthus, because he had killed his glorious father. And then the one who killed him set out a funeral feast for the Argives, on behalf of his hateful mother and the cowardly Aegisthus.)

(3.306–10)

Nestor's account omits an explicit reference to Orestes' murder of his mother, although, as Lesky says; "if we retain [3.310], the conclusion is unavoidable that Clytemnestra is fully complicit in the deed and for that reason was killed by Orestes" (1967:15); Kunst agrees, adding that "the adjective used for her, στυγερή, seems to be conventional for an adulteress" (1924–25:26).[45] Thus, Nestor alludes to Clytemnestra's complicity and to

---

[43] On the "curiosity" of this device, and the view of the scholiasts that "the minstrel who was captured beside Clytemnestra used to prevent her from having evil thoughts (πονηρὰς ἐπινοίας) by relating to her the accounts of the virtuous actions of men and women" (διηγούμενος ἀνδρῶν καὶ γυναικῶν ἀρετάς; scholium to EM), see West (1988:176–77 ad 3.267), and Dindorf (1962:142–44 ad 3.267).

[44] For a discussion of the problems raised by discrepancies in geography and setting between the various accounts in the Telemachy (and in particular the contradiction between "to his [Aegisthus's] home" (ὅνδε δόμονδε) here and "at his [i.e., Agamemnon's own] hearth" (ἐφέστιος) in 3.234, see Kunst (1924–25:19–26) and Lesky (1967:12–14).

[45] Griffin, citing the scholiast to *Iliad* 9.456 (διὸ οὐδὲ περὶ τοῦ φόνου τῆς Κλυταιμήστρας φησίν), refers to the "silence in the *Odyssey* about the way in which Clytemnestra died" (1977:44 n. 32).

the retribution that her son exacted. And he sets before Telemachus a situation analogous to the one that Telemachus had contemplated earlier: "If I should hear that he has died . . . I will come home . . . and pile up a tomb for him . . . and give my mother to a husband" (2.220ff.).

The account, then, of the House of Atreus story in Book 3 replicates and underscores the paradigm outlined in Book 1, but adds the significant new element of Clytemnestra's betrayal of Agamemnon. What is more, in this account, and in this one only, Clytemnestra is characterized in terms applicable to Penelope: ". . . Noble Clytemnestra; for she was a woman of virtuous thoughts" (δῖα Κλυταιμήστρη· φρεσὶ γὰρ κέχρητ' ἀγαθῇσι, 3.266); we can compare Agamemnon's praise of Penelope at 24.194: "How virtuous were the thoughts of excellent Penelope" (ὡς ἀγαθαὶ φρένες ἦσαν ἀμύμονι Πηνελοπείῃ).[46] The House of Atreus story has now been expanded to provide a paradigm for the potential negative outcome of Penelope's situation, and the expansion is phrased in terms that make it possible to accommodate Penelope within its limits. She, like Clytemnestra, is a woman of ἀγαθαὶ φρένες; she is now, like Clytemnestra was, without male supervision (cf. "beside her there was a minstrel, whom Atreides had instructed carefully as he went off to Troy to protect his wife" [πὰρ δ' ἄρ' ἔην καὶ ἀοιδὸς ἀνήρ, ᾧ πόλλ' ἐπέτελλεν / Ἀτρεΐδης Τροίηνδε κιὼν εἴρυσθαι ἄκοιτιν, 3.267–68] with "and to him [Mentor] as he left upon the ships he entrusted his whole household, and [he told him] to obey the old man [Laertes] and to keep everything secure" [καὶ οἱ ἰὼν ἐν νηυσὶν ἐπέτρεπεν οἶκον ἅπαντα, / πείθεσθαί τε γέροντι καὶ ἔμπεδα πάντα φυλάσσειν, 2.226–27]). And we can observe also that, as Kunst remarks, "at first, in the Telemachia at any rate Clytemnestra stands . . . almost on the same level as Penelope, whom this *sprechender Name* [*Klytaimnēstrē* meaning "renowned for being wooed"] would fit at least as well" (1924–25:26, citing 3.266 and comparing Κλυτομήδης in *Iliad* 23.634).

Furthermore, Clytemnestra's capitulation to Aegisthus's seduction is traced to the operation of fate, in striking contrast to the assignment to Aegisthus of responsibility for his own downfall: "But when the fate of the gods constrained her to be overwhelmed" (ἀλλ' ὅτε δή μιν μοῖρα θεῶν ἐπέδησε δαμῆναι, 3.269); in Book 1, by contrast, Aegisthus was said to have died "beyond what was fated" (ὑπὲρ μόρον, 1.34). Thus, the story of a wife's betrayal is told in Book 3 from a perspective in which a woman of fundamentally good character is overwhelmed by fate and circumstances; and this paradigm is directly applicable to Penelope. It is not without reason, then, that Nestor draws the moral for Telemachus as follows:

---

[46] Cf. Kunst 1924–25:26. The phrase used of Clytemnestra is a formulaic one; it is applied to Eumaeus in 14.421, and to Amphinomus in 16.398.

καὶ σύ, φίλος, μὴ δηθὰ δόμων ἄπο τῆλ' ἀλάλησο,
κτήματά τε προλιπὼν ἄνδρας τ' ἐν σοῖσι δόμοισιν
οὕτω ὑπερφιάλους, μή τοι κατὰ πάντα φάγωσι
κτήματα δασσάμενοι, σὺ δὲ τηυσίην ὁδὸν ἔλθῃς.

(And so don't you, my friend, wander far and long from your house,
leaving behind your property, and men in the house
so high-spirited, lest they divide up all your wealth
and consume it, and you will have gone on a fruitless journey.)

(3.313–16)

Clytemnestra does not figure prominently in the account of the House of Atreus story in the fourth book, and is mentioned only at an early point when Menelaus refers to the death of Agamemnon at the hands of "another, [who] killed him secretly, unseen, and by the trickery of his dread wife" (ἄλλος ἔπεφνε / λάθρῃ, ἀνωιστί, δόλῳ οὐλομένης ἀλόχοιο, 4.91–92). In Book 4 the story appears principally in the form of the report that Menelaus extracted from Proteus concerning the *nostoi* of the Achaeans; in that account Clytemnestra is omitted entirely, and the focus is exclusively on the ambush set for Agamemnon by Aegisthus (4.512–37). This is the only instance of the House of Atreus story in the *Odyssey* that reports the ambush: in Agamemnon's account in the first *nekyia*, which is otherwise complementary to this one (see below), it is not related.

The relevance of the particulars of this account to Telemachus's situation becomes clear almost immediately, when the scene shifts back to Ithaca, and the suitors devise and put into motion plans for ambushing Telemachus (4.669–72; 4.778–86; note the correspondence between "having selected from among the people twenty noble youths, he set them in ambush" [κρινάμενος κατὰ δῆμον ἐείκοσι φῶτας ἀρίστους / εἷσε λόχον, 4.530–31] and "he selected twenty noble youths" [ἐκρίνατ' ἐείκοσι φῶτας ἀρίστους, 4.778]). The *lokhos* ("ambush") motif is an important one in the *Odyssey*, as Edwards has shown, and it is brought into correlation with the House of Atreus story: "The example of the ambush which the suitors set for Telemachus is of importance equal to the tale of how Aegisthus killed Agamemnon. This λόχος is mentioned no less than eight times in references scattered between books 4 and 17" (A. T. Edwards 1985:27–41; citation p. 28).

By the end of the fourth book, then, there are indications once again (as earlier, at 2.335–36; see above) that the House of Atreus story threatens to intrude into the narrative proper, and there are other features of the narrative and of the narrative structure in Book 4 that also point to parallels with the situation on Ithaca and suggest a need for urgency. First, it is significant, following the emphasis on Clytemnestra's betrayal of Agamemnon in Book 3 (and Menelaus's mention of it in 4.91–92), that Helen's past conduct now comes under scrutiny in the form of two contradictory narratives, each told from a manifestly self-interested point of view. As Andersen has pointed out, these stories foreshadow the later situation on Ithaca (Andersen 1977; see also Dupont-Roc and Le Boulluec 1976; Zeitlin 1981:204–6; Bergren 1981:207–10; I discuss this parallel further in Chapter Four below).

Second, there are aspects of the narrative structure of Book 4 and of the House of Atreus story within it that provide for a transition back to Ithaca and indicate elements of continuity between the two stories. Menelaus, having heard from Proteus the account of Agamemnon's murder, was overcome with grief ("thus he spoke, but as for me, my heart was broken," ὣς ἔφατ', αὐτὰρ ἐμοί γε κατεκλάσθη φίλον ἦτορ, 4.539), whereupon Proteus aroused "the heart and manly spirit in his breast" (κραδίη καὶ θυμὸς ἀγήνωρ ... ἐνὶ στήθεσσι, 4.548–49) by suggesting that he hasten home: "For you might find him [Aegisthus] alive, or if Orestes has anticipated you and killed him, you might get there in time for the funeral feast" (ἢ γάρ μιν ζωόν γε κιχήσεαι, ἢ κεν Ὀρέστης / κτεῖνεν ὑποφθάμενος· σὺ δέ κεν τάφου ἀντιβολήσαις, 4.546–47). On the next morning, as Menelaus reports it, he set sail for his native land (4.585–86). He breaks off the account of his history abruptly at this point, and turns to invite Telemachus to stay for a while in Lacedaemon.

We know from the beginning that Menelaus was not ultimately to become his brother's avenger, and we know too from Nestor's account in Book 3 that he did arrive on the day of the funeral feast: αὐτῆμαρ δέ οἱ ['Ορέστῃ] ἦλθε βοὴν ἀγαθὸς Μενέλαος, 3.311). But the narrative in Book 4 nevertheless is interrupted at the moment when the issue is still undecided, and a rapid return to the narrative present is effected. And it is just at this juncture that a second transition returns us to Ithaca, where the suitors are plotting an ambush against Telemachus that, we observed above, resembles Aegisthus's ambush of Agamemnon.

This narrative move is interpreted variously in the literature. Allione insists that "the Telemachy does not have the effect ... of creating a mood of dramatic uncertainty and expectation in the reader" (Allione 1963:37),[47] but her notion of uncertainty is more literal than mine. Klingner's interpretation seems to me a more convincing one: "It seems as though Telemachus must fall into the trap. . . . Thus the fourth book ends. In effect, the message of the narrative is: . . . in the homeland of Odysseus there is terrible danger" (1964:67–68).[48] Fenik discusses the passages at

[47] "La Telemachia non vale perciò a creare un'atmosfera di drammatica incertezza e aspettazione nel lettore."

[48] "Es scheint, als müsste Telemach alsbald in die Falle laufen. . . . So endet das vierte Buch. . . . Die Erzählung besagt etwa . . . : in der Heimat des Odysseus ist es todgefährlich geworden."

the end of Book 4 and the middle of Book 16 under the rubric of "doublets," explaining that one can apply the term to passages that "have no symmetrical form individually ... [but] simply emerge as a pair when taken together" (Fenik 1974:163).

The House of Atreus story disappears from the narrative at this point, to be resumed only in the first *nekyia* (11.405–34). But its last instance in Book 4 is constructed so as to leave it open-ended, with vengeance not yet taken. This is the structural equivalent of the warning in Book 3 with which Nestor concludes his account of Agamemnon's fate, and of his advice to Telemachus to hasten home (3.313–16). What is more, the last-mentioned narrative element in the story, the ambush, is replicated immediately in the ensuing narrative. And I would argue, against the traditional interpretation, that the effect of these and the other poetic devices associated with the story is a dynamic one, suggesting continuity into the narrative proper of the House of Atreus story rather than the figuration of a static point of reference for the *mythoi* of the *Odyssey*. When the story surfaces again, in Book 11, it forms part of the "background" that Odysseus must assimilate prior to his return to Ithaca and that, consequently, will influence the interpretation of events in that section of the poem as well.

PENELOPE AND CLYTEMNESTRA: THE FIRST *NEKYIA* (BOOK 11)

Discussions of the use of the House of Atreus story commonly distinguish between its use in the Telemachy, where it is understood to apply to the young hero, and its development in the *nekyia* and following, where it takes on the character of the "bad wife theme." Hölscher, for example, says, "It is ... clear ... that the story of the Atreidae in the Telemachy serves a paradigmatic function. ... The story in the *nekyia* is tuned to a different key" (1967a:4, 5).[49] Similarly, Lesky argues, "The first group of references [make up] the paradigm according to which Telemachus is supposed to pattern his actions.... The story of Agamemnon's murder here [in the *nekyia*] provides a different comparison from the story in the Telemachy. Here it is a matter of the contrasting picture to Penelope's faithfulness ..." (1967:11, 15).[50]

From the analytic point of view, this discrepancy in outlook is attributed to "older" and "younger" parts of the text (e.g., Kunst 1924–25:27–28). From the neoanalytic perspective, however, the different versions are re-

---

[49] "Es ist ... offenbar ... dass die Atridengeschichte in der Telemachie einem paradigmatischen Zwecke dient.... Auf einen anderen Ton ist die Geschichte in der Nekyia gestimmt."

[50] "Die erste Gruppe von Erwähnungen [make up] das Paradeigma, nach dem Telemachos sein Handeln einrichten soll.... Die Geschichte von der Totung Agamemnons dient hier [in the Nekyia] einem anderen Vergleiche als in der Telemachie. Hier geht es um das Gegenbild zu Penelopes Treue...."

garded as contemporaneous: "In contrast to the . . . tendency to interpret all individual parts as changing reflections of one and the same story, the tradition seems to lead us to the conclusion that already at the time in which the Telemachy and *nekyia* were composed different variants existed. These variants allowed the poet to make first Aegisthus, then Clytemnestra prominent in the report of the deed, or to name both together" (Lesky 1967:17).[51] But from the unitarian point of view, which is the one closer to my own here, the variation becomes an issue in compositional technique: ". . . The fact that the reports of the murder in the *Odyssey* first emphasize Aegisthus, then Clytemnestra does not convince me of the necessity of assuming different, preexisting variants—especially when one considers, on the one hand, the different poetic aims at each point and, on the other hand, the basic coherence of the accounts" (Eisenberger 1973:181 n. 79).[52]

Thus, Agamemnon's account of his murder in *Odyssey* 11.405–34 bears a close relation to the story reported in Book 4 by Menelaus (especially to lines 534–37; 4.535 = 11.411) and is commonly regarded as a complement of the earlier version. But from the perspective of my own emphasis on narrative effect, I would not interpret this complementarity with reference to authorial intention, as Eisenberger does: "As is well known, the narrative of the Atriedae at 405ff. is constructed and only to be understood as a supplement to the report of the Telemachy, especially in the fourth book" (Eisenberger 1973:181).[53] Rather, the effect of the echo is to establish a continuity with Menelaus's story despite the distance in narrative time between Books 4 and 11. This same continuity, however, underscores the difference in narrative focus and picks up elements from Book 3: Clytemnestra, we recall, was not mentioned in the Book 4 story.

In the speech of Agamemnon here and its companion discourse in 24.192–202, the central feature is the transfer to Clytemnestra of (sole) responsibility for the murder. At the opening of the speech, in 11.410, to be sure, she is only Aegisthus's accomplice ("[Aegisthus] killed him to-

---

[51] "Im Gegensatz zu der . . . Tendenz, alle Einzelpartien als wechselnde Reflexe ein und derselben Geschichte zu deuten, scheint uns die Überlieferung darauf zu führen, dass bereits zur Zeit, in der Telemachie und Nekyia gedichtet wurden, verschiedene Varianten bestanden, die es erlaubten, in den Berichten über die Tat einmal Aigisthos, dan wieder Klytaimestra hervortreten zu lassen, oder beide vereint zu nennen."

[52] ". . . Hat mich die Tatsache, dass die Berichte über die Ermordung in der Odyssee bald Aigisth, bald Klytaimnestra oder beide zusammen hervortreten lassen, in Anbetracht einerseits der jeweils verschiedenen poetischen Zwecke, andererseits der grundsätzlichen Vereinbarkeit der Berichte nicht von der Notwendigkeit der Annahme verschiedener, dem Dichter vorgegebener Varianten überzeugt."

[53] "Bekanntlich ist die Erzählung des Atriden 405ff. als Ergänzung der Berichte in der Telemachie, besonders im vierten Buche . . . angelegt und nur als solche zu verstehen."

gether with his dread wife," ἔκτα σὺν οὐλομένῃ ἀλόχῳ), although she is the sole agent indicated for the murder of Cassandra:

> οἰκτροτάτην δ' ἤκουσα ὄπα Πριάμοιο θυγατρὸς
> Κασσάνδρης, τὴν κτεῖνε Κλυταιμήστρη δολόμητις
> ἀμφ' ἐμοί· αὐτὰρ ἐγὼ ποτὶ γαίῃ χεῖρας ἀείρων
> βάλλον ἀποθνήσκων περὶ φασγάνῳ.

> (And I heard the most pitiful cry of the daughter of Priam, Cassandra, whom tricky-crafty (*dolomētis*) Clytemnestra killed on top of me. But I, raising my hands to the sword as I died, let them fall to the ground.)
>
> (11.421–24)

The enjambment at 11.422–23 is striking, and its effect is to associate Clytemnestra closely with the murder of Agememnon. The sentence immediately following poses formidable problems of interpretation and translation, and mine is only one of several possibilities, all of them unsatisfactory (see further Stanford 1978, 1:396 ad 423–24; Ameis-Hentze-Cauer 1964, 1(2):163 ad 423; and Heubeck 1989:102–3 ad 422–26). The general thrust of Agamemnon's complaint is clear; however: Cassandra was slaughtered on top of him, as he was in the process of expiring. This portrait involves Clytemnestra even more intimately in the slaughter, and at the end of the speech she is assigned full responsibility for it:

> οἷον δὴ καὶ κείνη ἐμήσατο ἔργον ἀεικές,
> κουριδίῳ τεύξασα πόσει φόνον.

> (Such was the unseemly thing that that one devised, fashioning murder for her wedded husband.)
>
> (11.429–30)

In the discourse as a whole, the pathetic element is strongly emphasized (Besslich 1966:32–33). Agamemnon reports: "Thus I died by a most pitiful death" (ὣς θάνον οἰκτίστῳ θανάτῳ, 11.412; cf. 11.416ff.),[54] and this is defined especially through the betrayal of affection ("But that dog-faced one turned her back on me, and though I was going into the house of Hades, she could not bring herself to shut my eyelids with her hands or to close my mouth," ἡ δὲ κυνῶπις / νοσφίσατ' οὐδέ μοι ἔτλη, ἰόντι περ εἰς Ἀίδαο, / χερσὶ κατ' ὀφθαλμοὺς ἑλέειν σύν τε στόμ' ἐρεῖσαι, 11.424–26). Similarly, Agamemnon describes his disappointed hopes for a happy homecoming: "Indeed, I had expected to come home welcome to my children and servants" (i.e., entire household) (ἤτοι ἔφην γε / ἀσπάσιος παί-

---

[54] And in particular 11.418: ἀλλά κε κεῖνα μάλιστα ἰδὼν ὀλοφύραο θυμῷ ("but upon seeing such things especially would you have sorrowed in your heart"; and cf. οἰκτροτάτην . . . ὄπα ("a most pitiful sound") at 11.421, of Cassandra's cry.

δεσσιν ἰδὲ δμώεσσιν ἐμοῖσιν / οἴκαδ' ἐλεύσεσθαι, 11.430–32); and he refers also to having missed his child's greeting: "But my wife did not even allow me the pleasure of seeing my son" (ἡ δ' ἐμὴ οὐδέ περ υἱὸς ἐνιπλησθῆναι ἄκοιτις / ὀφθαλμοῖσιν ἔασε, 11.452–53).

In the course of this speech Agamemnon twice formulates a moral condemning all women, and this underscores his shifting of the responsibility for his death to Clytemnestra: "So there is nothing more dreadful or shameless than a woman who conceives such deeds in her heart" (ὣς οὐκ αἰνότερον καὶ κύντερον ἄλλο γυναικός, / ἥ τις δὴ τοιαῦτα μετὰ φρεσὶν ἔργα βάληται, 11.427–28); "and so she has poured shame upon herself and upon the race of female women who shall be, and even upon the one who acts well" (οἵ τε κατ' αἶσχος ἔχευε καὶ ἐσσομένῃσιν ὀπίσσω / θηλυτέρῃσι γυναιξί, καὶ ἥ κ' εὐεργὸς ἔῃσιν, 11.433–34). Concerning line 11.427, there is general agreement that it stands as a condemnation of all women, even with 11.428, which is omitted in many of the manuscripts.[55] Odysseus agrees with Agamemnon's general moral insofar as it is drawn on the basis of the experience of Helen, "on whose account many of us died" (Ἑλένης μὲν ἀπωλόμεθ' εἵνεκα πολλοί, 11.438), and of Clytemnestra, who "fashioned a snare for you while you were far away" (σοὶ ... δόλον ἤρτυε τηλόθ' ἐόντι, 11.439).

Agamemnon, however, goes on to assimilate Odysseus's situation to his own. He warns him against gentleness and even honesty before his wife ("now don't you too then be gentle even with your wife, and don't tell her the whole account that you know, but tell her part, and keep part hidden," τῳ νῦν μή ποτε καὶ σὺ γυναικί περ ἤπιος εἶναι / μηδ' οἱ μῦθον ἅπαντα πιφαυσκέμεν, ὅν κ' ἐὺ εἰδῇς, / ἀλλὰ τὸ μὲν φάσθαι, τὸ δὲ καὶ κεκρυμμένον εἶναι, 11.441–43), assuring him all the while that he has no reason to expect murder from Penelope ("but not for you, Odysseus, will there be murder by a woman at any rate," ἀλλ' οὐ σοί γ', Ὀδυσεῦ, φόνος ἔσσεται ἔκ γε γυναικός, 11.444).

In the closing segment of the speech, however, just after he has thought of Orestes and just before he asks Odysseus about him, Agamemnon once again insists on Clytemnestra's sole responsibility for his death: "But before that [i.e., before I saw Orestes] she killed me even myself" (πάρος δέ με πέφνε καὶ αὐτόν, 11.453); and he delivers another warning, which concludes with a condemnation of all women:

ἄλλο δέ τοι ἐρέω, σὺ δ' ἐνὶ φρεσὶ βάλλεο σῇσι·
κρύβδην, μηδ' ἀναφανδά, φίλην ἐς πατρίδα γαῖαν
νῆα κατισχέμεναι, ἐπεὶ οὐκέτι πιστὰ γυναιξίν.

---

[55] "Verse 427 contains, at any rate, a generalization, even if verse 428 is genuine" (Besslich 1966:30 n. 38; cf. Heubeck 1989:103 ad 436–39).

(And I will tell you something else, and do you store it in your heart;
secretly, and not openly, bring your ship upon the shore
of your own fatherland, since women are no longer trustworthy.)

(11.454–56)

Many of the ancient manuscripts omit these lines, since as Hölscher explains, "they appeared to contradict the praise of Penelope" (1967a:7).[56] The scholiast to H remarks, "These are not carried in most on the grounds that they conflict with the preceding lines" (οὐδὲ οὗτοι ἐφέροντο ἐν τοῖς πλείστοις ὡς μαχόμενοι τοῖς προκειμένοις, Dindorf 1962:514 ad 452), and many of the modern editors follow suit: e.g., Ameis-Hentze states that "it is inappropriate for Agamemnon to return to warning and suspicion, after he has just celebrated the faithful Penelope as the opposite of Clytemnestra" (1877–90, 2:118 ad 454–56).[57]

There is no reason to omit the line, however, since the structure of this discourse anticipates precisely that of the encomium to Penelope in Book 24 (24.192–202);[58] here, as there, the example of Clytemnestra represents the general type, and displaces that of Penelope. In 24.192–202, the praise of Penelope is juxtaposed with the blame of Clytemnestra, and the latter is generalized over the former through the same formulaic tag that appears in a similar context in Book 11: "for all female women, even she who acts well" (θηλυτέρῃσι γυναιξί, καὶ ἥ κ' εὐεργὸς ἔῃσιν, 24.202 = 11.434). Here in the first *nekyia*, the praise of Penelope and the assurances of her faithfulness are enclosed on either side by warnings, and inserted into a general framework of betrayal and mistrust. Agamemnon concludes his discourse with the all-encompassing warning to Odysseus that "women are no longer to be trusted" (ἐπεὶ οὐκέτι πιστὰ γυναιξίν, 11.456).

We should note also that Odysseus, too, when he announces to Alcinous the subject of the second half of his *mythos*, regards Agamemnon's fate as a generalized form of *nostos*: "the sufferings of my companions, who indeed perished afterwards, and who escaped out from under the groaning battle-cry of the Trojans, but upon their homecoming died by an evil woman's working of her will" (κήδε' ἐμῶν ἑτάρων, οἳ δὴ μετόπισθεν ὄλοντο, / οἳ Τρώων μὲν ὑπεξέφυγον στονόεσσαν ἀυτήν, / ἐν νόστῳ δ' ἀπόλοντο κακῆς ἰότητι γυναικός, 11.382–84). Clytemnestra is certainly the "evil woman" meant here, both because "upon homecoming" is specified, and because in what immediately follows Odysseus does in fact go on to relate the story of Agamemnon's slaughter (cf. Ameis-Hentze-Cauer 1964, 1(2):160 ad 384).

[56] "Sie schienen in Widerspruch zu stehen zu Penelopes Preisung."
[57] "Denn diese Rückkehr des Agamemnon zur Warnung und Verdächtigung, nachdem er so eben die treue Penelope als Gegenbild zur Klytämnestra gefeiert hat, ist ungehörig."
[58] Besslich discusses the rhetorical structure of Agamemnon's discourse, and draws attention to the ring-composition of 11.441–56 (1966:30–33).

The pattern whereby Clytemnestra displaces Penelope as the general female type, then, is appropriate to Agamemnon, but, as its reinforcement through generalizing maxims suggests, it is not peculiar to him. It is repeated in Book 13, when Odysseus finally arrives in his own fatherland, and this, as I shall argue, conditions the interpretation of the scenes on Ithaca.

Chapter Three

COMING HOME/GOING HOME (BOOKS 13, 15, 16)

IN THE EXCHANGE between Agamemnon and Odysseus in the first *nekyia*, at approximately the midpoint in the narrative, Clytemnestra, Penelope, and Helen appear together for the only time in the poem. Odysseus, having heard the sad story of Agamemnon's murder, reflects sorrowfully on the disasters brought to the House of Atreus "through women's counsels" (γυναικείας διὰ βουλὰς, 11.437) and refers to both Clytemnestra and Helen. Whereupon Agamemnon warns Odysseus about Penelope, while assuring him at the same time that he has nothing to fear from her (11.441–44). The conjunction of the three women is a significant one, and I shall argue in this chapter that in the books that are transitional from the first to the second half of the poem, the narrative paradigm for Odysseus's return is reformulated from the parallel of Clytemnestra and *nostos* to the model of Helen and *xenia*.

This reformulation is constructed in the text principally through the parallelism between Odysseus and Telemachus. This parallelism operates throughout the poem, but it is brought into the foreground in this middle section of the narrative. In Book 13 Odysseus finally comes home, while in Book 15 Telemachus, at Athena's urging, goes home. Both heroes confront the threat of ambush, and both have something to fear from the woman who waits in the halls. The danger that Odysseus might suffer Agamemnon's fate is raised in Book 13 only to be dismissed, in accordance with Agamemnon's own earlier assurances to him that "you, Odysseus, will not meet with murder from your wife" (ἀλλ' οὐ σοί γ', Ὀδυσεῦ, φόνος ἔσσεται ἔκ γε γυναικός, 11.444); but the possibility remains that Penelope will abandon the house, taking part of its property with her: Athena warns Telemachus to "watch out lest she [Penelope] carry some property out of the house without your consent" (μή νύ τι σεῦ ἀέκητι δόμων ἐκ κτῆμα φέρηται, 15.19). We can compare here the necessity in the *Iliad* to recover, not just Helen herself, but "Helen and all her possessions" (Ἑλένην ... καὶ κτήματα πάντα, *Iliad* 3.282, 285, 458; cf. Ἑλένῃ καὶ κτήμασι πᾶσι μάχεσθαι in 3.70, 91).

After Telemachus and Odysseus are reunited as father and son in Book 16, Odysseus adopts the disguise of a beggar and comes into his own house as a stranger/guest (*xeinos*). *Nostos* is thus conflated with *xenia*, and the parallel between Penelope and Helen is now extended to encompass the double tales of Helen's conduct at Troy. This raises the question whether Penelope will recognize Odysseus and welcome him home, or betray him through the seduction of other men. This alternative is an important structuring feature of Books 18 and 19, and accordingly I take it up in Chapters Four and Five; it is prefigured in Book 16, however, through a reformulation of the alternatives confronting Penelope.

Warnings about Penelope (Books 13, 15)

At the beginning of Book 13, the Phaeacians leave Odysseus asleep on the shores of Ithaca; he awakens not knowing where he is and encounters Athena disguised as a young native boy. Odysseus attempts to conceal his own identity with the first of his lying-tales, and Athena thereupon reveals herself. In the course of their subsequent dialogue, Athena chides Odysseus for being, as she says, "glib[1] ... and suspicious and watchful" (ἐπητής ... καὶ ἀγχίνοος καὶ ἐχέφρων, 13.332). She instances his hesitation to proceed home eagerly in expectation of a warm welcome (ἀσπασίως ... ἐλθὼν / ἵετ', 13.333–34) and his intention to put his wife to the test (πρίν γ' ἔτι σῆς ἀλόχου πειρήσεαι, 13.336)—despite the fact, as Athena assures him, that Penelope sits waiting for him "as always" (αὔτως, 13.336), lamenting for him always (αἰεί, 13.337), day and night.

These lines (13.333–38), like most of those in which suspicion attaches to Penelope, were athetized by Aristarchus, and suspected by the older editors. In this case, the grounds adduced are that Odysseus has not yet indicated an absence of desire to see his wife and child: "These six verses are athetized because she has received no sign from him that he does not yet want to see his wife" (ἀθετοῦνται στίχοι ἕξ, ὅτι οὐδὲν εἴληφε παρ' αὐτοῦ σημεῖον τοῦ μήπω βούλεσθαι τὴν γαμετὴν ἰδεῖν, scholium to HQ [Dindorf 1962:573 ad 333–38]).

Commentators differ, however, about whether they think Athena has correctly anticipated Odysseus's own thoughts, as Erbse argues (1972:158–60),[2] or whether she has misread them. The scholiast, supporting athetesis of the passage, deduces from a later passage (see below) that "the opposite to this [a reluctance to run and see his family] appears to be the case ... he himself was eager to see his wife" (scholium to HQ, Dindorf 1962:573 ad 333–38),[3] and Clay argues that Athena is employing

---

[1] On the meaning of ἐπητής, see Hoekstra 1989:185 ad 332 and Russo 1985:200–201 ad 128, who translate as "well-spoken," "polite."

[2] Similarly, Ameis-Hentze-Cauer explains, "He wants, as Athena surmises, to test them [his wife and son] himself," although they add, "this supposition is, however, not confirmed by his surprised answer at 383ff." (1964, 2(1):21 ad 335).

[3] τοὐναντίον γὰρ διὰ τοῦτο αὐτῷ ἐπιφαίνεται, ἵνα κρύψῃ αὐτοῦ τὴν εἴσοδον· διὸ καί φησι

here a diversionary tactic: "She flatters Odysseus and attempts to deflect his distrust of her to another object" (Clay 1983:203).

Stanford explains more convincingly that Odysseus has learned from the example of Agamemnon (1978, 2:211 ad 332ff. and 2:213 ad 383–84). And indeed there is in Athena's speech a faint echo of Agamemnon's earlier words: Athena had contrasted with Odysseus "another man [who] upon returning home from his wanderings would have happily (ἀσπασίως) run to see his children and wife in his halls" (ἀσπασίως γάρ κ' ἄλλος ἀνὴρ ἀλήμενος ἐλθὼν / ἵετ' ἐνὶ μεγάροις ἰδέειν παῖδάς τ' ἄλοχόν τε, 13.333–34),[4] and Agamemnon had explained to Odysseus in the underworld how "in fact, I had expected to come home welcome (ἀσπάσιος) to my children and servants" (ἤτοι ἔφην γε / ἀσπάσιος παίδεσσιν ἰδὲ δμώεσσιν ἐμοῖσιν / οἴκαδ' ἐλεύσεσθαι, 11.430–32).

This motif is further strengthened a little later in the same episode when Athena and Odysseus sit down together to "devise destruction for the arrogant suitors" (13.372–73), and Athena gives Odysseus further details of the situation on Ithaca. She reports:

> ἡ δὲ σὸν αἰεὶ νόστον ὀδυρομένη κατὰ θυμὸν
> πάντας μέν ῥ' ἔλπει καὶ ὑπίσχεται ἀνδρὶ ἑκάστῳ,
> ἀγγελίας προϊεῖσα, νόος δέ οἱ ἄλλα μενοινᾷ.

(And she [Penelope], though grieving over your homecoming in her heart, arouses hopes in all of them, and makes promises to each man, sending them messages, but her mind yearns for other things.)[5]

(13.379–81)

Odysseus's reaction is swift and forceful:

> ὦ πόποι, ἦ μάλα δὴ Ἀγαμέμνονος Ἀτρεΐδαο
> φθίσεσθαι κακὸν οἶτον ἐνὶ μεγάροισιν ἔμελλον,
> εἰ μή μοι σὺ ἕκαστα, θεά, κατὰ μοῖραν ἔειπες.

(Oh no! Surely I was just about to die by the evil fate of Agamemnon son of Atreus in my own halls unless you had told me precisely, goddess, each of these things.)

(13.383–85)

The context here can only suggest betrayal by Penelope, although editors and commentators have attempted to palliate the obvious force of the

---

[383–85]. οὕτως οὖν αὐτὸς ἠπείγετο ἰδεῖν τὴν γαμετήν (scholium to HQ, Dindorf 1962:573 ad 333–38).

[4] Cf. Ameis-Hentze-Cauer (1964, 2(1):21 ad 333), "ἀσπασίως .. with ἵετο, elsewhere joined with ἰδεῖν."

[5] Athena's account here recalls that of Antinous in the assembly in Book 2; 13.380–81 = 2.91–92.

implied comparison between Penelope and Clytemnestra. Wilamowitz, for example, complains concerning the logic of Odysseus's response, "she [Athena] has neither related everything to him κατὰ μοῖραν ἕκαστα, nor is it apparent wherein the similarity to Agamemnon should reside" (1884:107),[6] and he goes on to argue that Athena's speech in 13.376–81 is an interpolation that has displaced an original full exposition of the situation on Ithaca.[7] Concerning the present speech Wilamowitz says: "I have no reservations that this stupidity cannot belong to the poet of Book 13" (1927:12).[8] Focke argues that Athena's original speech had to do exclusively with the suitors, that Odysseus was hearing about them now for the first time, and that indeed "the artistic sensibility of the poet of O has been preserved in that the suitor question has been delayed so long" (1943:278).[9] Merkelbach, too, explains the force of Odysseus's reaction in 382ff. with reference to information concerning the suitors: "Athena must also have described the arrogance and the violence of the suitors. Thus is Odysseus's outcry justified" (1969:61).[10]

The scholiast's explanation of the lines is an especially peculiar one, but it is partially adopted by Erbse in his defense of the passage. In support of the athetesis of lines 13.333–38 (cited above), in which Athena chided Odysseus for his suspiciousness, the scholiast (cited above) says that 13.383–85 imply the presence of intention to go and see his wife from which the goddess must inhibit him. Erbse, then, argues in defense of the two passages that in the first, when Odysseus hesitates to proceed home immediately, the goddess correctly divines his thoughts; the second passage, however, implies that Odysseus had not in fact hesitated, but had originally intended to go home right away—thus, the goddess had to prevent him from doing so. Erbse does not reconcile the contradiction here, but resorts to the weak supposition that "the goddess remains—as is proper—the wiser one in the end" (1972:159–60).[11]

The concern with Penelope is pronounced throughout this episode, and it is difficult to explain the coherence of the text without imputing to Odysseus a mistrust of Penelope based in part on what he had heard from Aga-

---

[6] "Sie [Athena] hat ihm jetzt weder κατὰ μοῖραν ἕκαστα erzählt, noch ist ersichtlich, worin die Ähnlichkeit mit Agamemnon liegen soll."

[7] Cf. Merkelbach, "in A the situation on Ithaca must have been explained at this point" (1969:61). The present speech is believed to have displaced an account of the weaving trick, which now appears in Book 2 (ibid.).

[8] "Ich halte mich nicht dabei auf, dass diese Stümperei dem Dichter des 13 nicht gehören kann."

[9] "Der Kunstverstand des O-Dichters hat sich auch darin bewährt, dass er die Freierfrage so lange hinausgeschoben hat."

[10] "Auch den Übermut und die Gewalttätigkeit der Freier muss Athene beschrieben haben. Da ist der Ausruf des Odysseus wohl berechtigt."

[11] "Die Göttin bleibt—wie es sich gehört—am Ende doch die Klügere."

memnon in the underworld.¹² The contrast of 13.383–85 with Anticleia's reassurances in 11.181–87 is sometimes stressed, although those lines are themselves problematic on account of an internal contradiction; Page, for example, observes that Anticleia cannot be both ignorant of the suitors' presence and aware of Telemachus's status as an adult male (1955:41). Hoekstra remarks concerning Erbse's defense of the lines that "πειρήσεαι [in line 336] remains offending" (Hoekstra 1989:185 ad 333–38), and unitarian readers in general put the case as Thornton does: "Why does Odysseus approach his own wife Penelope like a potential enemy and traitor? The background to this is what happened to Agamemnon at the hands of Clytemnestra" (1970:91).

Murnaghan and other recent feminist readings are correct, I think, to stress the generic rather than particular form of this mistrust: "Penelope is as dangerous as Clytemnestra because the nature of her position as Odysseus' wife means that, whether she wants to or not, she eventually attracts his enemies to his house" (Murnaghan 1987:126). The presence of this misogynistic bias should not be regarded as self-explanatory, however, or as a simple reflex of the social system in which it was encoded; its function in the text demands further investigation.

Athena's warning to Odysseus constitutes the last instance of the House of Atreus story in the narrative, except for its invocation by Agamemnon in Book 24. It occurs at an important moment, and amidst several indications of the need for ascertaining Penelope's loyalty: Athena had already warned Odysseus at their first encounter to reveal himself to no man or woman (13.308), and Odysseus instructs Telemachus in 16.300ff. to conceal the news of his return, specifying there the need to withhold the announcement from Laertes and Penelope, as well as from Eumaeus and all of the household servants. The House of Atreus theme is consolidated for Odysseus, then, on the threshold of his reentry into his palace, and it serves to condition his approach to Penelope with the expectation that she might betray him. Before we encounter her again, however, there is a somewhat different warning about Penelope delivered by Athena, this time to Telemachus, in order to speed his departure from Sparta, and it forms part of the bridge that connects Books 4 and 15.

Book 15 is the point where the two principal plot lines of the narrative converge into a single narrative direction that is maintained consistently throughout the remaining second half of the poem.¹³ The compositional

---

¹² As Wilamowitz remarks, by way of explaining the Bearbeiter's train of thought, "To be sure it has been seven years since Odysseus spoke to Agamemnon and heard his fate, but it has only been a few hundred verses since the parallel was drawn between Clytemnestra and Penelope in Book 11" (1884:108).

¹³ Hoekstra understands the compositional unity of this section similarly: "The lines [of the main and secondary plots] gradually approach one another and meet in the recognition

form of this section of the narrative is admired even by analysts—"the weaving of the two threads into a single strand in the Fifteenth book reveals an uncommonly skilful hand" (Page 1955:72)—and Hoekstra extends this judgment to apply to the episode of the ambush in Book 16: "The three threads appear to have been skilfully interwoven. In spite of the objections made by analytic critics, and whatever the genesis of the *Odyssey* may be, xiii–xvi show a well-considered composition" (Hoekstra 1989:147).

The *nostoi* of Odysseus and Telemachus are joined to the narrative that precedes and follows by means of repetition, recapitulation, and redefinition of narrative motifs, and through the use of what Delebecque identifies as "bridge episodes" (charnières) (Delebecque 1958:71–107; for discussion, see below). The "internal chronology" of this section of the poem has also been discussed fully (see esp. Delebecque 1958:11–17, 1980:1–35), in particular because it appears that two days elapse for Telemachus and only one for Odysseus between 14.532–15.6 (the point at which they are both asleep at night) and 15.495–16.2 (the dawn on which Telemachus arrives in Ithaca and Odysseus awakens).[14]

At the opening of Book 15, Athena prefaces her instructions to Telemachus with a repetition of Nestor's earlier warning:

>Τηλέμαχ', οὐκέτι καλὰ δόμων ἄπο τῆλ' ἀλάλησαι,
>κτήματά τε προλιπὼν ἄνδρας τ' ἐν σοῖσι δόμοισιν
>οὕτω ὑπερφιάλους· μή τοι κατὰ πάντα φάγωσι
>κτήματα δασσάμενοι, σὺ δὲ τηυσίην ὁδὸν ἔλθῃς.

(Telemachus, it is no longer good for you to wander so far
  and long from your house,
leaving behind your property, and men in the house
so high-spirited, lest they divide up all your wealth
and consume it, and you will have gone on a fruitless journey.)
                                              (15.10–13 [15.10b–13 = 3.313b–16])

In Book 3 this warning had operated as the moral drawn from the story of Clytemnestra's betrayal of Agamemnon. Here, it prefaces Athena's elaboration of the dangers that await Telemachus upon his return; these include the courtship of Penelope and the suitors' ambush. Athena's repetition in this new context of Nestor's warning now instantiates a structural equiva-

---

scene [of Book 16]. After attention has been shifted towards the suitors by Odysseus' and Telemachus' plotting to kill them, there begins, in connection with them, a short third episode [16.322–451] which takes up the narrative broken off in 4.847 and points forward to the development of the action in Books 17–24" (Hoekstra 1989:147).

[14] On this apparent temporal discrepancy, see Page 1955:66–68 and 77–80 n. 14; cf. also Eisenberger 1973:91 n. 1; Delebecque 1958:31–41, 1980:16–19; and Fenik 1974:187 n. 90.

lence between Penelope's remarriage and Clytemnestra's betrayal. This adds considerably to the complexity of the narrative, since that same remarriage, as we shall see, is later presented as authorized by Odysseus and in Telemachus's own interests.

As the context shows, Penelope's remarriage and Clytemnestra's betrayal each represent an obstacle to the hero's *nostos* and a threat to the integrity of the *oikos*. Here too, as in the case of Odysseus's fears expressed at 13.383ff., ancient and modern commentators alike resist the surface implications about Penelope. Aristophanes of Byzantium, for example, athetizes line 19 (see below) because of its "mean-spiritedness" (ἐπὶ σμικρολογίᾳ), although Austin explains that "the somewhat slanderous aspersions which Athena makes on Penelope's character must be seen in the perspective of Telemachos' recognition of his adult duties at home . . ." (1969:51); and Finley regards the episode as a "particularly young and unworthy dream" (1978:8). In Ameis-Hentze-Cauer, Athena's concern is thought to be illogical: "This information also does not accord with the picture that the poet otherwise gives us [at 13.78]. He has invented the remarkable requirement in order to achieve an effective motivation for Athena's warning speech" (1964, 2(1):60 ad 15.18). Page, however, objecting to Kirchhoff's complaint that Athena arouses Telemachus "through the pretense of things . . . which she knows do not correspond to the truth" (Kirchhoff 1879:504 ad 15.9),[15] explains that "if they do not correspond to the truth, they do correspond to what Telemachus expects and fears; and I do not know what further justification they need" (Page 1955:80).

Athena warns Telemachus that although Penelope is still in the house, "already her father and her brothers are urging her to marry Eurymachus" (15.16–17). This is a particularly perilous situation, since the intrusion of Penelope's father and brothers means the active presence on the scene of a set of competing interests from another household. It is not until we have specific evidence of litigation concerning inheritance, in fourth-century Athens, that we have the wherewithal to document a situation of rivalry and hostility between competing lineages.[16] It is a widely recognized feature of the marriage pattern that we see reflected in the *Odyssey*, however, that the exchange of women around which it is organized generates a structural antagonism between the woman's father and brothers on the one

---

[15] ". . . Durch die Vorspiegelung von Dingen . . . von denen sie weiss, dass sie der Wahrheit nicht entsprechen."

[16] See the discussion of problems in the Athenian system of marriage and inheritance in MacDowell 1978:84–108; cf. also Pitt-Rivers (1977b:113–25) on the conflict that inheres in the Mediterranean marriage-system between the exogamous and endogamous principles. Monro (1901:302 n. 22) discusses the older suggestion that the suitors represent vestiges of a system in which the prerogative of disposing of a widow fell to the "kinsmen" who made up the tribal council.

hand, and her husband and his family on the other. Athena is certainly alluding in this warning to some danger of this kind. She goes on to specify:

μή νύ τι σεῦ ἀέκητι δόμων ἐκ κτῆμα φέρηται.
οἶσθα γὰρ οἷος θυμὸς ἐνὶ στήθεσσι γυναικός·
κείνου βούλεται οἶκον ὀφέλλειν, ὅς κεν ὀπυίῃ,
παίδων δὲ προτέρων καὶ κουριδίοιο φίλοιο
οὐκέτι μέμνηται τεθνηότος οὐδὲ μεταλλᾷ.
ἀλλὰ σύ γ᾽ ἐλθὼν αὐτὸς ἐπιτρέψειας ἕκαστα,
δμῳάων ἥ τίς τοι ἀρίστη φαίνεται εἶναι,
εἰς ὅ κέ τοι φήνωσι θεοὶ κυδρὴν παράκοιτιν.

(Watch out lest she [Penelope] carry some property out of the house
without your consent.
For you know what kind of heart a woman has in her breast;
she wants to increase the house of the man who marries her,
and of her former children and of her beloved wedded husband
she has no memory once he is dead, nor does she ask after them.
But as for you, go and yourself hand over everything
to whichever one of the serving-women seems to you the best one,
until the gods make clear who is to be your honored wife.)

(15.19–26)

The dangers that Athena anticipates here represent a variation on the House of Atreus motif, a variation, formulated in light of the motif, which comes to the fore increasingly in the second half of the poem. The anticipated dangers center on the implications of Penelope's legitimate remarriage, which is now envisioned as a form of abandonment, rather than on the possibility of an act of betrayal such as that attributed to Clytemnestra. Thus, as we shall see, this envisioned remarriage, although specifically authorized by Telemachus's coming of age (18.269–70) and earlier anticipated by Odysseus as an apparently reasonable alternative to waiting (11.177–79), is attracted first into the paradigm of the House of Atreus motif, and then, by the end of Books 15 and 16, into the model represented by the stories of Helen. Here, its threatening aspect is formulated with specific reference to Telemachus, and Athena's contrast draws attention especially to the impermanence of the bond that joins husband and wife in the patriarchal setting.[17] Her formulation is a general one, but it

[17] On this important feature of patriarchal society, see the discussions in Arthur 1973, 1982 and Vernant 1969, which, drawing on Gernet's classic discussion of the communal hearth (Gernet 1976), elaborates especially the symbolic dimensions of the *epiklēros*. Murnaghan's discussion of Penelope in the *Odyssey* is particularly attentive to "relationships [that] are not based on any natural tie but are artificial social constructs" (1987:38, cf. 163–64), although she does not treat the passage that is before us.

amounts to a sociological truth for which the case of Helen serves as a particular instance: Helen had earlier, in the account she presented to Menelaus, Telemachus, and Peisistratus, claimed to have regretted the "abandon[ment] of my child and bedchamber and husband" (παῖδά τ' ἐμὴν νοσφισσαμένην θάλαμόν τε πόσιν τε, 4.263).[18]

The reformulation of Penelope's situation around the model of Helen is signaled in the narrative by a formulaic shift. In Book 13, Athena's description of Penelope replicates that of Antinous in the assembly of Book 2 and provokes Odysseus's outburst of mistrust: "She arouses hopes in all of them, and makes promises to each man, sending them messages; but her mind yearns for other things" (2.91–92 = 13.380–81). And in Book 16, Telemachus's description of the situation for the disguised Odysseus repeats what he had told the disguised Athena in Book 1: "She neither refuses the hatefull marriage nor is she able to bring things to a conclusion" (ἡ δ' οὔτ' ἀρνεῖται στυγερὸν γάμον οὔτε τελευτὴν / ποιῆσαι δύναται, 16.126–27 = 1.249–50).

In the course of Book 16, however, new alternatives appear for Penelope that dominate the action for the remainder of the poem. As Telemachus first formulates it when he questions Eumaeus: "Does my mother remain still in the halls or has some other man has married her already?" (ἤ μοι ἔτ' ἐν μεγάροις μήτηρ μένει, ἦέ τις ἤδη / ἀνδρῶν ἄλλος ἔγημεν, 16.33–34 = 11.178–79). Telemachus implies here what he states more clearly later, that Penelope's remarriage would represent a form of both private and public betrayal, entailing lack of regard (*anaideia*) for both Odysseus and the people's opinion:

> μητρὶ δ' ἐμῇ δίχα θυμὸς ἐνὶ φρεσὶ μερμηρίζει,
> ἢ αὐτοῦ παρ' ἐμοί τε μένῃ καὶ δῶμα κομίζῃ,
> εὐνήν τ' αἰδομένη πόσιος δήμοιό τε φῆμιν,
> ἢ ἤδη ἅμ' ἕπηται Ἀχαιῶν ὅς τις ἄριστος
> μνᾶται ἐνὶ μεγάροισιν ἀνὴρ καὶ πλεῖστα πόρῃσιν.

> (My mother's heart within her mind debates this way and that,
> whether to remain beside me and keep the house,
> having regard for her husband's bed and the people's report,
> or whether to follow after whoever is best of the Achaeans
> that woo her in the halls and offers the most gifts.)
>
> (16.73–77)

This evaluation, it should be remarked, conforms with that of Penelope herself (compare 16.73–77 with 19.524–29). West, following Wehrli

---

[18] In the *Iliad*, Helen speaks of having "left behind her bedchamber and family and beloved child and the lovely companionship of young women" (θάλαμον γνωτούς τε λιποῦσα / παῖδά τε τηλυγέτην καὶ ὁμηλικίην ἐρατεινήν, *Iliad* 3.174–75).

(1959:232–33 n. 15) and others, dismisses its importance: "We should not attach too much importance to gossip as a deterrent, [since] elsewhere [Penelope] admits that both her son and her parents wish her to decide on a second husband" (West 1988:58). But this amounts to overreading the complicating factor in the narrative of Telemachus's coming of age; for while from Telemachus's perspective Penelope's remarriage is thereby rendered legitimate, this same remarriage from Odysseus's point of view constitutes a betrayal in the form of desertion.

In the early books of the narrative, the representation of Penelope's dilemma—and her behavior—left open possibilities that were both vague and ominous and were thereby associated with the paradigm of Clytemnestra. Throughout the final books, however, the question for Penelope is articulated as a specific choice between marrying one of the suitors or remaining by the side of Telemachus. This alternative—the choice between abandonment or faithfulness—recapitulates Helen's choice at the beginning of the Trojan War. And as we shall see, when this alternative is played out in the narrative, it is represented so as to suggest an analogy to the diptych of tales about Helen in Troy that were related in Book 4, which similarly juxtaposed loyalty and seduction of other men.

On the surface of the narrative, to be sure, Penelope repudiates the suitors' attentions and remains steadfastly faithful to Odysseus until signs appear that Telemachus has reached maturity. She thereupon regretfully decides upon remarriage, in accordance with Odysseus's earlier instructions. But the straightforward meaning of this behavior is complicated by the network of alternative scenarios in which it is encased, and by the variety of implications that are attached to the options that lie before Penelope. It is against this background of conflicting outcomes and multiple meanings that the narrative action of the subsequent books must be interpreted.

Telemachus's *Kleos*

The transition in this middle section of the poem from the narrative paradigm of Clytemnestra and the House of Atreus to Helen and the assault upon Troy is mediated through Telemachus, specifically, as I shall argue, through the theme of his *kleos*. A. T. Edwards has argued that *kleos* in the *Odyssey* entails both *nostos* and revenge, and that consequently, "κλέος from revenge . . . is formulated so that Telemachus, Penelope, and Odysseus are mutually dependent" (1985:87; cf. also Nagy 1979:38–40). As the full extention of the argument makes clear, however, this *kleos* belongs primarily to Odysseus, for whom it functions in addition to "preserve . . . [the *kleos*] which he won at Troy" (Edwards 1985:85): "In the *Iliad* κλέος is something won through warfare, and its most common source is victory. . . . In the *Odyssey* the κλέος of victory is primarily that of revenge. . . .

There is also, however, a κλέος associated with death. . . . Death while fighting does in fact bring κλέος. . . . However, just as a hero's death can enhance and preserve κλέος, so a wretched, unworthy death can destroy it" (ibid.:73–74). According to this pattern, Penelope and Telemachus act principally to facilitate the *nostos* and revenge of Odysseus, so that they participate almost vicariously in the *kleos* he thereby gains. This reading, though attractive and convincing insofar as it applies to Odysseus, does not adequately comprehend, it seems to me, the specificity of the kleos belonging either to Penelope or to Telemachus.

The subject of Telemachus's *kleos* is ordinarily approached from two slightly different perspectives. First, the question is raised: In what might the *kleos* of Telemachus consist? And second, critics argue that Telemachus has no identifiable *kleos* of his own, but that his *kleos* is a matter either of recovering that of his father and transferring it to himself, or of approximating himself to his father and thus acquiring his father's *kleos* by association.

A *kleos* belonging specifically to Telemachus is never described as such in the poem, although Athena alludes to it prospectively in 1.93–95: "I shall send him [Telemachus] into Sparta and into sandy Pylos, to find out about his own father's *nostos*, if he hears anything of it, and so that noble *kleos* might accrue to him among men" (πέμψω δ' ἐς Σπάρτην τε καὶ ἐς Πύλον ἠμαθόεντα / νόστον πευσόμενον πατρὸς φίλου, ἤν που ἀκούσῃ, / ἠδ' ἵνα μιν κλέος ἐσθλὸν ἐν ἀνθρώποισιν ἔχῃσιν), and again in 13.422–23: "I myself sent him off, so that he might garner noble *kleos* in going there" (αὐτή μιν πόμπευον, ἵνα κλέος εσθλὸν ἄροιτο / κεῖσ' ἐλθών). Concerning these two passages, Focke remarks, "There is no doubt, κλέος here [13.422] and also at 1.95 refers unequivocally to the journey and only to it" (1943:59).[19] In addition, Focke attributes to the "poet of T" the heroization of a conception of κλέος meaning "report": "And with κλέος the poet of T usually thinks not only of valor at arms, the daring of a sea traveler and adventures in foreign lands. He uses the word mostly in the sense of rumor, report, information" (ibid.: 59–60).[20] And recently, Peter Jones (1988) has offered an extensive defense of the notion that Telemachus's *kleos* is constituted by his journey around the Peloponnese. Jones argues that Telemachus in the first four books, and especially in Books 3–4, is offered an account of himself (a *kleos*) that stresses his similarity to Odysseus; in the later books, this potential similarity is acted out in the narrative, and in this way Telemachus's potential *kleos* is consolidated in reality.

[19] "Kein Zweifel, κλέος bezieht sich hier [13.422] und somit auch 1.95 unzweideutig auf die Reise und nur auf sie."

[20] "Und bei κλέος pflegt der T-Dichter nicht nur an Waffenruhm, an Seefahrerkühnheit und Abenteuer in fremden Ländern zu denken. Er gebraucht das Wort zumeist im Sinne von Gerede, Gerücht, Kunde."

Rüter, too, argues that Telemachus, in encountering "the fame of Odysseus," thereby also confronts his own: "Thus, as an unknown, Telemachus encounters the fame of Odysseus; his tears betray how deeply he is affected. Menelaus and Helen recognize him, and he is also led to self-recognition, to the recognition that he is the son of such a father" (1969:239).[21] Klingner says that "Telemachus encounters his and his father's affairs . . . everywhere played out through memory . . . (1964:77).[22] Murnaghan argues along the same lines, but she identifies Telemachus's *kleos* with that of Odysseus even more closely: the purpose of Telemachus's journey, in her view, is "to create the conditions that will allow him to take his father's place. . . . His aim is to recover his father's *kleos* . . . so that that *kleos* is available to be transferred to him . . ." (1987:157).

In general it is the case that Telemachus's adequacy to his role—his maturity, as it is sometimes called—is gauged throughout the *Odyssey* with reference to the male figures who function as paradigms for him, and particularly against the example of his father. As Rüter puts it, "The characters and the roles of Telemachus and Odysseus are . . . doubtless created to be parallel" (1969:142).[23] This has been shown in detail by a number of scholars,[24] and both Hansen and Apthorp have drawn attention especially to the parallels developed between Odysseus's sojourn in Scheria and Telemachus's in Sparta, both of which immediately precede homecoming (Hansen 1972:48–57; Apthorp 1980:12–22).

There is another dimension to Telemachus's *kleos*, however. When he is first enjoined to its pursuit, he is exhorted to imitate the *kleos* of Orestes (1.298–300). Later, he despairs of his ability to meet the challenge:

> αἲ γὰρ ἐμοὶ τοσσήνδε θεοὶ δύναμιν περιθεῖεν,
> τείσασθαι μνηστῆρας ὑπερβασίης ἀλεγεινῆς,
> οἵ τέ μοι ὑβρίζοντες ἀτάσθαλα μηχανόωνται.
> ἀλλ' οὔ μοι τοιοῦτον ἐπέκλωσαν θεοὶ ὄλβον
> πατρί τ' ἐμῷ καὶ ἐμοί· νῦν δὲ χρὴ τετλάμεν ἔμπης.

(If only the gods would grant me the strength
to take vengeance upon the suitors for their grievous arrogance,
for they outrage me with their foolish devisings.

---

[21] "Telemach begegnet als ein Unbekannter dem Ruhm des Odysseus; die Tränen verraten seine Betroffenheit. Menelaos und Helena erkennen ihn, und auch er wird zur Erkenntnis seiner selbst geführt, zur Erkenntnis, dass er der Sohn eines solchen Vaters ist."

[22] "Telemach findet sein und seines Vaters Sache . . . allenthalben in der Erinnerung gespiegelt vor. . . ."

[23] "Die Gestalten und die Rolle des Telemach und des Odysseus sind . . . zweifellos bewusst parallel gestaltet."

[24] For discussion and references, see Clarke 1967:30–44; Apthorp 1980:12 n. 53; A. T. Edwards 1985:28–30; and Jones 1988:501–6.

> But for me the gods have spun out no such satisfaction,
> for my father and me. For now it is necessary altogether to endure.)
>
> (3.205–9)

In these last remarks, as Edwards points out, Telemachus extends the validity of Orestes' example to include Odysseus, which he interprets as a sign that "Telemachus . . . depends on the return of his father to win this κλέος" (A. T. Edwards 1985:80). And Nagy, citing 2.360 ("to find out about the *nostos* of my dear father, if I might hear something of it," νόστον πευσόμενος πατρὸς φίλου, ἤν που ἀκούσω) and 3.83 ("I am pursuing the wide *kleos* of my father, if I might hear something of it," πατρὸς ἐμοῦ κλέος εὐρὺ μετέρχομαι, ἤν που ἀκούσω), remarks, "In his quest for his own heroic identity, Telemachus is confronted with a double frame of reference in the figure of his father" (1979:39–40).

As we have seen, Telemachus's *kleos* is closely bound up with that of Odysseus, both in that it is modelled upon it and in that Telemachus's *kleos* is acquired or even "inherited" from Odysseus. It is also the case, however, that the story of Telemachus, like that of Penelope, has its own narrative logic within the *Odyssey*, a logic at variance with the *mythos* of Odysseus and accommodated to it only at the end.[25] This logic is given, as we have seen, by the House of Atreus story, and this motif includes especially a model for Telemachus's *kleos* in Orestes.[26]

It is important not to downplay the dynamic force of this paradigm for Telemachus, or to modify the character of its implications for the action of the second half of the poem. The House of Atreus motif was set before Telemachus as an object-lesson by both Athena and Nestor, and it was elaborated as a three-stage process entailing: (1) the death of the father; (2) vengeance exacted by the son for his murder, and honor paid him in funeral rites; and (3) the disposition of the mother. Similarly, according to the second option that Athena had offered to Telemachus in her *parainesis* in Book 1.279ff.—the scenario now in force as the plot of the narrative—Telemachus was enjoined: (1) to undertake a journey to discover if his father is alive or dead; (2) to commemorate his father's death if he received news of it and to give his mother to a husband; and then (3) to plot revenge against the suitors.

The first stage of the Orestes paradigm is incorporated into the poem as an ambiguity about Odysseus's fate that resolves itself on the surface of the

---

[25] And particularly at the point where Thornton—correctly, in my view—locates the "turning point" of Telemachus's maturity, at 21.369ff. (Thornton 1970:76–77). Austin (1969:52, 61–62), on the other hand, thinks that Telemachus is transformed by Athena's first appearance, and that his laughter in 21.105 should be read as the culmination of his newly acquired *polymechania*. For further discussion, see below in Chapter Five.

[26] See Edwards's remark, "The κλέος of Orestes, the avenging son, is . . . presented as a paradigm for Odysseus' return" (1985:80).

narrative with a lamentation *as if* he were dead. Such is the scene that Menelaus calls to mind for Telemachus in 4.110ff., before the latter has revealed his identity:[27]

> ὀδύρονται νύ που αὐτὸν
> Λαέρτης θ' ὁ γέρων καὶ ἐχέφρων Πηνελόπεια
> Τηλέμαχός θ', ὃν ἔλειπε νέον γεγαῶτ' ἐνὶ οἴκῳ.

(To be sure, they are mourning for him [Odysseus],
the old man Laertes, and mindful Penelope,
and Telemachus, whom he left newborn in his house.)

(4.110–12)

Menelaus's words arouse in Telemachus the desire for *goos* (4.113), a term that designates the private lamentations sung by family members over the dead, as opposed to the *thrēnos* or public lamentation performed by professional mourners.[28] The *goos*, as Redfield has shown, functions in the mourning process as the means for transcending the loss of the dead person, and for accommodating oneself to a world in which he no longer exists: "The . . . *gooi* do not speak of the dead man as he was in life; rather they speak of how things are now that he is gone, the difference made by his absence. Mourning is not so much memory of the past as a definition of the new situation; mourning . . . celebrates the departed, not for what he did, but for how much he will be missed. The living person is thus dismissed, and a new social figure, the absent one, is created" (Redfield 1975:180).

Similarly, the two episodes of *goos* in Book 4—both introduced with the same formula ("arouse [in him/them] the desire for *goos*," ὑφ' ἵμερον ὦρσε γόοιο, 4.113, 4.183)—surround Telemachus's own lamentation with representations of absence, and both situations bear some resemblance to that of Telemachus. Menelaus explains to Telemachus that, although he is lord over much property, it brings him no joy, because his brother Agamemnon was killed by "another" and by "his dread wife's treachery" (δόλῳ οὐλομένης ἀλόχοιο, 4.92). Peisistratus mourns for a brother also, for Antilochus, whom he "never met or saw" (οὐ γὰρ ἐγώ γε / ἤντησ' οὐδὲ ἴδον, 4.200–201).

In the *Iliad*, as Nagy has shown, public grief (*penthos* or *akhos*) is regularly figured as the opposite of *kleos*; it is the legacy of the failed heroic quest (Nagy 1979:94–117; cf. Nagy 1974:256–59; Frame 1978:121–24). The

---

[27] Cf. Murnaghan 1987:161: "The narrative of the Telemachy, in particular the account of Telemachus' encounter with Menelaus with its stress on the conquest of grief, acts out the process of reconciliation to loss that is a condition of the world in which it is set."

[28] See Alexiou 1974:11–13 for a discussion of this distinction in Homer; and cf. Nagy 1979:112–13.

Trojan who wounded Menelaus, early in the poem, for example, is said to have thereby gained κλέος for himself, but to have caused grief for the Achaeans: ". . . for him *kleos*, for us *penthos*" (*Iliad* 4.207; cited by Nagy 1979:94). By extension, a given epic situation can call forth *kleos* or *penthos/akhos*, depending upon the personal involvement of the participants (Nagy 1979:94–117; cf. Nagy 1974:256ff.). Thus Odysseus in Book 8 is personally affected by Demodocus's lay concerning the Trojan horse and grieves when he hears it.[29] Furthermore, as the example of Achilles' grief for Patroclus makes particularly clear, *penthos/akhos* can function as a rationale for *kleos*, inciting the hero to take revenge for the death of his fallen comrade (Nagy 1979:102–12). *Penthos* functions as the flipside of *kleos*, then, and is inscribed in a rhythm of reciprocity with it.

This function of grief, and its close relationship to *kleos*, conditions the pervasive theme of lamentation in the *Odyssey* and provides a context for understanding Telemachus's grief in Book 4.[30] His lamentation is not simply the expression of personal sorrow, but a stage in the development of his own preparation for the pursuit of *kleos*. For him, as for Orestes, his father's death would provide the occasion for the exercise of his own heroic capacities; the public acknowledgment of this loss thus functions as the prelude to *kleos*. In the *Odyssey*, or course, Odysseus does not perish. Yet the governing paradigm for the development of *kleos* in the poem requires that we envision it. As Murnaghan remarks: "[The Telemachy] is inspired by an assumption, the assumption that Odysseus will not return, that is in conflict with the central message of the poem as a whole" (1987:158).

In Book 4, Odysseus's absence is fictionalized as death with reference to Menelaus's own loss, and Telemachus is consequently drawn into the role of Orestes, which Menelaus himself had failed to fulfill. For in the account of his history, Menelaus does not omit an element of self-reproach: Menelaus links his wandering ("while I was wandering," ἧος . . . ἠλώμην) with Agamemmnon's death and with his own present failure to enjoy the riches that he accumulated ("and so it is without joy that I am lord over these possessions," ὡς οὔ τοι χαίρων τοῖσδε κτεάτεσσιν ἀνάσσω, 4.93). And when Telemachus first heard about the murder of Agamemnon, he asked Nestor if "Menelaus was not in Argos or Achaea, but wandering somewhere else among men, that he [Aegisthus] had the courage to kill him [Agamemnon]" (3.251–52). In this way the House of Atreus story serves to potentiate the situation of Telemachus, to draw out the implications of its elements and to indicate their logical coherence.

---

[29] This aspect of song is discussed by Nagy (1979:101). Cf. also the discussions of Walsh (1984:3–21), Thalmann (1984:157–67), and Murnaghan (1987:148–75); and see Pucci 1987:225–26 for a discussion of the Odyssean "discourse of pity."

[30] Goldhill's recent discussion draws attention to the peculiarity of Telemachus's expression of grief in 4.291–95 (1988:19–24).

The second stage of the Orestes pattern entails the exacting of vengeance from his father's murderers; in the adaptation of the motif that applies to Telemachus, however, the matter of Penelope's marriage precedes the *mnēstērophonia*—both in the paradigm as given by Athena (1.279ff.) and adopted by Telemachus (2.214ff.), and in the action of the narrative. We saw earlier that the issue of Penelope's courtship was tied closely to the House of Atreus story when it surfaced in connection with Odysseus's return to Ithaca. Athena's *parainesis* to Telemachus in Book 15.10–26 also draws on this parallel, but it shifts the attention away from the suitors and onto Penelope's father and brothers. This is an important move in the poem, and it must be regarded as more consequential than simply a facilitating mechanism for returning Telemachus to Ithaca.

For Athena's warning implies the fulfillment of something like the first scenario outlined in Book 1, whereby Penelope was returned to the *kyrieia* of her father's household and Telemachus assumed that of his own *oikos*. As Telemachus's later remarks to Menelaus show, he has taken Athena's advice to heart:

βούλομαι ἤδη νεῖσθαι ἐφ' ἡμέτερ'· οὐ γὰρ ὄπισθεν
οὖρον ἰὼν κατέλειπον ἐπὶ κτεάτεσσιν ἐμοῖσιν·
μὴ πατέρ' ἀντίθεον διζήμενος αὐτὸς ὄλωμαι,
ἤ τί μοι ἐκ μεγάρων κειμήλιον ἐσθλὸν ὄληται.

(I want now to return to my own home; for I left behind me
  when I came here no one to watch over my property.
[And I must watch out] lest I myself die/disappear while
  searching for my godlike father,
or some fine piece of property disappear from my halls.)
(15.88–91)

Telemachus speaks here as *kyrios* of his *oikos*, even to the point of identifying his own survival with that of his property—see ὄλωμαι/ὄληται in lines 90 and 91 above—and hence with the *oikos* itself. In addition, he is concerned both for his own *nostos* (see νεῖσθαι ἐφ' ἡμέτερ' in line 88) and for his own *kleos*—his disappearance, as well as his inability to protect his *oikos*, would relegate him to the *akleia* to which, in the end, Agamemnon was consigned (24.95ff.). A. T. Edwards has shown that the ideology of *kleos* in the Homeric poems includes its destruction through an ignoble death (1985:74), and Nagy argues that in the epic tradition, Odysseus is figured as the "best of the Achaeans" precisely in that "he has won both *kléos* and *nóstos*" (Nagy 1979:39).

But as Nagy especially has also made clear, unless a hero dies in battle, a successful *nostos* is not only a *ne plus ultra*, as it were, of the hero's *kleos*, it is also its *sine qua non*. And just as Clytemnestra and Penelope are the key to the *nostoi* of Agamemnon and Odysseus, so for Telemachus *nostos* must entail the assertion of his rights over his household—his *kyrieia*, in a word. Thus, Athena envisions and Telemachus assimilates a scenario that presumes the assumption by Telemachues of his *kyrieia*, and the anticipation of danger consequently is recast to take account of the particularities of Telemachus's situation. The threat is now construed as the abandonment of the *oikos* by Penelope and its consequent exposure to appropriation by outsiders.

Furthermore, it is clear that Telemachus, in assuming his *kyrieia*, will to some extent displace Penelope.[31] We can compare, for example, Athena's and Telemachus's concern that the property be kept intact with Odysseus's inquiry of his mother in the first *nekyia*, whether Penelope still "stays by my son and guards everything safely" (ἠὲ μένει παρὰ παιδὶ καὶ ἔμπεδα πάντα φυλάσσει, 11.178). According to the scenario that Athena outlines, by contrast, Telemachus will assume the role of *kyrios*, and consequently the role of caretaker of the household property will pass first to "the best of the serving-women," and then to his own "wedded wife" (15.25–26). It is noteworthy in particular that *kyrieia* in this system requires the active collaboration of a female partner—a trusted one of the δμῷαι before marriage (15.25; cf. οὖρον in 15.89), one's wife afterwards (15.26). Thus Odysseus, following the completion of his *nostos*, explicitly turns over his household property to Penelope: "[You] attend to my property which is in the halls" (κτήματα μέν, τά μοί ἐστι, κομιζέμεν ἐν μεγάροισι, 23.355).

Athena's second *parainesis*, then, functions to incorporate into the narrative the anticipation of a *nostos* for Telemachus that will consolidate the *kleos* he has begun to acquire and prepare the way for the revenge against the suitors. From the Telemachean point of view, this *nostos*, unlike that of Agamemnon or Odysseus, must entail the withdrawal of the woman ἐν μεγάροις rather than her faithfulness, or, at the very least, the assertion of his rights over her. This aspect of Telemachus's situation is projected early in the poem: as Murnaghan observes, "The difference in Telemachus brought about by his voyage is reflected in Athena's apparently contradictory commands: before being told to go, he is advised to send Penelope home to her father (*Od.* 1.274–78); after his voyage is projected, the advice is changed, reflecting the change it will make on him, and he is told to arrange her remarriage himself (*Od.* 1.292)" (1987:106–7 n. 22).[32]

From Telemachus's point of view, the danger of betrayal is also configured differently, projected now as the loss of property instead of wife.

---

[31] For a neounitarian analysis of the discrepancy in the plot of the *Odyssey* between Penelope's and Telemachus's interests, see Wehrli 1959.

[32] As my earlier discussion makes clear, I interpret this discrepancy in advice differently. But it is clear that one of the results of Telemachus's voyage is to alter his status with reference to Penelope.

These two themes are merged in Telemachus's question to Eumaeus in 16.33–35: "Does my mother remain still in the halls, or has some other man wed her now, and the bed of Odysseus lies widowed of coverlets, covered with foul cobwebs?" (ἤ μοι ἔτ' ἐν μεγάροις μήτηρ μένει, ἦέ τις ἤδη / ἀνδρῶν ἄλλος ἔγημεν, Ὀδυσσῆος δέ που εὐνὴ / χήτει ἐνευναίων κάκ' ἀράχνια κεῖται ἔχουσα;). Fenik's summary of the question brings out its implications clearly: "'What of my mother? Has she remained true, or is Odysseus' bed deserted and empty?'" (1974:237).

This second stage of the adaptation of the Orestes paradigm—Telemachus's assumption of *kyrieia*—does not, of course, come to pass, any more than does its first stage—the death of the father. But in both cases, narrative logic requires that we envision and even to some extent anticipate an outcome different from that which is inscribed in the poem's *mythos*. The operation of this logic, in turn, conditions the meaning of the action in the final segment of the poem. For as we shall see, the configuration of Telemachus as *kyrios* allows him to function as the head of his household and thus to demonstrate concretely his assumption of that role. Similarly, with the remaining stage of the paradigm—the revenge against the suitors—Telemachus's participation is qualified, in this case by the presence of Odysseus. Odysseus nods to Telemachus as he is about to string the bow, and the son voluntarily yields to the authority of the father (21.129). The notion of competition between them, however, is preserved in the final scene of the poem, when Laertes rejoices (ἦ μάλα χαίρω) that "my son and my son's son are striving together for virtue" (υἱός θ' υἱωνός τ' ἀρετῆς πέρι δῆριν ἔχουσι, 24.515).

When Telemachus is dispatched to Ithaca in the section immediately following Athena's warning, Helen's gift to him is accompanied by instructions that act to return the narrative to its proper course. The gift itself, a robe woven by Helen's hands, is given "in anticipation of your longed-for marriage, for your bride to wear" (πολυηράτου ἐς γάμου ὥρην, / σῇ ἀλόχῳ φορέειν, 15.126–27). But until that time arrives, she tells him, "let it lie in the halls in the keeping of your dear mother" (τῆος δὲ φίλῃ παρὰ μητρὶ / κεῖσθαι ἐνὶ μεγάρῳ, 15.127–28). Helen does not envision, then, Telemachus's assumption of *kyrieia* and Penelope's departure from the *oikos*. Rather, while anticipating Telemachus's coming of age, she regards Penelope still as the guardian of the household, and this, of course, accords with the existing narrative situation.

What is more, in the same section of the narrative, just prior to his departure, Helen interprets for Telemachus an omen that anticipates Penelope's dream in Book 19:[33]

---

[33] Cf. 19.536–50, esp. 19.536–39: χῆνές μοι κατὰ οἶκον ἐείκοσι πυρὸν ἔδουσιν / ἐξ ὕδατος . . / ἐλθὼν δ' ἐξ ὄρεος μέγας αἰετὸς ἀγκυλοχείλης / πᾶσι κατ' αὐχένας ἦξε καὶ ἔκτανεν ("I

ὡς ὅδε χῆν' ἥρπαξ' ἀτιταλλομένην ἐνὶ οἴκῳ
ἐλθὼν ἐξ ὄρεος, ὅθι οἱ γενεή τε τόκος τε,
ὣς 'Οδυσεὺς κακὰ πολλὰ παθὼν καὶ πόλλ' ἐπαληθεὶς
οἴκαδε νοστήσει καὶ τίσεται·

(Just as this [eagle] snatched up the goose that was bred in the house, itself coming from the mountain, where are its race and begetting, so will Odysseus, who has suffered many evils and wandered much, return home and take his revenge.)

(15.174–78)

Helen's prophecy ratifies the expectation of Odysseus's return and explicitly envisions the *nostos* and *tisis* ("revenge") of Odysseus. Thus, as Telemachus departs from Sparta, the House of Atreus paradigm is redefined for him through Helen, away from the expectation suggested earlier by Athena that he will himself assume the *kyrieia* of his household and take vengeance upon the suitors. For Telemachus now, a new confidence about his father's return displaces his own earlier hopeless diffidence and prepares him to assume the role of his father's ally. Earlier, Telemachus had responded to Mentor's encouragement to action with a confession of despair: "For that one [Odysseus] there will be no true *nostos*, but for him already the immortals ones have designed death and black fate" (κείνῳ δ' οὐκέτι νόστος ἐτήτυμος, ἀλλά οἱ ἤδη / φράσσαντ' ἀθάνατοι θάνατον καὶ κῆρα μέλαιναν, 3.241–42). Now, he replies both to Helen's prophecy and to the later one of Theoclymenus with an expression of confident anticipation that their visions will be fulfilled: "Thus may Zeus now bring it about, the loud-thinking spouse of Hera" (οὕτω νῦν Ζεὺς θείη, ἐρίγδουπος πόσις Ἥρης, 15.180); "if only, oh stranger, this word [of yours] might find fulfillment" (αἲ γὰρ τοῦτο, ξεῖνε, ἔπος τετελεσμένον εἴη, 15.536).

FROM *NOSTOS* TO *XENIA* (BOOK 16)

By the beginning of Book 16, the *mythos* of Telemachus merges with that of Odysseus, and this pattern dominates the remainder of what Schadewaldt refers to as "die innere Heimkehr" ("the internal homecoming") that begins in Book 13 and continues until Book 23 (Schadewaldt 1970b:57). The convergence of the stories of Odysseus and Telemachus is especially marked in the episode of the suitors' *lokhos* ("ambush"), which closes Book 16 (16.322–451). The ambush, with its surrounding material, forms one of what Delebecque identifies as the "bridge" episodes joining the second half of the narrative to its first section. Thus, 16.322–451 resumes the ac-

---

had twenty geese about the house, eating grain from the water . . . and a huge eagle with crooked talons came and broke all their necks and killed them").

tion that was interrupted at 4.847 and is complementary to the last episode of Book 4 (4.624–847), in which the action of the narrative returned to Ithaca and the suitors' plans for the ambush were formulated and put into place.

A. T. Edwards's investigation of the *lokhos* motif in the *Odyssey* has established its presence as a narrative pattern in the epic tradition generally. Edwards has shown also that its adaptation in the *Odyssey* revises the Iliadic view of the *lokhos* as "a strategem of desperation, cowardice, and deceit" and configures it instead as "a strategem by which the weak defend themselves against the injustice of a more powerful foe" (1985:41). In my view, however, this development does not occur in the poem by means of a simple "reversal of values normally assigned to ambusher and victim" (ibid.:33), but rather it occurs as the transformation of the *lokhos* of Agamemnon upon his return from Troy, which is narrated in Book 3, into the *mnēstērophonia* of Book 22, which is, as Edwards has argued, represented as an ambush (ibid.:35–38). This transition is mediated in several ways, including, as Edwards points out, through the lying-tales of Odysseus in which the *lokhos* motif appears prominently (ibid.: 32–35); it is conditioned also, in my view, by the displacement of the *lokhos* motif from Odysseus to Telemachus.

"The suitors," as Edwards notes, "plot against [Telemachus] as lord of his estate and a potential king of Ithaca—as replacement for Odysseus" (1985:28). To be sure, it is also true that in Book 1 "Telemachus' initiative [in embarking on a voyage] signals his intention to assume the role of master in his house and claim the position of authority left vacant by his absent father (1.292–305)" (Edwards 1985:28). It is also the case, as Edwards points out, citing 1.383–98, that a dispute between Telemachus and the suitors concerning Odysseus's *geras* on Ithaca and the hegemony of his *oikos* is part of the plot from the beginning. But it is only in Book 16 that the threat posed by Telemachus is specifically articulated as such. Earlier, Antinous had proposed an ambush in outrage at the boldness of one whom he had thought of as nothing but a "young boy" (νέος πάϊς), as he calls him in 4.665; and he expects further trouble from Telemachus as a result of this adventure (see esp. 4.667). But the ambush itself is designed only to "teach him a lesson": "so that he might regret this journeying after his father" (ὡς ἂν ἐπισμυγερῶς ναυτίλλεται εἵνεκα πατρός, 4.672).

In Book 16, by contrast, the proposal for a second ambush is specifically formulated around the issue of hegemony, in recognition of Telemachus's legitimate claims to lordship of his *oikos*:

ἀλλὰ φθέωμεν ἑλόντες ἐπ' ἀγροῦ νόσφι πόληος
ἢ ἐν ὁδῷ· βίοτον δ' αὐτοὶ καὶ κτήματ' ἔχωμεν,
δασσάμενοι κατὰ μοῖραν ἐφ' ἡμέας, οἰκία δ' αὖτε

κείνου μητέρι δοῖμεν ἔχειν ἠδ' ὅς τις ὀπυίοι.
εἰ δ' ὑμῖν ὅδε μῦθος ἀφανδάνει, ἀλλὰ βόλεσθε
αὐτόν τε ζώειν καὶ ἔχειν πατρώια πάντα,
μή οἱ χρήματ' ἔπειτα ἅλις θυμηδέ' ἔδωμεν
ἐνθάδ' ἀγειρόμενοι, ἀλλ' ἐκ μεγάροιο ἕκαστος
μνάσθω ἐέδνοισιν διζήμενος· ἡ δέ κ' ἔπειτα
γήμαιθ' ὅς κε πλεῖστα πόροι καὶ μόρσιμος ἔλθοι.

(But let us seize Telemachus first in the field far away from the city
or on the road. And let us ourselves possess his livelihood and his possessions,
dividing them by lot amongst ourselves, although as for his house,
we will give it to his mother to have together with whoever weds her.
But if this plot displeases you, and you want instead
for him to live and possess all his inheritance,
then let us not go on devouring his lovely wealth,
gathering here, but let each man from his own halls
woo [her], advancing his suit with bride-gifts; and then she
would marry whoever offers the most and comes as [her] fated [husband].)
(16.383–92)

At this point in the narrative, then, an important element of the House of Atreus story is reformulated so as to cast Telemachus rather than Odysseus in the role of Agamemnon—the returning hero ambushed upon his *nostos*. Thus, the plot against Telemachus displaces the threat of the House of Atreus paradigm from Odysseus to his son. When Antinous's proposal fails to be adopted,[34] the suitors return to their feasting: "And so, rising up immediately they proceeded into the house of Odysseus, and once there sat down upon polished thrones" (αὐτίκ' ἔπειτ' ἀνστάντες ἔβαν δόμον εἰς Ὀδυσῆος, / ἐλθόντες δὲ καθῖζον ἐπὶ ξεστοῖσι θρόνοισιν, 16.407–8). Concomitant with the suitors' abandonment of plans for ambush, the House of Atreus story disappears from the text, and the problematic of Odysseus's *nostos* is now formulated around the theme of *xenia*.

Athena had proposed to Odysseus in 13.393ff. that he return home in disguise, and this suggestion conforms with that of Agamemnon in the first *nekyia*, where it is specifically conceptualized as an alternative to the House of Atreus story (11.441–56). At this point, Odysseus becomes a stranger in his own land, and his return, his *nostos*, is now a matter of whether *xenia* will be extended to him. The problem of a hostile reception to the master of the house has been converted into one of a friendly reception to a stranger. The figure who mediates this transition is Theocly-

---

[34] Amphinomus objects to an assault upon a member of a "kingly race" (γένος βασιλήιον, 16.401) without authorization from Zeus. On the suitors as equivalent to regicides by virtue of their intentions, see Bader 1976:20.

menus, who Page even suggests may have been Odysseus himself in disguise in "another version of the story" (1955:88).[35] Theoclymenus operates at a number of points as a doublet for Odysseus,[36] and Telemachus's acceptance of his supplication and offer of conveyance to Ithaca introduce the model by which Odysseus's *nostos* will be effected.

The structure of this section of the *Odyssey*, then, instantiates an equivalence between *nostos* and *xenia*, as Bader has argued in detail. She points out that there is both a chronological succession between the two themes,[37] and also a unity of content: the crimes of the suitors and their allies among the servants, she argues, are equivalent to the murder of Agamemnon and the seduction of Clytemnestra. In my interpretation of the relation between *nostos* and *xenia*, however, I focus instead on the equivalence between the welcoming home of the returning husband/father and the incorporation into the household of a *xeinos*—on "welcome" and "hospitality," therefore, rather than on "murder"/"seduction" and "inhospitality." My interpretation differs, too, from that of Murnaghan, who argues that "hospitality serves as a substitute or alternative for recognition of identity," and that there is a "correlation between social acceptance and recognition of identity" (1987:107, 103). The latter claim seems valid, and is well substantiated by the text. The revelation of identity, however, whether *de novo* or in the form of a recognition scene,[38] is not equivalent to the *xenia* scenario but rather forms part of it. In the end, therefore, I do not see a "conflict between the role of guest that Odysseus has earned in Penelope's eyes and the role of husband that he wishes to claim" (ibid.:114), but rather its opposite—a close equivalance. I argue this point in detail in Chapter Six.

Odysseus's *nostos* and *xenia* is eventually constituted around the parallel represented by the episode on Phaeacia. In Books 17–21, however, the more immediately relevant model is that of Helen, who, along with Menelaus, sends Telemachus on his way at the end of Book 15. As we shall see, this section of the *Odyssey* is organized around the question of whether

---

[35] The apparent inconsistency of Theoclymenus's role has been critized by Page, who complains that Theoclymenus "is introduced at great length and with much ado; thereafter the part he plays is very small and confused until the end" (Page 1955:86–87). Page goes on to suggest that his part in the poem had originally been much fuller, and that in another version of the story his part may have been played by Odysseus in disguise. For a defense of Theoclymenus's role and function in the text, see Hoekstra 1989:262–63 ad 15.513–22; Erbse 1972:42–54; Eisenberger 1973:95–96; and Fenik 1974:233–44.

[36] This is particularly the case as concerns *xenia*; for discussion, see Chapter Five below.

[37] "An allusion to the story of Aegisthus and Agamemnon occurs for the last time in Book 13, whereas the theme of the inhospitality of the suitors and of their allies begins immediately thereafter, in Book 14" (Bader 1976:21–22).

[38] On the typology of these scenes in the *Odyssey*, which I outline briefly in Chapter Five, see Richardson 1983; Emlyn-Jones 1984; and Murnaghan 1987:20–55.

Penelope will extend to Odysseus the kind of *xenia* that Helen offered to Telemachus in Book 4 and to Odysseus himself at Troy, or whether she will instead seduce other men and abandon her household, like Helen did in Menelaus's story in Book 4 and in connection with the origins of the Trojan War, to which Odysseus had alluded in Book 11.

Chapter Four

WHAT DOES PENELOPE WANT? (BOOKS 18, 19)

PENELOPE'S ACTIONS and intentions in the section of the *Odyssey* where she figures prominently have long constituted what scholars call a *crux* ("point of difficulty") of interpretation or *zetema* ("interpretive issue"). Her appearance before the suitors and solicitation of gifts from them has exposed her to the suspicion of lasciviousness; and her failure to recognize Odysseus in Book 19 has raised questions about the direction of her thoughts. The debate on these matters began in antiquity and was elaborated into a subordinate tradition that competed with the "vulgate" of a chaste and faithful Penelope (Jacobson 1974:246). For example, the scholia to the beginning of Book 13 record the hypothesis that Odysseus did not reveal himself to Penelope before the slaughter of the suitors because he may have "suspected that she would want to save some of them" (ἴσως δὲ καὶ μὴ σῶσαι τινὰς βουληθεῖσα ὑπείδετο, Dindorf 1962:789 ad 556–57). Seneca, chastising the rhetoricians for their critical nit-picking, regards it as fruitless to inquire "whether Penelope was unchaste, whether she deceived her whole generation, whether she suspected that it was Odysseus whom she saw before she knew it" (*an Penelope impudica fuerit, an verba saeculo suo dederit, an Ulixem illum esse quem videbat antequam sciret suspicata sit*, Seneca *Ep.* 88.8). Servius, in his commentary to the *Aeneid*, summarizes the scandalous tradition that was common in antiquity: "For when he [Odysseus] returned home to Ithaca after his wanderings, it is said that he found among his household gods Pan, who was reported to have been born from Penelope and all the suitors, as the name itself Pan seems to indicate;[1] although others report that he was born from Hermes, who transformed himself into a goat and slept with Penelope.[2] But after Odysseus saw the deformed child, it is said that he fled [again] to his wanderings" (Servius in *Aen.* 2.44).[3]

In the following two chapters I deal in some detail with this long interpretive history, concentrating on scholarly approaches from the time of Wilamowitz to our own, in order to show how inconsistencies in the text

---

[1] A false etymology that connects Pan with *pantes*, meaning "all."
[2] This tradition appears as early as Pindar (fr. 100 Snell; see Jacobson 1974:246 n. 8).
[3] Nam cum Ithacam post errores fuisset reversus, invenisse Pana fertur in penatibus suis, qui dicitur ex Penelope et procis omnibus natus, sicut ipsum nomen Pan videtur declarare: quamquam alii hunc de Mercurio, qui in hircum mutatus cum Penelope concubuerat, natum ferunt. sed Ulixes posteaquam deformem puerum vidit, fugisse dicitur in errores.

itself have generated an unusual set of problems that defies easy critical solution. Furthermore, as I indicate below, I think that this history is less variegated than it appears, and that it is dominated by an ideological bias toward the unitary subject. Accordingly, what I offer to the reader is not an explanation or solution as such, but an interpretation of how these "inconsistencies" function in the narrative to endow it with meaning.

THE APPEARANCE BEFORE THE SUITORS (BOOK 18)

In Book 18, Penelope is inspired by Athena to appear before the suitors, and Odysseus interprets her solicitation of bridal gifts as a deliberate deception of the wooers (18.281–83). In Book 19, following the *homilia* with the disguised stranger, Penelope decides to set the bride-contest, a plan that Odysseus approves (19.582–87). The announcement of the contest is postponed until Book 21, and the contest culminates in the *mnēstērophonia* of Book 22. In this sequence of events there are, broadly speaking, two principal scenarios: in one, Penelope "remains beside [Telemachus] and keeps everything secure" (16.74 = 11.178, 19.525), in accordance with the *nostos* paradigm; in the other, she "follows after whoever is best of the Achaeans" (16:76 = 11.179, 19.528). This alternative of remarriage, as we have seen, has been brought into association with the House of Atreus story. In the text as we have it, there are indications that these two contradictory scenarios are being enacted simultaneously, and the resulting incompatibility has been explained in a number of different ways, as we shall see.

Seen as part of the text's system of meaning, the "illogicality," as Kirk calls it (1962:247), of *this double plot corresponds in its broad outlines to the diptych of narratives in Book 4*, as I suggested in Chapter Three.[4] The two complementary and contradictory accounts of Helen's behavior at Troy compose a double view of her that has engendered the suspicion that, like the two "versions" of Penelope, they must derive from different epic sources: "These [two] episodes cannot possibly be inventions of one and the same poet, since each tale presupposes a different conception of Helen's personality" (Kakridis 1971a:49).

In the first of these stories, which Helen herself narrates, Odysseus enters Troy disguised as a beggar whom she recognizes and questions, and he attempts unsuccessfully to evade her discovery of him: compare "and he tried to avoid her with his cunning" (ὁ δὲ κερδοσύνῃ ἀλέεινεν, 4.251) with "[Odysseus] turned quickly toward the darkness; for he suddenly reflected in his heart that . . ." (ποτὶ δὲ σκότον ἐτράπετ' αἶψα· / αὐτίκα γὰρ

---

[4] For a recent penetrating analysis and critique of the notion of "structural anomaly" in this section of the *Odyssey*, see Goldhill 1988:1–9.

κατὰ θυμὸν ὀίσατο κτλ., 19.389–90). After Helen finds him out, Odysseus swears her to secrecy and proceeds to slaughter many Trojans; the account concludes with an affirmation of Helen's ultimate faithfulness to Menelaus. This story was part of the epic tradition, and was summarized by Proclus from the *Ilias mikra* of Lesches (Kakridis 1971a: 41, 41–42 n. 39).

In Menelaus's tale, by contrast, Helen calls out seductively to the Greek warriors in an effort to entice them from their ambush in the Trojan horse. As Menelaus reports it, he and Diomedes were overcome with longing, and were on the verge of responding (4.282ff.). Andersen suggests that this story, which does not appear to have been part of the epic tradition, represents an invention of the poet of the *Odyssey* in the service of providing a "Motivverdoppelung" or "foreshadow[ing of] the return of the Hero—the hidden Hero" (1977:9, 11).

Dupont-Roc and Le Boulluec have demonstrated in detail the linguistic and thematic complementarity of the two discourses in Book 4 (1976:32–36), and Andersen has shown how the tales of Helen and Menelaus foreshadow the later situation on Ithaca (Andersen 1977). The similarity between Helen and Penelope begins as early as the point of their entrances (Lattimore 1969:100), which, although they contain formulaic elements and represent a typical scene or motif sequence (Nagler 1974:64–86), combine these elements in this manner in only Books 4 and 19.[5] Thus, both women issue forth from their bedchambers (ἐκ δ' Ἑλένη θαλάμοιο θυώδεος ὑψορόφοιο / ἤλυθεν, 4.121–22; ἡ δ' ἴεν ἐκ θαλάμοιο περίφρων Πηνελόπεια, 19.53) looking like golden Artemis ('Αρτέμιδι χρυσηλακάτῳ ἐικυῖα, 4.122; 'Αρτέμιδι ἰκέλη ἠὲ χρυσῇ 'Αφροδίτῃ, 19.54) and immediately begin to question the men about each particular (αὐτίκα δ' ἥ γ' ἐπέεσσι πόσιν ἐρέεινεν ἕκαστα, 4.137; ἔμελλον ἐνὶ μεγάροισιν ἐμοῖσιν / ἀμφὶ πόσει εἴρεσθαι, 19.94–95; and ἐθέλω δέ μιν ἐξερέεσθαι, 19.99). In addition, in Book 4 Helen's golden distaff and silver basket are identified as a gift and descriptively elaborated; in Book 19 the same applies to the chair on which Penelope sits.

Furthermore, insofar as the two narratives of Helen conflate poetic truth and falsity with sexual fidelity and betrayal, they serve as models for Penelope. As Zeitlin has formulated it: "These ambiguities [of poetics and erotics] are not only recollections of a past which belong to Helen and Menelaus, but potential forecasts for Penelope. This future depends upon Penelope's choice of one of the two possible roles which the two stories offer her—that of the faithful woman who receives the beggar in disguise and welcomes him, or that of the woman who, surrounded by men (read

---

[5] The similarities are demonstrated in greatest detail by Forsyth 1979, who also compares other versions of what he calls "allurement scenes."

suitors for Greeks), practices the wiles of seduction, although another man's wife" (1981:206).⁶

Thus, in Book 18, Penelope appears before the suitors and seduces them into showering her with bride-gifts; at her appearance, the suitors' "knees were loosened, and their hearts were enchanted with desire, and they all prayed to lie in bed beside her" (τῶν δ' αὐτοῦ λύτο γούνατ', ἔρῳ δ' ἄρα θυμὸν ἔθελχθεν, / πάντες δ' ἠρήσαντο παραὶ λεχέεσσι κλιθῆναι, 18.212–13). Similarly, in Book 4, Diomedes and Menelaus are overcome with desire, and "both of us sprang up, longing to go out or to answer from within" (νῶι μὲν ἀμφοτέρω μενεήναμεν ὁρμηθέντες / ἢ ἐξελθέμεναι ἢ ἔνδοθεν αἶψ' ὑπακοῦσαι, 4.282–83). The narrative action of Book 19 bears a more complex and subtle relationship of similarity to the tale told by Helen, since although the elements of the narrative action in Helen's tale are replicated, they are distributed among different agents. Nevertheless, taken together, the narrative elements of this sequence of events cohere into a paradigm for loyalty that is in fact close to that imagined by the suitors (see below on the discrepancy between the accounts of the bow-trial in Books 21 and 24).

Penelope throughout this section of the poem is neither in open collusion with Odysseus, like Helen was, nor does she secretly betray him, as Clytemnestra did Agamemnon. In this respect Penelope composes for herself in the course of Books 18–21 a revisionary *mythos* like that of Odysseus and Telemachus, which is defined, like theirs, against the existing paradigms in the tradition—in Penelope's case, the paradigms for women's behavior are at issue. Odysseus alludes to these in Book 11, when he instances Helen and Clytemnestra as sources of suffering brought about "through female plotting" (γυναικείας διὰ βουλάς, 11.436–39). As Klingner remarks on this passage, "The one unfaithful woman [Helen] is responsible for the beginning of the Trojan disaster, while the other [Clytemnestra] closes this disaster with the attack on the life of her husband when he returns home. On the other hand, there is Penelope, who preserves the home for her husband and, standing with him and his cause, is united with him in the end. The three women are emphatically placed together in the journey to the realm of the dead at 11.436ff." (Klingner 1964:79).⁷ Penelope

⁶ See also Olson's recent study, which relates the story of Helen to what he calls "the sexual dynamics of the epic and the struggle between male and female that persists there" (1989:394).

⁷ "Die eine Ungetreue verschuldet den Anfang des trojanischen Unheils, die andere beschleisst es mit dem Anschlag auf das Leben des heimkehrenden Mannes. Dagegen steht Penelope, die dem Manne die Heimat rettet und, zu ihm und seiner Sache stehend, am Ende mit ihm vereint wird. Die drei Frauen sind ausdrücklich so zusammengeordnet in der Fahrt zum Totenreich 11, 436ff."

does not ever refer to Clytemnestra, but she knows Helen's story, and she instances it at an important point in the narrative (23.218–24).

The double discourse of Book 4 did not allow for a resolution of the questions of either sexual truth or narrative fidelity. The issue is not left open in precisely the same way in Books 18–21, since it is not a question of conflicting *mythoi*, but rather of one narrative whose direction cannot be fixed. This indeterminacy of narrative direction is incorporated into the plot at 18.158ff., when Athena inspires Penelope to appear before the suitors:

> τῇ δ' ἄρ' ἐπὶ φρεσὶ θῆκε θεὰ γλαυκῶπις Ἀθήνη,
> κούρῃ Ἰκαρίοιο, περίφρονι Πηνελοπείῃ,
> μνηστήρεσσι φανῆναι, ὅπως πετάσειε μάλιστα
> θυμὸν μνηστήρων ἰδὲ τιμήεσσα γένοιτο
> μᾶλλον πρὸς πόσιός τε καὶ υἱέος ἢ πάρος ἦεν.
> ἀχρεῖον δ' ἐγέλασσεν ἔπος τ' ἔφατ' ἔκ τ' ὀνόμαζεν·
> "Εὐρυνόμη, θυμός μοι ἐέλδεται, οὔ τι πάρος γε,
> μνηστήρεσσι φανῆναι, ἀπεχθομένοισί περ ἔμπης."

(Then the goddess, grey-eyed Athena, put it in her heart,
the daughter of Icarius, watchful Penelope,
to show herself to the suitors, so that she might open
their spirits all the more, and [so that she] might be all the more honored
before her husband and son even than she was before.
She laughed pointlessly, and said to her, calling her by name,
"Eurynome, my spirit impels me, though it did not before,
to appear before to the suitors, hateful though they are.")
(18.158–65)

Several interconnected interpretive problems appear in this brief passage. Two of them are lexical, and concern the meaning of the phrases "open [their] spirits" (πετάσειε ... θυμόν, 18.160–61) and "she laughed pointlessly" (ἀχρεῖον δ' ἐγέλασσεν, 18.163). A third debated issue is the assignment of intention in the two parts of the purpose clause: "so that she might open ..." and "so that she might be honored" (ὅπως πετάσειε ... ἰδὲ τιμήεσσα γένοιτο, 18.160–62). As Büchner points out, since Penelope is unaware of Odysseus's presence in the hall, ὅπως τιμήεσσα γένοιτο must describe Athena's rather than Penelope's intentions: "As Penelope does not know that Odysseus will be present at the scene, and thus also cannot expect that her behavior toward the suitors she will earn greater honor in his eyes, the sentence with ὅπως must be understood from the perspective of the goddess" (1940:143).[8] And Russo explains that "the

---

[8] "Da Penelope nicht weiss, dass Odysseus der Szene beiwohnen wird, also auch nicht hof-

construction of ὅπως with the optative can describe either the intention behind an action or the results achieved as a consequence of the action" (1985:204 ad 18.160–62).

Büchner goes on to inquire in what sense Penelope's intentions can be conceived as ὅπως πετάσειε θυμόν. He explains the phrase by interpreting Penelope's laugh in 18.163 (ἀχρεῖον δ' ἐγέλασσεν) as "sardonic," on the analogy of Odysseus's μείδησε . . . σαρδάνιον ("he smiled sardonically") in 20.301–2, and as a sign, therefore, that Penelope intends a deliberate deception of the suitors. Thus, πετάσειε θυμόν means not "astonish them, arouse them to desire" (ἐκπλήξειε, ἀναστήσειε πρὸς ἐπιθυμίαν), as the scholiast reads it, but "enchant" (θέλξειε), which also has ancient authority (Büchner 1940:143). Similarly, Allione translates "in order that she might gladden to the highest degree" (*per allietare massimamente*), noting that this is the only instance in Homer of the transitive use of the verb (1963:76 and n. 27). As Russo explains, however, this interpretation reflects "an early confusion of πετάννυμι [meaning] 'expand' with πέτομαι [meaning] 'to fly' " (1985:204 ad 18.160).

Thornton translates the phrase as "spread out the spirit of the suitors" (1970:97) and explains, "This image [the *hapax* ἀγχίνοος in 13.332] of tight-togetherness, with no gaps or interstices, and its opposite of 'spread-outness' or 'being relaxed' are characteristic of Homeric and later Greek notions about a self-possessed and intelligent person and a stupid, impulse-driven person" (ibid.:146 n. 30). And Russo says, "πετάσειε here means she would 'enlarge' or 'open up' the Suitors' spirit, the metaphor being to expand it with a new influx of strong emotion" (1985:204 ad 160). Similarly, in Ameis-Hentze-Cauer the phrase is rendered, "das Herz weit machte" ("open wide [their] heart[s]"), and explained, "mit freudiger Hoffnung schwellte" ("arouse [in them] joyous expectation[s]") (1964, 2(1):154 ad 160). Byre, in connection with the interpretation of the scene discussed below, argues that the phrase means "something like 'expose the passions of the suitors [to the observation of Odysseus]' " (1988:170).

The understanding of this phrase depends either on the intention assigned to Penelope in this scene or that derived from the purpose clause. In Büchner's view, Penelope intends at this juncture to deceive the suitors. Aroused by the recent news concerning Odysseus and distressed by the awareness of the suitors' plot against Telemachus, she has realized that she must attempt to gain some time, and to this end has conceived the novel plan: "She must try to win time and in a different way to turn away the threat of violence that threatens Telemachus and herself. To this end she

---

fen kann, durch ihr Verhalten gegenüber den Freiern grössere Ehre bei ihm zu erlangen, so muss der Satz mit ὅπως aus dem Sinn der Göttin verstanden werden."

devises a completely new approach" (1940:139).[9] Büchner goes on to explain, "With her present explanation it is only a question of a new scheme, which like the earlier ones is supposed to fill the suitors with hope and hold them back from their planned violence" (ibid.:140),[10] and he cites a scholium to 18.272: "She arouses them to hope concerning the marriage out of the fear of being compelled" (ἐλπίδα πᾶσαν αὐτοῖς ὑποβάλλει τοῦ γάμου δεδοικυῖα ἵνα μὴ βιασθῇ). Similarly, the scholium to 18.160 says: "Penelope does not approach [the suitors] seductively, but she inspires them with the expectation that she is planning to marry one of them in order to forestall their violence" (οὐκ ἀλαζονικῶς δὲ πρόσεισιν ἡ Πηνελόπη, ἀλλ' ὅπως μὴ βιασθῇ προνοουμένη καὶ ἐλπιδοποιοῦσα τὸ δοκεῖν τινι συνοικῆσαι). Allione raises against this interpretation a cogent objection: "The promise of marriage would not have saved the young man. The suitors, in fact, intended to kill him not because he prevented Penelope from marrying again, but in order that they might divide among themselves Odysseus's riches" (1963:70 n. 12; cf. also Eisenberger 1973:246).[11]

Nevertheless, Allione too regards "la richiesta dei doni" ("the solicitation of gifts") as a deliberate deception ("un inganno") on Penelope's part.[12] In her view, Penelope's behavior in Book 18 should be interpreted against both the γέλασσε of 17.542, in which Penelope laughs in response to Telemachus's sneeze, and the ἀχρεῖον ἐγέλασσε of the passage before us, which Allione sees as "a smile that may manifest a confident hope" (1963:74).[13]

The phrase ἀχρεῖον ἐγέλασσε is usually translated as "she laughed helplessly" or "she laughed inanely," in connection with an interpretation of the passage that sees the gesture "not as an expression of a definite emotion or as a reflection of a definite intention, but rather as an index of Penelope's uncertainty and perplexity at how to react to an impulse that is inexplicable and . . . probably even repulsive to her" (Byre 1988:163).[14] As Allione

[9] "Sie muss versuchen, Zeit zu gewinnen und die Telemach und auch ihr selbst drohende Gefahr einer Gewalttat auf andere Weise abzuwenden. Zu diesem Zweck schlägt sie ein ganz neues Verfahren ein."

[10] "Es handelt sich bei ihrer jetzigen Erklärung nur um eine neue List, die wie die früheren die Freier mit Hoffnungen erfüllen und von der geplanten Gewalttat zurückhalten soll."

[11] "La promessa di nozze non poteva salvare il giovane. I pretendenti volevano infatti ucciderlo no perché egli trattenesse Penelope dal nuovo matrimonio, ma per potersi spartire tutte le ricchezze di Odisseo."

[12] Similarly, Reinhardt interprets the scene as a deliberate deception of the suitors, but one specifically formulated for the purpose by the poet on the analogy of the weaving trick (1960a:19–20).

[13] ". . . Un sorridere che manifesti fiduciosa speranza."

[14] For a full discussion of the possible meanings of the phrase, see Büchner 1940:141–43 and Allione 1963:71–74. On the meaning of laughter in the *Odyssey*, see Levine 1982–83 and Colakis 1986.

observes, however, "That Penelope might be laughing 'without knowing why' must be . . . absolutely denied, since nothing suggests here that Athena's inspiration forces the woman to perform an action that is contrary to what her heart would advise to her" (1963:71–72).[15]

In the view of Allione and others, Penelope is emboldened by the recent reports concerning Odysseus and attempts to trick the suitors by promising marriage in the hope and expectation that Odysseus will return before she is obliged to make good on her offer: "Just now Penelope has smiled, thinking about the trick, which surely would work, and about her hopes, which perhaps would come true. But, if Odysseus does not return, then the wedding that she is about to promise will truly have to come to pass" (1963:77).[16] Similarly, Levine argues, on the analogy of the *Dios apatē* of *Iliad* 14, that "besides reflecting her confusion at the sudden notion to show herself to the suitors, her laugh also anticipates her hoodwinking of them. Her laughter expresses more confidence than surprise" (1983:174).

Such interpretations take account of the discrepancy in 18.158–65, even if, in the absence of any explicit reference in the text to Penelope's intentions, they cannot be fully convincing. As Murnaghan remarks, "Penelope's motives . . . are difficult to assess because the poet is generally uncommunicative about her thoughts, as he is not about Odysseus' . . ." (1986:104). And we can observe also that in Book 19, Penelope confesses to the disguised Odysseus that, after the trick of the web, she was not able to "find another device" (νῦν δ' οὔτ' ἐκφυγέειν δύναμαι γάμον οὔτε τιν' ἄλλην / μῆτιν ἔθ' εὑρίσκω, 19.157–58). Büchner does not appear to regard this statement as inconsistent with his interpretation of Book 18 (Büchner 1940:146), and it is not mentioned in this connection by either Allione or Levine. Russo, by contrast, who also thinks that the ascription to Penelope of a deliberate deception is "the most convincing interpretation of the scene," regards Penelope's use of the plural *doloi* in 19.137 (ἐγὼ δὲ δόλους τολυπεύω) as significant in this regard (1985:213 ad 18.283).

Nevertheless, it is worth noting that the "inconsistencies" of this section of the *Odyssey* begin here, with a segment that cannot easily be athetized or otherwise brought into alignment with a single plot-line. Fenik avoids explaining the discrepancy by attributing it to a kind of willful oversight on Homer's part: "The poet . . . loses sight of (or willingly ignores) strict motivation in direct proportion to the extent to which he develops his favorite

---

[15] "Che Penelope rida 'senza sapere il perché' mi pare assolumente da escludere, perché nulla lascia qui intendere che l'ispirazione di Atena faccia compiere alla donna un gesto contrario a quello che l'animo le suggerirebbe."

[16] "Or ora Penelope ha sorriso pensando all'inganno che certo sarebbe riuscito e alle speranze che forse si sarebbero avverate. Ma, se Odisseo non torna, le nozze che ella si appresta a promettere dovranno essere davvero conchiuse."

situations..." (Fenik 1974:120;[17] cf. Levine 1983:177). Fenik argues further that it is Eurynome's reply that gives Penelope the idea to remarry (1974:116–20). But in Wilamowitz's reading of the scene, the intention to remarry is fully Penelope's: he refers to her "actual feelings" ("eigentliches Gefühl") and explains further, "Trusty Eurynome is completely in agreement.... The matron perceives Penelope's wish as a concession" (1927:19–20).[18] Vester, on the other hand, argues implausibly that "in the course of the conversion with the suitors—key word: dining (δαῖτα [18.279])—Penelope first has the idea of allowing presents to be given to her; in this she is thinking above all of Telemachus, who is angry at both her *and* the suitors because his possessions are being wasted" (1968:432; emphasis in the original).[19]

The analytic approach as exemplified by Merkelbach attributes the discrepant impulses of the whole "Geschenkszene" ("gift scene") in Book 18 to the influence of different authors. For one of these (A), Penelope "knew ... quite well what she wanted: she wanted to lead the suitors on and to win a rich reward" (1969:13).[20] This intention is consciously formulated, since in the older A poem, the foot-washing scene of Book 19 led to a recognition between Penelope and Odysseus, and then to their collusion in setting the bow-trial (ibid.:9). It is this scenario of which the gift scene of Book 18 preserves only traces.[21] For the other author (B), "Penelope herself does not properly know what she wants" (ibid.:13).[22] In the case of B, Penelope is more or less an instrument of Athena's will, which she herself does not fully understand. Some contemporary unitarians adopt a similar reading of Penelope throughout this section of the narrative: "This is not, *expressis verbis*, the intention of Penelope, but rather the intention that Athena pursues with her acquiescence"[23] (Vester 1968:430; cf. Thornton 1970:97; Erbse 1972:81; and J. H. Finley 1978:9–12).[24]

[17] The "favorite situation" here is what Fenik identifies as an "interruption sequence"; see the discussion in Fenik 1974:73–74, 95.

[18] "Die vertraute Eurynome ist ganz einverstanden.... Die Dueña sieht in Penelopes Wunsch ein Einlenken."

[19] "Erst im Verlauf der Unterhaltung mit den Freiern—Stichwort: speisen (δαῖτα [18.279])—kommt Penelope der Einfall, sich Geschenke geben zu lassen; dabei denkt sie vor allem an Telemachos, der es den Freiern *und* ihr verargt, dass sein Besitztum verschleudert wird."

[20] "... Wusste ... ganz genau, was sie wollte: sie wollte die Freier nasführen und reiche Beute machen."

[21] For the older analytic interpretation of the scene, according to which it interrupts the sequence between 18.157, when Amphinomus resumes his seat, and 18.304, when the suitors get up to dance, see Wilamowitz 1884:28–34; and cf. Wilamowitz 1927:19–50, esp. 19–26.

[22] "Penelope selber nicht recht weiss, was sie eigentlich will."

[23] "Dies ist also *expressis verbis* nicht die Absicht der Penelope, sondern die Absicht, die Athene mit ihrer Eingebung verfolgt."

[24] Page argues similarly, though from an analytic viewpoint (1955:124).

Similar impulses are understood to be at work in the neounitarian interpretation of the scene, which, however, attributes their presence in the text to the influence of a folktale version in which Penelope willingly agrees to a new alliance, in accordance with Odysseus's instructions to remarry upon Telemachus's coming of age: "The fixing of the time in the directions of Odysseus, 'when our son's beard begins to grow,' seems to me to bear the stamp of folktale"[25] (Hölscher 1967b:28; cf. Hölscher 1978:59–64).[26] In this reading, Penelope's character remains a constant, so that although the text preserves traces of the folktale version, they are thoroughly worked over and adapted to the epic context: "In short, she is *not* the deceiver of the fairy tale, but rather the understanding, grieving figure of the epic" (Hölscher 1967b:30; emphasis in the original).[27]

From an altogether different point of view, Nortwick interprets the scene in Book 18 against a parallel with the Nausicaa episode in Book 6 and develops a convincing argument that the "clustering of . . . motifs which are contrary in their signification" has the effect of associating Penelope's "divided mind" with Nausicaa's "confused adolescent sexuality" (Nortwick 1979:272, 270).[28] Although the psychological implications of this reading are, in my view, problematic (see below), those concerning narrative structure are not, and could be extended further, along the lines suggested by Forsyth (1979). Both Nausicaa and Penelope repudiate the desire for marriage, although for different reasons. In neither case is it culturally appropriate for a woman to openly acknowledge such longings, but in Penelope's case they are also absent from the surface of the text. Concerning Nausicaa, the narrative is explicit: "Thus she spoke, for she was embarrassed to mention blossoming marriage to her dear father" (ὣς ἔφατ᾽· αἴδετο γὰρ θαλερὸν γάμον ἐξονομῆναι / πατρὶ φίλῳ, 6.66–67). In Book 18, by contrast, the narrative indicates only a change in direction, signaled by ἀχρεῖον δ᾽ ἐγέλασσεν, and by οὔ τι πάρος γε in the address that follows it: "Eurynome, my spirit impels me, though it did not before, to appear before the suitors, hateful though they are" (Εὐρυνόμη, θυμός μοι ἐέλδεται, οὔ πι πάρος γε, / μνηστήρεσσι φανῆναι, ἀπεχθομένοισί περ ἔμπης, 18.164–65). Similarly, in Book 6, Nausicaa's father divines the

---

[25] "Die Terminbestimmung in der Anweisung des Odysseus: 'Wenn unserem Sohn der Bart wächst,' scheint mir den Stempel des Märchenhaften zu tragen."

[26] Cf. Merkelbach 1969:11, " 'Sprouting of a Son's Beard' is a concept capable of being extended."

[27] "Kurz, sie ist *nicht* die Listige des Märchens, sondern die Verständige, Trauernde des Epos." Cf. also Hölscher's claim that "what once was cleverness is now superiority" (Hölscher 1967b:30), and the detailed demonstration (pp. 29–31), of the narrative integrity of the episode as a whole.

[28] As Nortwick points out, Austin also interprets Nausicaa with reference to later events of Ithaca, but he reads her principally as a "stand-in" for Telemachus (Austin 1975:201). Besslich also introduces a comparison with Book 6 (1966:91).

wishes concealed behind his daughter's request (ὁ δὲ πάντα νόει, 6.67), and in Book 18, Eurynome's response indicates that she has understood Penelope's intentions as constituting a decision to remarry.

The scene in Book 18 is clearly constructed as if it represented an acknowledgment on Penelope's part of her readiness to remarry, and this decision has generated significant difficulties in the interpretation of Penelope's character. As Hölscher explains, "The entrance has alienated interpreters since antiquity. It does not seem worthy of the regal, mourning, 'prudent' Penelope; *regina prope ad meretricias artes descendit* was the oft-cited judgment of critics" (1967b:28).[29] Ancient, nineteenth-century, and contemporary interpretations alike, from both the analytic and the unitarian viewpoints, then, have insisted on alienating from Penelope this aspect of her representation. It has been displaced onto Athena, onto a folktale Penelope, onto a Penelope in collusion with Odysseus, and onto Penelope's unconscious. The more moralistic of these readings have certainly conflated a prohibition against the open acknowledgment of sexually conditioned wishes with a denial of their existence. But even the more contemporary interpretations divide Penelope against herself and project into the text an "other" Penelope, an "unconscious" Penelope, for which the text itself gives no warrant.

Thus, Nortwick claims that "the preoccupation with marriage as a social (and political) necessity is accompanied by an unconscious resurgence of interest in men, which triggers the impulse to arouse the suitors" (1979:274) and refers also to Nausicaa's "submerged, unrecognized ... awakening of sexual interest in men" (ibid.:273). This sequence, by which sexual desire is understood to eventuate in marriage, represents our own experience and construction of understanding, but reverses the ancient paradigm, whereby the social institution of marriage is the instrument for awakening rather than for satisfying sexual desire.[30]

---

[29] "Der Auftritt hat seit dem Altertum die Erklärer befremdet. Er schein der hoheitsvollen, trauernden, 'verständigen' Penelope nicht würdig: *regina prope ad meretricias artes descendit*, war das oft zitierte Urteil der Wissenschaft." This strongly worded opinion is cited by Wilamowitz from K. L. Kayser, *Homerische Abhandlungen* (Leipzig, 1881, p. 41) as *ipsa regina ad artes prope meretricias descendit* (1884:33)—a judgment that Schadewaldt refers to as "the false prudery of the nineteenth century" (1970d:78). Wilamowitz interprets the scene, which he attributes to the Penelopedichter (the poet also of Book 1), as a parody, and he compares Penelope to the Angelica of Ariosto: "Penelope, the faithful widow, is of course faithful—just as Angelica is chaste. So much is clear. And still ... she conducts herself as women always have; she knows how to make men docile and perhaps knows how to exploit the favorable situation of so many admirers pining for her—just like Angelica" (1884:33–34, citation p. 34). Cf. Wilamowitz 1927:24–25.

[30] As Vernant points out, "The allure of erotic seduction is a part of marriage ... but it is neither its basis nor a constituent element in it. On the contrary, it remains, in principle, alien to the tie of marriage" (1980b:136). Nevertheless, the occasion of marriage itself is conditioned by the arousal of sexual desire, and this is characteristically represented in allegorical

The narrative itself, as we have seen, constructs a Penelope whose "heart" or "spirit" (θυμός), as she says in 19.524 and as Telemachus says of her in 16.73, "is divided" (δίχα; cf. Εὐρυνόμη, θυμός μοι ἐέλδεται, 18.164). The word used, θυμός, is the "heart as vital principal," the "urge to action."[31] The text of these passages presents a unique adaptation of an otherwise typical scene[32] in which the epic hero ponders a set of alternatives, and either chooses himself or is impelled toward a choice by another character or by a god: the description of Penelope in 19.524 ("my heart springs up this way and that," θυμὸς ὀρώρεται ἔνθα καὶ ἔνθα) may be compared with those of Telemachus in 16.73 ("the heart in her mind is pondering," θυμὸς ἐνὶ φρεσὶ μερμηρίζει) and of Odysseus in 5.365 ("while he was pondering these things in his mind and in his heart," εἷος ὁ ταῦθ' ὥρμαινε κατὰ φρένα καὶ κατὰ θυμόν). These "*mermērizein* scenes," or "scene[s] of 'introspection,' " as Pucci calls them, dramatize the notion of interiority, particularly in their Odyssean form, where they often result in the patient endurance for which Odysseus is known. Pucci discusses four *mermērizein* scenes in which "Odysseus' posture of endurance . . . illustrate[s that] the dramatic suspense of some of the Iliadic passages is replaced [in the *Odyssey*] by a more intimate, interior dialogue about issues" (Pucci 1987:74–75).

In Penelope's case, by contrast with that of Odysseus, the text suspends judgment and attempts to exteriorize this "drama of inmost being" by playing out both alternatives simultaneously in the action of the narrative.[33] As for ὅπως τιμήεσσα γένοιτο, while it is certainly a result of Penelope's appearance before the suitors, it *cannot* represent an intention formulated by her. Ὅπως πετάσειε θυμόν, on the other hand, *must* be her own intention, whether it is understood as a deliberate bit of trickery or not. In this way, the narrative indeterminacy that, in my view, characterizes this section of the poem (Books 17–23) insofar as it concerns Penelope, is brought into the text from the beginning as its defining quality.

From this perspective, ἀχρεῖον in ἀχρεῖον ἐγέλασσε is better explained

---

form on vase-paintings of wedding scenes. A particularly good example is the name-vase of the Eretria painter (ARV^2 1250 #34), in the form of an *onos* or *epinētron*, which was used as a knee-covering when carding wool. The marriage of Alcestis appears on one side, and on the other are represented and identified by name Aphrodite, Eros, Harmonia, Peitho ("Persuasion"), Hebe ("Youth"), and Himeros ("Desire"). See the discussion in Robertson 1975, v. 1:418–19; and cf. also Redfield 1982:195–97.

[31] As well as the "powerhouse that [in the *Iliad*] pushes heroes to their glorious death" (Pucci 1987:175; 165, 181; and see 157–208 *passim*). See also Onians 1988:49–56, 116–19; Snell 1960:9–17; and Wilamowitz 1927:189ff.

[32] Arend 1933:106–15; Müller 1966:124 n. 79; Pucci 1987:66–75.

[33] Schadewaldt similarly interprets the scene as dominated by a structural opposition, which he identifies as the contrast between "Wirkung der schönen Frau" ("the effect of a beautiful woman") and "die besorgte Mutter" ("the solicitous mother") (1970d:77–78).

narratologically or sociologically than linguistically. Thus, the "uselessness" of Penelope's laugh should be measured against Telemachus's sneeze in 17.541, which, unlike her own gesture, is understood as efficacious in signalling the future direction of events. This use of the adverb ἀχρεῖον is indirectly analogous to its use in *Iliad* 2.269, where Thersites looks around "helplessly" or "ineffectually" because his social position precludes the intervention of comrades to avenge his humiliation. And so, although it is true that "the soldier and the queen are worlds apart" (Levine 1983:173), they do both belong to a social order in which both words and gestures are characteristically endowed with a significance that extends beyond their immediate meaning. Thus, the phrase ἀχρεῖον ἐγέλασσε is analogous to the double vision inherent in the ὅπως clause of 18.160–62, since it incorporates both the representation of a significant act (ἐγέλασσε) and an indication that it is insignificant in the sense that it is devoid of its usual meaning (ἀχρεῖον).

The contradiction in the purpose clause of 18.160–62 (ὅπως πετάσειε ... ἰδὲ τιμήεσσα γένοιτο) is enacted in the subsequent scene, in which Penelope arouses the suitors' desire, and Odysseus "rejoiced, because she was extracting gifts from them, and she was charming their hearts with her honeyed words. But her mind had other intentions" (18.281–83):

> Ὣς φάτο, γήθησεν δὲ πολύτλας δῖος Ὀδυσσεύς,
> οὕνεκα τῶν μὲν δῶρα παρέλκετο, θέλγε δὲ θυμὸν
> μειλιχίοισ' ἐπέεσσι, νόος δέ οἱ ἄλλα μενοίνα.

Like the passage discussed above, this one contains a phrase whose meaning is disputed: "Her mind had other intentions" (νόος δέ οἱ ἄλλα μενοίνα, 18.283). Penelope herself, to be sure, had indicated a desire only to "say a word" to Telemachus.[34] But Odysseus here is constructing Penelope's intentions in accordance with the overall narrative action, and he is reading the incident against the paradigm articulated by Athena in 13.381 (cf. 2.92), where the goddess had assured him that, although she arouses the suitors, Penelope intends otherwise ("her mind intends otherwise," νόος δέ οἱ ἄλλα μενοινᾷ). Commentators commonly adduce the Book 2 passage, where the suitor Antinous, describing the trick of the web, says the same thing about Penelope, in support of the contention that Penelope intends a ruse here (e.g., Russo 1985:213 ad 18.283). Bona, however, argues that Antinous's parallel expression in Book 2 "does not allude to a specific trick of Penelope; it is the queen's whole mode of conduct ... the

---

[34] The discrepancy between 18.167–68 and what Penelope actually says to Telemachus in 18.215ff. is no longer regarded as a serious inconsistency; see Fenik 1974:73–74, 116–19. Cf. also Allione 1963:74. Eisenberger 1973:246–48 discusses Besslich's refutation of Schadewaldt's argument for the excision of the scene; and Byre's recent article contains an extensive discussion of the issue (1988:163–65).

whole situation on Ithaca that has come into being during these years that suggests to [Antinous in Book 2] that, despite appearances, the queen had something else in mind" (1966:151).[35] By the same token, Bona goes on to insist that Odysseus rejoices, not because he detects a specific deception at work, but because of Penelope's whole manner of handling the suitors (ibid.:151–52).

Hölscher, however, claims that in 2.92 and 13.381, as well as in 18.283, "the expression does not mean 'have designs on or plan something,' but rather, 'to wish passionately for something else.' She wants to win a delay; she wants the return of Odysseus" (1967b:29).[36] Similarly, Erbse argues that the phrase means here "in her heart she cherishes (cherished) other desires" (1972:82–87, citation p. 82).[37] And Austin claims unconvincingly that "those other things . . . are nothing else but the welfare of the beggar" (1975:210). From the analytic point of view, by contrast, Merkelbach insists, "Odysseus actually has no reason at all to rejoice in his wife; he should rather be furious over her faithlessness" (1969:11).[38] And Page insists that "this statement, 'her mind was set on other purposes,' is, in this context, absolutely false. Penelope's promise of re-marriage is made in good faith: there is no indication that she does not mean what she says" (1955:125), and he adds that 13.381 is irrelevant here, on the grounds that "it would be very unlike the manner of the *Odyssey* to expect the listener to remember such a detail from so long ago" (ibid.:133 n. 26).

It is true that a decision to remarry, in its narrowest sense (that is, apart from its function in the narrative as a whole), is fully justified by Penelope's judgment concerning Telemachus's maturity, as she explains to the suitors:[39]

> ἡ μὲν δὴ ὅτε τ' ᾖε λιπὼν κάτα πατρίδα γαῖαν,
> δεξιτερὴν ἐπὶ καρπῷ ἑλὼν ἐμὲ χεῖρα προσηύδα·
> "ὦ γύναι, οὐ γὰρ ὀίω ἐϋκνήμιδας Ἀχαιοὺς
> ἐκ Τροίης εὖ πάντας ἀπήμονας ἀπονέεσθαι. . . .
> . . . .

---

[35] "Antinoo non allude a un inganno determinato di Penelope . . . è tutto il modo di comportarsi della regina . . . è tutta la situazione che in quegli anni s'è creata in Itaca, a suggerire al pretendente la certezza che, nonostante le apparenze, la regina abbia ben altro in cuore."

[36] "Bedeutet das Wort nicht: etwas anderes im Schilde führen, sondern: sich leidenschaftlich etwas anderes wünschen. Sie wünscht sich Aufschub, sie wünscht sich Odysseus' Rückkehr."

[37] "So besagt auch die dreimal in der Odyssee vorkommende Wendung νόος δέ οἱ ἄλλα μενοινᾷ (bzw. μενοίνα) nichts anderes als 'im herzen hegt(e) sie andere Wünsche.'"

[38] "Odysseus hat eigentlich gar keinen Grund, sich über sein Weib zu freuen; er sollte eher wütend sein über ihre Untreue."

[39] See Eisenberger 1973:271 for a defense of Penelope's decision to remarry as a "realistic estimation of her position."

> τῷ οὐκ οἶδ᾽, ἤ κέν μ᾽ ἀνέσει θεός, ἤ κεν ἁλώω
> αὐτοῦ ἐνὶ Τροίῃ· σοὶ δ᾽ ἐνθάδε πάντα μελόντων·
> μεμνῆσθαι πατρὸς καὶ μητέρος ἐν μεγάροισιν
> ὡς νῦν, ἢ ἔτι μᾶλλον, ἐμεῦ ἀπονόσφιν ἐόντος·
> αὐτὰρ ἐπὴν δὴ παῖδα γενειήσαντα ἴδηαι,
> γήμασθ᾽ ᾧ κ᾽ ἐθέλησθα, τεὸν κατὰ δῶμα λιποῦσα."
> κεῖνος τὼς ἀγόρευε· τὰ δὴ νῦν πάντα τελεῖται.

(For indeed, when he departed from his fatherland,
taking my right hand by the wrist, he said to me:
"My wife, for I do not think that the well-greaved Achaeans
will all of them return unharmed from Troy. . . .
Therefore I do not know whether a god will send me back [here],
 or whether I shall be captured
there in Troy; but let everything here be in your care:
To be mindful of my father and mother in the halls
just as now, or even more so since I am far away;
but when you see our child with his beard grown,
marry whomever you wish, leaving your home behind."
So he said to me; and now it is all being brought to completion.)
(18.257–60, 265–71).

Commentators have seen, however, that the action of Book 18 cannot be rationalized solely in these terms, and they question why, with the signs of Odysseus's return all around her, Penelope does not postpone this admittedly requisite step for yet a short while longer. Hölscher, for example, regards αὐτὰρ ἐπὴν δὴ παῖδα γενειήσαντα ἴδηαι (18.269) as the *Terminangabe* ("predefined limit") of the folktale constituted by the Telemachy, but as inapplicable to the following books of the epic: "This time [i.e., 'as soon as our son's beard begins to grow'] is thus the moment of crisis, but simultaneously also the basic situation of the whole epic, which, however, is explicated in the Telemachy alone and not in the following Odysseus books" [40](1967b:32).[40]

The unitarian solution, as we have seen, requires that motives unexpressed in the text be attributed to Penelope. Allione, for example, claims, "It is clear that, reading the text as it stands, without excluding a single verse, one cannot help but detect a ruse on Penelope's part, and it is impossible, therefore, to consider her action as a simple promise of matri-

---

[40] "Dies [i.e., 'Sobald unserem Sohn der Bart wächst'] ist, als der Augenblick der Krise, zugleich die Grundsituation des ganzen Epos, die aber in der Telemachie allein, und nicht in den folgenden Odysseus-Büchern, expliziert wird." Contra Allione 1963:63: "What had begun with the Telemachy now [in Book 18] attains its fulfillment."

mony to which she is forced by circumstances" (1963:66).⁴¹ Allione also regards it as possible that the account of Odysseus's parting words is a fabrication devised, along with her protestations that a new marriage is a hateful necessity (18.272), in order to confer on her discourse "a complete verisimilitude" (ibid.:76). The analytic view regards Odysseus's parting words as a fabrication as well, although from a different interpretive viewpoint: e.g., "her account of the departure of Odysseus is on the same level as the stories of the begger's travels" (Wilamowitz 1927:24);⁴² "what Penelope begins to relate at 18.257, he [Odysseus] immediately recognizes as a *pseudos* ['lie'], while the suitors are taken in without further ado" (Focke 1943:314).⁴³

Most recently, Byre argues implausibly that Odysseus also experiences unexpressed reactions, or that, at the very least, the text records something like a transformation of affect. For according to this interpretation, Athena really intends to provoke the suitors into a display of their passion and thereby to arouse Odysseus's anger. But "the poet perhaps did not find it necessary explicity to show the fulfillment of this part of the plan.... [Odysseus's] pent-up rage finds both expression and release in the joyful recognition that things are not really 'going the suitors' way'" (Byre 1988:171, 172).

The action of Book 18, it is clear, can only be rationalized by devices such as these, which require a kind of reading between the lines demanded nowhere else in the poem. Combellack, for example, comments concerning one suggestion (by Whallon, "The Homeric Epithets," *Yale Classical Studies* 17 [1961]:128) that Penelope proposes the contest of the bow knowing that the suitors will prove unequal to the test: "This assumption ... requires us to endow Homer's audience with a kind of clairvoyance enabling the listeners to see what Homer's characters mean at times when they say just the opposite" (1973:39 n. 13). Hence, I think, the frequency with which scholars turn to a psychological reading of the text, which legitimates recourse to hidden motives.

I have suggested, by contrast, that the narrative of Books 18–21 is governed by the paradigm of alternatives introduced into the story by Telemachus at the beginning of Book 16, which Penelope acknowledges in Book 19.524ff. as her state of mind: either to remain in the halls by the side of Telemachus, or to marry whichever suitor brings the most gifts. In my

⁴¹ "E chiaro che, leggendo il testo così com'è, senza escluderne alcun verso, non si può fare a meno di scorgervi una astuzia di Penelope, ed è impossibile, quindi, considerare la sua azione come una semplice promessa di matrimonio a cui è forzata dalle circostanze."

⁴² "Ihr Bericht über den Abschied des Odysseus steht auch auf der Höhe der Reiseberichte des Bettlers."

⁴³ "Was Penelope [18.]257 zu erzählen beginnt, erkennt er sofort als ψεῦδος, während die Freier ohne weiteres darauf hereinfallen."

view, the scene as a whole retains its plausibility and its narrative integrity only if it is read not from the point of view of psychological realism, but rather of narrative strategy.[44] Thus Penelope repudiates Eurynome's suggestion that she beautify herself, but this same action nevertheless occurs in the text, brought about by Athena. Similarly, the purpose clauses in 18.158–63 displace the decision "to remain beside her son and keep everything safe" onto Athena and represent it as an intention behind Penelope's appearance before the suitors, which is inconsistent with what she herself articulates. In the exchange with Eurynome in 18.164ff., by contrast, the decision to remain faithful is represented through Penelope's own protestations of disinterest in her appearance, while the explicit articulation of the desirability of remarriage is left to Eurynome. And finally, in the appearance before the suitors, the option of faithfulness is displaced onto Odysseus, and represented as his paradoxical response to Penelope's behavior. Thus, in the epiphany of Book 18, the two options consistently appear side by side, with Penelope herself articulating or representing first one, then the other. The narrative action, beginning with Book 18, represents this state of indeterminacy. In this way, Penelope's state of mind is exteriorized, and the plot is enacted as the "drama of inmost being" that Telemachus attributes to Penelope in 16.73 (θυμὸς ἐνὶ φρεσὶ μερμηρίζει), though without permitting us access to any truth of ultimate intention.

The Character of Penelope's Character (Book 19)

In Book 19, the narrative discrepancies are less glaring, but ultimately of greater significance for the poem as a whole and for its interpretation. The inconsistencies have principally to do with the final section of the book, in which Penelope decides upon remarriage and the trial of the bow (560ff.), although questions about structure and authenticity have often extended to encompass the digression on the scar (388–466) and the recognition by Eurycleia (467ff.). These have been approached from three different interpretive perspectives, which may be divided into the analytic point of view on the one hand, and the two different orientations that make up the uni-

---

[44] Compare here Murnaghan's suggestion that Odysseus's interpretation "is a proleptic understanding of events as part of a larger strategy" (1987:132), and Felson-Rubin's distinction between characters as "unwitting agents who act within whatever plot is given to them . . . [and as] supreme plotters who seemingly control their lives" (Felson-Rubin 1988:64). Felson-Rubin regards both Odysseus and Penelope as examples of the second type, and her interpretation emphasizes the reader's response to the text (e.g., "in my view, the locus for a psychological interpretation is in the interpreter, who may legitimately base . . . inferences about Penelope's psyche on clues in the text" [ibid.: n. 14]). Allione's interpretation, though it regards Penelope's actions as a trick, also emphasizes the correlation between the inner struggle of the characters and structural tensions in the plot (1963:77–78).

tarian approach on the other: aesthetic and characterological/psychological. These readings, as we shall see in this section, not only propose different solutions for the textual discrepancies, but embody very different evaluations of the ultimate aim of the poem. The ideology informing the interpretive enterprise is perhaps easiest to discern in the case of the analysts, who refer explicitly to such notions as the "Ionian ideal of manhood," to the contrast between humanism and heroism, and to the corresponding opposition between the "wedded wife" and "hero's consort." As I shall suggest, however, the unitarian approach is informed by a comparable ideology, also oriented around specific notions of character integrity, that similarly refuses to countenance rifts and discontinuities in its idea of the subject. It will be the burden of my reading overall, by contrast, to suggest that the indeterminacy around which the character of Penelope is constructed undermines this notion of a coherent, essential self and presents us with a notion of the person instead as constructed—invented on the spot, as it were—and ultimately brought into being as such by time, place, and circumstance.

Penelope's resolution to institute the bride-contest is regarded by Kirk and other analysts as "a serious illogicality" in the structure of the poem (Kirk 1962:247), announced as it is in the context of an accumulation of evidence that Odysseus's return is imminent, and following immediately upon the report of a dream portending this same event. As Wilamowitz remarks, "[It is] incomprehensible that Penelope does not have at least some doubt about the clear assurance that Odysseus will be there within twelve hours" (Wilamowitz 1884:62).[45] Woodhouse discusses the decision in a chapter entitled "Penelopeia's Collapse" (Woodhouse 1930:80–91); Page describes it as "a surrender [to the suitors] which runs absolutely counter to all that has preceded," and which introduces into the poem a "fault in construction [that is] very great and very obvious" (Page 1955:126, 124). And Schwartz regards it as certain that it cannot be an "original poet . . . who makes the plan of the trial with the bow come into being immediately after the stranger has sworn—with the most binding and convincing proofs of his trustworthiness—that Odysseus will return home in a short time" (1924:111).[46] Combellack has rationalized the difficulties in the narrative by proposing an alternate scenario incorporating "the obvious solution that should have occurred to the kind of woman

---

[45] ". . . Unbegreiflich dass Penelope nicht dieser deutlichen Zusicherung, dass Odysseus innerhalb von zwölf Stunden da sein wird, mindestens mit Zweifel entgegentritt."

[46] ". . . Kein origınaler Dichter . . . erzählt haben kann, der den Plan der Bogenprobe in Penelope entstehen lässt, unmittelbar nachdem ihr der Fremde nach den bündigsten, sie selbst überzeugenden Beweisen seiner Glaubwürdigkeit, geschworen hat, Odysseus werde binnen kurzem heimkehren."

Homer has portrayed. Her failure to think of it has long seemed to me the great defect in the plotting of the *Odyssey*," namely:

> All she need do is pretend to the suitors that she has made up her mind to delay no longer. She has not, however, been able to decide which of her many suitors to choose, and so she will allow a contest with her husband's bow to make the decision for her. It could hardly have been unreasonable to the suitors if she added something like, "Since I am willing to choose my second husband in this way, I think it only fair of you to agree that, if it should happen that none of you can string the bow and shoot through the axes, you will then abandon your suit and leave my house." (1973:39)

This suggestion endows Penelope's words and actions at the end of Book 19 with rationality. As we observed above in connection with a problematic episode in Book 18, however, the imputation by critics to Penelope of a set of thoughts and motives that they regard as logical serves to highlight rather than to explicate the problem of the text. Book 19 is divided, broadly speaking, into two major segments—the section preceding and including the foot-washing scene (lines 100–507), and the section following it (lines 508–604)—and there is a disjunction between these two sections on the surface of the narrative that requires interpretation.

Kirk, Page, and contemporary analysts refer the narrative discrepancies in Book 19 to an older version of the poem in which Penelope recognized Odysseus, and in which they proceeded to plan together the revenge upon the suitors. This "version" of the narrative is preserved in our present text as Amphimedon's interpretation of Odysseus's revenge and the suitors' defeat:

> αὐτὰρ ὁ ἣν ἄλοχον πολυκερδείῃσιν ἄνωγε
> τόξον μνηστήρεσσι θέμεν πολιόν τε σίδηρον.
>
> (But he directed his wife with great cleverness
> to set up for the suitors the bow and grey iron.)
>
> (24.167–68)

As Wilamowitz observed in his second treatise on the structure of the *Odyssey*, however, this passage does not necessarily preserve traces of "the true continuation" of Book 19, since the author of the *nekyia* includes other details of the plan as enacted in our present version, and since Amphimedon's remark makes sense as a reasonable inference from the narrative as presently constituted.[47]

---

[47] "The author of the *nekyia* . . . knows of Telemachus's trip to Pylos and of the hiding of the weapons, and since the pair discuss the shooting contest in the present Book 19, the expression of Amphimedon is justified even though Odysseus only approves an idea of Penelope" (Wilamowitz 1927:46).

In general, the older analysts, while regarding the passage in Book 24 as an important clue (e.g., Wilamowitz 1884:59), were more concerned to identify the original segments out of which the final text as we have it was put together. Thus, Wilamowitz argued that narrative of Book 19.51–475 eventuated originally in a recognition between Penelope and Odysseus, and that "the fragment of another *Odyssey* ends here [at line 476]" (ibid.:55). The segment itself belongs with a unit composed of sections of Books 17, 18, and 19, and this unit, extracted from an earlier account of Odysseus's wanderings (Books 5–14 and 17–19), was originally attached to a Telemachy (Books 2–4 and 15–19) (ibid.:227–32).

In Wilamowitz's view, the original "core of the saga of Odysseus's homecoming" (1884:58) was built up out of the central elements of "the faithful wife, the underage son, the hero educated in what had already become a characteristic figure, the Ionian ideal of manhood";[48] its outcome was conceived as the slaughter of the suitors. Its full description was as follows:

> After indescribable suffering and dangers, the kingly hero returns, naked and exposed, to his home: that was the goal of his suffering for which he yearned, and now he finds a much more difficult task. Unruly princelings have come to the fore, because the sovereign's throne was vacant, and keep his heir from the kingdom to which he was born, prey upon the possessions of the absent man, court his wife. He is too weak to confront them openly, and he has no resources but his just cause, his hero's strength, and his cleverness; yet these assure him of success, for the gods are on his side. With the help of the gods the unexpected can be accomplished, things reckoned impossible by mortals: justice triumphs.[49] (ibid.:57)

Furthermore, what now appears as the second major segment of Book 19, lines 476–604, represents "a piece of filler, patchwork poetry" ("ein Füllstück, Flickpoesie") (ibid.:63), which has displaced the earlier recognition scene. As for the original scene, "a patchwork poet, the editor, has cut this [the recognition] away and made pointless the recognition by Eurycleia, which he did not eliminate" (ibid.:66).[50]

---

[48] ". . . Die treue Gattin, den unmündigen Sohn, den schon zu einer charakteristischen Figur, zum ionischen Mannesideal, augebildeten Helden."

[49] "Der königliche Held kehrt nach unsäglichen Leiden und Gefahren allein nackt und bloss in die Heimat zurück: das hatte er als Ziel der Mühen ersehnt, und nun findet er eine noch viel schwerere Aufgabe. Unbotmässige Edelinge haben sich erhoben, da der Fürstensitz leer war, und hindern dem Erben das angestammte Herzogtum, sie zehren vom Gute des Verschollenen, umwerben sein Weib. Er is zu schwach, ihnen offen die Spitze zu bieten, nichts hat er für sich als sein gutes Recht und seine Heldenkraft und Klugheit: aber diese sichern ihm den Erfolg, denn die Götter sind auf seiner Seite. Mit der Götter Hilfe gelingt das Unerwartete, menschlichem Ermessen nach Unmögliche: das Recht triumphirt."

[50] "Diese [die Erkennung] ein Flickpoet, der Bearbeiter, abgeschnitten [hat], und die Erkennung durch Eurykleia, die er nicht beseitigte, wirkungslos gemacht."

Eduard Schwartz, partially in response to Wilamowitz, proposed a reconstruction of the oldest and second oldest epics of Odysseus's journey and homecoming, and of the successive stages of their transformation into our present text. Schwartz argued that in the oldest epic (which he designated as O), the *homilia* between Odysseus and Penelope in Book 19, beginning with line 105, represented the first meeting between the spouses in O, and that the final section of Book 17 was preliminary to it (Schwartz 1924:107, 102).[51] It eventuated, Schwartz argued further, in a recognition through the intermediary of the old nurse: "It may therefore be regarded as a confirmed finding of analytic criticism that in O, the oldest *Odyssey*, Odysseus allowed himself to be recognized by Penelope through the mediation of the nurse . . ." (ibid.:110).[52] Penelope and Odysseus together proceed to plan the revenge against the suitors. This poem, in Schwartz's view, was composed by a poet with an essentially dramatic rather than epic temperament (ibid.:229): the poet of O "wanted to elevate the epic hero to a new greatness by transporting him into an opposing existence, namely the existence that appears to the common consciousness to be the fulfillment of earthly happiness" (ibid.:193).[53] For such a poet, the scene of *anagnōrismos* represents "der Höhepunkt dramatischen Könnens" ("the high point of dramatic ability"; ibid.:195; cf. also 195–96).[54]

By a corollary argument, Penelope's appearance before the suitors in Book 18—"ein Höhepunkt der Dichtung" ("a high point of the poem"; Schwartz 1924:216)—was assigned to K, Schwartz's reconstruction of the second epic of Odysseus's wanderings and return, in which Penelope is not brought in on the secret, and recognizes Odysseus only after the revenge against the suitors.[55] This poem was "the product of an agon, of an artistic competition that the poet undertook . . . against the creator of the epic of

[51] For the full reconstruction of the recognition and revenge sequence in O, see Schwartz 1924:175–82.

[52] "Es darf also als ein sicheres Resultat der Analyse angesehen werden, dass in O, der ältesten Odyssee, Odysseus sich, bei der ersten Begegnung, der Penelope zu erkennen gab durch Vermittlung der alten Amme, die beim Fussbad die Narbe einer Wunde fand, die ihm in jungen Jahren, noch vor seiner Verheiratung, ein Eber geschlagen hatte; alte Diener und Ammen haben für solche Merkmale ihrer jungen Herren das beste Gedächtnis."

[53] ". . . Wollte den epischen Helden zu einer neuen Grösse steigern, indem er ihn hineinstellte in ein entgegengesetztes Sein, eben das Sein, das dem gemeinen Bewusstsein als des Erdenglückes Vollendung erscheint."

[54] See also Schwartz's further remarks: "The impetuous artistic temperament of O has welded together epic tradition, mythical fairy tale, and realistic novella; the internal unity that held the construct together was the epic hero, who in new surroundings—whether in the world of fairy tale or in the palace of his homeland—showed the cleverness and the power that the Trojan poets glorified" (1924:220).

[55] For the reconstruction of the revenge and recognition sequence in K, see Schwartz 1924:216–18.

the *Odyssey*" (ibid.:218),⁵⁶ and its central theme was the curse of the Cyclops, which was worked out through the narrative of the wanderings (ibid.:220–21). It was animated throughout by a heroic ideal quite different from that of O: "A kind of heroism, different from that of O, stands in opposition to the untroubled world of fairy tale: it is an internal heroism that is essentially independent of the epic splendor. There [in O] the heroic greatness of an epic hero casts its dark shadow on the uniform radiance of the Phaeacians' happiness: here [in K] the longing of a man for his sorrow-filled world, that is yet his own, resists for years the pleasure of life in a foreign land" (ibid.:222).⁵⁷ At the same time, Penelope has been transformed from the "Heldenweib" ("hero's consort") of O into the "Ehefrau" ("wedded wife") of K.⁵⁸

In his 1927 monograph, *Die Heimkehr des Odysseus*, dedicated to Schwartz, Wilamowitz modified slightly his view of Books 18 and 19.1–475, which are now regarded as a unit, "a consistent piece of very unusual character" (1927:19). This unit, to be sure, does not include the appearance before the suitors in Book 18, which, as discussed above, is now treated as a separate and self-enclosed unit with its own peculiar character (ibid.:25–26).

The analytic interpretation of Book 19, then, is linked closely with that of Book 18, with which 19 is understood to be inconsistent. Merkelbach interprets the scene before the suitors in Book 18 as the displaced aftermath of the recognition in 19. In his view, Penelope, after having recognized Odysseus, plots a two-stage revenge upon the suitors in concert with him. In the first, which is the episode now equivalent to part of Book 18, Penelope solicits bride-gifts, which are designed as recompense for the wasted property of the household; in the second, which now exists as an

---

⁵⁶ ". . . Das Produkt eines Agon, eines künstlerischen Konkurrenzkampfes, den ihr Dichter gegen den Schöpfer des Odysseusepos . . . unternommen hat."

⁵⁷ "Ein anderes Heldentum tritt hier zu einem ungetrübten Märchendasein in Gegensatz als in O, ein inneres, das von dem epischen Glanze im Grunde unabhängig ist. . . . Dort [in O] wirft einmal die heroische Grösse eines epischen Helden ihren dunklen Schatten in die eintönige Helligkeit des Phäakenglückes: hier [in K] wehrt sich Jahre hindurch die Sehnsucht des Mannes nach der leidvollen, aber ihm gehörenden Welt gegen ein geniessendes Dasein in der Fremde."

⁵⁸ The poet of K "Penelope aus einem Heldenweib umbildet zu der Ehefrau" (Schwartz 1924:231). On this point, see further Schwartz's remarks concerning objections to the idea that Odysseus and Penelope plotted the revenge together: "Only as a curiosity do I note that a respected Homeric scholar finds it unthinkable that Penelope again exposes her husband, whom she had just found, to the most terrifying danger; the critic has even won applause for this. If Odysseus and Penelope were such petits bourgeois, he would never have given up the pleasant life with Calypso and she would have consoled herself with a good-natured suitor. Royalty measures its happiness with other yardsticks than those of Philistines" (ibid.:180 n. 1).

episode in Book 21 (lines 311–58), Penelope contrives to put the instrument of revenge in Odysseus's hands (Merkelbach 1969:14–15).[59]

For Merkelbach, the narrative inconsistencies affecting the depiction of Penelope in the *Odyssey* constitute the conditions requiring the hypothesis of two parallel narratives.[60] Of these, one (the *Rachegedicht* or "Revenge poem" [R]) is characterized by a heroic spirit, the other (A) by a humanistic tenor: "In R we find the same heroic spirit that pervades the *Iliad*.... The *Odyssey* of A shows a different, more human spirit" (Merkelbach 1969:138).[61] The Penelope of the earlier, original poem (R), which Merkelbach ascribes to Homer (ibid.), is also more "heroic":

> In the novella, the wife of a man who has disappeared has already agreed to a second marriage, and only the coincidence of his timely return home preserves the wife for the hero.... Yet as soon as the story was transformed into heroic epic, the behavior of the wife also had to be judged according to a different, heroic standard, that a heroine should remain true to her husband.[62] (Ibid.:219)

Thus, the Penelope of our present Book 19 has been reworked under the influence of R: "It is perhaps clear that [in the construction of the recognition scene] A has partly employed the plot of R and consciously surpassed it" (ibid.:98).[63] Similarly, Wilamowitz argues that the poet of Books 18–19 was acquainted with the unit composed of Books 21–23 and reshaped 18–19 under its influence: "Its [Book 19's] creation is a transformation of older and original legend; and one can say that its author has, with full awareness, made the characters that appear in 21–23 more profound" (Wilamowitz 1927:77).[64]

---

[59] For a summary of the larger narrative segment of which this sequence forms part, see Merkelbach 1969:75.

[60] Merkelbach instances three specific narrative contradictions: (1) Amphimedon's report in 24.167–69; (2) the double announcement of the bow-contest in 21.311–53 (by both Penelope and Telemachus); and (3) the appearance before the suitors in 18.158–303. These points are taken up one by one by both Vester (1968:429–32) and Erbse (1972:76–90), and are convincingly refuted from the unitarian point of view.

[61] "Wir finden bei R den gleichen heroischen Geist, der die Ilias durchweht.... Die Odyssee von A zeigt einen anderen, menschlicheren Geist." The general contrast between Merkelbach's R and A is similar to that between Schwartz's O and K, but the construction of the "heroic" and "humanistic" Penelopes is quite different, as the following discussion shows.

[62] "In der Novelle hat die Frau des Verschollenen ihre Einwilligung zur zweiten Ehe bereits gegeben, und nur der Zufall der rechtzeitigen Heimkehr erhält dem Helden die Gattin.... Sobald die Geschichte aber ins heroische Epos umgesetzt wurde, musste auch das Verhalten der Frau nach einem anderen, einem heroischen Maßstab beurteilt werde, denn eine Heroine sollte ihrem Mann bis zum Tod die Treue halten."

[63] "Es ist wohl deutlich, dass [in the construction of the recognition scene] A die Handlung von R teilweise benützt und bewusst überboten hat."

[64] "Seine [Book 19's] Erfindung ist eine Umbildung der älteren und ursprünglichen Sage,

The interpretation of Book 19, then, is not a matter of structure and of inconsistencies alone; it concerns most especially the evaluation of Penelope's character. For Penelope's decision to hold the bow-contest is not only "illogical" (Kirk), a defect in plot (Combellack) or construction (Page), and unworthy of a genuine poet (Schwartz); it also calls into question Penelope's characterization as "the faithful wife":

> Yet it is a great pity that this exemplar of a good wife did not remain faithful to her husband for at least one day longer; then her fame would have been assured forever; but unfortunately she had given up her resistance precisely on the last day, and her husband was obliged to see her do this! If he had not coincidentally come back on that day she would be another man's wife. Indeed, one knows about the faithfulness of women; and with the best of them it was essentially not different. That is the way one must judge the Penelope of our *Odyssey*.[65] (Merkelbach 1969:5)

The remedy for this blemish, when Book 18 is assigned neither to a separate epic tradition, as by Wilamowitz, nor to an alternative *Odyssey*, as by Schwartz, nor to a different position in the existing one, as by Merkelbach, typically has assumed two principal forms. These can be distinguished as "aesthetic" on the one hand, and "psychological" on the other.

It was Wilamowitz who first argued the claims of the aesthetic reading of the text, by distinguishing between consistency of character in life and in poetry: "Again the critics think only about what the characters should do or not do so as to conduct themselves intelligibly in the sense of the average person, instead of paying attention to what the poet needs and wants" (Wilamowitz 1927:40).[66] Wilamowitz went on to refer the difficulties in the plot composition of this section of the poem to the conflicting needs of the audience on the one hand, and of the central figure of the narrative on the other:

> He must explain to his audience what Penelope's circumstances are, that it is really the last moment in which the savior appears. That must also be com-

---

und man darf aussprechen, dass sein Dichter mit vollem Bewusstsein die Charaktere, wie sie 21–23 bieten, vertieft hat." See also an earlier remark: "This book [19], on the other hand, was composed by a bold newcomer whom the characters of the main individuals had charmed" (Wilamowitz 1927:46).

[65] "Es ist doch sehr schade, dass dies Musterbild einer guten Frau nicht noch wenigstens einem Tag länger ihrem Mann die Treue gehalten hat; dann wäre ihr Ruhm auf immer gesichert; aber leider hatte sie ihren Widerstand gerade am letzten Tag aufgegeben, und ihr Mann hat das mit ansehen müssen! Wenn er nicht zufällig an jenem Tag zurückkam, war sie die Frau eines anderen. Man kennt ja die Treue der Weiber; und bei der besten war es im Grunde auch nicht anders. So muss man die Penelope unserer Odyssee beurteilen."

[66] "Wieder denken die Kritiker nur an das, was die Personen tun oder lassen sollten, um sich verständig im Sinne des Durchschnittsmenschen zu benehmen, statt auf das zu achten, was der Dichter braucht und will."

pletely clear to Odysseus. And at the same time he must have complete confidence that his wife has remained faithful to him: if indeed he confronts her himself, he must at least get assurance of this from her.[67] (Ibid.:40)

Woodhouse, too, explained Penelope's decision to remarry by what he called "the necessities of the plot," which are determined by "aesthetic" rather than "logical" considerations. Logical motivations for actions in a narrative, Woodhouse explains, are "grounded either in the nature of things, or in the psychology of the personages"; they are specifically "human" rather than supernatural, and they are "based in the character of the actor, that is to say in the law according to which the actor, being what he is, reacts to external circumstances or to the content of his own soul" (Woodhouse 1930:88–89). Aesthetic considerations, by contrast, spring from the necessities of the plot rather than of the character: "If the poet cannot find in his characters what he needs in the way of motive power, he must just contribute it out of his own head" (ibid.:87–88). In the *Odyssey*, the postponement of the recognition necessitated recourse to some such "ramshackle" devices, and the consequent interference with the integrity of Penelope's character: "The collapse of Penelopeia's resistance, without explanation, ruins the logic of the character, since she has not been exhibited to us from the outset as a specimen of pure caprice" (ibid.:89). Similarly, Allen argues that Homer has allowed "the requirements of the moment" to override considerations of character depiction throughout this section of the narrative: "The consistency of Penelope's character, what there was of it, has been sacrificed, but Homer agrees with Aristotle that plot is more important than character" (Allen 1939:119).

Van der Valk's reading of the end of Book 19 introduces the criterion of realism into the interpretation of the narrative, in contrast to the more straightforward aesthetic approach, which, while recognizing that "[a] complete reversal of form is not unexampled in real life," insists nevertheless that "fiction has . . . its own laws, and by virtue of these it differs from real life" (Woodhouse 1930:89). For Van der Valk, the overriding principle of interpretation is that the "poets [of the *Iliad* and *Odyssey*] represent man and his actions in a way which completely agrees with the actual situation in which human beings converse and with the motives that prompt them" (Van der Valk 1966:37). From this perspective, Penelope's reluctance to accept the evidence of Odysseus's imminent return is regarded as realistic: "It is quite natural that the omen of the dream moves Penelope,

---

[67] "Seinen Hörern muss er exponieren, wie es um Penelope steht, dass es wirklich der letzte Augenblick ist, in dem der Retter erscheint. Auch dem Odysseus muss das ganz bewusst werden. Und zugleich muss dieser die volle Sicherheit haben, dass seine Frau ihm treu geblieben ist; wenn er ihr gar selbst gegenüber tritt, muss er es durch sie selbst mindestens bestätigt erhalten."

but it cannot break the spell which was cast upon her by Odysseus' absence" (ibid.:40). Thus Van der Valk finds the construction of the plot "artful" in just that section most commonly attributed to the *Bearbeiter* by analytic readers—in 19.508–604, the *homilia* between Penelope and Odysseus following the foot-washing scene, in which the dream of the geese appears. The function of this dream, Van der Valk argues, is to provide an occasion for Penelope to reaffirm her devotion to her husband in the context of the announcement of her decision to remarry, and hence to heighten suspense and add drama to a plot that required that announcement ("because only in this way can the contest of the bow be arranged" [ibid.]).

For Van der Valk, then, the adjustments of the narrative necessitated by the postponement of the recognition between Penelope and Odysseus provide the occasion, not for "ruining" the logic of Penelope's character, as Woodhouse claimed, but for deepening it and endowing it with greater realism. This is the interpretive trend that has predominated in Anglophone scholarship in recent years and that appears also in some recent German interpretations that adopt a unitarian point of view. I have called this the "characterological" or "psychological" approach, because it attributes determinative force in the narrative to Penelope's emotional state and to the inner workings of her mind. It may be combined with an aesthetic interpretation of the text, as by Van der Valk as well as by Fenik (see below) and others, but it is often also allowed to stand on its own merits. And when it does, this approach assigns unity to Penelope's character, either on the basis of its construction around a dominant central theme (such as "sorrow," "longing," "disbelief"), or on the similar grounds of psychological realism.

Thus, Thornton argues that "Penelope's unbelief is . . . a consistent feature of her character" (1970:105) and that it triumphs finally over the hopes raised by the signs that appear in Books 17 and 19. Or as Eisenberger puts it: "We should not take offense at the disbelief with which she encounters the statements of the beggar, and at her decision to marry again. Instead, we must consider how many years she has waited in vain, how often she has been disappointed, and how much she sees herself compelled to the extreme necessity of remarriage" (1973:271).[68]

Similarly, of Penelope's refusal to lend credence to the dream-omen, Besslich remarks, "Penelope's spiritual condition is summarized in these two verses [19.568–69]. Disbelief and longing stand roughly side by side.

---

[68] "So dürfen wir an dem Unglauben, mit dem sie den Ankündigungen des Bettlers begegnet, und an ihrem Entschluss zur Wiedervermählung nicht Anstoss nehmen, sondern müssen bedenken, wie viele Jahre sie umsonst gewartet hat, wie oft sie enttäuscht worden ist und wie sehr sie sich in die äusserste Notwendigkeit zur Wiederverheiratung versetzt sieht."

In the end, longing is the basis for her disbelief" (1966:21).[69] Vester, too, argues, unconvincingly in my view, for an inverse but logical relationship between longing and despair: "The greater her longing for him [Odysseus], the further from her [Penelope] in reality he seems to be; her increasing longing thus manifests itself as an inversely proportional function, as it were, of her dwindling hopes for her husband's return" (Vester 1968:420).[70]

Even from an analytic point of view it can be argued that Penelope's characterization throughout Book 19 remains consistent, and that it is centered on her disbelief. As Focke, who regards Book 19 as the work of the O poet, but who attributes the Penelope scene of Book 18 to T (Focke 1943:309), puts it: "That Penelope no longer accepts this assurance [Odysseus's insistence in 19.585ff. that Odysseus will return before the suitors can string the bow] is understandable. At 309[71] she had already made clear what she thought about her husband's return" (ibid.:334).[72]

From this point of view, then, Penelope is a kind of *uxor dolorosa*, whom years of sorrowful waiting have rendered impervious to hope. She is beset by no conflict, and she arrives at the decision to hold the bow-contest without ambivalence. Telemachus's accession to manhood requires her to take this step, and signs of Odysseus's impending return are, understandably, given no credence: "To sum up, Penelope's decision in Book 19 to arrange for the bow contest is clearly motivated by Odysseus' parting words and by Telemachus having grown to manhood. Omens, prophecies and dreams ... cannot divert [her]" (Thornton 1970:105).[73]

There is no question from this perspective of Penelope's flirtatiousness, of the collapse of her resolve, of her betrayal of Odysseus. From this "characterological" point of view such issues, so prominent in analytic interpretations, are nothing more than "moral outrage serving the interests of philological argument," Fenik puts it (1974:46). As he goes on to explain:

---

[69] "In diesen beiden Versen [19.568–69] ist Penelopes seelische Haltung zusammengefasst. Unglaube und Sehnsucht stehen schroff nebeneinander. Letztlich ist die Sehnsucht der Grund ihrer Ungläubigkeit."

[70] "Je grösser die Sehnsucht nach ihm, desto ferner scheint er ihr realiter zu sein; ihre wachsende Sehnsucht zeigt sich so gleichsam als eine umgekehrte Funktion ihrer schwindenden Hoffnung auf die Rückkehr des Gatten."

[71] Where she first expresses disbelief in Odysseus's return: "If only, oh stranger, this word of yours might find fulfillment. . . . But thus does it seem to me in my heart, that it will be: neither will Odysseus come back home ever . . ." (19.309, 312–13).

[72] "Dass Penelope auf diese Versicherung nicht mehr eingeht, ist begreiflich. Sie hatte schon 309 zu verstehen gegeben, wie sie über des Gatten Heimkehr dachte."

[73] Thornton argues that the omens, prophecies, and dreams are irrelevant to Penelope so long as they are not validated through "signs" (1970:105), but Penelope *is* provided with a "sign" in Book 19—see σήματ' ἀναγνούσῃ (19.250)—and while this *sēma* does not provide specific proof of Odysseus's identity, it does guarantee the stranger's trustworthiness.

"The facts are otherwise. The scene [the *homilia*] has been if nothing else a depiction of the queen's tenacity and fidelity. Her capitulation occurs only with extreme reluctance, after twenty years of waiting, and under fierce pressure from the suitors, her son, and even her family. . . . To label her surrender, which she repeatedly describes as hateful to herself, . . . as a shameful betrayal is simply grotesque" (ibid.).

Such readings offer a corrective to the moralistic tendency of the older interpretations, but they take into account the texture of the narrative itself only under the rubric of "irony." Thus, Thornton argues that the poem incorporates "a masterpiece of poetic invention and a source of rich dramatic irony," in that a series of developments that are altogether consistent with Penelope's character serve also the necessities of the plot (Thornton 1970:96). As Fenik elaborates: "The scene [the *homilia*] is a triumphant exhibition of the poet's command of his narrative tools, his effortless control, his self-confidence and skill in variation. . . . Clear, logical cause and effect, airtight motivation or strict verisimilitude are not his concern. His interest is in emotion, irony, and pathos" (Fenik 1974:47).

Nevertheless, it remains the case that in the text as we have it significant discrepancies of narrative direction appear in the course of the unit consisting of Books 17–19, and extending over the course of only one day.[74] Unitarian interpretations of this sequence of events that focus on Penelope's character are obliged to overlook, to one degree or another, these discrepancies, and to ignore particularly the force of Penelope's responses in Book 17. I want to review briefly this whole sequence of events in the light of the claims about the unity of Penelope's character and behavior that we have just considered, in order to provide a background for examining the more psychologically oriented of the character approaches.

At the beginning of Book 17 Telemachus reports to his mother the account of Proteus, which he heard from Menelaus, to the effect that Odysseus was being held against his will on Calypso's island. The report of this news, the text tells us, "aroused the heart in her breast" (ὣς φάτο, τῇ δ' ἄρα θυμὸν ἐνὶ στήθεσσιν ὄρινε, 17.150). Immediately thereafter, Theoclymenus interrupts to proclaim the prophecy "that Odysseus is already in his fatherland, sitting somewhere or prowling about, and taking in these evil deeds, but for all the suitors he is hatching evil" (ὡς ἦ τοι Ὀδυσεὺς ἤδη ἐν πατρίδι γαίῃ, / ἥμενος ἦ ἕρπων, τάδε πευθόμενος κακὰ ἔργα, / ἔστιν, ἀτὰρ μνηστῆρσι κακὸν πάντεσσι φυτεύει, 17.157–59), and Penelope accepts the prophecy by affixing to it the wish that it might come to pass: "If only, oh stranger, this word might be fulfilled!" (αἲ γὰρ τοῦτο, ξεῖνε, ἔπος

---

[74] Dawn rises at 17.1 and at 20.91; late afternoon begins at 17.170; afternoon is divided from evening at 18.305–6. It is the "longest" day in the poem (amounting to 1,728 lines). See Delebecque 1980:7.

τετελεσμένον εἴη, 17.163). Finally, at the end of Book 17, when Penelope expresses to Eumaeus the fervent hope that "if only Odysseus might come and arrive in his fatherland, then he with his son would avenge the violence of [these] men" (εἰ δ' 'Οδυσεὺς ἔλθοι καὶ ἵκοιτ' ἐς πατρίδα γαῖαν, / αἶψά κε σὺν ᾧ παιδὶ βίας ἀποτείσεται ἀνδρῶν, 17.539–40), Telemachus sneezes, and Penelope readily interprets this as a confirming sign: "Don't you see that my son sneezed at all [those] words? Therefore would death not be unaccomplished for all the suitors; not one of them will escape death and the fates" (οὐχ ὁράᾳς, ὅ μοι υἱὸς ἐπέπταρε πᾶσιν ἔπεσσι; / τῶ κε καὶ οὐκ ἀτελὴς θάνατος μνηστῆρσι γένοιτο / πᾶσι μάλ', οὐδέ κέ τις θάνατον καὶ κῆρας ἀλύξει, 17.545–47).

Just following this scene, Penelope asks Eumaeus to arrange for her to speak with the beggar, and when the disguised Odysseus responds by requesting postponement of their interview until after the suitors have left for the evening, Penelope remarks on the discrepancy between the stranger's thoughtfulness and the arrogance and stupidity of the suitors (17.586–88). Penelope's next action in the narrative, some 150 lines later (at 18.158ff.), is to decide upon remarriage; and when the interview with the stranger does take place, in Book 19, the resolve to remarry is reaffirmed and strengthened. Thus, to summarize: (1) at the opening of this day Penelope greets Telemachus upon his safe return, and responds enthusiastically to the signs of Odysseus's imminent homecoming; (2) in the evening she appears before the suitors and solicits bride-gifts; (3) at the end of the day, by the light of the fire and following upon further trustworthy reassurances, she affirms her resolve to institute immediately the contest of the bow.

The aesthetic approach to the narrative, as we have seen, recognizes the inconsistencies here, but considers them appropriate to a poet who "loses sight of (or willingly ignores) strict motivation in direct proportion to the extent to which he develops his favorite situations with their special emotions and ironies" (Fenik 1974:120). Similarly, for Hölscher, the aesthetic pleasure we derive from the scenes renders questions about their logicality within the poem irrelevant. Thus, concerning the appearance before the suitors, he says: "There is often secret pleasure in the unrecognized, and always when someone does something good and right, about which he has not a clue to what extent it is right" (1939:63);[75] and of the *homilia*, which he interprets also as a "typical situation," Hölscher remarks: "Their purpose [scenes of 'failed' recognition] is not to introduce the discovery, but rather to wrap anew the hidden, that just now threatens to betray itself, in

---

[75] "Die heimliche Freude des Unerkannten gibt es noch öfter, und immer dann, wenn etwas Gutes und Richtiges tut, wovon er doch nicht ahnt, in welchem Masse es das Richtige ist."

mistrust, neglect, and doubt" (ibid.:71).[76] In Vester's analysis, too, narrative contradictions are referred to the principle of aesthetic effect.[77]

Unitarian interpretations centered on the characterological principle are similarly obliged to understand the inconsistency between Books 17 and 18 as irony. From this perspective, however, it is often explained as divine intervention. And indeed, the text explicitly attributes to Athena Penelope's idea to show herself to the suitors, along with the later plan to set the bow-contest, employing the same formulaic lines in both instances (18.158–59 = 21.1–2).[78] Thus Thornton remarks simply, "It is Athene who stirs in Penelope the desire to show herself to the suitors" (Thornton 1970:97), without elaborating further on the point. And Erbse argues, against Merkelbach, that "what Merkelbach describes as the intention of the queen is in truth the plan of the goddess, of which the human being, instrument of Athena, knows nothing" (Erbse 1972:81).[79] It is also true, however, that in each of these instances the text also represents the idea as Penelope's own (see below).

More common is the tendency to adopt a version of the characterological approach that emphasizes psychological factors and comprehends the unity of Penelope's character under a rubric such as "agitation" or "irrationality." From this perspective, Penelope either vacillates between hope and despair, or else is the victim of the play of irrational forces. Thus, Eisenberger explains the appearance before the suitors as a momentary lapse: "It is the feeling of joy in the reunion with Telemachus, which continues to have an effect during that morning but which dissipates in the hours before the conversation. As a result, during the night her normal condition of mind—longing, but despair and skepticism toward the reports about Odysseus—is reestablished" (Eisenberger 1973:271).[80] Besslich explains Penelope's decision to institute the bow-contest at the end of Book 19 in a similar manner: "The pessimistic decisiveness with which she now speaks

---

[76] "Ihr Sinn ist nicht, die Enthüllung herbeizuführen, sondern vielmehr das Verborgene, das soeben sich zu verraten droht, von neuem in Misstrauen, Nichtbeachtung und Zweifel einzuhüllen."

[77] See, e.g., Vester's distinction between Penelope's consciousness and "the knowledge of the audience" in the first group of speeches in Book 19 (1968:423), and his argument that "this ambiguity in his words [Odysseus's prediction in 19.555–58 that the dream will be realized], which is only clear to the listener, can hardly be overlooked and connects the second conversation again with the first [sc. with 19.296ff.]" (ibid.:428).

[78] On Penelope as "double agent" by virtue of this divine intervention in Book 21, see Nortwick 1983.

[79] ". . . Das, was Merkelbach als Absicht der Königin beschreibt, in Wahrheit Plan der Göttin ist, von dem der Mensch, Athenes Werkzeug, nichts weiss."

[80] "Es ist die Stimmung der Freude über das Wiedersehen mit Telemach, die darin am Morgen nachwirkt, aber in den Stunden bis zur Unterredung mit dem Fremden vergeht, so dass in der Nacht ihre normale Seelenlage—Sehnsucht, aber Hoffnungslosigkeit und Skepsis gegen Berichte über Odysseus—wiederhergestellt ist."

is a sudden reaction, the almost self-tormenting attempt to clarify her uncertain situation once and for all—with negative consequences; thus it is a defensive reaction with which she meets her nascent hope . . ." (Besslich 1966:21).[81] Allione, too, as we saw in our discussion of Book 18, regards "dolore e speranza" ("grief and hope") as "i sentimenti che caratterizzano la figura di Penelope" ("the feelings that characterize the figure of Penelope," Allione 1963:93). Finley, who follows Allione (Finley 1978:14 n. 6), speaks of "the intense oscillation of feeling that, in Book 18, produces the first of her two drastic and enigmatic acts; the other will be her decision for the test of the bow" (ibid.:8). Most recently, Dimock has claimed that "the pressure of events [in Book 18] led Penelope irrationally and almost involuntarily to encourage the suitors" (1989:262).

This focus on Penelope's irrationality amounts, I think, to a particular kind of "psychologizing" that has been prominent in Homeric studies since the 1930s and has come under increasing critical scrutiny in recent years.[82] Here I want only to point to the compatibility—indeed, the ultimate identity—between explanations of Penelope's behavior based on divine intervention and those founded on notions of irrationality. In both cases the idea of illogicality is reified—it is endowed with an essence and a determinative force, and comprehended as inherently inscrutable and consequently as impervious to further analysis. Thus, there is a certain equivalence implied between divinity and human irrationality. As Amory remarks on Penelope's decision to fetch the bow at 21.1–2: "Homer habitually objectifies internal mental processes in the figures of gods, and always with due regard for the psychological reality of his characters" (1963:113). Or, as M. Edwards has put it recently: "Forces that we would consider psychological may also be attributed to an external and divine power" (1987:129).[83]

This equivalence makes it possible to claim, at one and the same time, both that Penelope acts as a free agent and that she is manipulated by divinity. Thus, Wilamowitz explains that "Athena bears the responsibility for her conduct," but he adds: "That does not and cannot change the fact that she speaks the way that corresponds with her suggested motive; accordingly, the result must be that we notice it is contrary to her actual feelings"

---

[81] "Die pessimistische Entschiedenheit, mit der sie jetzt spricht, ist eine plötzliche Reaktion, der geradezu selbstquälerische Versuch, ihre unsichere Situation ein für allemal—in negativer Konsequenz—zu klären; eine Abwehrreaktion also, mit der sie der aufkeimenden Hoffnung begegnet. . . ."

[82] For recent discussion, see Arthur 1984; Monsacré 1984:51–62; and M. Edwards (1987:143–48).

[83] As this indicates, "psychological" is sometimes understood to be equivalent to "irrational."

(Wilamowitz 1927:19).[84] Similarly, Allione argues concerning the appearance in Book 18, "The twofold intention (ὅπως . . .) belongs jointly to the goddess and to Penelope . . ." (1963:76).[85] And, more recently, Finley claims: "The goddess is working in her [Penelope]—which is not to say that she herself is not acting" (1978:9).

This kind of characterological/psychological reading of Penelope, then, is close to the aesthetic interpretation of the text in that it ultimately bypasses the question of logical consistency in the narrative. It displaces the issue—not, as in the aesthetic reading, onto poetic form, but onto the forces of irrationality themselves, located either in the heights of the heavens or in the depths of human soul. This reading of Penelope comes close to explaining her responses through appeal to, as Woodhouse put it, "our general knowledge of human nature, or . . . some store of working maxims—such . . . as that pearl of masculine wisdom: *varium et mutabile semper femina*" (1930:89). The psychological interpretation of Penelope as we have discussed it so far saves her from becoming an exemplar of her sex (*così fan tutte*) only because her choices ultimately, and unbeknownst to her, are correct. As one commentator has put it: "She [Penelope] . . . does . . . unconsciously what is right. For as she . . . praises the unknown beggar [at the end of Book 17], she does not guess in what peculiar way she does what is right—and likewise her speech to the suitors [in Book 18]" (Hölscher 1939:63).[86]

An extension of this point of view that offers a more subtle and complex form of psychological explanation was first proposed by Amory in 1963 and was extended further by Russo in 1982, and both address themselves to what we might call the "logic" of irrationality.[87] Both Amory and Russo argue that Penelope's "illogical" behavior in this section of the narrative is guided by her intuitions, and that these, in turn, represent a kind of rationality that operates on a level just below that of conscious awareness (see also Nortwick 1979).

Amory's interpretation is focused on the profusion of signs, omens, and other forms of mysterious communication that fill this section of the poem, and on her view that Penelope is characterized by a "particular kind of

---

[84] "Die Verantwortung für ihr Benehmen trägt Athena. . . . Das hindert nicht und kann nicht hindern, dass sie so redet, wie der ihr suggerierten Absicht entspricht; es muss nur daneben herauskommen, dass wir merken, es ist wider ihr eigentliches Gefühl."

[85] "La duplice intenzione (ὅπως . . .) è insieme della dea e di Penelope. . . ."

[86] "Sie . . . tut . . . unbewusst das Richtige. Denn wie sie . . . den fremden Bettler schätzt, sie ahnt doch nicht, in welch besonderer Weise es das Richtige ist, was sie tut.—Und ebenso ihre Rede zu den Freiern." Erbse remarks similarly of the same scene: "For she unconsciously prepares for the execution of the plan of revenge and at the same time makes it clear how very objectionable a new marriage is to her" (Erbse 1972:84).

[87] Amory's thesis was formulated against that of Harsh, which I take up below; Russo saw his interpretation as an extension of Austin's (see below).

perception": she "thinks intuitively rather than rationally. She is always holding a veil in front of her face" (Amory 1963:104; see also Amory 1966:55–56). Thus, Penelope intuitively recognizes Odysseus in Book 19 and proposes the contest as a form of divination, and as a test of her intuitions (Amory 1963:106).

Allione, too, argues that Penelope's confidence in the stranger's predictions led her to consolidate her plans, and to confide them to him "in order that she might provoke a . . . suggestion that contains a more precise indication of time" (Allione 1963:91).[88] Allione concludes that "the human merit of Penelope's action . . . consists in her intuition of the approach of the decisive day" (ibid.:93).[89]

Russo's discussion, focused on the dream of the geese in Book 19 (on which see below) and the dream visions of Book 20, also claims that Penelope is influenced to set the bow-trial by a "swelling current of intuitions, intimations, and half-believed hopes" (Russo 1982:17), but Russo attempts to specify more fully the specifically Homeric understanding of "mental activity that belongs to the lower levels of consciousness" (ibid.).[90] All of these readings, it should be noted, presume a Penelope who, insofar as she is "innately irrational, impulsive, and passive," is also stereotypically feminine, and who notably "lack[s] rather than share[s] the mental power that is so central to Odysseus' success" (Murnaghan 1987:138).[91]

The narrative inconsistencies of this section of the poem, then, have been explained in accordance with three principal lines of interpretation. The analytic and neoanalytic views have assigned the discrepant sections to different sources of origin. The unitarian approach has been divided into aesthetic and characterological trends, with the former understanding narrative illogicality as a negligible consequence of the poem's formal structure, and the latter comprehending it as a feature of the poetic depiction of Penelope.

[88] ". . . Per provocare un . . . suggerimento, che contiene una più precisa indicazione di tempo."

[89] "Il valore umano dell'azione di Penelope . . . consiste nell'aver essa intuito l'avvicinarsi del giorno decisivo." Austin, too, argues that Penelope throughout Book 19 is in a "hectic state" characterized by the "dynamics of mental conflict" (Austin 1975:218, 234), and that she "subconsciously" recognizes Odysseus as her husband. Thus, she proposes the bow-contest as "a form of divination" (ibid.:235).

[90] Russo bases his argument in part on a suggestion of Devereux, who applied psychoanalytic principles to an interpretation of Penelope's character. But Devereux's argument is flawed, as Russo's is not, by inattention to the methodological difficulties of applying psychoanalysis to the literature of a premodern culture. Devereux resorts instead to complacent reassurances concerning "the universal and culturally neutral validity of psychoanalysis" (Devereux 1957:386).

[91] Cf. also Felson-Rubin's apposite remarks: "Amory's Penelope emerges as an unconscious and unreflective being, very 'female' in an old sense of the word but not so very 'like-minded' to Odysseus" (Felson-Rubin 1988:79 n. 13).

None of these interpretations is able to account for the textual coherence of the narrative—for the sense, in other words, that the poem operates as a unified whole, whether that coherence is understood to spring from the clumsy manipulations of the final redactor, or whether it is comprehended as an original feature of the epic. For, as one commentator has put it, "who in the camp of the analytic critics ever wanted to dispute that the *Odyssey*—despite undeniably existent objections to individual parts—is meaningful in its totality?" (Vester 1968:418).[92] The question, to be sure, is a matter of accounting not only for the overall structure of Book 19, but also for its position in the whole course of development of the homecoming ("[der] Gesamtverlauf des Heimkehrergeschehens" [ibid.]).

In recent years, some new dimensions have been added to this discussion by scholars influenced by feminist, socioanthropological, and narratological theory. The most ingenious of these new readings, that of John Winkler, harks back to an interpretation first put forward by P. W. Harsh in 1950, who argued in a well-known article that Penelope developed suspicions about the stranger's identity on the basis of the reports in Book 17, and that these were strengthened in Book 19; understanding, however, that open recognition in the presence of the maidservants would jeopardize Odysseus's life, she kept her thoughts concealed (Harsh 1950).[93] Winkler defends a similar reading, arguing, like Harsh, that Penelope's conduct in Book 19 is guided by her suspicion that the beggar is Odysseus, and that although Penelope does not necessarily recognize him, "she reaches a point where his answers are sufficiently Odyssean to justify her gamble in setting up the contest of the bow" (Winkler 1990:143).

Though their readings are quite similar, Harsh and Winkler base them on radically different interpretive premises. For Harsh, "cautious conservatism is the key to Penelope's character" (1950:4); Winkler regards Penelope principally as a figure of *mētis*. And while Harsh sees Penelope as "a keen and intelligent woman" (ibid.:6), he endows her character with psy-

---

[92] "Wer wollte etwa im Lager der Analytiker bestreiten, dass die *Odyssee* in ihrem Gesamtverlauf—trotz ohne Zweifel vorhandener Anstösse im einzelnen—sinnvoll ist?" And even Wilamowitz said of the Bearbeiter that "[he] is not a scheming fool or villain like the sciolous interpolator of a superseded textual criticism, at whose door one lays the blame for whatever is displeasing, but rather a rhapsode who first undertakes to unite the epic of the wandering with the Telemachia" (Wilamowitz 1927:165).

[93] For discussion of Harsh's thesis, see Merkelbach 1969:237 (n. to page 7); Allione 1963:82 n. 32; Amory 1963:103–4; Vester 1968:418 n. 9; Erbse 1972:86; Russo 1982:7 n. 9; Murnaghan 1987:137; and Winkler 1990:155. Stewart, alone among contemporary interpreters, adopts Harsh's reading outright (Stewart 1976:103). It is often reported (e.g., by Winkler 1990:155) that Harsh maintained "that Penelope actually recognizes the true identity of the beggar in Book 19," but this is not in fact the case; it is the point of Harsh's argument to insist rather that Penelope conceives and then acts upon "suspicions" or "secret suspicions" of the stranger's identity (1950:2, 5, 6, 7, 11, 13, 18, 19, 20).

chological plausibility by appealing to the stereotype of a transcultural and transhistorical female essence: Penelope is "feminine in her wealth of emotion"; she is characterized by "feminine resort to subterfuge" and "feminine intuition" (ibid.:4, 7). Winkler, by contrast, reads the *Odyssey* as "a story about Mediterranean social practices" (1990:130) and, accordingly, interprets what he calls Penelope's "faithful duplicity" (ibid.:147) as an example of the strategy of subterfuge that governs all social interactions in this world. For in a cultural system centered on the interplay of honor and shame, the deliberate use of lies, secrets, and silence operates as a sign of cultural competence, rather than of weakness or of moral laxity.[94]

These readings are ingenious, and even convincing in their way, when they are restricted to the action of Book 19. Winkler's in particular is attractive because he argues that the poet is manipulating rather than simply replicating female stereotypes, and this accords better with the overall sense of a narrative focused, after all, on the trope of duplicity. It must ultimately be admitted, however, that "this hypothesis, although brilliant and subtle, does not find a secure foundation in the text" (Allione 1963:82 n. 32, referring to Harsh).[95] In addition, as we shall see below, these readings founder when they attempt to bring the action of Books 20 and 23 within their compass, and they must resort as well to implausible accounts of the appearance before the suitors in Book 18.

Other recent readings are attentive to the implications of Penelope's social role, and they are similarly disinclined to regard her simply as its passive victim. Marquardt (1985) and Felson-Rubin (1988) perhaps take this line of interpretation furthest in arguing that Penelope consciously exploits and manipulates her situation, as part of a strategy of self-defense or from an otherwise self-interested perspective. Marquardt interprets Penelope's acquiescence in the suitors' wooing as part of a plan to keep her options open; she argues that when Penelope sets the bow-contest, she does not expect any of the suitors to succeed, and that her subsequent expressions of despair spring from "subconcious guilt" (Marquardt 1985:44). In Felson-Rubin's reading, Penelope, like Odysseus, plots her moves with care but, kept in ignorance of the larger plot, must design actions that "fit into more than one plot trajectory" (1988:73). Furthermore, although she intends to hold out against the suitors, various passages reveal also the simultaneous presence of "a sensuous Penelope under the influence of Aphrodite as well as Artemis" (ibid.:76). Penelope is, from this point of view, preeminently either *polytropos* ("of many turns") (Marquardt) or *periphrōn* ("circumspect") (Felson-Rubin), and she is in addition "far more prudent

---

[94] On the general applicability of the paradigms derived from Mediterranean social anthropology to ancient Greek culture, see Walcot 1970, 1977; Arthur 1981, 1982; and discussions throughout Winkler 1990.

[95] "Questa ipotesi, pur se brillante ed acuta, non trova sicuro fondamento nel testo."

about her own security and attentive to her own pleasures than others (both characters and critics) have acknowledged" (Felson-Rubin 1988:77).

This scandalous reading of the text, as we might call it, gives us a Penelope with greater psychological plausibility than does the analysts' scandalized interpretation, and it satisfies the desire for a realistic character-portrayal.[96] It is ultimately no more successful in accounting for the narrative structure of the poem, however—Marquardt resorts freely to the notion of Penelope's "instinctive timing" to explain the setting of the bow-contest; Felson-Rubin discusses the text by theme, and so elides the problem of narrative coherence.

Murnaghan, too, proposes that "Penelope's behavior is imposed on her by her impossible role as faithful wife of a man who is absent" (1987:138), but Murnaghan regards Penelope as victimized by her assimilation to a generalized form of misogyny that obliges Odysseus to conceal his identity from her. This results in an "illogically constructed plot" (ibid.:127) whose illogicality is, however, itself rendered meaningful. For Penelope, insofar as the particularity of her character is overwhelmed by her social role, comes to represent the fundamental instability of human social institutions,[97] and the necessary subjection of human beings, not only to social but to metaphysical pressures: "the doubleness that persists in Penelope's behavior . . . testifies . . . to an inevitable subjection to social pressures . . . [and this is a] manifestation of subjection to the passage of time" (Murnaghan 1986:109). Thus, through Penelope, the *Odyssey* undercuts its own central theme, the notion that human events can indeed be controlled through deception and *mētis* (Murnaghan 1987:134; cf. 143, 146).

Murnaghan insists on what she calls a "literal reading" of the text, which, as she says, requires a direct confrontation with the illogicality of its structure and the irreconcilability of its parts (Murnaghan 1986:113). This is an important interpretive maneuver, and it results in a sensitive reading of the poem. This reading is also a sentimental one, however, which imports into the narrative a tragic, or perhaps tragi-comic, element for which there does not otherwise appear to be warrant.[98] To be sure, misogyny in ancient Greece was tied closely to the exchange of women (e.g., Arthur 1982:535–38), and an analogy between women's social role and the human condition functioned as part of ancient Greek ideology (e.g., Arthur 1983:110–12), but the *Odyssey* does not thematize these issues as such.

---

[96] See esp. Felson-Rubin's remark, "We must treat [Penelope] as if she were a character in real life, with a world of her own" (1988:64).

[97] Penelope is "the figure who represents the potential unruliness at the heart of social organization" (Murnaghan 1987:146).

[98] Murnaghan refers to the setting of the bow-contest as "the poem's persuasive imitation of an act of despair" (1987:137).

Otherwise, then, the newer interpretations of Penelope in the *Odyssey* have modified the older ones in important respects, but they have not materially altered the terms of the discourse. For the analytic readers, in predicating their reading upon a unitary notion of character, were led to what one might regard as a correct diagnosis of schizophrenia (or multiple personality) in the text. Unitarian readers, likewise committed to a unitary notion of character, have adopted two different but ideologically compatible interpretive stances. On the one hand, the inconsistencies in Penelope's character are acknowledged, but are regarded as an unfortunately necessary by-product of the poem's narrative structure. I have discussed this as the aesthetic approach to the text. Other readers have imputed coherence to Penelope on the basis of thematic, psychological, or sociological concerns, but have largely disregarded issues of narrative texture and structure. This is what I have called the characterological/psychological approach, and I think the most recent readings of Penelope conform to it either explicitly or implicitly.

In my discussion of Book 18 in this chapter, I adopted a different interpretive strategy. First, I tried to show how the representation of Penelope functioned in concert with aspects of the poem's narrative structure, and I argued that as a consequence, what could be understood as characterological incoherence was in fact retrieved by the structure of the episode. In the first part of Chapter Five I argue more fully for a close relationship between "characterological incoherence" and narrative unity. I then suggest how the "problems" in the representation of Penelope's character are important and functional aspects of the narrative overall, and I show that they operate ultimately in the service of what I analyze in the last chapter as the poem's "ideology of exclusivity." I do not, then, subscribe to the unitarian notion that the discontinuities in the representation of Penelope either are only apparent or are devoid of a specific narrative function; nor, on the other hand, do I accept the analytic claim that the structure of the narrative must be adjusted to take them into account. I comprehend these ruptures in the coherence of character instead under the rubric of indeterminacy, and I argue that this indeterminacy has a specific and definable function in the poem as we possess it.

Chapter Five

THE CONSTRUCTION OF PRESENCE (BOOKS 17–21)

THE OVERALL homecoming sequence includes the omens and foreshadowings of Book 17, the appearance before the suitors in 18, the *homilia* and the decision to set the bow-contest in 19, the sorrowful dreams of Book 20, and the setting of the contest in Book 21; it culminates in the *anagnōrismos* ("recognition scene") of Book 23. It is this sequence which requires interpretation, and whose narrative coherence in the text as we have it must be explained. We have seen already that the analytic reading splits this narrative into two or more principal segments, and generally regards Penelope's appearance before the suitors in Book 18 as a "foreign body" (Wilamowitz 1927:19), the end of Book 19 and beginning of 20 as the work of the final redactor, and the resulting sequence of Books 17–19 as the work of a different poet than that of Books 21–23. The unitarian readings of this sequence, whether they appeal to the principles of aesthetic form or of character portrayal and psychological versimilitude, either disregard the sequence of actions as such, or explain it through the operation of emotions or thoughts that do not appear in the text.

In this chapter I address first the structural logic of the two principal instances of narrative discrepancy in this sequence, and I show how the text attempts to resolve them. I go on to discuss how the narrative action of Books 17–21 is conditioned, in different but analogous ways, by Odysseus's presence on Ithaca. For Telemachus, the *anagnōrismos* of his father authorizes the assumption of a "disguise" as the *kyrios* of what he now appropriates as his *oikos*. This same gesture legitimates for Penelope two apparently contradictory courses of action: on the one hand, she decides upon remarriage and moves to bring it into effect; on the other, she resumes her role as mistress of the household she is about to abandon and receives into it the stranger Odysseus. These actions, which are on one level of the text based simply upon a mistake—the erroneous conviction that Odysseus will not return—are on another level constitutive of reality. For they bring into being for Penelope a new relationship with "Odysseus," based on an abandonment of the old one. This, in turn, is what makes it possible for Penelope's *anagnōrismos* of Odysseus to be effected through a convergence of the stranger with the husband, rather than through a simple replacement of one by the other.

The logic of this narrative development is given by the Nausicaa se-

CONSTRUCTION OF PRESENCE (17–21)   115

quence of Books 6 and 7, in which Alcinous's proposal of marriage to Odysseus follows upon indications of Nausicaa's readiness for marriage and her initial reception of Odysseus as a stranger. Thus, my interpretation argues for a certain equivalence between husband and stranger, and it is also built around a reading of disguise that emphasizes its capacity not just to misrepresent reality, but also to instantiate it.

Narrative Disjunction and Textual Disguise (Books 18–19)

There are two principal moments of narrative incongruity in the segment of the *Odyssey* that stretches from Book 17 to Book 23, and these form the crux of the representation of Penelope: the appearance before the suitors in Book 18, and the decision to set the bow-contest in Book 19. This is well-known; but it is perhaps not so frequently acknowledged that these two incidents share certain important structural features.

Both follow immediately upon trustworthy signs of Odysseus's imminent return and are connected closely with them in the text. These appear in Book 17 as the omens and foreshadowings discussed above, to whose implications Penelope reacts with an enthusiastic endorsement; in Book 19 they consist first in the stranger's assurances that Odysseus is near and on the verge of homecoming (19.268–72),[1] which themselves follow upon Penelope's recognition of the *sēmata* ("signs"), and second, in the dream of the geese and its interpretation (19.535–58).

In the first episode, the discrepancy appears as the incompatibility between Penelope's decision to appear before the suitors at 18.158ff. and her explicit expectation of Odysseus's return, affirmed at 17.541–50. There intervenes between these two incidents only the fight with the beggar Irus, which provides the occasion for an important exchange between Penelope and Telemachus, to which we shall turn later. Let us note here, however, that Penelope's expectation of Odysseus's *nostos* is explicitly formulated in the context of the forthcoming *homilia* with the stranger; having heard from Eumaeus that the stranger has reported that Odysseus is near, Penelope wishes aloud for his return and revenge upon the suitors. And when Telemachus's sneeze confirms her wish, Penelope interprets the sign in light of an explicit expectation that the forthcoming *homilia* will substantiate the encouraging reports.

ὣς φάτο, Τηλέμαχος δὲ μέγ' ἔπταρεν, ἀμφὶ δὲ δῶμα
σμερδαλέον κονάβησε· γέλασσε δὲ Πηνελόπεια,

[1] "Pay attention to my account. For I will tell you truly and I will not hide it, that the homecoming of Odysseus I have heard is already near, and he himself is alive in the land of the Thesprotians" (ἐμεῖο δὲ σύνθεο μῦθον· / νημερτέως γάρ τοι μυθήσομαι οὐδ' ἐπικεύσω, / ὡς ἤδη Ὀδυσῆος ἐγὼ περὶ νόστου ἄκουσα / ἀγχοῦ, Θεσπρωτῶν ἀνδρῶν ἐν πίονι δήμῳ, / ζωοῦ).

αἶψα δ' ἄρ' Εὔμαιον ἔπεα πτερόεντα προσηύδα·
"ἔρχεό μοι, τὸν ξεῖνον ἐναντίον ὧδε κάλεσσον.
οὐχ ὁράᾳς, ὅ μοι υἱὸς ἐπέπταρε πᾶσιν ἔπεσσι;
τῶ κε καὶ οὐκ ἀτελὴς θάνατος μνηστῆρσι γένοιτο
πᾶσι μάλ', οὐδέ κέ τις θάνατον καὶ κῆρας ἀλύξει."

(Thus she spoke, and Telemachus sneezed loudly, and the house
resounded loudly all around. So Penelope laughed
and immediately addressed winged words to Eumaeus:
"Come now, call that stranger right here to me.
Don't you see that my son sneezed at all those words?
Therefore would death not be unaccomplished for all
the suitors; not one of them will escape death and the fates.")

(17.543–47)

Thus, Penelope's decision to appear before the suitors at 18.158ff. is incompatible, not only with the omens and foreshadowings of Book 17 generally, but more specifically with the immediately preceding indication of narrative direction, which is explicitly formulated around the presence in the house of the stranger.

In Book 19, Penelope's expressions of despair are similarly incongruous, but in this case with their immediate narrative context. Once the stranger has established this trustworthiness through the *sēmata* ("signs," 19.250) and has been accepted as a *xeinos* (19.253–54), he goes on to offer Penelope assurances that Odysseus is near and on the point of return (19.269–72, 300–302). He then ratifies them with an oath: "And I will give you a secure oath [on this] . . . that indeed all these things are being fulfilled just as I proclaim" (ἔμπης δέ τοι ὅρκια δώσω . . . ἦ μέν τοι τάδε πάντα τελείεται ὡς ἀγορεύω, 19.302, 305). He swears the same oath with which Theoclymenus had endorsed his own prophecy earlier the same morning,[2] and Penelope responds with the same formulaic wish: αἲ γὰρ τοῦτο, ξεῖνε, ἔπος τετελεσμένον εἴη ("If only, oh stranger, this utterance [of yours] might be fulfilled!" 19.309 [= 17.163, 15.536]). On this occasion, in contrast to the earlier one, however, Penelope inexplicably rejects the prophecy's import:

ἀλλά μοι ὧδ' ἀνὰ θυμὸν ὀίεται, ὡς ἔσεταί περ·
οὔτ' Ὀδυσεὺς ἔτι οἶκον ἐλεύσεται, οὔτε σὺ πομπῆς
τεύξῃ. . . .

---

[2] "First of all then, let Zeus stand [as my witness] of the gods, and the table of guest-friendship and the hearth of excellent Odysseus, at which I have arrived" (ἴστω νῦν Ζεὺς πρῶτα θεῶν ξενίη τε τράπεζα / ἱστίη τ' Ὀδυσῆος ἀμύμονος, ἣν ἀφικάνω, 17.155–56); compare this with: "First of all, then, let Zeus stand [as my witness], the highest and best among the gods, and the hearth of excellent Odysseus, at which I have arrived" (ἴστω νῦν Ζεὺς πρῶτα, θεῶν ὕπατος καὶ ἄριστος, / ἱστίη τ' Ὀδυσῆος ἀμύμονος, ἣν ἀφικάνω, 19.303–4).

(But this is how it seems to me in my heart that it will in fact be:
Neither will Odysseus ever come home, nor will you be equipped
with conveyance. . . .)

(19.312–14)

Penelope's response here is quite unexpected in the immediate narrative context. In addition, we should note that her words here specifically contradict and indeed invert the expectations of Book 17, and that they do so in a linguistic context that resonates with that earlier episode.

Finally, at the end of Book 19, just after Penelope has asked the stranger's advice whether she should "remain beside my son and watch over everything securely . . . or follow after whoever of the Achaeans is best at wooing me in the halls" (ἠὲ μένω παρὰ παιδὶ καὶ ἔμπεδα πάντα φυλάσσω . . . / ἢ ἤδη ἅμ' ἕπωμαι, Ἀχαιῶν ὅς τις ἄριστος / μνᾶται ἐνὶ μεγάροισι . . . , 19.525, 528–29) and has offered a rationale for waiting (the dream of the geese) that is confirmed as valid by the stranger, she rejects this advice and decides on the contest of the bow. In contrast to her earlier expressions of hopefulness, she now not only affirms her conviction of an unhappy outcome ("This dawn that is coming will be an ill-omened one, which will take me away from the house of Odysseus," ἥδε δὴ ἠὼς εἶσι δυσώνυμος, ἥ μ' Ὀδυσῆος / οἴκου ἀποσχήσει, 19.571–72), but takes immediate steps to insure that outcome by adding to her prediction a statement of intention to set up the contest of the bow. Thus, at this point in the narrative Penelope supplants Odysseus's own intentions as reported in her dream (ὃς πᾶσι μνηστήρεσσιν ἀεικέα πότμον ἐφήσω, 19.550) with her own: "For now I shall set up a contest" (νῦν γὰρ καταθήσω ἄεθλον, 19.572).

The incongruities of this section of the poem, then, are more than a matter of a confusing and irresolute narrative, although they are that as well. They consist more precisely in explicit contradictions, formulated, in one case, such that the language and situation of one episode (Odysseus's prophecy in Book 19) both replicate and specifically contradict another that occurs within the same narrative compass (Theoclymenus's prophecy in Book 17). What is more, the situation that occurs later (the *homilia*) and occasions the most extreme statements of diffidence is introduced early in the narrative of this segment, and in a context that would have led us to expect a ratification of the confidence expressed there. This same context, which brings into the foreground of the narrative not only the expectation of Odysseus's return, but also Penelope's specific affirmation of it, provides the immediate background for the appearance before the suitors as well.

The first of the two structural parallels between the appearance before the suitors and the decision to set the bow-contest, then, is their location in the context of specific and explicit indications of Odysseus's return. The illogicality in the first case, however, is inscribed in the narrative itself, in the "plot" (the *mythos*, as Aristotle calls it), and takes the form of an incompatibility between Books 17 and 18, whereas the contradiction in Book 19 appears as a disjunction in the content of the discourse, as Penelope's explicit rejection of the content of the prophecy and the dream whose authenticity is guaranteed by signs that she herself either solicits or provides.

The second structural parallel between the two episodes is the recuperation of the "illogicality" within the text itself, and in the same manner in both cases. In the first, as we saw above, Odysseus assigns a meaning to Penelope's actions and an intention to her thoughts at variance with the structure and surface meaning of the narrative:

> ὣς φάτο, γήθησεν δὲ πολύτλας δῖος Ὀδυσσεύς,
> οὕνεκα τῶν μὲν δῶρα παρέλκετο, θέλγε δὲ θυμὸν
> μειλιχίοισ' ἐπέεσσι, νόος δέ οἱ ἄλλα μενοίνα.

(Thus she spoke, but long-suffering godlike Odysseus rejoiced
because she was extracting gifts from them, and she was charming their hearts
with her honeyed words, but her mind had other intentions.)

(18.281–83)

In the second, Odysseus confirms Penelope's decision to institute the bow-contest in a manner that is inconsistent both with his interpretation of the dream in the exchange immediately preceding and with what she herself sees as the implications of such a step:

> ὦ γύναι αἰδοίη Λαερτιάδεω Ὀδυσῆος,
> μηκέτι νῦν ἀνάβαλλε δόμοισ' ἔνι τοῦτον ἄεθλον·
> πρὶν γάρ τοι πολύμητις ἐλεύσεται ἐνθάδ' Ὀδυσσεύς,
> πρὶν τούτους τόδε τόξον ἐΰξοον ἀμφαφόωντας
> νευρήν τ' ἐντανύσαι διοιστεῦσαί τε σιδήρου.

(Oh revered wife of Odysseus son of Laertes,
do not now any longer put off this contest within the house;
For before [it], Odysseus of the many counsels will return back here,
before, [that is,] these men here can take up that well-polished bow,
string the sinew [onto it], and shoot through the iron.)

(19.583–87)

In both instances, where a major inconsistency appears in the text, narrative direction is restored through the same device, an explicit interpretation of events by Odysseus at variance with the implicit orientation of these same actions. In both cases Penelope appears to consolidate her plans for remarriage, and both times Odysseus interprets her intentions in the light of his own. Thus, Odysseus's remarks have a recuperative effect, and serve to mitigate the jarring force of Penelope's words and actions; Odysseus assures us with the authoritative voice of the one whose interests are most at stake that Penelope "does not mean what she says."

Incorporated into the structure of the text, then, is what we might call a patriarchal maneuver, which restores coherence to the narrative surface of the poem at the price of denying to Penelope a set of interests or meanings different from Odysseus's own. Critics, too, are inclined to rationalize the text by adopting Odysseus's perspective and pointing to the ultimate compatibility of Penelope's actions with his plans.[3] As one commentator has warned, however, we must guard against the tendency "to project the knowledge of the audience onto Penelope" (Vester 1968:423). This audience's consciousness is itself close to that of the narrator, and hence to that of Odysseus.[4]

The feminist reading of this same text, as we have seen, emphasizes the discrepancy in perspectives, but endows Penelope with an autonomy that the text does not support. The Penelope of the feminist reading, moreover, pursues her own interests with a single-minded determination that obliges her willfully to disregard indications of her husband's impending return. This approach, then, occludes access to a different aspect of the text than does the "patriarchal" perspective. Neither of these approaches is successful in accounting for the text as we have it. As we have seen, a disjunctive conjunction is deeply imbedded in the poem's structure, and it is an intrinsic feature of its form. Thus, what requires explanation is the overall coherence of the text in the light of—not despite—its discordant texture.

As we have seen, up until the point when Telemachus's *anagnōrismos* effects the first stage of Odysseus's return to Ithaca, Penelope's conduct within the narrative is entirely one-dimensional. She longs for her husband's return and remains resolutely steadfast and faithful. Her actions are encased, however, in a narrative that suggests a different direction for them and the possibility of a different outcome. This is conveyed principally through the operation of the House of Atreus motif in the first four books, but it appears also in the form of specific doubts raised about Penelope in the narrative of Books 13 and 15, which are preliminary to Odysseus's return and constitute the thematic preparation for it. Beginning with Book 18, however, Penelope's own words and actions are drawn into this network of ambiguity. What is more, by Book 18 the background to Penelope's behavior has been expanded to include not only the alternative embodied in Clytemnestra, but the options represented by Helen as well—

---

[3] And it is, to be sure, the most patriarchal of critics who propose the most extreme solution: the analysts simply eliminate from the text a Penelope who will not conform to Odysseus's needs.

[4] As Murnaghan observes, Odysseus's perspective is in some way similar to that of the narrator, while Penelope's is more like that of a character unaware of the plot in which her actions take shape (Murnaghan 1987:128–29; cf. also Felson-Rubin 1988).

both that of the unfaithful wife who freely seduces other men, and that of the perspicuous helpmeet who functions as ally in the camp of the enemy. Odysseus's responses to Penelope's behavior, which are at variance with its implied meaning, now constitute a misreading that operates like a disguise. This misreading is endowed with authority through the association between the narrator's perspective and that of Odysseus, but the discrepancy remains nonetheless and informs the tenor of the narrative throughout these books.

Telemachus: Maturity and Misrepresentation

Penelope's appearance before the suitors is ascribed in the text to an unprecedented impulse ("Eurynome, my heart now urges me, though it did not before . . . ," Εὐρυνόμη, θυμός μοι ἐέλδεται, οὔ τι πάρος γε, 18.164), and it is rationalized as a need to admonish Telemachus:

> παιδὶ δέ κεν εἴποιμι ἔπος, τό κε κέρδιον εἴη,
> μὴ πάντα μνηστῆρσιν ὑπερφιάλοισιν ὁμιλεῖν,
> οἵ τ' εὖ μὲν βάζουσι, κακῶς δ' ὄπιθεν φρονέουσι.

> (And I would like to say a word to my son, as it would be better,
> [than he should] not associate with the arrogant suitors,
> who speak well, but have evil thoughts behind his back.)

(18.166–68)

When Penelope does address Telemachus, it is to reproach him for allowing—considering his newly achieved maturity—the suitors to mistreat the *xeinos*; and after he agrees with her that he is now an adult, she goes on, in response to Eurymachus's compliments, to report Odysseus's parting words, inviting her to remarry upon Telemachus's coming of age (cited in Chapter Four, above).

Throughout the first section of Book 18, then, the two themes of Telemachus's maturity and Penelope's remarriage are closely connected through juxtaposition. As we observed just above, when Penelope first addresses Eurynome both themes appear, as they do in Eurynome's response, urging her mistress to adorn herself before descending into the *megaron* on the grounds that Telemachus has now come of age. And in the appearance itself, Penelope converses both with Telemachus concerning his behavior as a mature young man, and with Eurymachus concerning her remarriage.[5]

This conjunction of the two themes is ordinarily interpreted as a causal one. That is, Penelope's decision to remarry is regarded as a simple conse-

---

[5] Schadewaldt remarks on this feature of the narrative: "This opposition [between beautiful woman and concerned mother] is the poetic principle which dominates and forms the structure of the scene . . . also in the second part [18.206ff.]" (1970d:78).

quence of her son's accession to maturity (e.g., Erbse 1972:89; Thornton 1970:105; Allione 1963:67; Eisenberger 1973:271; Finley 1978:8–9; Hölscher 1967b:31–33). If we first look more closely into the content and consequences of Telemachus's accession to maturity, however, we shall be in a better position to redefine the meaning of Penelope's behavior in this section of the poem.

As we observed in our discussion of *nostos* and *kleos* in Chapter Three, Telemachus's coming of age was associated in particular with his eligibility to acquire *kleos*. And Telemachus's *kleos*, like that of Odysseus, was dependent upon the completion of a successful *nostos*, which the suitor's ambush had threatened to disrupt. There is another aspect to Telemachus's *kleos*, however, which is fully actualized only after the *anagnōrismos* of Odysseus, namely its connection with *xenia*. For as A. T. Edwards remarks, referring especially to Alcinous's promise to Odysseus of conveyance home in Book 7, "The *Odyssey* . . . differ[s] from the *Iliad* . . . in regarding ξεινίη as a source of κλέος" (Edwards 1985:74). There, Odysseus responds to Alcinous's offer with a prayer to Zeus to bring it about, and concludes: "[For then,] for him [Alcinous] upon the life-giving earth there would be undying *kleos*, while I would arrive in my fatherland" (τοῦ μέν κεν ἐπὶ ζείδωρον ἄρουραν / ἄσβεστον κλέος εἴη, ἐγὼ δέ κε πατρίδ' ἱκοίμην, 7.332–33).

Edwards goes on to suggest that "the *Odyssey* organiz[es] κλέος in terms of the modes of violence and ξεινίη, and the locales of home and away. The κλέος of violent deeds at home is that of revenge, corresponding to the κλέος of victory in the *Iliad*" (Edwards 1985:75). It is rather the case, I think, that Odyssean *kleos* differs from its Iliadic counterpart in being organized principally around the correct treatment of *xeinoi*—the proper reception of guests whose demeanor is modest and dignified, and its corollary, the appropriate punishment of those who are arrogant, overbearing, or otherwise threatening. Thus, just as it is a sign of the well-functioning *oikos* that its head can both extend hospitality to strangers and protect the *oikos* against intruders, so it is the mark of Odysseus's resumption of his rights over his own *oikos* that he is able to take revenge upon the suitors and is no longer forced passively to endure their intrusion.[6]

Telemachus's incapacity to recieve *xeinoi* in his own house is particularly galling to him. As he says to Eumaeus, when the latter attemps to entrust to his care the disguised Odysseus (ἤλυθ' ἐμὸν πρὸς σταθμόν, ἐγὼ δέ τοι ἐγγυαλίξω, 16.66) and explains that the stranger is a suppliant (ἱκέτης δέ τοι εὔχεται εἶναι, 16.67):

---

[6] Indeed, as I suggested in Chapter One, and as I discuss more fully in Chapter Six, the *Odyssey*'s construction of the suitors' offense as a punishable crime is an innovation tied closely to its ideology of exclusivity.

Εὔμαι', ἦ μάλα τοῦτο ἔπος θυμαλγὲς ἔειπες.
πῶς γὰρ δὴ τὸν ξεῖνον ἐγὼν ὑποδέξομαι οἴκῳ;
αὐτὸς μὲν νέος εἰμὶ καὶ οὔ πω χερσὶ πέποιθα
ἄνδρ' ἀπαμύνασθαι, ὅτε τις πρότερος χαλεπήνῃ·
μητρὶ δ' ἐμῇ δίχα θυμὸς ἐνὶ φρεσὶ μερμηρίζει. . . .

(Eumaeus, very painful for me indeed is this thing that you say.
For how indeed shall I receive a *xeinos* in the house?
I myself am [still] a young man, and I do not yet trust in my hands
to defend a man when someone first provokes him with abuse;
and the heart in my mother is divided. . . .)

(16.69–73)

Earlier, just after his arrival in Ithaca, Telemachus had entrusted Theoclymenus to Peiraeus, and on that occasion he explained that, although there was no dearth of guest-gifts in his home, he himself would be absent from it, and his mother did not ordinarily appear in public (15.513–17).[7]

After the *anagnōrismos* of Odysseus at 16.186–219, however, Telemachus formally accepts Theoclymenus in the agora as his own *xeinos*, as he had indicated to Penelope that he would do:

αὐτὰρ ἐγὼν ἀγορὴν ἐσελεύσομαι ὄφρα καλέσσω
ξεῖνον, ὅτις μοι κεῖθεν ἅμ' ἕσπετο δεῦρο κιόντι.

(But I myself shall proceed to the agora, so that I might call
the *xeinos*, who followed after me as I came [home] here.)

(17.52–53)

And in addition, he now instructs Eumaeus to equip the *xeinos* Odysseus for begging among the suitors (17.342–46).

Furthermore, although Telemachus had behaved deferentially to Odysseus when he first encountered him (see below), following the *anagnōrismos* he is willing to display a certain haughtiness: he instructs Eumaeus to "bring the wretched stranger to the city, so that there he can beg for his supper. . . . It is not possible for me to take responsibility for everyone [who comes along], since I have my own troubles in my heart. If the stranger is angry at this, it will be so much the worse for him; I prefer to relate things as they are" (τὸν ξεῖνον δύστηνον ἄγ' ἐς πόλιν, ὄφρ' ἂν ἐκεῖθι / δαῖτα πτωχεύῃ. . . . ἐμὲ δ' οὔ πως ἔστιν ἅπαντας / ἀνθρώπους ἀνέχεσθαι, ἔχοντά περ ἄλγεα θυμῷ· / ὁ ξεῖνος δ' εἴ περ μάλα μηνίει, ἄλγιον αὐτῷ / ἔσσεται, 17.10–11, 12–15).

At the beginning of Book 18, Telemachus openly proclaims his assump-

---

[7] "Otherwise I would myself bid you to come to our house; for there is no dearth of *xenia* [among us]. But [as things are], it would be the worse for you yourself, since I shall be absent, and my mother will not see you; for she does not appear at all before the throng of suitors in the house, but she weaves her web in the upper room, away from them" (15.513–17).

tion of the role of host (*xeinodokos*) rather than, as before, deferring to Eurymachus's conspicuous excellence (15.518–24). And indeed, Hélène Kakridis argues that "Odysseus, once inside the house, and even though he is a beggar, is considered Telemachus's *xeinos* and is possessed of all a guest's rights" (1963:94).[8] Now Telemachus assures the disguised Odysseus of precisely the protection that he had before been unable to guarantee.[9]

> τοῖς δ' αὖτις μετέειφ' ἱερὴ ἲς Τηλεμάχοιο·
> "ξεῖν', εἴ σ' ὀτρύνει κραδίη καὶ θυμὸς ἀγήνωρ
> τοῦτον ἀλέξασθαι, τῶν δ' ἄλλων μή τιν' Ἀχαιῶν
> δείδιθ', ἐπεὶ πλεόνεσσι μαχήσεται ὅς κέ σε θείνῃ.
> ξεινοδόκος μὲν ἐγών, ἐπὶ δ' αἰνεῖτον βασιλῆε,
> Εὐρύμαχός τε καὶ Ἀντίνοος, πεπνυμένω ἄμφω."

(Then the prodigious strength of Telemachus[10] proclaimed among them:
"Stranger, if the manly heart and spirit arouse you
to defend yourself against this man, then do not be afraid
of any of the other Achaeans, since whoever strikes you will [have to] battle many men.
For I myself am the host [*xeinodokos*] here, with the approval of the two kings
Eurymachus and Antinous, who are both men of discretion."

(18.60–65)

Finally, following Penelope's appearance, and her recognition, in the course of it, of her son's accession to maturity, Telemachus twice challenges the suitors' treatment of his *xeinos*, occasioning both times an expression of amazement on their part. At the end of Book 18, when Eurymachus hurls a footstool at Odysseus and misses, striking the cupbearer, Telemachus rebukes the suitors, and in Book 20 he deliberately provokes them. Addressing the disguised Odysseus, he says:

> ἐνταυθοῖ νῦν ἧσο μετ' ἀνδράσιν οἰνοποτάζων·
> κερτομίας δέ τοι αὐτὸς ἐγὼ καὶ χεῖρας ἀφέξω
> πάντων μνηστήρων, ἐπεὶ οὔ τοι δήμιός ἐστιν
> οἶκος ὅδ', ἀλλ' Ὀδυσῆος, ἐμοὶ δ' ἐκτήσατο κεῖνος.
> ὑμεῖς δέ, μνηστῆρες, ἐπίσχετε θυμὸν ἐνιπῆς
> καὶ χειρῶν, ἵνα μή τις ἔρις καὶ νεῖκος ὄρηται.

---

[8] "Les passages qui nous montrent les rapports entre Ulysse, mendiant inconnu, et Télémaque, prouvent qu'une fois dans son manoir, même en tant que mendiant, Ulysse est considéré comme Τηλεμάχου ξεῖνος et a tous les droits d'un hôte."

[9] Cf. ἄνδρ' ἀπαμύνασθαι (16.72, cited above) with τοῦτον ἀλέξασθαι in 18.62; and cf. also κερτομίας δέ τοι αὐτὸς ἐγὼ καὶ χεῖρας ἀφέξω in 20.263

[10] For the discussion of this archaic periphrasis, see Russo 1966:195–97 ad 18.60, and West 1988:155 ad 2.409; I have adopted Russo's translation of the phrase.

(Sit there now among the men and drink your wine.
And I myself will protect you against the insults and violence
of all the suitors, since this house does not belong
to the people, but to Odysseus, and I acquire it after him.
You then, suitors, keep your spirited feelings under control,
and your hands too, so that strife and discord do not arise.)

(20.262–67).

On both occasions the suitors are taken aback: "Thus he spoke, and then they all bit their lips with their teeth in amazement at Telemachus, that he had spoken out so boldly" (ὣς ἔφαθ', οἱ δ' ἄρα πάντες ὀδὰξ ἐν χείλεσι φύντες / Τηλέμαχον θαύμαζον, ὃ θαρσαλέως ἀγόρευε, 18.410–11 = 20.268–69). And although in the second instance Antinous recommends that the suitors defer to Telemachus—for he recognizes that Telemachus is now under Zeus's protection—Ctesippus nevertheless takes up the challenge, hurling an ox-foot at the *xeinos* and missing. Telemachus proves equal to the challenge, claiming that had Ctesippus hit his mark, he (Telemachus) would have killed him. He adds:

τῶ μή τίς μοι ἀεικείας ἐνὶ οἴκῳ
φαινέτω· ἤδη γὰρ νοέω καὶ οἶδα ἕκαστα,
ἐσθλά τε καὶ τὰ χέρεια· πάρος δ' ἔτι νήπιος ἦα.

(Therefore let no one behave abusively
in my house. For I now understand and discern clearly the difference
between noble and base. But before I was still just a child.)

(20.308–10)

On this occasion too, the suitors acquiesce in the rebuke: "Thus he spoke, and they all kept very silent" (ὣς ἔφαθ', οἱ δ' ἄρα πάντες ἀκὴν ἐγένοντο σιωπῇ, 20.320).

The rebuke of Ctesippus represents the last of Telemachus's four specific claims to have acceded to full maturity, with their accompanying acknowledgment that before he was a mere child. The second and third of these occur in Books 18 and 19, the first as part of his response to his mother (18.229), the second as part of his explanation to Eurycleia why he now wants to store his father's armor away (19.19). The first was in Book 2, in his address to the assembly (2.313), and it was prompted by Athena's advice in Book 1 to leave off "clinging to childhood" (νηπιάας ὀχέειν, 1.297). And in the course of Book 19, both Odysseus (19.160–61) and Penelope (19.530ff.) acknowledge that Telamachus is now a grown man. In Book 21, by contrast, just following his feigned display of inability to string the bow, Telemachus pretends self-reproach:

ὢ πόποι, ἦ καὶ ἔπειτα κακός τ' ἔσομαι καὶ ἄκικυς,
ἠὲ νεώτερός εἰμι καὶ οὔ πω χερσὶ πέποιθα
ἄνδρ' ἀπαμύνασθαι, ὅτε τις πρότερος χαλεπήνῃ.
ἀλλ' ἄγεθ', οἵ περ ἐμεῖο βίῃ προφερέστεροί ἐστε,
τόξου πειρήσασθε, καὶ ἐκτελέωμεν ἄεθλον.

(Oh for shame! I will certainly turn out later to be base and feeble,
or else I am [still] too young, and I do not yet trust in my hands
to defend a man when someone first provokes him with abuse;
well, then, come, you who are more preeminent than I in strength,
make trial of the bow, and let us conclude the contest.)

(21.131–35)

It is particularly notable that Telemachus here repeats the lines by which he had earlier excused to Eumaeus his inability to accept Odysseus as a *xeinos* in his home (16.72–73 = 21.132–33). Here, his incapacity is feigned; there, it was felt as real.

In the course of the second half of the *Odyssey*, then, from the point when Telemachus first returns to Ithaca in Book 15 until the point in Book 21 when he feigns inability to string the bow, Telemachus's *kleos* as *xeinodokos* is consolidated; it is manifested as his capacity both to receive *xeinoi* in his home and to defend them from abuse within it. For as Hélène Kakridis has pointed out, "For the *xeinodokos*, it is a point of honor not to allow mistreatment of his guests" (1963:95).[11] This accession to maturity is a feature of Telemachus's characterization that has often been treated, especially in the unitarian school of thought, as an issue of character development, a phenomenon that Wilamowitz claimed was altogether absent, not only from the *Odyssey*, but from Greek literature in general: "Now I can no longer credit the poet with such an aim [of showing how Telemachus matured to manhood]. Tracing character development lies outside the province of Hellenic poetry, and is totally alien to the Hellenes. There is also no trace in the later books of a change in the nature of Telemachus" (Wilamowitz 1927:106).[12] Most recently, it has been claimed that in the course of the poem, and especially in the later books, Telemachus does undergo a transformation, and that its content is his closer identification with Odysseus, particularly with the latter's capacity for *dolos* (Jones 1988; cf. Austin 1969).

As the discussion of Telemachus's *kleos* in Chapter 3 made clear, how-

[11] "C'était pour le ξεινοδόκος une question d'honneur de ne pas permettre qu'on maltraite ses hôtes."

[12] "Jetzt traue ich dem Dichter eine solche Tendenz [uns zeigen wie Telemachos zum Manne ausreifte] nicht mehr zu. Charakterentwickelung zu verfolgen liegt der hellenischen Poesie, liegt überhaupt den Hellenen fern. Es ist auch in den späteren Büchern von einer Veränderung im Wesen Telemachs nichts zu spüren."

ever, an identification of Telemachus with Odysseus is a leitmotif running through the poem from Book 1 on, even if certain aspects of that similarity are not explored until the later books.[13] What does change dramatically is not Telemachus's character, but his status (cf. Murnaghan 1987:105–7 nn. 20, 22). When Telemachus returns to Ithaca, he is still a young man—if no longer a *nēpios* ("child"; literally, "infant"),[14] then certainly still a *neos* ("youth," "young man"). But once the *anagnōrismos* of Odysseus takes place in the middle of Book 16, a transformation is made possible, and it is signaled in the text by a change in the treatment of *xeinoi*.

The issue on the surface of the text has two aspects: as Telemachus explains to the stranger Odysseus at the beginning of Book 16, he is only one against "countless enemies" (δυσμενέες μάλα μυρίοι, 16.121); furthermore, his mother "neither refuses the hateful marriage, nor is she able to bring matters to a conclusion" (ἡ δ' οὔτ' ἀρνεῖται στυγερὸν γάμον οὔτε τελευτὴν / ποιῆσαι δύναται, 16.126–27). Thus, both physical incapacity and his mother's status are barriers precluding Telemachus's assertion of his mature potency. These issues are resolved, first by the *anagnōrismos* in Book 16, then by Penelope's apparent indication of readiness for remarriage in Book 18. As is clear from the sequence of passages cited above, Telemachus's readiness to receive *xeinoi* appears in the text just after the *anagnōrismos*, and his willingness to openly challenge the suitors follows upon Penelope's appearance in Book 18. These changes in Telemachus flow from alterations in the narrative conditions of the text and cannot properly be identified as "character development." Nevertheless, since these altered conditions make possible the manifestation of previously unarticulated aspects of Telemachus's characterization, it appears as though those aspects had been latent in him all along. It is the structure of the text itself, then, that brings about what we might call, not character development itself, but the "character-development effect."

There is another, more subtle transformation that is effected in the poem through the *anagnōrismos*. This has to do with what I shall call the poem's ultimate commitment to its own *telos* ("end," "goal"): the reestablishment of Odysseus as *kyrios* of his own *oikos*, and the punishment of the suitors for their transgressions against its integrity.[15] The principal alternative sce-

---

[13] Cf. the remarks of West 1988:67: "Telemachus's 'awakening' is an important element in this book [Book 1]; though many critics . . . have seen an educational purpose in his journey, the real change in him occurs in [Book 1]."

[14] *Nēpios*, derived from *nē*, indicating negation, and *epos*, meaning "word," is the Greek equivalent of Latin *infans*, derived from *in-*, indicating negation, and *fans*, meaning "speaking."

[15] What constitutes the *telos* of the poem, in both the literal sense (at what line it ends) and the metaphorical one (its poetic goal), is a matter of dispute. On the first issue, see below, Chapter Six; on the second, see, for example, Müller's argument for "the fulfillment of the νόος of Athena as the τέλος of the poem" (1966:166–68).

nario that threatened that outcome was articulated early in the poem through the House of Atreus motif, and its parts were assigned opposite moral valences: the betrayal by the wife on the one hand (the Clytemnestra paradigm), and the son's assertion of his claim to his father's property on the other (the Orestes paradigm).

With the return of Odysseus to Ithaca and his recognition by his son, the second alternative has been effectively eliminated. The outcome still remains uncertain, to be sure, but the condition originally attached to the Orestes paradigm—namely, "if you hear that he [your father] has died and is no longer alive" (εἰ δέ κε τεθνηῶτος ἀκούσῃς μηδ' ἔτ' ἐόντος, 1.289)— has been removed. At the same time, Odysseus's disguise now makes it possible for that same scenario to be played out fully without threatening to derail the plot. In other words Odysseus's return eliminates the Orestes paradigm from the narrative whereas his disguise reinstates it as the content of the plot.

Telemachus now assumes the role of *kyrios* of Odysseus's *oikos*; this is made clear especially through his claim, asserted just before the bow-trial, that "this house does not belong to the people, but to Odysseus, and I acquire it after him" [literally, "he acquired it on my behalf"] (ἐπεὶ οὔ τοι δήμιός ἐστιν / οἶκος ὅδ', ἀλλ' Ὀδυσῆος, ἐμοὶ δ' ἐκτήσατο κεῖνος, 20.264–65). As Russo and others have pointed out, "Telemachus's speech is his strongest assertion thus far of his personal authority in the face of the Suitors" (Russo 1985:276 ad 262–74). It is not the first time that Telemachus has made such a claim (cf. his insistence in Book 1 that "I will be the ruler over our *oikos* and its servants, which godlike Odysseus acquired as booty for me," αὐτὰρ ἐγὼ οἴκοιο ἄναξ ἔσομ' ἡμετέροιο / καὶ δμώων, οὕς μοι ληΐσσατο δῖος Ὀδυσσεύς, 1.397–98). But the condition attached to that statement in Book 1 ("since godlike Odysseus has perished," ἐπεὶ θάνε δῖος Ὀδυσσεύς, 1.396) is now no longer in danger of being instantiated through the actualization of Telemachus's authority. That authority can now be fully realized precisely because it is a fiction authorized by Odysseus's disguise.

At the first encounter between Telemachus and Odysseus, when Telemachus enters Eumaeus's hut, Odysseus rises and gives up his place to his son: "To him as he entered his father Odysseus yielded his seat" (τῷ δ' ἕδρης ἐπιόντι πατὴρ ὑπόειξεν Ὀδυσσεύς, 16.42). By Book 21 the situation has been reversed, so that now the son yields place to the father: "And now in fact he [Telemachus] would have strung the bow as he bent it back for the fourth time, but Odysseus nodded to him not to and held him back, eager as he was" (καί νύ κε δὴ ἐτάνυσσε βίῃ τὸ τέταρτον ἀνέλκων, / ἀλλ' Ὀδυσεὺς ἀνένευε καὶ ἔσχεθεν ἱέμενόν περ, 21.128–29). The limits of the fiction involving Telemachus are marked by these two acts of deference, the first one real on the narrative surface but disguised beneath it, and the second disguised on the surface but real below. In the second instance, Telemachus's own disguise as *xeinodokos* and *kyrios* of his household shifts so that he now "disguises" himself as the son, the *neoteros*, who must yield place to those "more preeminent in strength" (*biēi propheresteroi*, 21.134). At this point, then, his pretense instantiates reality, and the narrative continues its course with the proper relationship between son and father in place.

Now when the suitors insult the beggar, Telemachus does not rise to his defense, but, as in Book 18, Penelope does, and Telemachus must assert his authority diffrently—over Penelope in the first instance, when he claims the right to dispose of the bow (21.344–53), and over the household servants in the second instance, by instructing Eumaeus to ignore the suitors and follow his own orders (21.369–75). In the narrative that immediately follows, Telemachus plays out his proper role of mature son by standing beside his father as ally (ἄγχι δ' ἄρ' αὐτοῦ / πὰρ θρόνον ἐστήκει, 21.433–34) and as battle-companion (22.91–92).

Penelope: Return, Remarriage, and *Xenia* (Book 19)

Penelope's status also changes when Odysseus returns home. This is not signaled by any gesture involving Odysseus directly, but instead by the acknowledgment, "postponed," as it were, from the earlier part of the narrative, of Telemachus's accession to maturity and Penelope's consequent eligibility for remarriage. Concerning this development, W. Allen Jr. has remarked: "It always strikes one as odd . . . that Penelope had waited until now to mention to anyone the admonition of Odysseus in regard to her remarrying. If she had had no intention of marrying until Odysseus had been gone twenty years, why did she not tell the wooers that when they first came? . . . Why did she not tell them of this condition at the beginning of the epic?" (Allen 1939:117). Allen explains the discrepancy by appealing to the notion of "double-time," referring to the tendency in epic and drama to telescope relevant events so that they appear to transpire during the period of poetic enactment. And he concludes, "Penelope's announcing her marriage now is just the same as if she had announced it at the beginning of the poem" (ibid.:118), adding that here it serves the function of motivating the contest of the bow.

Other critics, as we have seen, have suggested that Penelope invents the account of Odysseus's parting instructions as part of a deliberate ruse. As Büchner argues it: "And why did Penelope not long ago explain to the suitors precisely her husband's instructions that she should remarry as soon as Telemachus came of age? She would thereby have removed all difficulties. One can see that her present explanation has to do only with a new trick, which will, like the earlier one, fill the suitors with hopes and deflect them from their intended deed of violence [Telemachus's murder]" (Büchner 1940:140).[16] Winkler agrees, adding, "We might well suppose that Penelope's account . . . is her own invention, on the spur of the moment, and that this is an added reason why Odysseus is perfectly sure of her fidelity" (Winkler 1990:147). Allione is less sure—"in reality, the reader remains uncertain about the veracity of this advice"[17] (Allione 1963:76)—but she adds the important observation that an earlier acknowledgment would have operated as an added incentive to murder Telemachus (ibid.:76 n. 25).

Penelope's appearance before the suitors, then, is not only discrepant with the indications of narrative direction in Book 17, as we discussed earlier, but it is problematic also in that it introduces an unexpected alteration of the narrative circumstances. The argument cannot be sustained, in my view, that Penelope has invented this account of Odysseus's parting words—no textual evidence can be adduced to support such a contention, and furthermore, the logic of Eurynome's address to Penelope at the beginning of Book 18 seems to presuppose some such understanding (see Russo 1985:205–6 ad 175–76).

Rather, it seems that Telemachus's accession to maturity serves the same function in the narrative for Penelope that the *anagnōrismos* of Odysseus did for Telemachus. That is, on the surface of the text Odysseus's return resolves the problem of Telemachus's isolation and physical incapacity, and thus enables the realization of Telemachus's authority as head of his household. At the same time, however, at the level of the poem's structure—with reference to what I have called its commitment to its own *telos*—Odysseus's disguise operates to ensure the fictional status of Telemachus's authority.

Similarly, in Penelope's case, Telemachus's *coming of age* effects a transformation in her status that, on the surface of the text, allows the legitimate possibility of marriage to one of the suitors to be brought into the narrative. The possibility, together with its corollary acknowledgment of Penelope's authority to act independently, is fully developed in Book 19. At the level of narrative structure, however, this same option is inconsistent with the poem's *telos* precisely because there is no device, as there was in Telemachus's case, to endow it with fictionality. Consequently, as we have seen, commentators are inclined themselves to fill this lacuna from the

[16] "Und warum hat Penelope den Freiern nicht schon längst erklärt, gemäss der Weisung ihres Gatten solle sie sich, sobald Telemach volljährig geworden sei, wieder verheiraten? Sie wäre dadurch allen Schwierigkeiten aus dem Weg gegangen. Man sieht, es handelt sich bei ihrer jetzigen Erklärung nur um eine neue List, die wie die früheren die Freier mit Hoffnungen erfüllen und von der geplanten Gewalttat zuruckhalten soll." For discussion of Büchner, see Allione 1963:89–90 and n. 51; Erbse 1972:85–86; and Eisenberger 1973:269 n. 44.

[17] "In realità, il lettore resta incerto sulla veridicità di questo consiglio."

stores of their own critical sensibilities and, without warrant from the text itself, to interpret Penelope's gesture as a deliberate deception.

Here as elsewhere, however, it is important not to resolve artificially what the poetic structure of the narrative leaves open, but instead to inquire into the function of that irresolution. As we have seen, Penelope's behavior in this section of the narrative is now conditioned not only by the implications of the House of Atreus motif, but by those attaching to the stories of Helen. Thus, while Penelope's appearance before the suitors suggests Helen's willingness to seduce men other than her husband, the appearance itself is enclosed in the narrative on either side by the *homilia*—by the arrangements for it in 17.553–88 and by its actual occurrence in Book 19—and the *homilia* itself resonates with the representation of Helen as ally and helpmeet.

Intervening between the appearance before the suitors and the *homilia* in Book 19 are the two episodes in which the maid Melantho rebukes Odysseus. These are the only two such instances in the poem, and they are located strategically so as to deflect from Penelope the disapproval attaching to the behavior of the women of Odysseus's house. On the first occasion, Odysseus addresses the serving women directly, inviting them to go and sit beside their mistress—in effect, to associate themselves with her—while he holds the torchlights:

δμῳαὶ Ὀδυσσῆος, δὴν οἰχομένοιο ἄνακτος,
ἔρχεσθε πρὸς δώμαθ', ἵν' αἰδοίη βασίλεια·
τῇ δὲ παρ' ἠλάκατα στροφαλίζετε, τέρπετε δ' αὐτὴν
ἥμεναι ἐν μεγάρῳ, ἢ εἴρια πείκετε χερσίν·

(Maids of Odysseus, of a master who has been away for a long time,
go, all of you, into the house, where your respected queen is.
Turn your distaffs beside her, and comfort her
by sitting with her in the hall, or comb the wool with your hands.)

(18.313–16)

In response, Melantho rebukes Odysseus shamefully (τὸν δ' αἰσχρῶς ἐνένιπε Μελανθὼ καλλιπάρῃος, 18.321), and her rebuke is contextualized through both the report of her ingratitude to Penelope and her identification as the lover of Eurymachus (ἀλλ' ἥ γ' Εὐρυμάχῳ μισγέσκετο καὶ φιλέεσκεν, 18.325), the suitor earlier described by Telemachus as the best of them, and the one who "most desires to marry my mother and to get hold of Odysseus's privilege" (καὶ γὰρ πολλὸν ἄριστος ἀνὴρ μέμονέν τε μάλιστα / μητέρ' ἐμὴν γαμέειν καὶ Ὀδυσσῆος γέρας ἕξειν, 15.521–22). Thus, Melantho dissociates herself from Penelope by engaging in that behavior which comes closest to fulfillment of the Clytemnestra paradigm—by becoming the lover of the husband's chief rival. This association between Melantho and Eurymachus is reinforced at the end of Book 18 through Eurymachus's repetition, in his abuse of Odysseus, of Melantho's taunt of a few lines earlier (18.330–33 = 18.390–93).[18]

Odysseus had earlier formulated with Telemachus his plan to put the serving-men and -women to the test, a plan that is set forth as part of an overall injunction to secrecy, which, significantly, had included both Laertes and Penelope:

> μή τις ἔπειτ' Ὀδυσῆος ἀκουσάτω ἔνδον ἐόντος·
> μήτ' οὖν Λαέρτης ἴστω τό γε μήτε συβώτης
> μήτε τις οἰκήων μήτ' αὐτὴ Πηνελόπεια,
> ἀλλ' οἶοι σύ τ' ἐγώ τε γυναικῶν γνώομεν ἰθύν.
> καί κέ τεο δμώων ἀνδρῶν ἔτι πειρηθεῖμεν,
>
> (Let no one from now on hear that Odysseus is within,
> do not let either Laertes or the swineherd know it,
> nor any of the house servants nor Penelope herself.
> But you and I alone will find out right away about the women;
> and we could test the men servants as well.)
>
> (16.301–5)

Father and wife are here conjoined with servants, though without any explicit indication of suspected loyalties. The female servants, however, are put to the test in connection with the examination of Penelope herself. As Odysseus explains to Telemachus at the beginning of Book 19, "You then go off to sleep, and I shall be left behind here, so that I might provoke the maidservants further, along with your mother" (ἀλλὰ σύ μὲν κατάλεξαι, ἐγὼ δ' ὑπολείψομαι αὐτοῦ, / ὄφρα κ' ἔτι δμῳὰς καὶ μητέρα σὴν ἐρεθίζω, 19.44–45).[19]

And again, just before the *homilia*, Melantho spontaneously abuses Odysseus, accusing him this time of sexual interest in the women of the house: "Stranger, do you plan to go on causing trouble here at night, wandering about the house and peeping at the women?" (ξεῖν', ἔτι καὶ νῦν ἐνθάδ' ἀνιήσεις διὰ νύκτα / δινεύων κατὰ οἶκον, ὀπιπεύσεις δὲ γυναῖκας; 19.66–67). Odysseus's rejoinder to Melantho is very full, containing both a fictional account of his own past and assessment of the present situation in the house of Odysseus. It functions, then, as a first stage in the *erethisma* or provocation of Penelope herself, which thus transpires in an atmosphere charged with the accusation of sexual misconduct.

---

[18] For an interesting statement on the contrast between the *flens matrona* and *meretrices gaudentes*, see Levine 1987.

[19] *Erethizō*, meaning "provoke," like the closely analogous *peiraomai* ("test," "put to the test"; Russo 1985:226 ad 19.45), denotes provoking someone to a statement or to behavior that is self-revelatory—in this case, of course, concerning their disposition toward Odysseus.

This episode, like the earlier, similar one of Melantho's abuse, resolves the Clytemnestra paradigm within the poem by bringing into the narrative foreground a figure who enacts the scenario of female betrayal. It displaces the question of sexual misconduct from Penelope onto her faithless serving-woman and thus functions to absolve Penelope from the suspicion of wrongdoing. In the meantime, however, as we have seen, the issue of impropriety has been reformulated in the text around the alternatives offered by the stories of Helen. In Book 18, Penelope's appearance before the suitors resonates with Menelaus's account of Helen's attempt to seduce the Greek leaders; in Book 18, as in Book 4, the issue of veracity is left undecided.[20]

Helen's own account of her conduct at Troy was a story of perspicuity and faithfulness, and the *homilia* of Book 19 is organized around the expectation that Penelope will exhibit these same qualities. The first section (19.103–360) culminates with Penelope's reception of Odysseus as her *xeinos*; the *niptra* ("foot-washing") makes up the middle section (19.361–507); the last section consists in the dream of the geese and the decision to institute the bow-contest.[21]

The *homilia* opens with Penelope asking about the stranger's identity. The scene, as many commentators have observed, is a typical one.[22] Its elements were first identified by Hölscher, who compared the *homilia* with Odysseus's meeting with Eumaeus in Book 14, and with the scene featuring Nestor, Telemachus, and Athena in 3.195–248. Hölscher identified the typical sequence in these scenes as "promise–doubt—passionate affirmation—disbelief" (Hölscher 1939:72)[23] and concluded that their function "is not to bring about the revelation, but much more to cloak the hidden, which just now threatens to reveal itself anew, in mistrust, neglect, and doubt" (ibid.:71).[24] Vester argues similarly, and adds concerning Odysseus that "an Odysseus who in five speeches attempts to lead his wife to recognition and yet does not accomplish this goal can hardly be called

---

[20] Bergren 1981 is especially good on this aspect of the Book 4 narratives. I am not persuaded by Olson's recent argument that Helen's story is the "wrong" one, and Menelaus's the "right" one (1989:392–93).

[21] For slightly different versions of the structure of this highly structured book, see Vester (1968:419), who sees it, as I do, organized around "drei grossen Bauglieder," and Russo (1985:155–56), who divides it into seven sections, of which the central five making up the *homilia* are organized in an ABCBA symmetry. See also Fenik (1974:82–83), who dicusses the *homilia* under the rubric of scenes of interrupted action or conversation.

[22] See, in addition to the discussions treated above, Fenik 1974:39–47, 155–58; Thornton 1970:104; and Emlyn-Jones 1984:6–8.

[23] "Verheissung—Zweifel—leidenschaftliche Beteuerung—Unglaube."

[24] ". . . Ist nicht, die Enthüllung herbeizuführen, sondern vielmehr das Verborgene, das soeben sich zu verraten droht, von neuem in Misstrauen, Nichtbeachtung und Zweifel einzuhüllen."

πολύμητις; he is rather a bungler, to whom the poet must accord the good fortune of a footbath . . ." (1968:421).[25]

At the same time, the structure of the *homilia*, and particularly of the foot-washing scene, also contains elements drawn from what Emlyn-Jones has identified as a "recognition sequence" (1984:6–9, 13–14), and it may be that the pattern identified by Hölscher should be regarded as a variation of the recognition sequence, and as constituting an interrupted or "failed" version of it.[26] Thus, Emlyn-Jones describes the *homilia* as a "spoof recognition" (ibid.:8; see also Murnaghan 1987:46–52), and the orientation of the narrative toward this outcome of recognition is unmistakable. It is played out in the text itself as the *anagnōrismos* which occurs in the foot-washing scene. Eurycleia thus appears to take up the narrative action just where Penelope had left it off. As Austin remarks on this feature of the poem: "The rhythm of Penelope's recognition has brought her almost to the syntatic identification of the stranger and her husband.[27] . . . Then Eurykleia enters and she continues Penelope's line of thought, almost as if the whole scene had been hers" (Austin 1975:221). Thornton adds: "All through the long history of the scar, the audience probably expected comfortably that Penelope would share the recognition, and that a conspiracy between her and Odysseus would follow. When this does not happen, it has the charm of surprise, and the expectation of the 'recognition' continues" (Thornton 1970:102).[28]

Eurycleia, then, through her recognition of Odysseus and eager offer of herself as ally, plays out the role that otherwise Helen had assigned to herself—that of perspicuous helpmeet.[29] It is worth noting in this regard that both Helen and Eurycleia recognize their visitors' resemblance to their persons: both employ the formulaic line, "but I declare that I have never seen anyone so like . . ." (ἀλλ' οὔ πώ τινά φημι ἐοικότα ὧδε ἰδέσθαι, 4.141 = 19.380), with reference in Helen's case to Telemachus and in Eurycleia's

[25] "Ein Odysseus, der in fünf Reden versucht, seine Frau zur Wiedererkennung zu führen, dieses Ziel aber nicht erreicht, kann kaum als πολύμητις bezeichnet werden; er ist vielmehr ein Stümper, dem der Dichter das Glück der Fusswaschung zuteil werden lassen muss. . . ."

[26] Emlyn-Jones's "recognition sequence" is similar too to Fenik's scene-type of "the nameless stranger" (1974:1–60).

[27] Austin is referring to the structure of line 19.358a, in which Penelope instructs Eurycleia to "wash your lord's agemate" (νίψον σοῖο ἄνακτος ὁμήλικα). Penelope goes on to take into account the effect of the passage of time on the resemblance, whereas Helen and Eurycleia (see below) do not.

[28] And see also Erbse's comment: "In fact, the charm of the evening conversation consists in the fact that the recognition, despite all the critical moments, does not take place" (Erbse 1972:246). Cf. also Focke 1943:332. The ancient commentators, beginning with Aristotle, were especially impressed by the conjunction of *peripeteia* ("reversal") with recognition in this scene. See Büchner 1931 and Richardson 1983:229–35.

[29] Indeed, Olson argues that it is principally the influence of Helen's story that creates the expectation that the stranger will admit his identity to Penelope (1989:391).

to Odysseus. And so, just as Melantho, through her abuse of the stranger and her sexual misconduct with Eurymachus, attracted to herself the censure that in the plot paradigms of the narrative was associated with Clytemnestra, so the role of faithful accomplice is displaced in this scene onto Eurycleia. At the same time, this tendency to attract Eurycleia rather than Penelope into the paradigm of ally is forestalled by Odysseus's refusal of Eurycleia's offer to inform on the faithless women (19.500–502). Penelope's position in the narrative of Book 19 is thus located between that of the faithless traitor Melantho and that of the loyal helper Eurycleia; and her role, similarly, remains suspended between Clytemnestra and Helen, drawn toward both but conforming to neither.

There are, then, two opposite and complementary narrative impulses structuring the *homilia*, one leading toward revelation, recognition, and the restoration of Odysseus as head of his household, the other toward secrecy, concealment, and the maintenance of Odysseus's estrangement. These contradictory impulses are resolved in the scenario of *xenia*, which, as Eisenberger observes, structures the encounter as a whole: "This [the principle of *xenia*] confirms the original unity of the presentation: it is conceived as a narrative of the first togetherness of the queen and her husband who has returned, and in it the couple come nearer to one another on the basis and in the spirit of guest-friendship" (Eisenberger 1973:272).[30]

Xenia functions as the unifying principle of the *homilia* by virtue of its capacity as a ritual both to incorporate Odysseus into his household and simultaneously to continue his estrangement from it. The sequence resonates as well with the episode on Scheria, but not only, in my view, on account of the equivalence between the two occurrences of "the nameless stranger" sequence (Fenik 1974:1–60), or between recognition and *xenia* (Murnaghan 1987:107).[31] Rather, the resonance springs, as I see it, from the homology developed in the narrative between *xenia* and *gamos* ("marriage") on the one hand, and *xenia* and *nostos* on the other.

The equivalence between *xenia* and *nostos* is particular to the *Odyssey*, as I argued in Chapter Three; that between *xenia* and *gamos*, while part of the *Odyssey's* narrative structure, is also a feature of Greek culture in general. The institution of *xenia* functions generally as what anthropologists refer to as a "rite of incorporation": "In order that the rules of social intercourse

---

[30] "Dies [die Prinzipien der *xenia*] bestätigt die ursprüngliche Einheit der Darstellung: sie ist als Erzählung des ersten Beisammenseins der Königin und ihres heimgekehrten Gemahls konzipiert, in der die Gatten auf der Grundlage und im Geiste der Gastfreundschaft einander näherkommen." See also Thornton's remark, "It is interesting to note how the two meetings between Penelope and Odysseus in Books 19 and 23 are built on the themes of 'testing' and 'guest-friendship' " (1970:108).

[31] As I indicated in Chapter Three, I regard *anagnōrismos* as a feature of the *xenia* sequence rather than as an equivalent scenario.

may operate with regard to him the hostile stranger must be converted into a guest. This transformation is achieved through some ritual of incorporation which places the host and guest outside the bounds of the rivalry that governs relationships in a neutral setting" (Pitt-Rivers 1977b:115–16; cf. Pitt-Rivers 1977a).

The institution of *xenia* in its peculiarly Greek form, as Jean-Pierre Vernant has shown, operates to counter the strong tendency toward introversion that is otherwise characteristic of the Greek *oikos* (1969:139), and it is the household's central circular space, its hearth, that in particular has "the property of opening the domestic circle to those who are not members of the family, of enrolling them in the family community" (ibid.:146–47). The stranger and the suppliant are the paradigmatic outsiders of Greek culture, and Gould has argued that the distinction between them "is one of circumstance only" (1973:92). The *xeinos* and the suppliant are incorporated through rituals that endow them with kinship, and thus, as Alcinous remarks to Odysseus, "the stranger and the suppliant come to be equivalent to a man's brother" (ἀντὶ κασιγνήτου ξεῖνός θ' ἱκέτης τε τέτυκται / ἀνέρι, 8.546–47).[32] (It is relevant also that, in the case of Odysseus, when Alcinous accepts him as a suppliant, he displaces his favorite son Laodamas and installs Odysseus in his seat [7.170–71]—a gesture that is the source of later friction between the two men [8.132ff.]).

The woman, too, is an "outsider" in the patriarchal household, and like the suppliant and stranger, she is converted into an insider and bound to the *oikos* through rituals centering on the hearth (Gould 1973:97–98; Vernant 1969:136). A Pythagorean saying that represents an archaic tradition instructs the husband concerning his wife that a man "must not prosecute [her] because she is a suppliant; therefore we lead her from the hearth and we take her by the hand" (γυναῖκα οὐ δεῖ διώκειν τὴν αὐτοῦ· ἱκέτις γάρ, διὸ καὶ ἀφ' ἑστίας ἀγόμεθα καὶ ἡ λῆψις διὰ δεξιᾶς; for citation and discussion, see Gould 1973:98; cf. also Vernant 1969:147); and Greek tragedy also exploits the equivalence between "wife" and "stranger" (Vernant 1969: passim; see also Arthur 1982:545–46). As Vernant explains it: "The bonds between the man and his wife are the same as those which unite two antagonistic groups who have become guest-friends and allies after an exchange of oaths has substituted a peace agreement between them instead of a state of war" (1969:147 n. 79).

In the *Odyssey*, this equivalence between *xenia* and *gamos* appears as the recognition that a good *xeinos* makes a good husband (*posis*, 6.244) as well as a good son-in-law (*gambros* 7.313). Thus, Alcinous offers marriage to Odysseus (7.313), in response both to his own (7.312) and the Phaea-

[32] I am attempting in my translation to render the sense of "fabrication" present in the verb τέτυκται, though in only a very weak sense in the perfect forms of it.

cians' general approval of his conduct as a stranger (7.226–27), and to the report of *xenia* that Nausicaa extended to him (7.295–96). It is precisely because he is distinguished as a *stranger* ("since he spoke appropriately," ἐπεὶ κατὰ μοῖραν ἔειπεν, 7.227; "since you are such as you are, in your thinking just like I [Alcinous] am," τοῖος ἐὼν οἷός ἐσσι, τά τε φρονέων ἅ τ' ἐγώ περ, 7.312) that Odysseus will make a good *husband*: "If only . . . you would remain here, take my daughter and be called my son-in-law" (αἲ γάρ . . . / παῖδά τ' ἐμὴν ἐχέμεν καὶ ἐμὸς γαμβρὸς καλέεσθαι, / αὖθι μένων, 7.311, 313–14).[33]

Nausicaa recognizes that Odysseus's exemplary conduct toward her makes him ideal as a husband, and she wishes aloud to her companious that "such a man [as Odysseus] might be called my husband" (αἲ γὰρ ἐμοὶ τοιόσδε πόσις κεκλημένος εἴη, 6.244). This speech was condemned in antiquity as "inappropriate and licentious" (δοκοῦσιν οἱ λόγοι ἀπρεπεῖς παρθένῳ εἶναι καὶ ἀκόλαστοι, Dindorf 1962:314 ad 6.244; cf. ibid.:317 ad 6.275), although it is also reported that Ephorus regarded it as revealing Nausicaa's natural disposition to virtue (Ἔφορος μέντοι τοὔμπαλιν ἐπαινεῖ τὸν λόγον ὡς ἐξ εὐφυοῦς πρὸς ἀρετὴν ψυχῆς, Dindorf 1962:314 ad 6.244). Similarly, the ancient critics regarded Alcinous's eagerness to have Odysseus as a son-in-law as peculiar on the grounds that he was insufficiently acquainted with his character, and that Odysseus had not yet been subjected to the tests of virtue traditional in such situations (μὴ γὰρ ἐπιστάμενος ὅστις ἐστὶ μηδὲ πειραθεὶς εὔχεται σύμβιον αὐτὸν λαβεῖν καὶ γαμβρὸν ποιήσασθαι. ἦν μὲν παλαιὸν ἔθος τὸ προκρίνειν τοὺς ἀρίστους τῶν ξένων καὶ δι' ἀρετὴν ἐκδιδόναι τὰς θυγατέρας, Dindorf 1962:350–51 ad 7.311), although they allowed at the same time that Alcinous's proposition might constitute a "test" (ἴσως δὲ καὶ πεῖραν αὐτοῦ λαμβάνων τοῦτο εἴρηκεν, ibid.; cf. Hainsworth 1988: 339 ad 311–16).[34]

At the opposite end of the interpretive spectrum, Woodhouse and others have reconstructed from the text a hypothetical precursor, which Woodhouse calls "Nausicaa's Romance": "In the original old story . . . everything went as the heart would have it. There the Unknown is revealed in the end as a handsome and powerful prince, who marries the princess he has won against all competitors" (Woodhouse 1930:64; Vallillee 1955; contra, see Austin 1975:201). This reading, like that of the scholiasts, departs arbitrarily from the text as we have it. Contemporary commentators more plausibly regard the Nausicaa episode as a parallel or foreshadowing

[33] Odysseus is not received into the relationship of *xenia* only on the following day in the public gathering as Murnaghan claims (1987:95); see below on the λῆψις διὰ δεξίας ("taking up by the right hand") as the formal gesture that constitutes the *xeinos* as such.

[34] Vernant (1980a:61) discusses this anomaly in the context of a general assessment of marriage practices in ancient Greece.

of the later scenes on Ithaca, although the comparison is normally limited to Penelope's appearance before the suitors in Book 18 (Nagler 1974:64–86; Nortwick 1979; Forsyth 1979; cf. also Austin 1975:201).[35]

In my view, one effect of the Phaeacian episode is to construct the homology between *xenia* and *gamos*, both through explicit indications such as I discussed above, and through the implicit identification developed in the text between Nausicaa, who extends *xenia* to Odysseus, but for whom he is principally a potential husband, and Arete, who claims Odysseus as her *xeinos* (ξεῖνος δ' αὖτ' ἐμός ἐστιν, 11.338).[36] It is important to note, however, that in neither case is the woman's *xenia* formally efficacious: Nausicaa's reception of Odysseus transpires in the liminal space of the seaside beyond the city proper and must be kept concealed (6.285ff.); and the elder Echeneus, who is identified in terms that justify regarding him as a repository of ritual expertise (7.156–57),[37] twice redirects the ritual away from Arete and toward Alcinous (7.155f.; 11.342ff.). Thus, although Odysseus first approaches both Arete and Alcinous in supplication (σόν τε πόσιν σά τε γούναθ' ἱκάνω, 7.147), it is Alcinous who extends to him what is, as Gould shows, the efficacious gesture that constitues the *xeinos* as such—the raising up by the right hand (7.168–69; Gould 1973:79).

The *homilia* of Book 19 is conducted in the *megaron* by the fire, and this site—by the hearth (παρ' ἐσχάρῃ) or by the fire (πὰρ πυρί)—is conventional for the reception of *xeinoi*, as we discussed above. It is occupied in the *Odyssey* only by Odysseus in his role as *xeinos* or by his hosts (e.g., 6.52, 6.305, 7.153–54, 7.160, 17.572, 19.55, 19.389,[38] 19.506, 23.71, 23.89; see Segal 1974:483), and thus it operates as the staging for the scene of *xenia*. The *homilia* occurs there in accordance with a suggestion that Odysseus had advanced earlier:

>τῷ νῦν Πηνελόπειαν ἐνὶ μεγάροισιν ἄνωχθι
>μεῖναι, ἐπειγομένην περ, ἐς ἠέλιον καταδύντα·
>καὶ τότε μ' εἰρέσθω πόσιος πέρι νόστιμον ἦμαρ
>ἀσσοτέρω καθίσασα παραὶ πυρί·

[35] In Austin's view, Nausicaa in the Phaeacian episode is principally "the stand-in for Telemachus... [although she also] plays a courtship role" (1975:201).

[36] Nortwick extends his discussion of the parallel between Nausicaa and Penelope in Book 18 to encompass the *homilia* of Book 19, which he interprets as an "allurement scene" (1979:274–76).

[37] See especially "and knowing much ancient lore" (παλαιά τε πολλά τε εἰδώς, 7.157).

[38] On the manuscript variant ἀπ' ἐσχαρόφιν ("away from the fireplace") for ἐπ' ἐσχαρόφιν ("by the fireplace") here, see Monro 1901:168 ad 19.389, who defends it as a reading; it is printed in Allen's Oxford text. Stanford (1978, 2:331 ad 19.389–91) argues for ἐπ' ἐσχαρόφιν which is the reading printed without discussion in Russo's edition.

(Therefore instruct Penelope now to wait
in the halls, eager though she is, until the sun goes down;
and then let her question me about her husband's day of homecoming,
sitting close to me here by the fire.)

(17.569–72)

Odysseus diverts from himself any suspicion of impropriety by referring to his ragged clothes and his consequent need for the fire's warmth: "For I am wearing wretched clothing, as you yourself know, since I first came as a suppliant to you" (εἵματα γάρ τοι / λύγρ᾽ ἔχω· οἶσθα καὶ αὐτός, ἐπεί σε πρῶθ᾽ ἱκέτευσα, 17.572–73).

This location of the *homilia* in the *megaron* by the hearth also provides the occasion for Penelope to resume her role as mistress of her household, for she had earlier shared with Telemachus the incapacity to serve as *xeinodokos*. As Telemachus had explained it to Theoclymenus, "I shall be absent, and ... my mother ... does not appear among the suitors" (15:515–17); and before Eumaeus, Telemachus had claimed that he himself was too young, and that "the heart in my mother's mind is divided" (16.71–77).

So long as Penelope was fixed in her attitude of sorrowful longing for Odysseus's return, she remained in her room upstairs, except when situations that could be construed as emergencies called her forth: Phemios's "sad song" (1.340–41) in Book 1, or the suitors' plan to "murder her son in the halls" (16.411) in Book 16. Otherwise, Penelope is kept informed about events in the palace by Medon (4.675ff., 16.412), Eurycleia, or Eurynome, but does not herself descend into the *megaron*. If wanderers appear whom she wishes to question, she does so upstairs in her own quarters. Thus, when she first hears about the stranger, she is sitting in the upper room conversing with her maidservants. She summons Eumaeus to her presence (ἡ δ᾽ ἐπὶ οἷ καλέσασα προσηύδα δῖον ὑφορβόν, 17.507) and instructs him to go and tell the stranger to come to her, so that she can befriend him and question him (ἔρχεο, δῖ᾽ Εὔμαιε, κιὼν τὸν ξεῖνον ἄνωχθι / ἐλθέμεν, ὄφρα τί μιν προσπτύξομαι ἠδ᾽ ἐρέωμαι, 17.508–9). She repeats her instructions at the end of the conversation with Eumaeus: "Go and call the stranger right here to me" (ἐρχεό μοι, τὸν ξεῖνον ἐναντίον ὧδε κάλεσσον, 17.544). She is surprised when Eumaeus returns at the end of Book 17 unaccompanied by the stranger: "Didn't you bring him, Eumaeus?" (οὐ σύ γ᾽ ἄγεις, Εὔμαιε; 17.577).

Odysseus's suggestion of an interview in the *megaron*, then, combines with Penelope's awareness of Telemachus's maturity to provide the circumstances justifying both her active encouragement of the suitors' wooing and the resumption of her role as mistress of the household. Thus, in the first segment of the *homilia*, Penelope assures the *xeinos* that "I waste my heart away in longing for Odysseus" (ἀλλ᾽ Ὀδυσῆ ποθέουσα φίλον κατατήκομαι ἦτορ, 19.136), but that nevertheless circumstances require her to remarry: "Now I am no longer able to escape from marriage nor to devise another *mētis*" (νῦν δ' οὔτ' ἐκφυγέειν δύναμαι γάμον οὔτε τιν' ἄλλην / μῆτιν ἔθ' εὑρίσκω, 19.157–58). She goes on to appeal to the force of her family's insistence and her son's maturity: "For my parents are urging me strongly to marry, and my son is vexed to see [the suitors] consuming his livelihood" (μάλα δ' ὀτρύνουσι τοκῆες / γήμασθ', ἀσχαλάᾳ δὲ πάις βίοτον κατεδόντων, / γιγνώσκων, 19.158–60).

In the course of her appearance before the suitors in Book 18, and in the first interview with Odysseus, both Eurymachus and Odysseus evoke from Penelope a repudiation of *kleos*, Eurymachus by complimenting the superiority of her "appearance and stature and mind within" (ἐπεὶ περίεσσι γυναικῶν / εἶδός τε μέγεθός τε ἰδὲ φρένας ἔνδον ἐίσας, 18.248–49), and Odysseus by comparing her *kleos* to that of a righteous king: "Oh woman, no one of mortals upon the broad earth could reproach you, for your *kleos* reaches to the wide heavens" (ὦ γύναι, οὐκ ἄν τίς σε βροτῶν ἐπ' ἀπείρονα γαῖαν / νεικέοι· ἦ γάρ σευ κλέος οὐρανὸν εὐρὺν ἱκάνει, 19.107–8). On both occasions, Penelope responds with the same lines:

> ἦ τοι μὲν ἐμὴν ἀρετὴν εἶδός τε δέμας τε
> ὤλεσαν ἀθάνατοι, ὅτε Ἴλιον εἰσανέβαινον
> Ἀργεῖοι, μετὰ τοῖσι δ' ἐμὸς πόσις ᾖεν Ὀδυσσεύς.
> εἰ κεῖνός γ' ἐλθὼν τὸν ἐμὸν βίον ἀμφιπολεύοι,
> μεῖζόν κε κλέος εἴη ἐμὸν καὶ κάλλιον οὕτω.
> νῦν δ' ἄχομαι· τόσα γάρ μοι ἐπέσσευεν κακὰ δαίμων.

> (In fact my virtue and my form and my shape
> were all destroyed by the immortals, when the Argives embarked
> for Ilium, and along with them went my husband Odysseus.
> If he should return and *amphipoleuoi* my life,
> then my *kleos* would be just that much greater and finer.
> But as it is, I am grieved; for such are the troubles that fate has
>   brought upon me.)

(19.124–29 = 18.251–56)

The imagery upon which Penelope's language draws in 18.254 (= 19.127) is that of enclosure: the scholia to B gloss *amphipoleuoi* as περιπέσοι, περὶ τὸν ἐμὸν βίον πολοῖτο καὶ ἀναστρέφοιτο ("encounter," "patrol around my life and dwell [in it]"), and it is explained in Ameis-Hentz-Cauer as "to surround my life (with his concern)" (1964, 2(1): 159 ad 254). Thus, Allione's claim that Penelope is here conditioning all of her happiness on her husband's return insofar as *kleos* itself is conditioned by its association to felicity and prosperity (1963:82 and n. 34) is true, although too general to be relevant here.

In alluding to the need for Odysseus's return (εἰ κεῖνός γ' ἐλθών), Penelope emphasizes the association that the *Odyssey* develops between *kleos* and *nostos*. The *kleos* of which Penelope speaks here, like that of Books 2.125 and 24.196, is the *kleos* of unwavering fidelity, which in her case requires Odysseus's *nostos* for its completion and ratification. With this *kleos*, so it appears, Penelope has now ceased to be concerned, and this is consistent with her expressions of abandoned hope in Odysseus's *nostos*. In referring to the need for enclosure (*amphipoleuoi*), however, Penelope is concerned with a different aspect of her *kleos*, and one by which male and female claims to *kleos* are differentiated. For as the references to the veil before her face and to the maids who accompany her when she appears in public indicate, the social convention of female seclusion also requires the barrier of protection that only male presence can offer.[39]

There is only one occasion in the poem when Penelope appears in the *megaron* unprotected, as it were, and this, in Book 16, is occasioned by the emergency of the threat to Telemachus's life. Otherwise, Telemachus is present in the *megaron* when Penelope appears in both Books 1 and 18, and in Book 19 the suitors have withdrawn for the evening. On the two occasions when he is present in the hall, Telemachus offers to his mother unexpected demonstrations of his own maturity, asserted, in both cases, as his capacity to fulfill the expectations of the role of mature male. Telemachus's coming of age, then, not only authorizes Penelope's remarriage in a general way, but also specifically legitimizes her appearance in the public spaces of the house, and the resumption of her position as its mistress.

In the course of her first interview with the stranger, Penelope abandons her mourning and resigns herself to the loss of Odysseus. This is signaled in the narrative by a linguistic shift, in which Penelope's mournful weeping, previously represented principally through the verb κλαίω (see below), now becomes *goos*, the term that as we noted above in connection with Telemachus's lamenting in Book 4, is associated with the formal lamentation for the dead. Penelope, who is characterized especially by mourning, regularly dissolves into tears, and this is described through the formulaic lines, "then she bewailed Odysseus, her dear husband, until grey-eyed Athena cast sleep over her eyelids" (1.363–64 [= 16.450–51; 19.603–4; 21.357–58]). Similarly, in Book 19 she is aroused to tears by the stranger's reports concerning Odysseus, and as the text describes it, "Just so did the tears pour down her lovely cheeks, as she bewailed the husband who was

---

[39] The analogue or complement to seclusion and male protection, as well as its prelude, is life as a virgin among women: e.g., "and they gave them to the hateful Erinyes to care for" (καί ῥ' ἔδοσαν στυγερῇσιν Ἐρινύσιν ἀμφιπολεύειν, 20.78). West remarks concerning Penelope's use of the veil: "That Penelope goes veiled in the presence of the suitors even in her own home is probably to be interpreted as a gesture advertising her aversion to any familiarity and discouraging any notion that they are her guests" (1988:118 ad 1.334).

sitting before her" (ὡς τῆς τήκετο καλὰ παρήϊα δάκρυ χεούσης, / κλαιούσης ἑὸν ἄνδρα, παρήμενον, 19.208–9). On this occasion, however, the rare conjunction of disguise with reality, through which the poem draws attention to its own status as fiction, effects a transformation in the significance of Penelope's tears.

As Penelope weeps, Odysseus observes her: "But Odysseus pitied in his heart his wife as she mourned [him]" (αὐτὰρ 'Οδυσσεὺς / θυμῷ μὲν γοόωσαν ἑὴν ἐλέαιρε γυναῖκα, 19.209–10). Now the verb γοάω ("mourns"; γοόωσαν, 19.210) replaces κλαίω ("bewails"; κλαιούσης, 19.209). Thus, in 19.213, when Penelope leaves off crying, in 19.249 and 251, when she is aroused to it again, and in 19.264 and 268, when Odysseus enjoins her to leave off mourning, the same language appears (see also 19.513). The verb γοάω in the *Odyssey* otherwise principally connotes that mourning which is associated with loss through actual or imagined death—Telemachus's mourning for his father in Book 4; Penelope's lamenting after she hears that Telemachus has gone away (4.721, 4.758, 4.800, 4.801; cf. 17.8)— or its equivalent (Circe's transformation of the companions into swine in Book 10; 10.209, 10.248, 10.398, 10.457).

At this point in the poem, then, Penelope abandons hope of Odysseus's return. As she puts it just following the lying-tale that substantiates the stranger's claim to have met Odysseus: "I shall never again welcome him as he returns home to the dear land of his fathers" (19.257–59). To be sure, Penelope continues to "bewail" (κλαῖεν, 19.603; 20.58, 59, 84, 92) the loss of Odysseus in the same terms that had indicated her earlier lamenting over his absence, and in Book 21, when she takes up the bow for the *toxou thesis*, she both bewails (κλαῖε, 21.56) and mourns (γόοιο, 21.57) his loss. What transpires in Book 19, then, is a transformation of language that also brings about a potentiation of the connotations of *goos*.

Telemachus's mourning in Book 4 for the father he presumed dead functioned there as a prelude to his pursuit of *kleos*. Similarly, Penelope's expressions of depair in the *homilia* preface the display of her willingness to take on the role of *xeinodokos*. For the stranger's tale was validated through the *sēmata* ("signs") that Penelope recognized—the description of Odysseus's clothing—and this leads her to accord him a new status that, at the same time, entails her own assumption of a new role: "Oh stranger, whereas before you were pitiable to me, now you will be a beloved and respected *xeinos* in my halls" (νῦν μὲν δή μοι, ξεῖνε, πάρος περ ἐὼν ἐλεεινός, / ἐν μεγάροισιν ἐμοῖσι φίλος τ' ἔσῃ αἰδοῖός τε, 19.253–54). The structure of Penelope's thought here replicates that of Nausicaa, who had earlier remarked to her maids, "For before he had in fact appeared to me to be wretched, but now he seems like the gods" (πρόσθεν μὲν γὰρ δή μοι ἀεικέλιος δέατ' εἶναι, / νῦν δὲ θεοῖσιν ἔοικε, 6.242–43). In Penelope's speech here we can note especially the connotation of the phrase "in my halls" (19.254), by which Odysseus described his *oikos* just after the *anagnōrismos* by Telemachus (16.269). And earlier, addressing Penelope, the disguised Odysseus had invited her to question him "in your house" (19.115). As Ameis-Hentze-Cauer explains, that phrase "conveys the entitlement of Penelope as hostess to interrogate the stranger" (1964, 2(2): 9 ad 19.115).[40] In welcoming the stranger into the bond of *xenia*, then, Penelope has laid claim to her own authority as mistress of the household, and this transformation in her own status is associated with a loss of confidence in Odysseus's return.

Thus, when Penelope's *xeinos* now goes on to offer her the prophecy of Odysseus's return, she rejects it, explaining:

> ἀλλά μοι ὧδ' ἀνὰ θυμὸν ὀίεται, ὡς ἔσεταί περ·
> οὔτ' Ὀδυσεὺς ἔτι οἶκον ἐλεύσεται, οὔτε σὺ πομπῆς
> τεύξῃ, ἐπεὶ οὐ τοῖοι σημάντορές εἰσ' ἐνὶ οἴκῳ,
> οἷος Ὀδυσσεὺς ἔσκε μετ' ἀνδράσιν, εἴ ποτ' ἔην γε,
> ξείνους αἰδοίους ἀποπεμπέμεν ἠδὲ δέχεσθαι.
>
> (But this is how it seems to me in my heart that it will in fact be:
> Neither will Odysseus ever come home, nor will you be equipped
> with conveyance, since there are no masters in the house
> like Odysseus was among men—if he ever in fact existed—
> to send off reverent *xeinoi* and to receive them.)
>
> (19.312—16)

This is the first occasion on which Penelope employs the formula εἴ ποτ' ἔην γε ("if he ever was"), and it marks the turning point at which she resigns herself to the loss of Odysseus and abandons her mourning. As commentators observe, the formula εἴ ποτ' ἔην γε regularly refers to irretrievable and irreparable loss, and most often that associated with death. It is used by Priam of Hector in *Iliad* 24.426; by Telemachus of Odysseus in *Odyssey* 15.268 before the *anagnōrismos*; by Laertes of Odysseus before his recognition; by Helen at *Iliad* 3.180, to refer to lost happiness; and by Nestor at *Iliad* 11.762 (εἴ ποτ' ἔον γε), when he speaks, at a low point of morale among the Achaeans, of his own former prowess as a young man.

Thus, Penelope reaffirms her earlier belief that Odysseus will never return, and withholds acceptance of the stranger's prophecy; but at the same time she rewards him with the tokens of confidence in his reliability—a bath, fresh clothing, and a bed. It is significant here that earlier in the narrative, this treatment is specifically identified as the reward for validated goods news: Odysseus had requested fine clothing from Eumaeus as a

---

[40] "... Deutet auf die Berechtigung der Penelope, als Wirtin an den Gast Fragen zu richten."

euaggelion ("a reward for good news") when he had first announced Odysseus's return (14.151–54; cf. 391–97); and in Book 17, Penelope had promised to reward the *xeinos* in the same way "if I recognize that everything he says is true" (αἴ κ' αὐτὸν γνώω νημερτέα πάντ' ἐνέποντα, 17.549).[41]

Like other *xeinodokoi*, then, Penelope offers her guest a bath and bed, and she promises him also a place at the feast beside Telemachus; she cannot, however, extend to the him the promise of conveyance.[42] For, as she explains, "there are no masters in the house / like Odysseus was among men" (19.314–15). In this way, then, Penelope recognizes both the absence of male authority within the house and, by her suggestion that the *xeinos* dine alongside Telemachus, her son's as yet not fully actualized capacity to take on the role. For in explaining that the stranger will be bathed before the feast the next morning, she adds, "And it will be so much the worse for the one of them [the suitors] who molests or annoys him [the *xeinos*]" (τῷ δ' ἄλγιον, ὅς κεν ἐκείνων / τοῦτον ἀνιάζῃ θυμοφθόρος, 19.322–23), implying that Telemachus will be adequate to the task of defending the honor of a guest-friend within the house. And a little later we see that she is correct: when the next day's feast occurs, the suitors do in fact set before Odysseus "an equal portion with their own"; for so, as the text goes on to explain, "did Telemachus order": μοῖραν θέσαν . . . / ἴσην, ὡς αὐτοί περ ἐλάγχανον· ὡς γὰρ ἀνώγει / Τηλέμαχος, φίλος υἱὸς Ὀδυσσῆος θείοιο (20.281–83).

For Penelope as for Telemachus, then, *xenia* is a source of *kleos*, as she herself explains:

πῶς γὰρ ἐμεῦ σύ, ξεῖνε, δαήσεαι, εἴ τι γυναικῶν
ἀλλάων περίειμι νόον καὶ ἐπίφρονα μῆτιν,
εἴ κεν ἀϋσταλέος, κακὰ εἱμένος ἐν μεγάροισι
δαινύῃ;
. . . .
ὃς δ' ἂν ἀμύμων αὐτὸς ἔῃ καὶ ἀμύμονα εἰδῇ,
τοῦ μέν τε κλέος εὐρὺ διὰ ξεῖνοι φορέουσι
πάντας ἐπ' ἀνθρώπους, πολλοί τέ μιν ἐσθλὸν ἔειπον.

---

[41] My colleague James O'Hara proposes to me the convincing suggestion that Eumaeus puts Odysseus off because he doubts him, and this leads us to expect Penelope to do the same.

[42] *For the conventions governing the scene, see* the discussions in Arend 75:39–53 and Edwards 1975:61–71. On the adaptation of the motif to scenes with goddesses, see Tsagarakis 1979:38–41. Pedrick 1988 discusses the adaptation of the motif to the "noble woman," but she does not distinguish between goddesses and mortal women; nor does she take up the provision of conveyance. There are points, however, where poetic conventions appear to incorporate a status distinction between divinities and mortal men on the one hand, and mortal women and men of low status on the other (see Houston 1975). On clothing, see Schadewaldt 1970e; Block 1985; and Pedrick 1988:99 n. 13.

> (For how ever would you know about me, oh stranger, whether
> I surpass other women at all in intelligence and careful forethought
> if you feast in [my] halls all squalid and in filthy
> clothes?
>
> . . . .
>
> But as for the one who is himself blameless and who has blameless thoughts,
> his *kleos* is carried far and wide to all men
> by his *xeinoi*, and many men speak about him as noble.)
>
> (19.325–28, 332–34)

In this speech, Penelope's train of thought leads from women (γυναικῶν, line 325), to human beings in general (ἄνθρωποι, line 328), to the excellence of men (ὃς δ' ἂν ἀμύμων, line 332). And thus, in lieu of the *kleos* of the *basileus amumōn* ("excellent king," 19.109), which Penelope had earlier repudiated, and of the *kleos* tied to Odysseus's *nostos*, of which she is no longer convinced, Penelope here seeks to appropriate for herself the *kleos* that, properly speaking, belongs to the male head of household. We can note here that, although Penelope had earlier specifically excluded from her offer the provision of conveyance (πομπή, 19.313), it is precisely this factor upon which the dissemination of the *kleos* of the noble host depends: see ξεῖνοι φορέουσι ("strangers carry," i.e., "transmit") in line 333, and compare Odysseus's attribution of *kleos* to Alcinous when the latter agrees to provide him with conveyance (πομπή, 7.317).

The two discourses in which Penelope accepts Odysseus as her *xeinos* (19.253–60) and makes provisions for his care (19.309–34) end and begin with statements of disbelief in the possibility of Odysseus's return (19.257–60; 19.309–15), and these, in turn, enclose the discourse in which Odysseus offers his strongest assurances to the contrary (19.262–307). Penelope's refusal to believe the *xeinos* here can certainly be attributed, as is ordinarily the case, to her habitual mistrust, a feature of her character to which she herself alludes in the opening of the *homilia*: "Therefore I pay no attention to strangers or suppliants or heralds" (19.134–35). Likewise, Eumaeus had reported that Penelope regularly listens to what itinerant beggars (ὃς δέ κ' ἀλητεύων Ἰθάκης ἐς δῆμον ἵκηται, 14.126) have to say, and that she "receives them well and is kind to them and questions them about each particular" (ἡ δ' εὖ δεξαμένη φιλέει καὶ ἕκαστα μεταλλᾷ, 14.128); but he also insists that such types never succeed in gaining the confidence of either Penelope or Telemachus: "Old man, no wanderer who comes with reports about him [Odysseus] could persuade his wife and own son" (ὦ γέρον, οὔ τις κεῖνον ἀνὴρ ἀλαλήμενος ἐλθὼν / ἀγγέλλων πείσειε γυναῖκά τε καὶ φίλον υἱόν, 14.122–23).

Penelope's disbelief here, however, should be interpreted also in conjunction with the representation of the *homilia* as a scenario of *xenia*. For just as *xenia* both incorporates Odysseus into his *oikos* and keeps him a stranger within it, so Telemachus's coming of age both make it possible for Penelope to resume her role as mistress of the household and necessitates her severance from it. Both of these developments are founded upon the belief that Odysseus will not return—the same assumption that makes it possible in Book 20 for Telemachus to assure the suitor Agelaus that "I do not delay my mother's marriage, but rather I tell her to marry whomever she likes, and in addition I offer boundless gifts" (οὔ τι διατρίβω μητρὸς γάμον, ἀλλὰ κελεύω / γήμασθ' ᾧ κ' ἐθέλῃ, ποτὶ δ' ἄσπετα δῶρα δίδωμι, 20.341–42). Agelaus had prefaced his own statement to Telemachus with the provocative observation that "it is now already clear that he [Odysseus] is no longer going to return home" (νῦν δ' ἤδη τόδε δῆλον, ὅ τ' οὐκέτι νόστιμός ἐστιν, 20.333), and Telemachus does not dispute this (20.339–40).

In Telemachus's case, of course, the notion that his father will not return is the fiction upon which his own claim to *kyrieia* is founded. The growth of the same conviction on Penelope's part, by contrast, runs counter to the logic of the narrative. The resulting illogicality in the text is repaired, as it were, through Odysseus's "misreading" of the narrative action, which operates to disguise its implications. The first instance of such misreading is constituted by Odysseus's response to Penelope's appearance before the suitors. But the most striking example occurs at the end of Book 19, when the *homilia* is resumed following the foot-washing scene, and Penelope consolidates her decision to remarry.

Dream and *Toxou Thesis*

Penelope explains to her *xeinos*, in a brief concluding discourse to the *homilia* following the foot-washing scene, that her nights, like those of Pandareus's daughter, are filled with "bitter anxieties [that] cluster constantly around my heart and distress me further in my grief" (πυκιναὶ δέ μοι ἀμφ' ἀδινὸν κῆρ / ὀξεῖαι μελεδῶναι ὀδυρομένην ἐρέθουσιν, 19.516–17). The myth of Pandareus to which Penelope alludes may be intended, as Russo argues, to suggest that there is a danger that Penelope might, like Procne, bring about the death of her son "in her senseless folly" (δι' ἀφραδίας, 19.523).[43] But Penelope herself explains the simile with reference to the heart-rending dilemma that has dominated this section of the narrative: whether to retain her association with Odysseus's household, or to abandon it for the best wooer among the Achaeans (19.524–31).

Penelope goes on to explain that her grown son urges on her the second

---

[43] Russo suggests that the myth as recounted by the BV scholia on this passage may be a fiction invented to account for a misunderstanding of ἀηδών in 19.518 as a proper noun (1985:252–53 ad 19. 518–24).

course of action, but before drawing the logical conclusion she interposes an account of a dream and its interpretation, which she asks the *xeinos* to confirm for her.[44] The dream is divided into two parts: the dream proper, which Penelope identifies as an *oneiron* (see below), and in which an eagle swoops down and kills her pet geese; and its interpretation, rendered within the dream by the eagle, who identifies himself as her husband and explains that the geese are the suitors (19.536–50). In interpreting the dream, the eagle claims that it was not in fact an *onar* ("dream" = *oneiron*)[45] but a *hypar esthlon* ("true vision"): οὐκ ὄναρ, ἀλλ᾽ ὕπαρ ἐσθλόν, ὅ τοι τετελεσμένον ἔσται (19.547).

Odysseus confirms the dream's interpretation, adding that death and destruction await all the suitors (19.555–58), whereupon Penelope insists that the dream issued forth through the gates of horn and hence bore "words not destined to be accomplished" (ἔπε᾽ ἀκράαντα φέροντες, 19.565). The logic of Penelope's disbelief in the dream, after it is validated by the stranger, is hard to discern. Commentators have suggested that, like the report of Odysseus's parting words in Book 18, it is a deliberately composed fiction (Büchner 1940:149 n. 1; Harsh 1950:16; Winkler 1990:154), that it represents a form of divination (Amory 1963:106; Allione 1963:90–91; cf. Austin 1975:229–31), or of unconscious wish-fulfillment (Devereux 1957:382; Rankin 1962:622; Russo 1982:8–10, 1985:254–55 ad 541), or of both (Kessels 1978:98–100). Vester's proposal that we regard it simply as "a tormented woman's need for communication" (1968:427) amounts to confessing a despair of explaining the episode, whereas Finley's claim that "the geese . . . do not signify the suitors . . . but the state of half-orderliness that had been her comfort" (1978:19) disregards the obvious meaning of the text.

Just as it is important not to overinterpret the text, as in Devereux's claim that the dream represents unconscious wish-fulfillment, so we must not underinterpret it either, as Kurtz does, for example, in dismissing the most obvious implications of the surface narrative: "Surely Homer is not suggesting that Penelope seriously entertains a real affection for any of her suitors" (1989:24). The dream is remarkable as an imagistic representation of the divided state of mind that has characterized Penelope throughout the *homilia*, which has taken the form both of explicitly expressed ambivalence ("so for me too my heart springs up this way and that," 19.524) and of a conflict between wish ("If only, oh stranger, this utterance of yours

---

[44] Kessels argues that Odysseus is not asked to interpret the dream, but to confirm its interpretation; for discussion of the complex history of the debate over the meaning of ὑποκριτής and ὑποκρίνεσθαι, see Kessels 1978:29–31, 63–65 n. 16, 97, 121–22 n. 44.

[45] For discussion of this terminology and its meaning, see Kessels 1978:174–89; and note Russo's remark that the gloss ὅ τοι τελεσμένον ἔσται "in effect defines ὕπαρ as a vision of what will come true" (1985:268 ad 20.90).

might be fulfilled!" 19.309) and reality ("But this is how it seems to me in my heart that it will be," 19.312).

Only here, in the dream, the emotional valences are reversed, so that lamentation, which had earlier been associated with accommodation to reality (Odysseus's absence; cf. 19.570), is now attached to the event that was represented previously as a wish whose fulfillment was much desired (Odysseus's return and the slaughter of the suitors; cf. 19.569). At the same time, the belief in Odysseus's return is now, through the trope of the dream, converted from a wish to an "unreality." The new reality, as Penelope explains to the *xeinos* at the end of the homilia, is the *toxou thesis* and her imminent departure from the house; "the house of Odysseus" itself (19.570ff.), and her life in it, is now consigned to the world of dreams: "I think I shall remember it sometime even though in a dream" (19.581). The trope of the dream, then, fills the narrative function of allowing the expectation of Odysseus's return to be displaced from the surface of the narrative and consigned to the realm of unreality.

We run the risk of occluding the narrative function of the dream if we subject it too readily to the hermeneutics of suspicion, and claim that Penelope "really" enjoys (ἰαίνομαι, 19.537) feeding the suitors and would "really" bewail (αὐτὰρ ἐγὼ κλαῖον καὶ ἐκώκυον ἕν περ ὀνείρῳ, 19.541) their slaughter. For this amounts to reading the first part (the *onar*) in the light of the second (the *hypar*).[46] The narrative attempts to preclude this interpretation by introducing a distinction between *onar* and *hypar*, and by consigning the content of the dream itself to the realm of the former. In confirming the dream's interpretation, Odysseus himself does not reread the first part in the light of the second, and its implication is consequently left suspended in the narrative between Penelope's innocence of its meaning, and Odysseus's disregard of its implications.

Nevertheless, the context of the dream—in the course of a deliberation concerning marriage to one of the suitors—demands that we mistrust this surface of the text. Thus, the *homilia* concludes with a striking example of the narrative disjunction that generally characterizes the presentation of Penelope in the *Odyssey*, by which the narrative context is at variance with the literal or superficial meaning of the episode. And so Penelope's disbelief, and the consequent decision to set the bow-contest, have in the end the effect of assimilating her decision to a repudiation of Odysseus. Odysseus himself, however, appears wilfully to disregard the implication of her decision, and to misread them as assurances of faithfulness.

The *homilia* as a whole is governed by what could be called a discordant harmony, in which the rhythm of the stranger's concord with Penelope is

---

[46] See here Kessels's observation that Penelope "was not aware [when she experienced the dream] of the equation of geese with suitors" (1978:94).

developed against the theme of her gradual dissociation from Odysseus. Thus, the bond between Penelope and Odysseus is forfeited even as that with the *xeinos* is forged: as Hélène Kakridis has shown, the passages in which Penelope explicitly refers to the stranger show a modulation of meaning in the course of Book 19 toward greater feeling and friendliness (H. Kakridis 1963:100). Accordingly, the tendency in the critical interpretation of this scene—even among analysts—has been to focus on its representation of *homophrosynē* ("like-mindedness") and to comprehend the contradictory movement under the rubric of irony.[47] Vester's analysis, for example, calls attention to the "as if" structure of the *homilia*, and shows that the scene as a whole is characterized by a subtle shift whereby Odysseus, "the eternally absent one," gradually recedes from the foreground of Penelope's concern and is replaced in her esteem by the present stranger: "In the reality as she conceives it but which is nevertheless decisive, he moves ever further away, remains the eternally absent one . . . [but] the stranger grows in Penelope's eyes in a scarcely expected manner" (1968:420, 421).[48]

Such readings, as we have discussed earlier, amount to an identification of the critic's perspective with that of Odysseus, a point of view that, to be sure, the trope of disguise invites. Thus, Winkler argues that part of the effect of Penelope's trick in Book 23 is that it forces us to the recognition that our perspective had been Odysseus's all along (1990:158; cf. 159). And Murnaghan, who acknowledges the operation of a double perspective in this section of the poem, nevertheless regards Penelope as unable "to understand and to control the ambiguity of her own actions" (1987:130). Penelope is not unaware of her own perspective, however, nor is her perspective—consciously or unconsciously—that of Odysseus. She moves steadily, though ambivalently, toward remarriage with one of the suitors. This development is legitimated by Telemachus's coming of age, and it is not the decision as such which is problematic, but rather its incorporation into the ongoing narrative, as we have discussed.

Thus, Book 20 opens, as 19 did, with a reference to female betrayal, displaced, as in the earlier episode, from Penelope and her decision to marry one of the suitors onto the serving-maids—here referred to as γυναῖκες ("women") rather than δμῶαι ("housemaids")—and their ready willingness to sleep with the intruders: "The women issued forth from the *megaron*, the ones who used to sleep with the suitors before, laughing amongst themselves and full of good cheer" (ταὶ δ' ἐκ μεγάροιο γυναῖκες / ἤισαν, αἳ μνηστῆρσιν ἐμισγέσκοντο πάρος περ, / ἀλλήλῃσι γέλω τε καὶ

---

[47] Austin's (1975:179–238) is the fullest discussion of the development of *homophrosynē*; but see also Foley 1978.

[48] "In der von ihr gedachten, aber entscheidenden Wirklichkeit rückt er immer ferner, bleibt er der ewig Abwesende . . . der Fremde wächst bei Penelope in einer kaum erwarteten Weise."

εὐφροσύνην παρέχουσαι, 20.6–8). Even Penelope's striking prayer to Artemis for a quick and painless death (20.62–90) is ambiguous, since the wish to maintain virginity forever and the sorrow at its impending loss is a regular prelude to marriage for women in archaic poetry (Redfield 1982:190–91). Here, Penelope longs to assimilate herself to the daughters of Pandareus who, in a myth otherwise unknown to us, are snatched away by the storm winds on the eve of their marriage and given over to a life of immortality and sterility. This must be the meaning of their consignment to "the hateful Erinyes for them to *amphipoleuein*" (καί ῥ' ἔδοσαν στυγερῇσιν Ἐρινύσιν ἀμφιπολεύειν, 20.78).

Accordingly, Penelope's wish for death is followed by an anticipation that she will soon find herself bringing pleasure to a lesser man than the one whom she thinks is about to become her former husband: "And may I not bring gladness to the mind of a lesser man" (μηδέ τι χείρονος ἀνδρὸς εὐφραίνοιμι νόημα, 20.82). As Russo points out, "[Penelope's] complaint confirms the fact that she has no suspicion that her husband has already returned in the disguise of the beggar" (1985:267–68 ad 20.82), and this makes it impossible to argue that she has recognized the stranger as Odysseus in Book 19 without further assuming a resurgence of doubt at the beginning of Book 20, of which the text gives no sign. Penelope goes on here to report a vision of Odysseus lying beside her (20.88), which Russo interprets as "a premonition of Odysseus' return" (ibid.:268 ad 20.87–90; see also the longer discussion in Russo 1982:11–18). Since it is described as *oneirata kaka* (20.87)[49] and entails a representation of Odysseus as he was "when he went off with the army" (20.89), however, it is more likely that this represents a vision of the old marriage evoked as part of the process of accommodating to the new one.

In Book 21, Penelope appears in the *megaron* to set the bow-contest,[50] and she repeats the resolution at which she had arrived at the end of the *homilia*:

> ἀλλ' ἄγετε, μνηστῆρες, ἐπεὶ τόδε φαίνετ' ἄεθλον·
> θήσω γὰρ μέγα τόξον Ὀδυσσῆος θείοιο·
> ὃς δέ κε ῥηίτατ' ἐντανύσῃ βιὸν ἐν παλάμῃσι
> καὶ διοϊστεύσῃ πελέκεων δυοκαίδεκα πάντων,
> τῷ κεν ἅμ' ἑσποίμην, νοσφισσαμένη τόδε δῶμα
> κουρίδιον, μάλα καλόν, ἐνίπλειον βιότοιο,
> τοῦ ποτε μεμνήσεσθαι ὀίομαι ἔν περ ὀνείρῳ.

[49] Penelope *wishes* that it had been a *hypar*, but recognizes that it was not (20.90).

[50] For discussion of Penelope's appearance in Book 21 as an "allurement scene," see Forsyth 1979; the typological elements in the scene are more plausibly interpreted as part of the attendance motif, in my opinion (Nagler 1974:73–86).

> (Come, suitors, since this is the contest before you:
> for I shall set up the great bow of godlike Odysseus,
> and whoever is able to string it easily in his hand,
> and to send an arrow through all twelve axes,
> him would I follow along after, abandoning this house
> of my marriage, which is a lovely one, and full of good livelihood,
> which I think I shall remember always, even in my dreams.)
> (21.73–79 [21.75–79 = 19.577–81])

Here, as earlier, the marriage with Odysseus is consigned more and more to the realm of dreams, and Penelope accommodates herself ever more thoroughly to marriage with another.

Along with the readiness to remarry, as we have seen, Penelope resumes her role as mistress of the household, and the most forceful representation of her transformed status appears at this juncture in the narrative. Penelope remains in the *megaron* throughout the contest, and witnesses the failure of Leodes, then Telemachus and Eurymachus, to string the bow. After Antinous suggests an interlude, Odysseus entreats Antinous and Eurymachus for permission to attempt the bow. When Antinous demurs, Penelope intervenes to support the request: compare "but come, give me the polished bow, so that among you . . ." (ἀλλ' ἄγ' ἐμοὶ δότε τόξον ἐύξοον, ὄφρα μεθ' ὑμῖν, 21.281) with "but come, give him the polished bow, so that we may see . . ." (ἀλλ' ἄγε οἱ δότε τόξον ἐύξοον, ὄφρα ἴδωμεν, 21.336). It is her most potent claim yet to authority in the household, and in this respect its function is analogous to Telemachus's threat to Ctesipus, "the strongest speech Homer puts in Telemachus's mouth," as Russo notes (1985:278 ad 20.304–9).

Telemachus's words are spoken in the context of competition among men, and they derive their force from the struggle for honor that characterizes the male world of challenge and riposte (Gould 1973:94–95; Redfield 1990:318–22). Penelope deliberately marginalizes these concerns in pressing instead her own claims to authority in the house: "Eurymachus," she says, in answer to his argument that the suitor's reputation will be affected if the stranger succeeds in stringing the bow, "there is no longer the possibility of good *kleos* among the people for those who dishonor the house of a noble man by consuming it" (Εὐρύμαχ', οὔ πως ἔστιν εὐκλείας κατὰ δῆμον / ἔμμεναι, οἳ δὴ οἶκον ἀτιμάζοντες ἔδουσιν / ἀνδρὸς ἀριστῆος, 21.331–33). She goes on to insist ("for thus I will tell you, and this is the way it will come to pass," ὧδε γὰρ ἐξερέω, τὸ δὲ καὶ τετελεσμένον ἔσται, 21.337) that the *xeinos* be allowed to attempt the bow, and promises, if he succeeds, the rewards and gifts that it is otherwise the office of the *xeinodokos* to bestow upon his guest:

CONSTRUCTION OF PRESENCE (17–21)

ἕσσω μιν χλαῖνάν τε χιτῶνά τε, εἵματα καλά,
δώσω δ' ὀξὺν ἄκοντα, κυνῶν ἀλκτῆρα καὶ ἀνδρῶν,
καὶ ξίφος ἄμφηκες· δώσω δ' ὑπὸ ποσσὶ πέδιλα,
πέμψω δ' ὅππη μιν κραδίη θυμός τε κελεύει.

(I shall dress him in a cloak and tunic, to serve as lovely clothes,
and I shall give him a sharp sword, to ward off from himself both dogs and men,
and a double-edged sword as well. I shall give him sandals for his feet,
and I shall send him wherever his heart and mind want.)

(21.339–42)

Penelope here envisions extending to Odysseus the offer of conveyance (*pompē*) and a gift of guest-friendship (*xeinēion*) which otherwise the *kyrios* of the household presents to his *xeinos* (on *xeinēia*, see West 1988:114 ad 1.311–13). In Book 13, for example, the departing Odysseus thanks Alcinous for πομπὴ καὶ φίλα δῶρα (13.41). Further, the scene of *xenia* in Book 8 makes clear that the presentation to the *xeinos* of weapons is tied directly to the male world, specifically to the renunciation of rivalry; there, Alcinous directs all of the *basileis* ("men of preeminence") to endow Odysseus with clothing and gold (8.392–93), but he instructs Euryalus to issue an apology and to ratify it with a gift. In complying, Euryalus offers Odysseus a silver-studded bronze sword, and such a gift presumes on the part of the *xeinos* too the renunciation of the power to affront (Pitt-Rivers 1977a:101–2, 109–12; cf. Bourdieu 1966; Hainsworth 1988:373).[51]

Penelope intervenes here in the context of a struggle for honor in the *oikos* of Odysseus, and she assumes here the role that had belonged to Alcinous in the earlier episode. It is a critical moment in the narrative, the second occasion on which Penelope has extended *xenia* to the stranger, and the second on which he has avoided its full reception. For just as Penelope's offer of *xenia* effects the reestablishment of her own authority within the household, so Odysseus's full acceptance of it would represent an efficacious gesture on his part, one that would consolidate his role as *xeinos* within the household. Russo points out that by his partial refusal of *xenia*, Odysseus avoids assimilating himself to the status of the suitors, men who take their ease in another man's household (Russo 1985:244 ad 19.336–48), and we can add that, by evading here the status also of Penelope's *xeinos*, Odysseus preserves the liminal position within the *oikos* that is essential to allow his transformation in the end into its *kyrios*.

Consequently, Telemachus's intervention, by which he reappropriates his own temporary status as the *kyrios* of Odysseus's *oikos*, not only represents a gesture of epic economy, which preserves the integrity of the

---

[51] Note that Odysseus had also given Iphitus a sword and spear, in the same exchange of *xeinēia* through which he himself had acquired the bow (21.34).

poem's *telos*, but also functions, as Odysseus's nod had in his own case, to instantiate the appropriate relationship between wife and mature son:

> μῆτερ ἐμή, τόξον μὲν Ἀχαιῶν οὔ τις ἐμεῖο
> κρείσσων, ᾧ κ' ἐθέλω, δόμεναί τε καὶ ἀρνήσασθαι.
> . . . .
> τῶν οὔ τίς μ' ἀέκοντα βιήσεται, αἴ κ' ἐθέλωμι
> καὶ καθάπαξ ξείνῳ δόμεναι τάδε τόξα φέρεσθαι.
> ἀλλ' εἰς οἶκον ἰοῦσα τὰ σ' αὐτῆς ἔργα κόμιζε,
> ἱστόν τ' ἠλακάτην τε, καὶ ἀμφιπόλοισι κέλευε
> ἔργον ἐποίχεσθαι· τόξον δ' ἄνδρεσσι μελήσει
> πᾶσι, μάλιστα δ' ἐμοί· τοῦ γὰρ κράτος ἔστ' ἐνὶ οἴκῳ.

> (Mother of mine, no one of the Achaeans has more authority
>   over this bow than I myself,
> to bestow it and refuse it to whomever I wish.
> . . . .
> No one [of the suitors] will forcibly prevent me if I want
> even to give it to this stranger and to let him have it.
> But do you go within and attend to your own work,
> the loom and the spindle, and bid the maidservants
> apply themselves to it. For the bow is a concern to all the men,
> and especially to me. For mine is the authority in the household.)
>   (21.344–45, 348–53)

Telemachus here realizes fully the position of authority toward which he had gestured in Book 1, when he appropriated from Penelope the prerogative of determining the bard's song (1.345–59), and the repetition here of the formulae used there of both Telemachus (21.350–53 = 1.356–59) and Penelope (21.354–58 = 1.360–64) invests the lines with transformative force. As I have argued elsewhere, in the *Iliad* these same formulaic lines appear at the point where the confusion of realms between Hector and Andromache is resolved, and each returns to the appropriate sphere (*Iliad* 6.490–93; see Arthur 1981:37). Similarly, their use here resolves the anomalous exercise of *kyrieia*—first by the son, and then by the wife—to which Odysseus's absence had led.

Odysseus's nod to Telemachus earlier in Book 21 had served to instantiate the proper relationship between son and father, and to signal the point at which Telemachus surrendered to Odysseus the role of male authority within the house. Telemachus's assertion of authority over Penelope here marks the point at which she relinquishes her own claims to preeminence, which had similarly extended to encompass the role of male head of the household. Consequently, at a later point in the narrative, Odysseus must reappropriate from Telemachus his own prerogative of authority over Penelope; and as we shall see, when Telemachus yields it, he alludes specifically to the matter of competition for preeminence among men.

Summary and Conclusion

In the course of Books 17–21, during the time that Odysseus is in Ithaca disguised as a beggar, the statuses and roles of both Telemachus and Penelope are affected. The case of Telemachus is the simpler one. Odysseus's disguise, together with Telemachus's awareness of it, makes possible the actualization of the state of maturity to which he had acceded in Book 1. Thus, Telemachus is able to assume the role of *xeinodokos* and to assert his own male potency against that of the suitors, without compromising the necessity for him to resume, at the poem's end, the status of son. Penelope's situation is more complex. Telemachus's accession to maturity makes it possible for her both to decide upon remarriage and to assume the role of mistress of the household. By means of this double movement in the plot, Penelope dissociates herself from Odysseus's *oikos* at the same time that she consolidates her position within it. In this respect, her representation in the narrative is analogous to that of Odysseus, who, as a *xeinos*, is both incorporated into his household and kept estranged from it.[52]

In Penelope's case, however, the decision to remarry, while authorized by Telemachus's maturity, is also represented as a form of betrayal. Thus, although Penelope in this section of the narrative is no longer in danger of becoming Clytemnestra, she is nevertheless drawn toward the paradigm of Helen, the woman who, while still the wife of one man, seduces others and yields to their blandishments. The resolution of the question of Penelope's ultimate faithfulness is forestalled, however, by its displacement from her actions onto her intentions. Odysseus's misreading of her intentions precludes the judgment that the narrative surface invites, and this device in turn enables Penelope to act out fully the role of independent and autonomous agent. Penelope thereby appropriates for herself the right to decide on her husband without fully assimilating herself to the paradigms of the women who claim sexual independence, to the examples of Clytemnestra and Helen.

Odysseus's misreading of Penelope's intentions within the poem has the same authorizing effect for her that his disguise had for Telemachus. In both cases the integrity of the poem's commitment to its own *telos* is preserved, even as its principal characters are enabled to act out roles that are inconsistent with that same outcome. This playing out of roles, like Odys-

---

[52] Cf. Segal 1962:46: "The whole of the second half of the *Odyssey* consists in Odysseus' rediscovery of the familiar through alienation, of himself through being other than himself."

seus's own disguise and lying-tales, does not simply misrepresent reality, but also transforms it.

Odysseus first enters his palace at 17.325, just at the moment when his dog Argus expires.[53] Argus is the only figure in the poem who recognizes Odysseus intuitively and spontaneously; his death is a sign that Odysseus's former life cannot simply be entered upon and resumed, and that a narrative of uncomplicated return is a negative option. Throughout Books 17–21, as he contructs his presence on Ithaca, Odysseus must confront the effects of his absence—his son's capacity to displace him, his wife's obligation eventually to remarry. The structure of the *Odyssey*, and particularly of this section of the narrative, effects a complex and forceful representation of Odysseus's return as a process of accommodation to and transformation of the situation engendered by his absence. Thus, Telemachus's replacement of his father as *kyrios* is represented as a capacity enacted to the point of realization, but foregone voluntarily. Penelope's remarriage is represented differently. Its construction as an event is conditioned in part by the question of her intentionality, which the narrative renders both problematic and indiscernible. It is conditioned also by the concomitant development of a relationship of *xenia* with the stranger; this relationship, by virtue of its construction as a homologue to marriage, operates to subvert the decision to remarry.

The scenario of *xenia* is the paradigm that structures the *homilia* overall, and this, as we observed earlier, is what makes it possible for the encounter to effect a kind of reunion between Penelope and Odysseus. For as Vester and Eisenberger in particular have shown, the *homilia* brings about what Eisenberger called "the first togetherness of the queen and her husband . . . [conceived] in the spirit of guest-friendship" (1973:272).[54] At the same time, the equivalence developed in the poem between *xenia* and marriage enables the relationship between Penelope and Odysseus that is constructed through the *homilia* to be refigured in Book 23, in the reunion proper, as one of marriage. As I will argue in Chapter Six, the reunion and the marriage that it brings into being are not constituted on the basis of an essential affinity between Penelope and Odysseus, but develop instead out of the relationship between them which is constructed in the course of Book 19, and which is represented as a form of *xenia*.

---

[53] On the complex meaning of this scene, see the illuminating discussion in Goldhill 1988:9–18.

[54] "Das erstes Beisammensein der Königin und ihres . . . Gemahls . . . [konzipiert] . . . im Geiste der Gastfreundschaft."

Chapter Six

DUPLICITY, INDETERMINACY, AND THE IDEOLOGY OF EXCLUSIVITY (BOOK 23)

Duplicity, Disguise, and Indeterminacy

As many commentators have observed, the principal narrative trope of the second half of the *Odyssey* is disguise and recognition. Hölscher, for example, describes "the basic motifs of the return of Odysseus [as] 'hiding' and 'revelation'" ("Verbergung und Enthüllung," 1939:67), and Thornton remarks, "'Concealment' and 'Disclosure'—which are of course complementary to each other—are the dramatic ideas on which the second half of the *Odyssey* is built" (1970:124–25).[1] In addition, this aspect of the poem has been the subject of two full-length studies in recent years. Murnaghan's book (1987) addresses the theme directly, and Pucci's investigation of the intertextual relationship between the *Iliad* and the *Odyssey* takes up also the philosophical and psychological implications of the strategy of disguise, as well as its relation to the poetics of the *Odyssey* (1987; see esp. 76–109).

In my interpretation of indeterminacy in the *Odyssey*, I have tried to show that the narrative is structured according to a principle of duplicity that, as I have presented it, includes disguise but is not limited to it. This duplicity appears in the text initially as a form of "doubling" of the plot—first, the development of the House of Atreus story as an alternative paradigm that threatens to displace the *Odyssey*'s own plot of Odysseus's return, and second, the substitution of the plot of *xenia* that resonates with Helen's story for the plot of *nostos* centered on the House of Atreus paradigm. Thus, Odysseus's return is acted out in the text as the welcoming into the house of an outsider—a kind of naturalization of the foreigner. Furthermore, since the plot of *xenia* is a close analogue and structural equivalent to that of *nostos*, the affinity between them also calls into question the relation between representation and reality, or, as Pucci refers to it, the connection between semblance and being (Pucci 1987:81–82). In other words, does Odysseus actually return home, or is it the case instead that a stranger who is exactly like Odysseus is incorporated into his household?

[1] See also Stewart 1976:103: "The question of recognition is a key to the meaning of the second half of the poem. . . ." Cf. also Starobinski 1975:345–48.

The popularization in film a few years ago of an incident in sixteenth-century Lyons played on this same trope, and the plot of this "real-life drama" centering on the figure of Martin Guerre was in some respects remarkably close to that of the *Odyssey*:

> The new Martin did not go straight to Artigat. As Le Sueur reported it, he went first to a hostelry at the next village, probably Pailhès. He told the hotelkeeper he was Martin Guerre and wept when his wife and family were mentioned. The word spread to his four sisters, who rushed to the inn, greeted him with delight, and went back for Bertrande [his wife]. When she saw him, however, she recoiled in surprise. Not until he had spoken to her affectionately, reminding her of things they had done and talked about, specifically mentioning the white hosen in the trunk, did she fall upon his neck and kiss him; it was his beard that had made him hard to recognize. (Davis 1983:42)

Martin was eventually declared an imposter and executed for fraud (ibid.:82–93). In the *Odyssey*, as I have argued, the concern is not so much with establishing the truth as such—which at one level is not in doubt—but with rendering problematic the relation between reality and disguise by focusing on the slippage between them.

For it is as a *xeinos* that Odysseus first establishes his claim to the *oikos* of Odysseus, the only question being whether he is a "wretched one of strangers" (δειλὲ ξείνων, 21.287), a "stranger and beggar" (ξεῖνος καὶ πτωχὸς, 21.292), a "wandering beggar" (πτωχὸς ἀνὴρ ἀλαλήμενος, 21.327), and a "wanderer experienced in evil things" (κακῶν ἔμπαιος ἀλήτης, 21.400), as the suitors think, or a "big, solid man, and he claims to be the son by birth of a noble father" (μάλα μὲν μέγας ἠδ' εὐπηγής, / πατρὸς δ' ἐξ ἀγαθοῦ γένος εὔχεται ἔμμεναι υἱός, 21.334–35), as Penelope's keener insight leads her to believe. When Odysseus shoots through the axes, he is still in disguise, and so he claims victory as "Telemachus's *xeinos*" (Τηλέμαχ', οὔ σ' ὁ ξεῖνος ἐνὶ μεγάροισιν ἐλέγχει / ἥμενος, 21.424–25) and goes on as the stranger (ξεῖνε, 22.27) to kill Antinous as an act of simple murder (φόνος, 22.11), rather than of revenge (οὐδέ κεν ὣς ἔτι χεῖρας ἐμὰς / λήξαιμι φόνοιο, / πρὶν πᾶσαν μνηστῆρας ὑπερβασίην ἀποτεῖσαι, 22.63–64).[2]

Thus, when Odysseus announces his return, this revelation is not so much a replacement of disguise with truth, of semblance with substance, as it is a convergence of the persona of the *xeinos* with that of Odysseus, of the *xeinos* with the *kyrios*. He proclaims, "You dogs, you kept on saying that I would never come back home!" (ὦ κύνες, οὔ μ' ἔτ' ἐφάσκεθ' ὑπότρο-

---

[2] Houston (1975) observes that Odysseus rises from a *diphros* (ordinary chair; 21.420) to shoot through the axes, but returns to sit down upon a *thronos* (seat occupied in the Homeric poems only by persons of high rank; 21.434).

που οἴκαδε νεῖσθαι, 22.35). He goes on as Odysseus to shoot the arrows that as a *xeinos* he had just let fly, and to slay as Odysseus the second leader of the suitors (Eurymachus), whose first leader (Antinous) he had killed as the *xeinos*. We recall that Telemachus had first claimed to be host with the permission of both Antinous and Eurymachus (18.65), and Fenik has shown in detail how these two suitors operate as character doublets in the poem (Fenik 1974:198–207). So in one respect Odysseus's slaughter of Eurymachus replicates or doubles his killing of Antinous, with the difference that he is the *xeinos* in the first instance and Odysseus in the second.

Duplicity or doubling in the plot, then, is resolved, as we shall see in this chapter, through the convergence of the absent "host" with the present "guest"—in other words, through the conflation of the *kyrios* or "insider," whose condition or attribute is that of *outsider*, with the *xeinos* or "outsider," whose condition or attribute is that of *insider*.

Telemachus, too, I have argued, is characterized by duplicity in that he adopts a kind of disguise, but one which is at the opposite end of the spectrum from that of Odysseus, since Telemachus "pretends" to be just who he in fact is—the son of Odysseus, born of his blood (16.300), and thus entitled to replace him as *kyrios* of the *oikos* in the way that Odysseus had replaced Laertes, and Laertes, presumably, Arcesius. This form of "duplicity," literally rendered, entails Telemachus's representation as Odysseus's double, and this is in fact a well-recognized feature of his characterization in the poem (see e.g., Clarke 1967:30–44; Apthorp 1980; Jones 1988; Austin 1969),[3] one that I discussed briefly above in Chapters Three and Five. In Telemachus's case, then, semblance and being are never fully disjoint, and this aspect of the narrative calls attention to the capacity of disguise not simply to misrepresent reality, but also to bring it into being.

Thus, Telemachus himself claims, from the beginning to the end of the poem, to be the one to whom the *kratos* ("authority") in the *oikos* belongs (τοῦ γὰρ κράτος ἔστ' ἐνὶ οἴκῳ, 21.353 = 1.359). But it is only as a fiction that he is represented in this capacity, for Odysseus's presence, as we have seen, both authorizes Telemachus's assumption of this role and denies it authenticity. Nevertheless, the disguise itself proves to be efficacious, and so at the point when Telemachus's enactment of the *role* of *kyrios* is about to converge with the reality of his *being* the *kyrios*—when he is about to string the bow (21.129)—he desists, deferring to the authority of the father. Now Telemachus disguises himself as one who is "wretched" (*kakos*), "feeble" (*akikus*), and "too young" (*neoteros*; 21.131–32), and thus his very adequacy to the role of Odysseus's son and heir is represented in the nar-

---

[3] Austin especially has demonstrated how Telemachus's ability to master the strategies of disguise and revelation is an important feature of his assimilation to the role of adult male in the poem (Austin 1969:54ff.).

rative as its displacement by the fiction of its nonexistence. In other words, when the fiction of Telemachus's ability to replace Odysseus as *kyrios* of the *oikos* is on the verge of realization, it is now itself replaced by the fiction of his incapacity to do so.

The resolution of Telemachus's disguise in the poem is effected through his representation as Odysseus's equal, as is shown especially in the poem's final episode. There Telemachus fights alongside his father as the equal in strength to him that he had earlier pretended not to be. By the same token, Odysseus arouses Telemachus's martial vigor in the end of the poem by reminding him of his sameness with him:

> Τηλέμαχ', ἤδη μὲν τόδε γ' εἴσεαι αὐτὸς ἐπελθών,
> ἀνδρῶν μαρναμένων ἵνα τε κρίνονται ἄριστοι,
> μή τι καταισχύνειν πατέρων γένος, οἳ τὸ πάρος περ
> ἀλκῇ τ' ἠνορέῃ τε κεκάσμεθα πᾶσαν ἐπ' αἶαν.

> (Telemachus, as you yourself will know as you go forth,
> where the best are distinguished among the fighting men,
> do not bring shame upon the race of our fathers, since always before
> we have been superior in manly strength over all the earth.)

(24.506–9)

Telemachus acknowledges the equation of his prowess with that of his father and male progenitors (24.510–12), and he and Odysseus go on to fight alongside one another: "And Odysseus and his shining son fell upon their first ranks . . . and they would have slaughtered them all and rendered them devoid of homecoming . . ." (ἐν δ' ἔπεσον προμάχιοσ' Ὀδυσεὺς καὶ φαίδιμος υἱός . . . καί νύ κε δὴ πάντας ὄλεσαν καὶ θῆκαν ἀνόστους, 24.526, 528).

By contrast, Telemachus's claim to assume *kyrieia* over Penelope—his disguise, that is, as her *kyrios*—is fully abandoned in the poem. When Telemachus reproaches her as "bad mother" (δύσμητερ, 23.97) for her failure to recognize and accept her husband, Penelope reminds him gently of the exclusivity of the relationship between husband and wife (see the discussion below), and Odysseus ratifies her view by turning Telemachus's attention from his mother to those matters which he and his son *do* have in common: "[Your mother] will think this through better presently" (τάχα δὲ φράσεται καὶ ἄρειον, 23.114); "let us together think how [other] matters might come out best" (ἡμεῖς δὲ φραζώμεθ', ὅπως ὄχ' ἄριστα γένηται, 23.117); "this [the dead suitors lying in the halls] is what I tell you to give thought to" (τὰ δέ σε φράζεσθαι ἄνωγα, 23.122). It is significant, however, that Telemachus's representation in the *Odyssey* as Penelope's potential *kyrios* is kept alive in the tradition, and appears in the *Telegony* as the story that Telegonus, Odysseus's son by Circe, killed his father and married Penelope afterwards, and that Telemachus married Circe (Eugammon, *Telegonia* [Allen, *Hom. Op.* vol. V, 109:23–27] cf. Griffin 1977:42; Monro 1901:382–83; cf. also Merkelbach 1969:142–55).

The duplicities of the alternative and substitute plots, as well as that of Telemachus's characterization, are directly tied to indeterminacies that are part of the poem's mise-en-scène: those of Odysseus's whereabouts and Telemachus's maturity. These uncertainties are resolved at the end of the narrative. But the most complex representation of duplicity in the *Odyssey*—that having to do with Penelope—is tied to an indeterminacy in the narrative which is not ever fully settled. For the uncertainty of Penelope's sociological status is generalized within the narrative to encompass her actions, their meaning, and their relation to her intentions. And while Penelope's sociological status is clarified in Book 23, this does not serve to dispel the more generalized form of indeterminacy that characterizes her representation in the poem. This indeterminacy is in fact, as I shall argue, incorporated into her *kleos* in the end.

As we have seen, Penelope's self-presentation in the *Odyssey* is organized around a set of contradictory and complementary scenarios by which one outcome or intention is suggested while at the same time its actualization in the text is consistently inhibited. I have argued that this textual strategy is not simply a matter of ambiguity, or of its psychological correlate, indecision, but rather that it is a narrative device analogous to the trope of disguise. Penelope, to be sure, does not in the course of the poem ever adopt a disguise in the manner of Odysseus, nor is her identity as such ever concealed or withheld, like that of Telemachus in Books 3 and 4. And I am not suggesting, as Murnaghan does, that Penelope, Telemachus, Laertes, and Eumaeus undergo a "genuine experience of . . . powerlessness . . . and lowered social status . . . [which] take[s] on the character of disguises because they prove reversible and . . . are removed with the revelation of [Odysseus's] return" (1987:25). My argument is constructed around the roles that Telemachus and Penelope assume as a result of Odysseus's disguised *presence*, rather than of his "actual" absence, and around the empowering effect of disguise, rather than its function as a token of helplessness.

Thus, although Penelope is never "disguised" or "revealed" as such in the narrative, nevertheless the character of her "duplicity" in the text is altered in the course of Book 23, with the result that she is brought into close alignment with Odysseus. In this way a complementarity between Odysseus and Penelope comes to be substituted in Book 23 for the duplicity of Odysseus's disguise and for the duplicity of Penelope's divided mind. As Hölscher puts it: "Here [in the recognition scene of Book 23] Penelope has thoroughly taken over the character of Odysseus: she is the cautious, the suspicious, the devious one. From that insight one can conclude that everything happens for the sake of this scene and for this plot and that the characters must from time to time accommodate themselves to it. The scene type has developed from the character of Odysseus, but it transfers this character now to Penelope" (1939:74).[4]

This complementarity, as Foley's analysis of reverse similes and Austin's discussion of *homophrosynē* ("like-mindedness") have shown, is signaled in various ways throughout the narrative (Foley 1978; Austin 1975:205–38),[5] but it is not brought into being as such until Book 23. In the first part of this chapter I discuss the construction of this complementarity, and I go on in the second half of the chapter to interpret the resulting *homophrosynē* as part of what I call the *Odyssey*'s ideology of exclusivity. I conclude with a discussion of the *Odyssey*'s construction of its own *mythos* against the examples of Helen and Clytemnestra.

Duplicity and Complementarity

The discourse with Eurycleia at the beginning of Book 23 (23.1–84) replicates and inverts a recognition scene, and it is followed immediately by the recognition scene proper (23.85–230). Recognition scenes in the *Odyssey* typically follow a sequence of doubt, proof, and embrace: "In their typical form, the *Odyssey*'s recognition scenes . . . involve a process of identification and testing leading to emotionally-charged reunions, which are experienced in gestures of physical union . . ." (Murnaghan 1987:22).[6] This pattern occurs in the recognitions by Telemachus (16.172ff.) and by Eumaeus and Philoetius (21.203ff.), and there is a similar pattern in the recognitions by Laertes (24.321ff.) and Dolius (24.386ff.).[7]

The awakening scene at the beginning of Book 23, whose structure Schadewaldt has analyzed in detail (1970c:64–65),[8] is composed of

---

[4] "Penelope hat hier durchaus den Charakter des Odysseus bekommen, sie ist die Vorsichtige, Misstrauische, Listenreiche. Man kann daraus sehen, dass alles um der Szene und der Handlung willen geschieht, die Charaktere sich zuweilen ihr fügen mussen. Der Typ der Szene hat sich aus dem Charakter des Odysseus entwickelt, gibt aber diesen Charakter jetzt an Penelope weiter."

[5] See also the remarks of Thornton: "Penelope's unbelief is . . . a consistent feature of her character. . . . Penelope is certainly much in need of this quality in order to protect herself and her loyalty to Odysseus; and she is a worthy partner for him in her exercise of it" (1970:105).

[6] On this aspect of the recognition scenes of the *Odyssey*, see also Erbse 1972:55–109.

[7] The Dolius recognition does not explicitly narrate an episode of doubt and proof, but its function is played in this case by stunned hesitation (οἱ δ' . . . ἔσταν ἐνὶ μεγάροισι τεθηπότες, 24.391, 392) and reassurance (αὐτὰρ Ὀδυσσεὺς / μειλιχίοισ' ἐπέεσσι καθαπτόμενος προσέειπεν, 24.392–93).

[8] Schadewaldt interprets the scene as a foreshadowing of the recognition scene proper, arguing that its development demonstrates an analogous fluctuation of doubt and belief culminating in an approximation of Penelope's position to that of Eurycleia (ibid.; cf. also Erbse 1972:55–57).

four episodes: (1) Eurycleia's excited announcement of Odysseus's return and slaughter of the suitors, followed by Penelope's skeptical expressions of disbelief (23.1–24); (2) Eurycleia's insistence that the *xeinos* is Odysseus, followed by Penelope's joyful acceptance of the news and embrace (23.25–38); (3) Eurycleia's full account of the events of Book 22, followed by a renewal of Penelope's skepticism (23.39–68); and (4) Eurycleia's further insistence, to which she now adds the proof of the scar, followed by Penelope's dismissal of her claims and decision to descend into the *megaron* to see Telemachus and the "one who killed [the suitors]" (23.69–84).

This scene follows the sequence doubt, proof, embrace; doubt, proof, refusal to extend recognition. Thus, here the *anagnōrismos* is doubled, with the effect that it is given once, in a tearful embrace, and it is withheld once. For, following the tearful embrace of Eurycleia, Penelope requests proof of the already accepted report, in contrast to the other recognition scenes, in which the *sēma* of the scar, or, in the case of Telemachus, assurances concerning divine assistance, precede the tearful embrace.[9] In Book 23, by contrast, Eurycleia's account following the embrace is unconvincing, and Penelope begins to doubt again, sure now that it is a case of divine intervention—a parallel to Telemachus's expression of doubt in Book 16, which had preceded the tearful embrace: "You are certainly not Odysseus my father, but a god is bewitching me so that I may weep and groan even more" (οὐ σύ γ' Ὀδυσσεύς ἐσσι, πατὴρ ἐμός, ἀλλά με δαίμων / θέλγει, ὄφρ' ἔτι μᾶλλον ὀδυρόμενος στεναχίζω, 16.194–95). It is at this point that Eurycleia proffers the evidence of the scar, the *sēma* by which Eumaeus, Philoetius, and Laertes are convinced. But Penelope appears to dismiss this proof, and agrees to descend into the *megaron* only in order to see her son, the slain suitors, and "the one who killed them" (ἀλλ' ἔμπης ἴομεν μετὰ παῖδ' ἐμόν, ὄφρα ἴδωμαι / ἄνδρας μνηστῆρας τεθνηότας, ἠδ' ὅς ἔπεφνεν, 23.83–84).

In the first section of the scene, the recognition as such is displaced onto Eurycleia. As Murnaghan remarks, "At *Od.* 23.32–34, where for a moment Penelope accepts the news of Odysseus' return, this embrace is displaced from Odysseus to his messenger Eurycleia" (1987:22 n. 4). Thus, Penelope initially accepts Eurycleia's report, and embraces her and weeps as Telemachus had done in his *anagnōrismos*:

ὣς ἄρα φωνήσας κατ' ἄρ' ἕζετο, Τηλέμαχος δὲ
ἀμφιχυθεὶς πατέρ' ἐσθλὸν ὀδύρετο δάκρυα λείβων.

(Thus having spoken, he sat down, and Telemachus, embracing his noble father, wept and shed tears.)

(16.213–14)

---

[9] Müller regards the miraculous transformation of Odysseus as the equivalent of a *sēma* (1966:109–10); cf. also Kearns 1982:4.

ὣς ἔφαθ', ἡ δ' ἐχάρη καὶ ἀπὸ λέκτροιο θοροῦσα
γρηὶ περιπλέχθη, βλεφάρων δ' ἀπὸ δάκρυον ἧκε

(Thus she spoke, and [Penelope] rejoiced and, leaping up from her bed, embraced the old woman, and let fall the tears from her eyelids.)

(23.32–33)

The displacement of the recognition onto Eurycleia in Book 23 renders the scene as a whole analogous to the foot-washing scene of Book 19, in which the expected recognition of Odysseus by Penelope is displaced onto Eurycleia, and in which Eurycleia's expressions of joy similarly provoke a response of displeasure and threats of violence (cf. 19.480, 488–90 with 23.21–24). In the foot-washing scene Eurycleia had assumed Penelope's role; in the awakening scene Penelope plays the part of Odysseus—greeting Eurycleia's expression of joy with the threat of violence. This is the first stage, then, of the transformation of duplicity into complementarity, and the consolidation of Penelope's character as stubborn, hard-hearted, and devious, like Odysseus's own.

In Book 23, the displacement of the *anagnōrismos* onto Eurycleia functions in two different ways on two different levels of the poem. On the structural level, it resumes the narrative action where it was interrupted in Book 19, and thereby endows the reunion of Penelope and Odysseus with elements drawn from the scenarios of both *xenia* and *anagnōrismos*. This aspect of the reunion has to do with what I call the poem's ideology of exclusivity, which I discuss below. On the surface of the text, the displacement of the *anagnōrismos* onto Eurycleia also allows Penelope to descend into the *megaron* knowing who Odysseus is without having acknowledged it explicitly. This has implications for the resolution within the text of other thematic issues; in particular, it makes possible the incorporation within the *anagnōrismos* of elements drawn from the scenario of betrayal.

When Penelope descends into the *megaron*, she debates, in one of the rare episodes in the poem where the inner workings of her mind are described, "whether standing apart to question her dear husband closely" (ἢ ἀπάνευθε φίλον πόσιν ἐξερεείνοι," 23.86), or "whether standing close she should kiss his head and clasp his hands" (ἢ παρστᾶσα κύσειε κάρη καὶ χεῖρε λαβοῦσα, 23.87). Penelope's state of mind here recuperates the narrative action of the awakening scene. For there Penelope had both joyfully welcomed the news of Odysseus's return and suspiciously questioned the report. Now, these double and contradictory actions appear in the narrative posed as alternatives. Thus, a link is established here, as elsewhere in the poem, between the narrative action and Penelope's state of mind.

There is a further function to this new, doubled state of mind. For the debate whether to welcome Odysseus or to withhold recognition now replaces for Penelope the dilemma that had dominated Books 18–21, whether to remain by her son and guard the house, or whether to marry "the best of the Achaeans." This represents the second stage, then, in the transformation of duplicity into complementarity, namely, the replacement of one set of alternatives, in which Odysseus is either awaited or abandoned, by another, in which he is either welcomed or not accepted. This alternative for Penelope complements Odysseus's initial dilemma whether to proceed home forthwith or to put his wife to the test (13.333–38), which is resolved in favor of the latter course of action (16.301–8), but which is recapitulated anew in the approach to Laertes (24.235–40). For Penelope, the alternative of withholding recognition has now also replaced that of failing to recognize, which had provided the basis for a decision to remarry. But when Penelope continues to withhold recognition (see esp. ἀγνώσασκε, "kept on not recognizing" in line 95), Telemachus reproaches her for her hard-heartedness:

> οὐ μέν κ' ἄλλη γ' ὧδε γυνὴ τετληότι θυμῷ
> ἀνδρὸς ἀποσταίη, ὅς οἱ κακὰ πολλὰ μογήσας
> ἔλθοι ἐεικοστῷ ἔτεϊ ἐς πατρίδα γαῖαν·
> σοὶ δ' αἰεὶ κραδίη στερεωτέρη ἐστὶ λίθοιο.

(No other woman would [have] such a stubborn spirit
as to hold aloof from her husband, who after toiling through
   many wretched labors
had come back to her in the twentieth year into his fatherland;
but the heart within you is always harder than stone.)

(23.100–103)

This speech parallels Odysseus's own initial hesitation to approach his family, for which Athena had rebuked him in similar terms: "Any other man who returned home after wandering would hasten to the welcoming sight of his wife and children" (13.333–34).[10] This, then, is another of the points at which the figure of Penelope is brought into conformity with that of Odysseus, and it is thus the second stage in the development of the complementarity between them.

There is, however, another function to Penelope's reticence here. Odysseus's hesitation in Book 13, as we saw earlier, was developed against the House of Atreus motif, which was explicitly evoked in the earlier context. And we can observe that although Odysseus had more to fear from the suitors, Athena had nevertheless attributed his hesitation solely to the desire to test his wife (13.336ff.).

---

[10] Cf. Hölscher's remark concerning Penelope's "hard-heartedness" throughout the recognition scene: "That it is a typical scene for the *Odyssey* . . . is clear from a comparison with a very similar scene in Book 13" (1939:74).

Here, in Book 23, Penelope's reticence takes on the character, as Telemachus (and later Odysseus, 23.168–72) sees it, of hard-heartedness: "The heart within you is always harder than stone" (σοὶ δ' αἰεὶ κραδίη στερεωτέρη ἐστὶ λίθοιο, 23.103). Penelope here, then, is playing a role similar to that of Clytemnestra, the paradigm of the wife who refuses to welcome her husband home. We can compare Agamemnon's complaint that "the bitch turned her back on me" (ἡ δὲ κυνῶπις / νοσφίσατ', 11.424–25) as he was dying, with Telemachus's impatient demand: "Mother mine, unmother, woman with an unyielding heart, why do you turn away from father so?" (μῆτερ ἐμή, δύσμητερ, ἀπηνέα θυμὸν ἔχουσα, / τίφθ' οὕτω πατρὸς νοσφίζεαι, 23.97–98). As we observed earlier, Agamemnon had focused in his speech in the first *nekyia* on the element of personal and emotional betrayal,[11] alleging against Clytemnestra her failure to perform funeral rites for him, to welcome him warmly, and to grant him the sight of his son.

Here, the coldness of Penelope's welcome upon Odysseus's homecoming provides an associative link with her negative exemplar. And this association, like the celebration of the fictional wedding and the trick of the bed discussed below, configures the *anagnōrismos* in the text as if it were a betrayal. The transformation of duplicity into complementarity for Penelope, then, is configured in part around the duplicity that characterizes Odysseus, but it incorporates also those aspects of *dolos*, *mētis*, and inflexibility which are associated with Clytemnestra and, consequently, with the alternative of Penelope's betrayal. Thus, both Telemachus and Odysseus, in reproaching Penelope for her stubborn refusal to welcome Odysseus, refer to the same "hard-heartedness" (τετληότι θυμῷ, 23.168=23.100) with which Odysseus clung to the underside of the ram in Book 9 (9.435) and endured the insults of the suitors (18.135, 24.163), and which, in its many guises, makes up one of his principal epithets (πολύτλας δῖος Ὀδυσσεύς).[12]

Similarly, Odysseus concludes his expressions of exasperation with Penelope's stubbornness by exclaiming to Eurycleia about her: "For indeed the heart in her mind is iron" (ἦ γὰρ τῇ γε σιδήρεον ἐν φρεσὶν ἦτορ, 23.172). The situation resonates with an earlier one where, in the face of Penelope's tearful expressions of anguish, Odysseus's own eyes "stayed still under his eyelids, as if they were horn or iron" (ὀφθαλμοὶ δ' ὡς εἰ κέρα ἕστασαν ἠὲ σίδηρος / ἀτρέμας ἐν βλεφάροισι, 19.211–12). In Book 19, Odysseus conceals his own feelings, as the text reports it, by means of *dolos* (δόλῳ δ' ὅ γε δάκρυα κεῦθεν, 19.212). But it is significant that, in Penel-

---

[11] Such that, to at least one commentator, the adultery and murder seemed downplayed by comparison (Wender 1978:41).

[12] The formulaic phrase τετληότι θυμῷ has a positive valence for Penelope, too, and characterizes the steadfastness with which she waits for Odysseus in 11.181 (= 16.37).

ope's case, although the text invites us to assume the operation of similar impulses, it does not identify them as such. This textual reserve parallels Penelope's own, and its effect is to withhold from the audience outside of the poem as from Odysseus within it any certainty regarding Penelope's thoughts and motives.

Odysseus attempts to counter this indeterminacy by converting Penelope's "stubborn heart" from an attitude of the moment into an attribute that makes her an exemplar among women; thus, he attempts to endow her behavior here with paradigmatic force: "Especially in you of all female women have the gods who hold Olympus placed a stubborn heart" (περὶ σοί γε γυναικῶν θηλυτεράων / κῆρ ἀτέραμνον ἔθηκαν Ὀλύμπια δώματ' ἔχοντες, 23.166–67). This figuration, in turn, implies that this is the decisive moment, the point in the poem at which Penelope's *kleos* will be fixed. When this does occur, through the trick of the bed, Penelope's *kleos* as the faithful wife is guaranteed through the fiction of betrayal. Thus, the concern with fictionality in the *Odyssey*, and the commitment of the text overall to the principle of indeterminacy, is such that even the final moment of truth in the narrative is structured ambiguously.[13]

This final moment of duplicity is also structured as an actual "doubling" of Odysseus's words by Penelope, and this device operates as a formal sign of the complementarity between them. Erbse remarks on this scene: "Penelope now has . . . two possibilities: she could, if she should still doubt his identity, ask the question that would trap him; or she could say to the stranger that she thinks he is Odysseus. . . . In the second case, of course, the scar could indeed still be mentioned, but it would not be the crucial element in the anagnorisis. The poet chose to take neither of these two paths, but rather found a third possibility: in conjunction with the words just cited he allows Penelope . . . to pick up on the order that Odysseus directed at Eurycleia and to instruct the nurse to prepare Odysseus's bed outside of the bedchamber . . ." (1972:69).[14]

Odysseus had opened his speech with a direct address to Penelope, but at its close he speaks of her in the third person, a shift modulated by an aside to Eurycleia: "Come, my nurse, spread out a bed for me, where I

---

[13] As Pucci remarks concerning this scene, "Penelope's recognition [is] effected by a representation of Odysseus as dispossessed of what determines his identity as husband and lord of the house" (1987:93).

[14] "Penelope hat nun . . . zwei Möglichkeiten: Sie könnte, falls sie an der Identität noch immer zweifeln würde, die Fangfrage stellen, oder die könnte dem Fremden sagen, dass sie ihn für Odysseus halte. . . . Im zweiten Fall könnte das Zeichen zwar noch erwähnt werden, aber es würde den Ausschlag bei der Agagnorisis nicht geben. Der Dichter hat keinen dieser Wege eingeschlagen, sondern eine dritte Möglichkeit gefunden: Er lässt Penelope im Anschluss an die zuletzt ausgeschriebenen Worte . . . die Anordnung, welche Odysseus an Eurykleia gerichtet hat, aufgreifen und der Amme Weisung geben, Odysseus' Bett aus dem Schlafgemach zu schaffen. . . ."

myself will lie down" (ἀλλ' ἄγε μοι, μαῖα, στόρεσον λέχος, ὄφρα καὶ αὐτὸς / λέξομαι, 23.171–72). Penelope's reply follows the same pattern, opening with a direct address, and shifting to Eurycleia. In addressing Eurycleia, Penelope picks up Odysseus's own line: "Come, spread out a thick bed for him, Eurycleia" (ἀλλ' ἄγε οἱ στόρεσον πυκινὸν λέχος, Εὐρύκλεια, 23.177), she instructs, adding the details that provoke Odysseus's revelation of the *mega sēma*. Erbse remarks on this "Übereinstimmung" in defending the authenticity of the passage: "Against the assumption of an interpolation speaks, not least of all, the correspondence in the disposition of the speeches at 23.166–172 and 174–180" (1972:70–71).[15] For Penelope, then, the transformation of duplicity into complementarity incorporates elements of characterization that stress her affinity with Odysseus, but these same characteristics also associate her with Clytemnestra, and endow the *anagnōrismos* with ambiguity.

The Wedding Digression (23.117–73)

Telemachus's rebuke provokes an intervention by Odysseus that interrupts the recognition and leads to the plan to celebrate the fictional wedding. This digression has been the center of interpretive contention between neoanalytic and unitarian interpreters. Schadewaldt regards this whole segment of the *Odyssey* as a test case for his construction of a "positivsynthetischen Analyse," much as Merkelbach had based his own more traditional analytic approach to the text on the disjunction between Books 18 and 19 (see above, Chapter Four). For Schadewaldt, the recognition scene of Book 23 is a section "which, in its current state of preservation, may well represent the most fundamental basis for an analysis of the *Odyssey*" (Schadewaldt 1970c:62).[16]

Schadewaldt's argument is based principally upon his analysis of the recognition scene as an "Übereckgespräch" (crosswise dialogue") among Telemachus, Odysseus, and Penelope, followed by a "Reizgespräch" ("flirtatious dialogue") between Odysseus and Penelope, each of which he interprets as "a dialogue of a very special fixed form" and the second of which he compares to a ball game (Schadewaldt 1970c:66–67).[17] Schad-

---

[15] "Gegen die Annahme einer Interpolation zeugt nicht zuletzt auch die Übereinstimmung in der Disposition der Reden 23.166–172 und 174–180."

[16] "Zu diesem Zweck sei die Wiedererkennung des Odysseus mit Penelope im dreiundzwanzigsten Gesang der Odysee herausgegriffen, die in ihrem gegenwärtigen überlieferten Zustand wohl als die grundlegendste Fundamentalstelle einer Analyse der Odysee gelten mag."

[17] A simile on which Schadewaldt does not fail to follow through: for example, "What is broken up by that digression of over fifty versus is the fixed form of that flirtatious dialogue, the ball game of the two spouses" (1970c:68); "the ... intolerable breaking apart of the fixed form of the flirtatious dialogue, which brings it about that the ball thrown by Odysseus to

ewaldt argues that the digression in which Odysseus and Telemachus plan their defense, the two arrange for the fictional marriage celebration, and Odysseus is bathed and transformed (lines 117–72) intrudes into this structure. When the recognition scene is purged of this digression, it complements fully, in Schadewaldt's view, the "rigid and at once organic structure" of the exchange with Eurycleia that opens the book (ibid.:64–65; citation p. 65; for further discussion from the analytic point of view, see Page 1955:114–15).

A number of critics have argued against Schadewaldt's reading of this scene and have defended a unitarian interpretation of the recognition in Book 23. Fenik, for example, has shown that the scene is an example of an interruption sequence, which is "a standard Homeric, and especially Odyssean, scene type" (Fenik 1974:64–65, 68–69, 98, 104; citation p. 104). But the most convincing arguments, in my view, are brought forward by Besslich (1966:83–96; cf. Erbse 1972:55–72; Eisenberger 1973:303–13), who demonstrates that the two parts of Odysseus's speech to Telemachus at the beginning of the suspected passage are "inseparably connected gramatically," and also directs attention to the efficacious aspects of the representations in the scene of Odysseus as "father of his son and master of his house" (Besslich 1966:90).

Besslich, who regards the digression as a "Zwischenstück" ("connecting piece") between Books 23 and 24,[18] argues that both the exchange with Telemachus and the celebration of the fictional marriage operate to constitute the relation of Odysseus with his wife, and that Penelope's silent presence throughout is a functional part of the scene: "Her [Penelope's] silent presence is the background against which everything takes place" (1966:94). Thus, Penelope comes to recognize Odysseus as her husband in a series of stages, in the first of which his relationship with Telemachus functions to mediate his relationship with her. "For Penelope her son is the only true certainty. He is, so to speak, reality's end, which she holds in her hands; and his behavior toward the stranger, the natural recognition of his authority, 'authorizes' him as the father, as Odysseus" (ibid.:88–89).[19]

Penelope remains in the air for over fifty-five verses" (ibid.:69). Cf. Besslich, who prefers to interpret Odysseus's words in 23.115–16 to the effect that Penelope withholds recognition because he is ragged and blood-spattered, as a " 'Seitenhieb' " rather than "Ballwurf" (1966:94).

[18] The "Zwischenstück" ("connecting piece") is in Besslich's view a particular theme and phenomenon in Homeric poetry, and he analyzes a number of parallel instances in both the *Iliad* and the *Odyssey* otherwise regarded as "Einschuben" ("intrusions"), in which he argues that "the silence of the person is made manifest [i.e., meaningful] . . . through an interposed event" (1966:97–119; citation p. 97). Compare Fenik (1974: 64–65, 68–69, 98, 104) on the scene as an example of the "interruption sequence."

[19] "Der Sohn ist für Penelope die einzige und eigentliche Gewissheit, er is sozusagen das Ende der Wirklichkeit, das sie in Händen hat; und sein Verhalten gegenüber dem 'Fremden,'

This is particularly true of the complimentary and deferential words that Telemachus addresses to his father following the first part of the digression:

> αὐτὸς ταῦτά γε λεῦσσε, πάτερ φίλε· σὴν γὰρ ἀρίστην
> μῆτιν ἐπ' ἀνθρώπους φάσ' ἔμμεναι, οὐδέ κέ τίς τοι
> ἄλλος ἀνὴρ ἐρίσειε καταθνητῶν ἀνθρώπων.
>
> (You yourself look to these things, dear father; for they say that yours
> is the best *mētis* among men, and that no other man
> among mortal men could contest with you in this regard.)
>
> (23.124–26)

Similarly, arranging for the fictional marriage not only gives Odysseus the opportunity in Penelope's presence to exert his authority as master of his house ("sich als Hausherr zu führen" [Besslich 1966:89]), but also allows him under the same conditions to become transformed from the beggar and stranger who was forced to follow orders into the *kyrios* of the *oikos* who issues them (ibid.).

The fictional marriage itself functions to deceive the outside world and postpone inquiries about the suitors. It is also, however, and more importantly, constitutive of the relationship between Odysseus and Penelope: "The thought . . . of creating a marriage scene is . . . not *only* a ruse, and deception, but it also contains truth: what is begun and prepared there *is* a kind of marriage, is remarriage" (Besslich 1966:89; emphasis in the original).[20] Segal too remarks that Odysseus "is indeed celebrating a wedding, in a sense," and he comments as well on the ironic function of the song in this episode (Segal 1983:44–45; citation p. 44; cf. also Pucci 1987:91). It is worth noting in this connection that, as we remarked above in Chapter Five, intimacy between man and woman in traditional societies characteristically follows rather than precedes marriage, and so Penelope's silence until after the "wedding" replicates the conventional sequence of events.

There is another aspect to this episode in the poem on which commentators remark less frequently–its representation also as the fictional enactment of what amounts to Penelope's betrayal of Odysseus:

> ὧδε δέ τις εἴπεσκε δόμων ἔκτοσθεν ἀκούων·
> "ἦ μάλα δή τις ἔγημε πολυμνήστην βασίλειαν·
> σχετλίη, οὐδ' ἔτλη πόσιος οὗ κουριδίοιο
> εἴρυσθαι μέγα δῶμα διαμπερές, εἷος ἵκοιτο."

---

die selbstverständliche Anerkennung von dessen Autorität 'autorisiert' diesen als den Vater, als Odysseus."

[20] "Der Gedanke . . . eine Hochzeitsszene aufzubauen, ist . . . nicht *nur* List und Täuschung, er enthält auch Wahrheit: Was sich da anbahnt und vorbereitet, *ist* eine Art Hochzeit, ist Wiedervermählung."

(And so someone hearing from outside the house would say:
"Indeed someone has married our much-courted queen;
The wretch! She did not hold out [for the sake] of her wedded husband,
to protect the great house [for him] all the way to the end, until he should return.")

(23.148–51)

These words constitute the "public rumor" alluded to earlier by both Telemachus and Penelope (δήμοιο φῆμις, 16.75 = 19.527); we can observe here especially the use of the iterative aorist εἴπεσκε ("would [repeatedly] say") in 23.148. Earlier, concern for "what people will say," along with respect for her husband's bed, had kept Penelope from remarriage: "Respecting her husband's bed and the voice of the people" (εὐνήν τ' αἰδομένη πόσιος δήμοιό τε φῆμιν, 16.75 = 19.527). Now, the "public rumor" is reported as if Penelope had remarried, and thus it functions as part of the final stage of the incorporation into the narrative of the alternative of Penelope's betrayal. Penelope's hesitation to recognize Odysseus, then, is developed in the narrative as if it actually were that which it has replaced, the decision to remarry and thereby betray him. As I remarked above, it is a particular feature of the consolidation of Penelope's *kleos* in the poem that the recognition itself of Odysseus is constituted as a betrayal—first through the association of Penelope's refusal to recognize him with Clytemnestra's cold rejection of Agamemnon, and then through the enactment of the fiction of Penelope's remarriage.

By its attribution to a hypothetical casual passerby, this alternative of betrayal is displaced from the inside of the house to the outside (see especially ἐκτὸς ἀκούων in 23.135 and δόμων ἔκτοσθεν ἀκούων in 23.148) and is now construed as a misunderstanding of reality: "Thus, then, would someone say, but they did not know how it was in fact" (ὣς ἄρα τις εἴπεσκε, τὰ δ' οὐκ ἴσαν ὡς ἐτέτυκτο, 23.152). The slight anacoluthon involved in the change of subject from the singular "someone" to the plural "they" effectively generalizes a casual and idiosyncratic reaction to the public world at large.

Telemachus and the household servants are also displaced from the scene of reunion to elsewhere inside the house by the fictional marriage, as Erbse and others note: "The so-called digression offered . . . yet a further advantage: the discreet removal of Telemachus [from the scene]" (1972:67; cf. Büchner 1940:158).[21] In this way, the participants in the moment of privacy between Odysseus and Penelope are reduced to the minimum consistent with the demands of female modesty in traditional society—Odysseus, Penelope, and Eurycleia, the trusted serving-woman. This displacement to

---

[21] "Die sogenannte Digression bot . . . aber noch einen weiteren Vorteil: die unauffällige Entfernung Telemachs."

the outside of public opinion, along with the elimination from the *megaron* of both outsiders (the suitors) and insiders (Telemachus and the servants), should be regarded, in my view, not simply as a gesture of sentimentality, but rather as constitutive of what we might call the *Odyssey*'s ideology of exclusivity.

HOMOPHROSYNĒ, ANAGNŌRISMOS, AND THE IDEOLOGY OF EXCLUSIVITY

The *Odyssey*'s construction of the suitor's wooing of Penelope as a crime is a widely acknowledged aspect of the particularity of its vision, which has most often been discussed in connection with the notion of divine justice in the Homeric poems. From the analytic perspective, as is well known, the criminalization of the suitors' and companions' activities marks the consciousness of a humanistically oriented later poet; e.g.; "He [B] is a reflective man, moved by legal, religious, and moral problems. The more profound justification of the suitors' murder was his main concern" (Schadewaldt 1970c:72).[22] From the unitarian point of view, this same aspect of the poem is believed to derive from a necessary contradiction between the worlds of reality and fantasy (e.g., Fenik 1974:226–27), or to represent the resolution of a "double theodicy" through the transformation of Athena's wrath into "righteous indignation against the suitors" (Clay 1983:238).

This is not the place to take up in detail the large subjects of the suitors' crimes[23] and of the *Odyssey*'s view of justice and the gods.[24] I want here instead to draw attention to certain aspects of the narrative techniques by which the suitors' behavior is construed as criminal in the poem, and to discuss some of their implications. To begin with, the suitors' wooing of Penelope, and their attempted murder of Telemachus, are, as we have seen, represented in the text against the paradigm of Aegisthus. As Fenik remarks, the "dominant ethical categories [in the poem are] exemplified by the suitors' fate and the paradeigma of Aigisthus" (1974:211; cf. also West 1988:57, 60).

---

[22] "Er ist ein nachdenklicher Mann, bewegt von rechtlichen, religiösen, moralischen Problemen. Die tiefere Rechtfertigung des Freiermords wie auch des Untergangs der Gefährten des Odysseus war sein Hauptanliegen."

[23] For comprehensive recent surveys, see Said 1979 and Bader 1976; cf. also Levine 1982. And for the interesting, though idiosyncratic, idea that the criminalizing of the suitors' behavior represents the epic adaptation of a hypothetical folktale motif of the unjust guest, see Levy 1963. Cf. also Kearns's argument that the return of Odysseus is modelled on a folktale version of a theoxeny (1982).

[24] For further discussion and references, see Allione 1963:38–48; Schadewaldt 1970b; Fenik 1974:209–27; Bader 1976:32–33; Clay 1983:213–39; and Heubeck 1986:395 ad 24.482–85.

In addition, there are specific accusations of improbity or impropriety raised against the suitors' behavior, such as Ctesippus's sarcastic claim that "it is not right nor just to abuse the *xeinoi* of Telemachus" (οὐ γὰρ καλὸν ἀτέμβειν οὐδὲ δίκαιον / ξείνους Τηλεμάχου, 20.294–95), which is later echoed by Penelope (21.312–13 [= 20.294–95]), and these may represent generally accepted conventions of behavior. But the *Odyssey* also articulates a specific standard of conduct with regard to *xeinoi*, whose authorization it ascribes to Zeus; as Eumaeus, addressing the disguised Odysseus, explains it:

> ξεῖν', οὔ μοι θέμις ἔστ', οὐδ' εἰ κακίων σέθεν ἔλθοι,
> ξεῖνον ἀτιμῆσαι· πρὸς γὰρ Διός εἰσιν ἅπαντες
> ξεῖνοί τε πτωχοί τε.
>
> (Stranger, it is not right for me to dishonor a *xeinos*, not even if one more wretched than you came along, for all strangers and beggars are from Zeus.)
>
> (14.56–58)

Such statements, which appear elsewhere in the *Odyssey* as well, represent the normalization of the poem's own distinctive ethical code.

Finally, both Odysseus and Penelope—but no one else in the poem—accuse the suitors of improper behavior toward Penelope.[25] Penelope herself, when she appears before the suitors in Book 16, complains that the suitors are "dishonoring his [Odysseus's] house by consuming it, and you are wooing his wife, and you are trying to kill his son, and you are causing me great grief" (τοῦ νῦν οἶκον ἄτιμον ἔδεις, μνάᾳ δὲ γυναῖκα / παῖδά τ' ἀποκτείνεις, ἐμὲ δὲ μεγάλως ἀκαχίζεις, 16.431–32). Odysseus, when he reveals himself to the suitors and begins to slay them, claims:

> ὦ κύνες, οὔ μ' ἔτ' ἐφάσκεθ' ὑπότροπον οἴκαδε νεῖσθαι
> δήμου ἄπο Τρώων, ὅτι μοι κατεκείρετε οἶκον
> δμῳῆσιν δὲ γυναιξὶ παρευνάζεσθε βιαίως
> αὐτοῦ τε ζώοντος ὑπεμνάασθε γυναῖκα,
> οὔτε θεοὺς δείσαντες, οἳ οὐρανὸν εὐρὺν ἔχουσιν,
> οὔτε τιν' ἀνθρώπων νέμεσιν κατόπισθεν ἔσεσθαι.
>
> (You dogs, you kept on saying that I would never return home
> from the city of the Trojans, so that you ravaged my house
> and you slept alongside my serving-women by force,

---

[25] We should distinguish here what Penelope and Odysseus allege against the suitors from such judgments as that of Menelaus, who is outraged that the suitors, "being strengthless themselves" (ἀνάλκιδες αὐτοὶ ἐόντες, 4.334), should aspire to occupy the bed of "a man of [such] bold strength" (κρατερόφρονος ἀνδρός, 4.333), but does not regard their desires as criminal.

and while I was still alive you deviously courted my wife,
with no fear of the gods who hold the broad heaven,
nor that there might come after some vengeance from men.)

(22.35–40).

The construction of the wooing of Penelope as a crime is an innovation of the poem, and it is signaled as such by the *hapax hypemnaasthe* in 22.38, which the scholia explain as "secretly anticipated him, imperceptibly courted" (ὑπεφθείρετε, λεληθότως ἐμνηστεύεσθε, Schol. to V at 22.38, Dindorf 1962:707), and which Cunliffe defines as meaning "to woo or court (the wife of a living husband) (the prefix implying that the wooers seek a right concurrent, and therefore in conflict, with the husband's rights)" (Cunliffe 1963:400). This accusation should be distinguished from what Eumaeus alleges against the suitors, which is that they "are not willing to court her properly" (οὐκ ἐθέλουσι δικαίως / μνᾶσθαι, 14.90–91), and it should be assimilated rather to the behavior of Aegisthus, who, despite the gods' warning, courted Agamemnon's wife (μνάασθαι ἄκοιτιν, 1.39) while her husband was still living. It is relevant in this connection to note also that ancient and modern commentators alike regard it as peculiar that Odysseus does not allege against the suitors their plot to kill Telemachus (Schol. to V at 22.38, Dindorf 1962:707).

One of the outstanding features, then, of the *Odyssey*'s ideology of exclusivity is its construction of the suitors' courting as a crime and, by implication, of the relationship between Odysseus and Penelope as inviolate. This contradicts our understanding of social practice generally; as West puts in, "The attempt to win Penelope should not be regarded as in itself improper or unconventional" (1988:57).[26] And in other respects the suitors' courting appears to correspond with archaic practice (Monro 1901:302–3 n. 22; West 1988:57–58). We do find in other archaic patriarchal systems institutions such as that in the Mishnah—the second century C.E. codification of Jewish law—whereby a woman remains bound (*agunah*) to her husband until proof of his death can be produced and is known technically by the title that characterizes her condition (as an *agunah*, a "bound woman").[27] But the representation of the suitors' wooing as criminal in the *Odyssey* is tied directly to the construction of the

---

[26] Contra Bader, who appears to characterize the tenor of its representation in the poem rather than what might be understood as the sociological referent, in claiming that "quant à la cour que les prétendants font à Pénélope, épouse légitime d'Ulysse (20.290, 21.158, etc.), c'est un adultère, lui-même sacrilège (cf. 15.522–524, où Zeus est invoqué)" (1976:21). The passages cited do not, in my view, support this interpretation.

[27] During the period intervening between the husband's disappearance and the proof of his death, any sexual relations in which the *agunah* engages are equivalent to adultery, and they subject both her and the man involved to the penalities prescribed for that offense. For further explanation and discussion, see Biale 1984:102–13, and Wegner 1988:63–64, 123–26.

relationship between Penelope and Odysseus as exclusive in the sense that it is unconditioned by its inscription in a broader social context.

There is a second, complementary aspect to this ideology of exclusivity, and this has to do with the meaning of Telemachus's elimination from the scene of reunion. At the beginning of the scene, as in the parallel encounter between Hector and Andromache in the *Iliad*, the son mediates the relationship between husband and wife, as Schadewaldt points out: "In such a bogged-down situation there is need—in interpersonal relations as much as in more momentous ones—of an intermediary, who breaks the silence and sets the dialogue in motion. This intermediary between man and wife is naturally the son, Telemachus" (1970c:66, cf. n. 10; and see Arthur 1981).[28] In the *Odyssey* however, as we have seen, the reunion itself takes place in the son's absence, and it is precisely the difference between the two poems that the relationship between husband and wife in the *Odyssey* is not constituted as the endpoint of the range that, in the *Iliad*, encompasses compatriots, parents, and siblings (on this point see the discussion and references in Arthur 1981).

The exclusivity of the relationship between Penelope and Odysseus, together with the *homophrosynē* by which it is represented in the poem, has a strongly romantic coloring, and this has led to a tendency to exempt it from further analysis, much in the same way, as I discussed in Chapter Four, that the apparent representation of Penelope's unconscious ambivalence in Books 18 and 19 has been assimilated to our own values and patterns of thought. *Homophrosynē* in the *Odyssey*, however, also has an ideological dimension.

In the *Odyssey* the intimacy between husband and wife is constituted as an exclusivity structured around a dialetic of inside and outside on the one hand, and "biological" or natural and social on the other. In his homecoming, as Foley has point out, "Odysseus renegotiates his social, not his natural relationships" (1978:25 n. 21), and Murnaghan has explained further: "The recognition scenes that cluster around the defeat of the suitors involve the recreation of . . . relationships with people to whom Odysseus is not related by blood: his loyal servants, Eurycleia, Eumaeus, and Philoetius, and his wife Penelope. . . . These relationships are not based on any natural tie but are artificial social constructs" (1987:38).[29]

This is true, however, only in limited sense, since it has been the burden

---

[28] "In einer solchen festgefahrenen Situation bedarf es—im Menschlich-Intimen genauso wie in grösseren Verhältnissen—eines Vermittlers, der das Schweigen bricht und das Gespräch in Gang bringt. Dieser Vermittler zwischen Mann und Frau ist naturgemäss der Sohn, Telemachos."

[29] The corresponding pattern whereby the recognition of non-kin occurs within or close to the home, and the recognition of kin outside the home (Murnaghan 1987:38), is, however, violated by the Dolius recognition (24.386ff.), which Murnaghan does not discuss.

of my discussion overall to argue that the indeterminacy that characterizes the *Odyssey* as a whole extends to all of the relationships of "identity" that constitute it, including that of self-identity. Thus, consanguinity in the *Odyssey* functions as the basis for establishing the relationship between Telemachus and Odysseus, rather than as its constitutive feature. Its actuality, by contrast, is constituted as such through the narrative action of Books 16–24. Similarly, the reunions with Eumaeus, Eurycleia, and Penelope are embedded in the narrative of an ongoing relationship in the present action of the poem, and it is this which brings them into being as realities within the text, rather than the moment of *anagnōrismos* proper.

We observed above that the displacement of the recognition proper onto Eurycleia allowed the scene of *anagnōrismos* to be replaced with one of *xenia*. Eurycleia announces to Penelope that her "husband [is] within, [seated] by the hearth" (πόσιν ἔνδον ἐόντα παρ' ἐσχάρῃ, 23.71), and this is where she finds him when she descends into the *megaron*: "Odysseus was sitting there opposite her, in the light of the fire" (ἕζετ' ἔπειτ' 'Οδυσῆος ἐναντίον, ἐν πυρὸς αὐγῇ, 23.89). This site by the hearth or by the fire, as we observed earlier, is the traditional locale for the reception of a *xeinos*.

Xenia in the *Odyssey*, as we discussed in Chapter Five, normally includes the provision to the *xeinos* of bath, meal and symposion, and bed, in addition to the gifts, tokens of guest-friendship, that are offered upon his departure—itself often provided by the host in the form of conveyance (Arend 1975:39–53; M. Edwards 1975:61–71; Tsagarakis 1979; Block 1985:3–11; Pedrick 1988). We must note also, however, that the *xenia* of Book 19, like Odysseus's parallel relationships with Nausicaa and Arete in Books 6 and 7, was a conditional and incomplete form of *xenia*. For properly speaking, it is only a man, specifically the *kyrios* of an *oikos*, who can accept another man as *xeinos*, even though the relationship of *xenia* is often mediated through the woman or women of the household (Pitt-Rivers 1977b; Abou-Zeid 1966; cf. Gould 1973:97–99). The representation of the *homilia* as a scenario of *xenia* in Book 19 was conditional, then, and this was indicated especially through the substitution of foot-washing for the bath, as Segal notes: "The bathing by Eurycleia [is] a ritual which is not fully or perfectly performed" (1974:476).

Incorporation into the household as a *xeinos* entails a status subordinate to that of the *kyrios*; similarly, uxorilocal marriage in the Homeric poems subordinates a husband to his father-in-law. This is clearest from Agamemnon's offer to Achilles (*Iliad* 9.141ff.), which the latter rejects (9.388ff.), and which is similar to Alcinous's proposal, as well as to the proposal that Menelaus would have liked to extend to Odysseus (4.174–77). The incorporation of the wife into the household through marriage is analogous to *xenia* because the wife assumes the same honored but dependent (and therefore subordinate) status relative to her husband as would a *xeinos*.

Insofar as Odysseus had been partially incorporated into the household in Book 19 as a *xeinos* then, his full presence as *kyrios* in Book 23 must be reconstructed in part as an appropriation from Penelope of the authority over *xenia*.

In Book 23, Odysseus himself arranges for his own bath and bed, and Pedrick has claimed that this indicates the presence of a conflict of authority between Penelope and Odysseus underlying the scene (Pedrick 1988:95–97; cf. Murnaghan 1987:114–17). Pedrick argues that Penelope "could deny [Odysseus] his homecoming even now by treating him like a guest" (Pedrick 1988:95); similarly, Murnaghan refers to "the conflict between the role of guest that Odysseus has earned in Penelope's eyes and the role of husband that he wishes to claim" (1987:114). But this emphasis on the undeniable disparity between the roles of husband and *xeinos* disregards the continuity between them that is otherwise developed in the poem, discussed in Chapter Five. Furthermore, the relationship of *xenia*, like that of marriage, entails both a certain measure of reciprocity and a difference in status. In my view, the *anagnōrismos* is represented as the culmination of a ritual of *xenia*, but in the course of it Odysseus is transformed from *xeinos* meaning "guest-stranger" to *xeinos* meaning "host." Thus, in Book 23 it is Penelope who appropriates from Odysseus the right to provide a bed for a guest (in this case, himself), rather than the other way around.

The configuration of the reunion as a scene of hospitality is premised, to be sure, on an "estrangement" between Penelope and Odysseus, but this aspect of the poem should be interpreted, in my view, as a rhetorical gesture with narratological implications, rather than as a moral one with psychological meaning. Odysseus is quite literally "estranged" by the device of his disguise as a stranger; Penelope's estrangement appears first as the silent posture she assumes upon her entrance ("but she sat down quite silent," ἡ δ' ἄνεω δὴν ἧστο, 23.93), and as the distance implied in her attitude of wonder ("wonder came over her heart," τάφος δέ οἱ ἦτορ ἵκανεν, 23.93; "the heart in my breast is amazed," θυμός μοι ἐνὶ στήθεσσι τέθηπεν, 23.105).

But a more significant representation of Penelope's estrangement from Odysseus is her refusal to recognize him, which is configured in the poem as a complex issue of identity. When she first enters the *megaron*, Penelope debates, "whether [standing] apart to question thoroughly her dear husband" (φίλον πόσιν, 23.86). This is the only such recognition scene, and the sole example in which the *knowledge* of who Odysseus is, is separated from the *acknowledgment* of his identity.[30] Thus, only from this *anagnōrismos* is

---

[30] Roisman draws attention to the implication of οἷος ἔησθα ("how you were") in line 175,

the proclamation of self that characterizes all the others absent: "I am he" (ἀλλ' ὅδ' ἐγὼ τοιόσδε, 16.205), Odysseus announces to Telemachus, and he speaks similarly to Eumaeus and Philoetius (ἔνδον μὲν δὴ ὅδ' αὐτὸς ἐγώ, 21.207) and to Laertes (κεῖνος μὲν δὴ ὅδ' αὐτὸς ἐγώ, 24.321). In the recognition by Eurycleia, it is she who proclaims his identity: "You are indeed Odysseus, dear child!" (ἦ μάλ' Ὀδυσσεύς ἐσσι, φίλον τέκος, 19.474). In all instances, Odysseus explains that after much wandering and suffering "I have come back to the land of my fathers in the twentieth year" (ἤλυθον εἰκοστῷ ἔτεϊ ἐς πατρίδα γαῖαν, 16.206 [= 19.484, 21.208, 24.322]).

Such passages, with their assertion of an equation between "I" (ἐγώ) and "he" (τοιόσδε, αὐτός, κεῖνος),[31] especially illustrate what Pucci has identified as the rhetorical function of the device of disguise and recognition, "through which the text tries to assure us of the self-identity of the hero" (Pucci 1987:87). Only in the case of the recognition by Penelope is "he" (Odysseus) kept separate from "I" (the stranger), so that here, as before the suitors, recognition is effected by a convergence of *xeinos* and Odysseus, rather than by a replacement of one by the other.

In the scene that constitutes the recognition proper, Odysseus characterizes himself by repeating the formula that, as we remarked above, appears in every other recognition scene in the poem: "Who after suffering many troubles has come back to his native land in the twentieth year" (ὅς οἱ κακὰ πολλὰ μογήσας / ἔλθοι ἐεικοστῷ ἔτεϊ ἐς πατρίδα γαῖαν, 23.101–2 = 23.169–70). Here, the lines make up part of a more comprehensive echo of Telemachus's earlier rebuke to Penelope (23.100–102 = 23.168–70). In Pucci's interpretation, this repetition "implies that [Odysseus's] offended reaction is generally 'masculine' and that he does not put anything personal or intimate in his reproach to Penelope" (1987:92–93); we can extend this observation by adding that Penelope's refusal to respond to this appeal marks the idiosyncrasy of this recognition, and its construction on a principle other than that of the replacement of the stranger with Odysseus, and of the substitution of truth for disguise.

Finally, when putting Odysseus to the test of the bed, Penelope prefaces her trick with an assertion of the impossibility of extending to him a recognition based on the past, a simple substitution of "now" for "then": "I know very well how you were when you went off from Ithaca upon a long-oared ship" (μάλα δ' εὖ οἶδ' οἷος ἔησθα / ἐξ Ἰθάκης ἐπὶ νηὸς ἰὼν δολιχηρέτμοιο, 23.175–76). Starobinski describes the crisis of identity here: "How does one go about revealing the true being which has been concealed and protected by lies? Here the word alone no longer serves; 'inner'

---

which, as a number of critics have pointed out, "suggest[s] that [Penelope] may actually know who [Odysseus] is at this point" (1987:63 n. 10).

[31] Or, in the case of Eurycleia, of "you" and "Odysseus."

certitude cannot manifest itself immediately in the declaration of the 'I am'" (1975:348).

Penelope's refusal to recognize Odysseus, and her insistence on the disjunction between her husband Odysseus and his first-person presence, should be interpreted, in my view, as a narrative strategy tied to the privileging within the poem of marriage as a constructed relationship. It is this feature to which the conjunction of elements of *anagnōrismos* and those of *xenia* draws attention, by configuring the reunion as a reconstitution of intimacy rather than as its simple resumption. For hospitality constructs a relationship in the same way that marriage does, and the emphasis on this feature contrasts with the assumption of identity underlying the notion of recognition. Thus the incorporation into the *anagnōrismos* of elements of *xenia* highlights the fictional aspects of intimacy, and the recognition itself is then based not so much on the certitude that "Odysseus is not simply an acceptable stranger but Penelope's husband" (Murnaghan 1987:116), but rather on its opposite—on the development of an identification between the stranger and Odysseus.

This identification is constituted at the opposite end of the spectrum from the notion that Penelope and Odysseus are reunited on the basis of a unique personal bond that persists through time (Murnaghan 1987:117). Rather, their reunion is the culmination of the ritual of *xenia* begun in Book 19 and resumed in Book 23. It is analogous in this respect to the offer of marriage that Alcinous extends to Odysseus on the basis of his conduct as a *xeinos*; Odysseus's suitability as Penelope's husband is similarly an extension and amplification of his fitness to be her *xeinos*.

The first element in the ideology of exclusivity in the *Odyssey*, then, is the representation of the suitors' courtship as a crime. Its complement, however, is not the essentializing of the relationship between Odysseus and Penelope—its representation as the "truth" of *homophrosynē*. Rather, it is the highlighting of the constructed and therefore fictional aspects of the complementarity between them and of their suitability for each other. This is particularly evident, in my view, in the trick of the bed, which constitutes the final stage in the transformation of the *xeinos* into Odysseus. Its first two stages are represented in Book 23 as Odysseus's provision for himself of the bath and fresh clothing normally offered by the host to the guest—a gesture by which Odysseus assumes concurrently the roles of both host and guest. This is marked especially by the phrase that locates the bath "in his [own] house" (ᾧ ἐνὶ οἴκῳ, 23.153) and signals his resumption of control over his *oikos* (cf. Müller 1966:146). It is when he moves to provide for himself also a bed that Penelope, in appearing to appropriate from him the role of *xeinodokos*, in actuality effects his transformation from *xeinos* to *kyrios*.

Penelope instructs Eurycleia to spread Odysseus's bed "outside the well-pillared bedchamber, which he himself built" (ἐκτὸς ἐϋσταθέος θαλάμου, τόν ῥ' αὐτὸς ἐποίει, 23.178). The transparent referentiality of this αὐτός ("he himself"), however, is only apparent, and this statement of Penelope's should be compared with the proclamation of self-identity in recognition scenes discussed above (e.g., "I am he," ὅδ' αὐτὸς ἐγώ). For Penelope appears to refer by the pronoun *autos* ("he himself") to the man standing in front of them, and thereby to indicate that she is aware of his "identity." But she is in fact claiming that Odysseus is Odysseus only insofar as that identity is a fact constituted as such in time and space—insofar as "he himself" is the man who built the bedchamber—not insofar as that identity exists as a (self-)referential truth. As Starobinski puts it, "The 'I have made,' together with the object made, are more probative than the 'I am' would have been" (1975:349).

This is the sole instance in the narrative of Penelope's "testing" (πόσιος πειρωμένη, 23.181; cf. πειράζειν ἐμέθεν, 23.114), and it should be interpreted as analogous with Odysseus's own—as a provocation designed to arouse self-revelation, not as an inquiry after the "truth." Penelope's provokes Odysseus to relate the story of the building of the bed and bedchamber, and afterwards she extends recognition to him, not so much because he has revealed his identity, but because through his narrative he has in fact instantiated it. Thus, the structuring of this moment of recognition in the text has elements in common with the structure of the scene overall, which, as I have argued, emphasizes the constructed aspects of identity.

The bed itself is most often interpreted as an emblem of permanence and stability—its immobility is a symbol of Penelope's own resolute faithfulness. But this interpretation does not exhaust its meaning in the text, nor does it take account of all of the features included in the description of its construction. In the first six lines of the speech, which is twenty-two lines long, Odysseus gives vent to his surprise and anger ("Oh woman, this is indeed a heartbreaking thing which you have said!" ὦ γύναι, ἦ μάλα τοῦτο ἔπος θυμαλγὲς ἔειπες, 23.183) and goes on to explain that no mortal man without a god's help would be able to move the bed, "since there is a *mega sēma* fabricated into the wrought bed" (ἐπεὶ μέγα σῆμα τέτυκται / ἐν λέχει ἀσκητῷ, 23.188–89). "This," he asserts, "I constructed and no other": τὸ δ' ἐγὼ κάμον οὐδέ τις ἄλλος (23.189).

It is this τὸ δ' ἐγὼ κάμον ("I constructed it") which replaces the ὅδ' αὐτὸς ἐγώ ("I am he") in the other recognition scenes, and which responds to and converges with Penelope's τόν ῥ' αὐτὸς ἐποίει ("which he himself made"). It effects not so much the recognition itself of Odysseus, or even the "proof" of his identity, but rather the constitution of it in much the same way that the earlier lying-tales had brought an identity for Odysseus into being. This "truth-tale" is thus analogous to the account that Odysseus gives his father later when, having offered the proof of the scar

(24.331–35), he realizes the insufficiency—or perhaps the inappropriateness—of this *sēma*, and goes on to provide a reckoning of the trees and the orchard that compose his patrimony.[32] These, he says to Laertes, "you once gave me, and I asked you about each of them when I was a little boy following you about the garden" (ἅ μοί ποτ' ἔδωκας, ἐγὼ δ' ᾔτευν σε ἕκαστα / παιδνὸς ἐών, κατὰ κῆπον ἐπισπόμενος, 24.337–38).

Odysseus then provides a reckoning of these trees, quoting, in all likelihood, Laertes' own words, and thus reconstituting the instance of the father's transmission to the son of the knowledge through which he effects the son's acquisition of the paternal inheritance. For trees, as fixed elements on a piece of land, serve as the land's identifying markers, and the possession of knowledge concerning them itself marks the son as their owner. In reciting to Laertes his own reckoning of his property, Odysseus identifies himself to his father not with reference to some permanent, essential truth of being, but rather by reconstituting the earlier instance when he became his father's legitimate heir, and thus his son in fact.

The "truth-tale" of the bed operates similarly for Penelope, and the continuity between the two recognition scenes is signaled by the employment in both instances of the same words to describe the moment of *anagnōrismos* "Thus he [Odysseus] spoke, and her knees and dear heart were loosened when she recognized the sure signs that Odysseus had recounted" (ὣς φάτο, τῆς δ' αὐτοῦ λύτο γούνατα καὶ φίλον ἦτορ, / σήματ' ἀναγνούσῃ, τά οἱ ἔμπεδα πέφραδ' Ὀδυσσεύς, 23.205–6 = 24.345–46). In describing the construction of the bed and bedchamber, Odysseus reconstructs the gesture whereby his marriage to Penelope was concretely embodied in time and space. For it is likely that the bedchamber, and perhaps also the house itself, was only constructed at the point of marriage, and thus functioned to instantiate the marriage as a physical reality. We can compare the construction in the *Iliad* of Paris's home, which, as it seems, was only completed once he brought Helen to Troy: "[The home] which he himself had wrought along with the men who were at that time the best carpenters in Troy of the fertile lands, who constructed the bedchamber and the house and the courtyard right near those of Priam and Hector, on the city's acropolis" (τά ῥ' αὐτὸς ἔτευξε σὺν ἀνδράσιν οἳ τότ' ἄριστοι / ἦσαν ἐνὶ Τροίῃ ἐριβώλακι τέκτονες ἄνδρες, / οἵ οἱ ἐποίησαν θάλαμον καὶ δῶμα καὶ αὐλήν, / ἐγγύθι τε Πριάμοιο καὶ Ἕκτορος ἐν πόλει ἄκρῃ, *Iliad* 6.314–17).[33]

[32] "But just as Penelope, in her response to the nurse, disregards the reference to the scar and appeals for a greater *sēma*, known only to the two spouses, i.e., the bed, just so does Odysseus spontaneously offer to his father, in the account of the trees, a further 'sign,' known only to the two men: no one could know whether these trees belong to the son. It is an unmistakable parallel with Book 23" (Heubeck 1986:378 ad 24.331–44; cf. also Besslich 1966:123–25; Erbse 1972:108–9).

[33] These homes should be distinguished from the rooms within the palace occupied by, in all probability, the sons of Priam by his many concubines: "But there were in it [Priam's

In the *Odyssey*, Odysseus constructs the bedchamber around an olive tree growing in the outer courtyard,[34] and the house as a whole thus appears to be centered on this bedchamber, in the same way that the bedchamber itself is centered on the bed, and the bed on the tree: "Building around this [tree] I constructed the bedchamber, until I completed it" (τῷ δ' ἐγὼ ἀμφιβαλὼν θάλαμον δέμον, ὄφρ' ἐτέλεσσα, 23.192); "starting with this [the planed-down tree stump], I built the bed, until I completed it" (ἐκ δὲ τοῦ ἀρχόμενος λέχος ἔξεον, ὄφρ' ἐτέλεσσα, 23.199). The symbolic meaning of this construction is perhaps enhanced by its opacity as a description in the more literal sense; as noted in Ameis-Hentze-Cauer concerning 23.199: "how this was accomplished in particular remains unclear" (1964, 2(2):142 ad 23.199). Because the bed and bedchamber themselves are constructed as the center of the *oikos*, they function symbolically in the poem as an analogue for the hearth. The hearth, as Vernant makes clear, "represents not only the centre of the domestic sphere. Sealed in the ground, the circular hearth denotes the navel which ties the house to the earth. It is the symbol and pledge of fixity, immutability, and permanence" (Vernant 1969:132).[35] The bed and bedroom fulfill this function in the *oikos* of Odysseus, and the description of their construction transfers to them as attributes the metaphorical qualities that otherwise characterize the hearth of the *oikos*.

An additional feature of its fabrication is that the bed was constructed through an acculturation of what is otherwise an object in nature.[36] Odysseus's bed thus resembles Achilles' sceptre in the *Iliad*, which, as he describes it there, "will never again sprout leaf and branch, since now it has left behind its stump in the mountains, nor will it blossom; for the bronze stripped off its leaf and bark" (τὸ μὲν οὔ ποτε φύλλα καὶ ὄζους / φύσει, ἐπεὶ δὴ πρῶτα τομὴν ἐν ὄρεσσι λέλοιπεν, / οὐδ' ἀναθηλήσει· περὶ γάρ ῥά ἑ χαλκὸς ἔλεψε / φύλλά τε καὶ φλοιόν, *Iliad* 1.234–37). Similarly, Odys-

---

palace] fifty bedchambers of polished stone, fashioned alongside one another. And there Priam's sons slept alongside their wooed and wedded wives" (αὐτὰρ ἐν αὐτῷ / πεντήκοντ' ἔνεσαν θάλαμοι ξεστοῖο λίθοιο / πλησίον ἀλλήλων δεδμημένοι· ἔνθα δὲ παῖδες / κοιμῶντο Πριάμοιο παρὰ μνηστῇς ἀλόχοισι, *Iliad* 6.243–46).

[34] Heubeck glosses ἕρκεος ἑωτός ("within the courtyard," 23.190) as " 'in the interior part of the field' (enclosed, which belonged to Odysseus, that is, to his father)" (1986:308 ad 23.190).

[35] On the homology operative in Greek culture generally between the hearth, the *thalamos*, and the *mukhos* of the *oikos*, see Vernant 1969:154–56.

[36] On this feature of the bed, see also Starobinski's remarks: "The tree commands the space that toil organizes round about it. It is a natural 'given,' invigorated by the sap that brings forth leaves in profusion and endows the trunk with great girth and solidity. Having been stripped and hewn, it goes on plunging its roots into the earth: the vegetal energy it carried inside itself is transmitted by a kind of metonymic continuity, to the bed ensconced within its wood" (1975:351).

seus "cut away the foliage of the slender-leafed olive tree, and trimming the bare trunk up from the root, I smoothed it around with the bronze" (καὶ τότ' ἔπειτ' ἀπέκοψα κόμην τανυφύλλου ἐλαίης, / κορμὸν δ' ἐκ ῥίζης προταμὼν ἀμφέξεσα χαλκῷ, 23.195–96). In Achilles' case, the separation of the branch from the tree, and the impossibility of its blossoming again, serve to mark the finality and irreversibility of his own resolve to abandon the fighting. The bed in the *Odyssey*, by contrast, retains its connection with the natural world from which it came, and thus represents the institution of marriage itself, which, centered on the biological realities of sexuality and procreation, nevertheless is configured in space and time as a social artifact. It may be, in fact, that this bed was in antiquity a *locus classicus*, as it were, for the union of art and nature (Lang 1982:331). For in refuting the argument that the nature (*physis* and *ousia*) of an object should be identified with its underlying matter (*to prōton enuparkhon*) rather than its form (*morphē* and *eidos*), Aristotle addresses himself especially to Antiphon's example of the "planted bed," which, if it acquired the power of regeneration, would produce not a bed but wood (Aristotle, *Physics* 2.1, 193a12–14); and it has been argued recently that Aristotle's use of this example represents a "Homeric echo" inspired perhaps by the popular currency of the Homeric *sēma* (Lang 1982).[37]

It is important also that the bed and the bedchamber were formed through a process of enclosure of the outside, so as to transform it into "inside." As Starobinksi remarks, "[Odysseus] fashions an enclosure within an enclosure; the image drawn here is that of a concentric structure, of a sealed place, of a protected *inside*" (1975:350; emphasis in the original). In a modern Greek ballad discussed by Kakridis as a parallel to the recognition of Odysseus in the *Odyssey*, the husband is similarly obliged to provide signs as proof of his identity, and these are arranged in three classes according to a progression toward intimacy of knowledge: in the ballad, the wife requires of the returning husband first "marks in the courtyard" (σημάδια τῆς αὐλῆς), and he mentions an appletree and vine growing beside the door; she then asks for "marks inside the house" (σημάδια τοῦ κορμιοῦ), and he tells her about the golden lamp that burns "right in the middle of the bedroom"; finally she asks him to tell her of "marks on my body, tokens of love" (σημάδια τοῦ σπιτιοῦ, σημάδια τῆς ἀγαπῆς) and he instances two moles and her husband's amulet, which she wears between her breasts (Kakridis 1971b:152–53; see also Emlyn-Jones 1984:7).

Kakridis suggests that the ballad preserves an ancient Greek folktale, and that the similarities with the recognition of Odysseus indicate that "the recognition of the returning husband was a popular, pre-Homeric motif,"

---

[37] I thank Helen Lang for drawing to my attention both this reference in Aristotle and her own speculations concerning it.

which in the *Odyssey* has been split into the recognitions of Books 23 and 24 (Kakridis 1971b:156–63; citation p. 157). In the *Odyssey*, the tokens are the *sēmata* of the scar, the bed, and the orchard,[38] and by contrast with the ballad, the bodily sign, the scar, is the least "intimate" detail. Intimacy in the *Odyssey* is conveyed rather through personalized knowledge about the outside (the trees in the orchard of Book 24), or through the privatization of the outside (the olive tree in the bed of Book 23).

The narrative of the bed and its construction, then, is a complex figuration for the moment in the poem when the marriage of Penelope and Odysseus is reconstituted. The account itself, like the reckoning of the trees through which Odysseus reacquires his patrimony, not only recalls the earlier episode, but also instantiates anew the relationship to which it refers. As an account, the description of the bed emphasizes the constructed, fabricated aspects of marriage as well as its uniquely private dimension. For it represents marriage as the moment in which outside is transformed into inside, in which natural impulses encounter the social institution that both conceals their existence and allows them to find expression, and in which the center of the house is constituted as such through its embodiment in space and time. But only in the case of Odysseus and Penelope are these essential and ideal aspects of marriage embodied in the construction of what Penelope, after the *anagnōrismos*, is now willing to call "our bed" (εὐνῆς ἡμετέρης, 23.226).

The second aspect of the ideology of exclusivity in the *Odyssey*, then, has to do with the meaning of the intimacy that constitutes the marriage between Penelope and Odysseus, and with the *homophrosynē* by which it is represented in the poem. As we have seen, the intimacy of their relationship is not an essential, permanent, and inalterable quality that inheres in it, but an originally constructed feature that must be reconstructed. Similarly, the *homophrosynē* between them must also be brought into being as such in the narrative, and it is constituted, as I suggested earlier, by the replacement of duplicity with complementarity.

Duplicity, Complementarity, and the Example of Helen

At the moment of *anagnōrismos*, Penelope embraces Odysseus and first addresses him by name: "Don't be angry with me, Odysseus . . ." (μή μοι, Ὀδυσσεῦ, σκύζευ, 23.209). She goes on to explain her reserve as a pre-

---

[38] Murnaghan's remarks on what she calls the "token" of the bow are interesting in themselves (1987:115–16), but it cannot be maintained that the bow constitutes a "sign." Eurycleia does not mention it when she reports Odysseus's presence, adducing as proof of his identity at first only the slaughter of the suitors and Telemachus's knowledge of his father's identity. On the significance of the bow, see also Nortwick 1983 and Fernández-Galiano 1986:ix–x, 152–53 ad 21.13.

caution against deception by "someone who might come along and trick me with his words" (μή τίς με βροτῶν ἀπάφοιτ' ἐπέεσσιν / ἐλθών, 23.216–17), and the supposition, as commentators observe, is a peculiar one, corresponding precisely to no situation represented or alluded to in the text.

This same speech also incorporates an extended and problematic reference to Helen, and its effect is to compromise this final moment of truth in the narrative. For, having alluded to the danger of deception by an imposter, Penelope goes on to explain:

> οὐδέ κεν Ἀργείη Ἑλένη, Διὸς ἐκγεγαυῖα,
> ἀνδρὶ παρ' ἀλλοδαπῷ ἐμίγη φιλότητι καὶ εὐνῇ,
> εἰ ᾔδη, ὅ μιν αὖτις ἀρήιοι υἷες Ἀχαιῶν
> ἀξέμεναι οἶκόνδε φίλην ἐς πατρίδ' ἔμελλον.
> τὴν δ' ἤτοι ῥέξαι θεὸς ὤρορεν ἔργον ἀεικές·
> τὴν δ' ἄτην οὐ πρόσθεν ἑῷ ἐγκάτθετο θυμῷ
> λυγρήν, ἐξ ἧς πρῶτα καὶ ἡμέας ἵκετο πένθος.

(For neither would Argive Helen, the offspring of Zeus,
have made love in her bed lying beside a stranger
if she had known that once again the valiant sons of the Achaeans
were going to lead her home to her own fatherland.
And in fact it was a god, you know, who aroused her to do the shameful deed;
for before that she did not lay up in her heart the bitter foolishness
from which from the very first grief has come upon us as well.)

(23.218–24)

These lines have been widely rejected since antiquity on account of the *non sequitur* that they appear to embody. As the ancient scholiast reports it, "The seven lines are athetized on the grounds that they contradict the sense" (ἀθετοῦνται οἱ ἑπτὰ στίχοι ὡς σκάζοντες κατὰ τὸν νοῦν, Dindorf 1962:720 ad 23.218). Kirchhoff explains more fully: "The elaboration of the underlying thought, which at this point it would hardly be worth even bringing up, is in fact so completely skewed and inappropriate that interpolation becomes palpable. The only thing that must remain in doubt is to whom should be ascribed the original authorship of this unhappy attempt to complete the text, which cannot originate with the poet himself" (Kirchhoff 1879:531–32).[39] Wilamowitz refers to the section as one "which the ancients correctly rejected" (1884:84 n. 8; cf. Wilamowitz 1927:74). Schadewaldt argues that the passage issues from the hand of the

---

[39] "Die Ausführung des zu Grunde liegenden Gedankens, der an sich schon hier kaum angemessen anzubringen gewesen wäre, ist in der That so völlig schief und zweckwidrig, dass die Interpolation handgreiflich wird und nur das Eine zweifelhaft bleiben muss, wem die Urheberschaft dieses verunglückten Erweiterungsversuches zuzuschreiben ist, der vom Dichter selbst nich herrühren kann."

Bearbeiter, along with 23.297–99 and 23.241–88; and he cites Van der Mühl, on the " 'illogical' Exemplum of Helen" (1970c:73; see also Monro 1901:252 ad 218–24 and Stanford 1978 2:401 ad 23.218–24).

The example of Helen has not seemed to apply to Penelope because, as Monro puts it, "the lesson would seem to be that men do wrongly from their ignorance of the future, and because they are led astray by higher powers. But this is not applicable in any way to Penelope" (1901:252 ad 218–24). Ameis-Hentze-Cauer attempt unconvincingly to explain the sequence of thought by arguing, "The thoughts of the speaker stray from the comparison [between Penelope and Helen] that she has begun and turn toward the significance that that woman's foolishness also has had for the fate of the two now reunited" (1964, 2(2):143 ad 220).[40]

One remedy has been to rewrite the passage so that the object-leson has to do with the danger of being deceived by a stranger. The scholia, for example, suggest the elimination of lines 220–22, so that Penelope would claim simply, "Helen would not have lain in love with a strange man, unless she had been deceived" (Dindorf 1962:720 ad 23.218). As Roisman points out, however, Penelope's fear of being deceived by a stranger is not analogous to Helen's love for a stranger by whom she was not deceived in any explicit sense (Roisman 1987:61, arguing against Marquardt 1985 and Amory 1963). The scholia, it is true, construct such an analogy by adding that there is a story that Paris was transformed by a device of Aphrodite into a likeness of Menelaus and in this guise seduced Helen (Dindorf 1962:720 ad 23:218). But this does not accord with the story of Helen as Penelope presents it.

Other recent commentators have maintained that the comparison with Helen reveals Penelope's unconscious feelings. Devereux's psychoanalytic reading, according to which the passage expresses Penelope's "innermost thoughts, temptations, and wishes," is the best-known example (1957:384). A variant upon this approach has been suggested recently by Felson-Rubin, who argues that in these lines Penelope "tacitly acknowledges to her husband how close she had come to adultery . . . and seeks to exonerate herself from blame" (1988:66, 67). Marquardt, though generally critical of psychoanalytic interpretation, refers in this case to "Penelope's subconscious guilt" in order to explain the comparison with Helen (1985:44–45; citation p. 44). In Marquardt's view, Penelope uses the reference to Helen in part "to bolster her defense of any 'folly' for which she herself might be criticized by Odysseus. . . . She does not yet know what Odysseus really thinks about her relationship with the suitors . . ."

---

[40] "Die Gedanken der Sprechenden schweifen von dem angeschlagenen Vergleich ab und wenden sich der Bedeutung zu, die der Leichtsinn jener Frau auch für das Schicksal der beiden jetzt wieder Vereinigten gehabt hat."

(ibid.:45). Similarly, Murnaghan suggests that "Penelope's caution stems from fear of her own susceptibility to desire," explaining further that "Penelope has been afraid that her recognition of the stranger as Odysseus might be based on desire rather than true knowledge" (Murnaghan 1987:142). Roisman, who regards a psychological approach as "especially justifiable in the analysis of Penelope's behavior" (1987:60 n. 4), argues that the comparison contributes to the establishment of what she regards as the speech's cool and distant tone, expressive of Penelope's "hurt and annoyance that Odysseus had kept his identity hidden from her" (ibid.:62). Roisman adds that "it must have been rather insulting that Odysseus chose to confide in his son rather than his wife" (ibid.).

Such interpretations, though convincing from the point of view of psychological realism, nevertheless require us to refer the passage to principles of coherence that lie outside the text. But within the text, the passage is most readily comprehensible with reference to the paradigms for female renown invoked by the narrative itself, as one of the earliest defenders of the lines saw (Platt 1899:382–84). For Clytemnestra, Helen, and Penelope are referenced together in Book 11, as we discussed earlier, and Agamemnon makes the comparison with Clytemnestra explicit in Book 24.

It is important to observe that Penelope regards herself as open to possible reproach *only* for having withheld recognition from Odysseus: "But do not now be angry and reproachful to me for this, because I did not welcome you warmly when I first saw you" (αὐτὰρ μὴ νῦν μοι τόδε χώεο μηδὲ νεμέσσα, / οὕνεκά σ' οὐ τὸ πρῶτον, ἐπεὶ ἴδον, ὧδ' ἀγάπησα, 23.213–14). The language of this passage is reminiscent of the kind of welcome that Agamemnon had originally expected (11.430–32) and that Odysseus, out of the fear that he might repeat Agamemnon's experience, elected to forego (13.333–34; for both passages, see above, Chapter Three). Penelope's anticipation of Odysseus's rebuke thus constitutes a kind of *hypophora*, whereby she dissociates herself from the heroine who preeminently did not welcome her husband home, but by the same token conscripts her own behavior into the same paradigmatic field.

Penelope's appeal to the example of Helen, by contrast with the implied reference to Clytemnestra, is explicit, and in it she employs the rhetorical figure *argumentum a minore*, whereby she attempts to deflect from herself any possibility of reproach: "If even Helen should be excused, then how much more so I. . . ."[41] Furthermore, Penelope here exonerates Helen in the same terms that Helen herself had employed earlier. In her own account of her actions at Troy in Book 4, Helen speaks of the time "when already my heart had turned to want to return back home, and I regretted

---

[41] The *argumentum a minore* is defined by Macrobius (*Sat.* 4.6.1) as follows: *cum aliquid proponitur quod per se magnum sit, deinde minus esse ostenditur quam illud, quod volumus augeri.*

the foolishness that Aphrodite endowed upon me when she led me there [to Troy] away from my native land" (ἐπεὶ ἤδη μοι κραδίη τέτραπτο νέεσθαι / ἄψ οἰκόνδ', ἄτην δὲ μετέστενον, ἣν Ἀφροδίτη / δῶχ', ὅτε μ' ἤγαγε κεῖσε φίλης ἀπὸ πατρίδος αἴης, 4.260–62).[42] Penelope too refers to the "foolishness" (atē) that led to Helen's error, and to a god's responsibility for it, but she describes it here as "wretched foolishness" (τὴν δ' ἄτην ... λυγρήν, 23.223–24), applying to it the same adjective that had earlier characterized the "sad song" (ἀοιδὴ λυγρή, 1.340–41) of the "wretched homecoming" (νόστος λυγρός, 1.326–27) of the Greek heroes, Agamemnon's "wretched death" (λυγρὸς ὄλεθρος 3.194; cf. 24.96), and the general temper of Clytemnestra's character: she is the woman who "preeminently cherished bitter wretchedness in her mind" (ἣ δ' ἔξοχα λυγρὰ ἰδυῖα, 11.432).

Penelope's reference to Helen here, then, is rhetorically equivalent to Agamemnon's formulation in Book 24. There, as I pointed out in Chapter Two, Penelope's *kleos* as the faithful wife was assured, but was displaced in the end by the paradigmatic force of Clytemnestra's example. Here, by suggesting an identification with her at the moment when Penelope enacts her differentiation from Helen, Penelope destabilizes the paradigm of her own behavior. It is particularly notable in this regard that by comparing her own refusal to recognize the husband/stranger Odysseus with Helen's willingness to accept the lover/stranger Paris, Penelope effects a conflation of betrayal with faithfulness. Thus, Penelope refuses closure to her own *mythos*, and the wide circulation in antiquity of stories depicting a wanton Penelope may have less to do with an inclination to "rebel against the superhuman ideal," as Jacobson suggests,[43] and more with ambiguities inscribed in the text of the *Odyssey* itself.

The references to Helen and, in Book 24, to Clytemnestra are part of a more general narrative pattern in the *Odyssey* whereby Penelope's *mythos* shifts direction, drawn toward the paradigm of Clytemnestra, which is held up as an imminent danger through Book 13, and toward that of Helen, which threatens to intrude upon the narrative from Book 18 on. Penelope's faithfulness, I have argued, is never an unproblematic category within this scheme, and this is particularly evident in Books 18 and 19, where the dissonance between what is said in the narrative about her and what is implied is particularly marked. I have argued that this ambiguity

---

[42] Allione discusses Helen's *atē* ("foolish deception") and notes that Helen's error is not the same as that of Aegisthus (1963:45 n. 58).

[43] Jacobson 1974:248; and see further pp. 246–49 for a discussion of the alternative traditions to the "vulgate" of Penelope as the *exemplum* of feminine virtue." For a discussion of the religious symbolism that can be attached to Penelope as a lunar Arcadian deity, particularly in relation to the stories about her reported by Pausanias, see Dietz 1971:15–17; cf. also Mactoux 1975:203–14 on mythical parallels between Helen and Penelope.

should be read not from a psychological point of view, as reflecting certain truths about Penelope's character, but from a narratological one, as embodying aspects of the poem's narrative structure. These have to do primarily with the postponement of truth, the withholding of identity, and the deferral of closure. This last feature figures especially in the closing sections of the poem, and Penelope is its particular agent. Thus, it is she who insists on postponing the culmination of their reunion until Odysseus has told her about the last trial that awaits him (23.257ff.). In this way, the finality of homecoming is deferred, and the ending of the story takes place instead under the sign of its indefinite continuity. As Peradotto remarks on this feature of the ending, "The *Odyssey* does not end with the dream of desire fulfilled, where the folktale would have ended, where both Aristophanes and Aristarchus—bad critics but good lovers—would have it end, in the nuptial embrace of Odysseus and Penelope. . . . That moment is marked by the shadow of the future, Tiresias' prophecy" (1985:453). Similarly, when Penelope instances Helen's betrayal of Menelaus as the story that might have been her own, she both consolidates her own *kleos* by differentiating herself from Helen and undermines the fixity of its meaning at the same time. In this way she incorporates into the narrative as a self-conscious statement about herself the indeterminacy of meaning that has characterized her throughout the poem.

The last stage in the tranformation in Book 23 of duplicity into complementarity between Penelope and Odysseus transpires in the paired narratives that they exchange following their lovemaking, in the first part of the section athetized by the ancient editors.[44] These paired narratives, along with the emphasis on the complementarity of their "trials" (ἄεθλα, 23.350), function in place of Odysseus's disguise and Penelope's divided mind as a concrete representation of the unity that now exists between them. As Thalmann has pointed out, Odysseus's and Penelope's shared memories operate as a counterpoint to "the interminable debate about the past" carried on by Helen and Menelaus (1984:166). Thus, the complementarity instanced here between the *mythoi* of Odysseus and Penelope contrasts with the contradiction developed earlier on the narrative between the stories of Helen and Menelaus.

There is a further revisionary aspect to the *mythoi* that Penelope and Odysseus speak to one another. For the language of their *mythoi*, as the text presents it, replicates the Iliadic forms of *kleos*, but from an Odyssean perspective. Thus, Helen in the *Iliad* weaves a robe depicting "the many contests of Trojans, breakers of horses, and bronze-armored Achaeans, the

---

[44] For recent discussion and bibliography concerning the long-standing problem of the end of the *Odyssey*, see Heubeck 1986:xxxix–xli. The most complete recent discussion of the problem is Erbse 1972:166–244, which includes a line-by-line commentary on disputed verses.

ones they suffered for her sake at the hands of Ares" (πολέας δ' ἐνέπασσεν ἀέθλους / Τρώων θ' ἱπποδάμων καὶ Ἀχαιῶν χαλκοχιτώνων, / οὕς ἔθεν εἵνεκ' ἔπασχον ὑπ' Ἄρηος παλαμάων, *Iliad* 3.126–28).[45] Penelope, by contrast, describes "what she endured in the halls as she looked upon the ruinous crowd of suitors, who for her sake slaughtered many animals, oxen and goodly sheep, and much wine was drawn off from the storage jars" (ἡ μὲν ὅσ' ἐν μεγάροισιν ἀνέσχετο δῖα γυναικῶν / ἀνδρῶν μνηστήρων ἐσορῶσ' ἀίδηλον ὅμιλον, / οἳ ἔθεν εἵνεκα πολλά, βόας καὶ ἴφια μῆλα, / ἔσφαζον, πολλὸς δὲ πίθων ἠφύσσετο οἶνος, 23.302–5). By the same token, Achilles in the *Iliad* had instanced his sufferings on behalf of the Achaean army, comparing himself there to a mother bird: "Nor does anything lie waiting for me, when I have endured the sufferings in my heart, always putting my life-spirit at risk in the battle, as a mother bird brings forth for her little ones morsels of food, whenever she gets them, but for herself there is only trouble" (οὐδέ τί μοι περίκειται, ἐπεὶ πάθον ἄλγεα θυμῷ, / αἰεὶ ἐμὴν ψυχὴν παραβαλλόμενος πολεμίζειν. / ὡς δ' ὄρνις ἀπτῆσι νεοσσοῖσι προφέρῃσι / μάστακ', ἐπεί κε λάβῃσι, κακῶς δ' ἄρα οἱ πέλει αὐτῇ. . . . *Iliad* 9.321–24).[46] Odysseus, for his part, recounts "the sorrows he inflicted upon men, and the ones he himself, in his suffering, toiled over" (αὐτὰρ διογενὴς Ὀδυσεύς, ὅσα κήδε' ἔθηκεν / ἀνθρώποισ' ὅσα τ' αὐτὸς ὀϊζύσας ἐμόγησε, / πάντ' ἔλεγ', 23.306–8).

When Odysseus later summarizes the account of their separate struggles, he emphasizes the *nostos* that in the *Odyssey*, as we have seen, operates as the index of *kleos*:

> ὦ γύναι, ἤδη μὲν πολέων κεκορήμεθ' ἀέθλων
> ἀμφοτέρω, σὺ μὲν ἐνθάδ' ἐμὸν πολυκηδέα νόστον
> κλαίουσ'· αὐτὰρ ἐμὲ Ζεὺς ἄλγεσι καὶ θεοὶ ἄλλοι
> ἱέμενον πεδάασκον ἐμῆς ἀπὸ πατρίδος αἴης.

(Wife, we are already sated full of many struggles,
both of us, you here bewailing my homecoming with its many sorrows;
but as for me, Zeus and the other gods held me back from my native land
with sufferings, though I was longing [to reach it].)

(23.350–53)

These *mythoi*, then, constitute the *kleos* of the *Odyssey* in its process of formation,[47] and thus they represent a narrative correlate to the Odyssean

---

[45] For a discussion of the relationship between the κλέα ἀνδρῶν of the *Iliad* and Helen's tapestry, see Bergren 1979; cf. also Kennedy 1986.

[46] See Pucci's discussion of the parallel between the passage and the *Odyssey* proem (Pucci 1982:41–43), and his more recent remarks: "The parallelism . . . emphasizes the opposite direction of their lives: Achilles' pain, grief, and labors in the work of war lead to his premature death; Odysseus' suffering and labors are the consequence of his attempts to preserve life . . ." (1987:57 n. 8).

[47] For a discussion of the implications for the ideology of *kleos* of the coincidence in the

ideology of *kleos*, which, as Nagy and Edwards especially have made clear, is ratified through *nostos* (see above, pp. 22–23, 69–70). Furthermore, as Thalmann points out, Odysseus in his tale here recapitulates the story he had told on Scheria, to which he now adds an account of his sojourn there. Thus, "his story is progressively updated; in the course of the *Odyssey* events narrated as they occur turn into past experiences, objects of memory."[48] But it is relevant as well that Odysseus's *mythos* breaks off just at the point where in the narrative he had fallen asleep, and that this same action now ensues for Penelope and Odysseus in bed. In lines 13.70ff., Odysseus goes on board the Phaeacians' ship and lies down to sleep; a few lines later, the Phaeacians deposit him, still sleeping soundly on the Ithacan shore (κὰδ δ' ἄρ' ἐπὶ ψαμάθῳ ἔθεσαν δεδμημένον ὕπνῳ, 13.119). Here in Book 23, his story is interrupted at exactly the point in the narrative that corresponds with his falling asleep in Book 13:

> καὶ πέμψαν σὺν νηὶ φίλην ἐς πατρίδα γαῖαν,
> χαλκόν τε χρυσόν τε ἅλις ἐσθῆτά τε δόντες.
> τοῦτ' ἄρα δεύτατον εἶπεν ἔπος, ὅτε οἱ γλυκὺς ὕπνος
> λυσιμελὴς ἐπόρουσε, λύων μελεδήματα θυμοῦ.

> (And they sent him on a ship into his own dear fatherland,
> after giving him plentiful amounts of bronze, gold, and clothing.
> He was still telling this last part of his tale, when upon him
> there suddenly came sweet sleep, which loosens the limbs and
>   releases the cares of the heart.)
>
> (23.340–43)

Thus here, as earlier in Book 4, the *Odyssey*'s stories merge with its narrative action, and so the boundary between the two levels of representation is blurred.

Within the narrative world of the *Odyssey*, the figure of Odysseus preeminently embodies the ambiguities of disguise precisely because Odysseus is "recognized," and as such is no longer disguised: "Disguise is of such an uncanny nature that it is perceived as 'disguise' only when it is detected and exposed—that is, precisely when it no longer functions successfully as a disguise" (Pucci 1987:83). This moment of revelation or recognition generates within the text an instance of what Pucci, drawing from

---

Odyssey between hero and bard, see Murnaghan 1987:148–54; and cf. the remark by Segal, who, instancing the expression *emon kleos*, notes that, in Iliadic passages with parallel usage, this phrase or its equivalent refers to a *kleos* that "the hero is in the process of creating" (1983:25–26).

[48] Thalmann 1984:162; Thalmann remarks further on the implications of this technique: "By noticing this progressive transformation of the present into the past ... we observe the *Odyssey* come into being as a poem and assume a poem's proper function" (ibid.:163). For a penetrating discussion of the comparable phenomenon in the *Iliad*, see Bergren 1979.

the analysis of psychological processes, has called "retroactivation" ("Nachträglichkeit"):

> Retroactivation... names the process through which some earlier experience becomes known, and significant, only when a later experience triggers a retroactivating reading of the earlier one. Analogously, a "disguise" is recognized as such only when the previous signs (the simulating ones) come to be perceived *as* simulating through the emergence of new signs that give significance to the first ones. (Pucci 1987:86)

As "readers" of the *Odyssey* rather than actors within its narrative world, we are not ourselves subject to this "retroactivation" in the case of Odysseus, whose assumption of disguise is described in the text and therefore known to us. The case of Penelope, however, is different. For just as the duplicity of her self-presentation functions like a disguise, so her recognition of Odysseus in Book 23 operates like a "retroactivation." The stratagem of the bed now raises the possibility that Penelope's earlier, more problematic words and actions should be read with the same mindset. And indeed, as we have seen, commentators freely resolve the narrative ambiguities of Books 18–21 by endowing Penelope with the requisite intentions. But although in Penelope's case the new signs (*sēmata*) enable the question to be perceived as such, it is still incapable of resolution. For even when Penelope is mistress of her own representation in the text, as in the recognition speech she delivers to Odysseus, her words are insufficient to counteract the opacity of her meaning.

Penelope's last words of direct speech in the poem are provoked by Odysseus's account of the last trial that awaits him. They express her wish for a peaceful old age, and they constitute a recognition of uncertainty, an acknowledgment that the *telos* lies in the gods' keeping:[49]

> εἰ μὲν δὴ γῆράς γε θεοὶ τελέουσιν ἄρειον,
> ἐλπωρή τοι ἔπειτα κακῶν ὑπάλυξιν ἔσεσθαι.
>
> (If the gods grant us a good old age,
> then there is hope for an escape from troubles.)
>
> (23.286–87)

With these words, as in her recognition speech to Odysseus, Penelope thematizes her own narrative presentation, by comprehending the future within the parameters of indeterminacy. Otherwise, however, the precise meaning of her words is obscure. Focke, responding to Bethe's judgment about the speeches of this section that " 'This pointless and soulless exchange destroys the tenor of the beautiful scene, and its elimination results

---

[49] Cf. the sentiments that opened her recognition speech: θεοὶ δ' ὤπαζον ὀϊζύν, / οἳ νῶϊν ἀγάσαντο παρ' ἀλλήλοισι μένοντε / ἥβης ταρπῆναι καὶ γήραος οὐδὸν ἱκέσθαι, 23.210–12).

in no hiatus' "⁵⁰ asks, "Are Penelope's confident concluding remarks in [23.]286f. really so soulless? . . . It is precisely their tenor of meaning that can hardly be misinterpreted" (Focke 1943:371).⁵¹ Peradotto remarks concerning the same lines, "It is hard not to find some disappointment, if not bitterness [in these words]" (Peradotto 1985:453). Stanford, by contrast, regards them as hopeful: "[These lines] speak of hope in the end, a peaceful evening after a life of storm."⁵² We can compare also Ameis-Hentze-Cauer, where Penelope's words are regarded as tentative: "The happy age presupposes overcoming the dangers not yet revealed" (1964, 2(2):147–48 ad 23.286). It is significant that even when Penelope speaks as Odysseus's confidante, with full knowledge of all of his own thoughts and concerns, the meaning of her words is not transparent. This last instance of a discrepancy in interpretive opinion, then, is perhaps the best sign of all that Penelope is a figure of indeterminacy in the *Odyssey*. For as we see here in her last words, even when Penelope speaks her mind, it is hard to know what is on it.

⁵⁰ "Zerstört dies zweck- und seelenlose Gerede die Stimmung der schönen Szene, und seine Streichung hinterlässt keine Lücke."
⁵¹ "Und sind denn Penelopes zuversichtliche Schlussworte 286f. wirklich so seelenlos? . . . Gerade ihr Stimmungswert ist doch kaum zu verkennen."
⁵² Stanford 1978, 2:404 ad 23.286–87, citing Hayman, *Odyssey*, 3 vols. (London, 1866–82).

Conclusion

INDETERMINACY IN THE *ODYSSEY*

AT THE BEGINNING of the *Odyssey* the story of Agamemnon's *nostos* displaces that of Odysseus from the narrative foreground: when Zeus first addresses the assembled divinities on Olympus, he begins by calling to mind the sorry fate of Agamemnon upon his return home from the Trojan War. At the end of the *Odyssey*, in the second *nekyia*, the story of Odysseus's *nostos* displaces that of Agamemnon: when Agamemnon is on the point of relating his own return to Achilles, the suitors appear, and Amphimedon's account of the return of Odysseus takes the place of Agamemnon's intended story. In Agamemnon's address to Odysseus, Odysseus's *kleos* is replaced, in turn, by that of Penelope. Finally, at the end of the speech, Clytemnestra's disrepute displaces Penelope's *kleos*. My discussion of Penelope's *kleos* in the *Odyssey* attempts to trace the logic of this narrative *polytropia*, which, as I interpret it, constitutes an indeterminacy of both narrative form and character representation.

I began by arguing that The House of Atreus story functions not just as a foil or warning motif in the poem, but as an alternative narrative structure already endowed by the force of tradition with a certain authority, toward which the *mythos* of the *Odyssey* is drawn. Penelope's indecision (1.249-50), which characterizes her throughout the narrative, is thus brought into juxtaposition at an early point in the poem with the paradigm of Clytemnestra's betrayal, although this parallel is not made explicit until Books 11 and 13. In the course of Book 4, however, another parallel *mythos* is introduced into the poem, in the form of a narrative diptych concerning Helen. These stories, which concern Helen's conduct at Troy, associate the paradigm of Helen with that of Clytemnestra in the second half of the poem, and refocus the question of Penelope's fidelity around remarriage rather than betrayal.

The representation of Penelope in Books 17-21, and especially in Books 18 and 19, brings into being a correlation between this indeterminacy of narrative direction and the representation of Penelope's character. For in this section of the poem Penelope appears to be pursuing simultaneously two contradictory courses of action—both remaining by the side of Telemachus and making herself available for remarriage. The structure of the narrative invites us to interpret this "doubleness" or duplicity on the analogy of the disguises assumed by Odysseus and Telemachus; but in Penelope's case, indications fixing the boundary between disguise and truth are absent from the narrative.

I have argued against an interpretation of this feature of the poem organized, from either the analytic or unitarian perspective, around a unitary notion of the subject—the idea, that is to say, that character is constituted around a core of true being represented by certain "characteristics." This absence of integrity can be understood instead as performing a specific function in the text, that of calling into question the relation between semblance and being, between disguise and truth. This disruption of the fixity of Penelope's character, then, functions, like Odysseus's disguise, as a strategy of estrangement—we do not know, in a certain sense, "who" Penelope is. Her "character" is thus rendered so as to represent an analogue to her state of sociological indeterminacy, which is defined by her lack of a *kyrios* or authorizing agent.

Both Penelope and Odysseus, then, are *xeinoi* in the second half of the poem, in different but comparable ways. Both are represented in a state of estrangement or alienation, and both play the role of *xeinos*—he as guest and she as host. Their reunion is thus effected as a convergence between *xeinos* and husband on the one hand, and wife and *xeinodokos* on the other. This representation of their reunion, and hence of their marriage—constructed anew in the narrative from a situation of alienation—constitutes, in my view, an important aspect of what I have called the *Odyssey*'s ideology of exclusivity. It focuses upon human relations as brought into being through efficacious words and actions, rather than as existing transcendentally, outside of the particularities of space and time.

In Odysseus's case, this convergence of husband and stranger attests also to the capacity of disguise not just to misrepresent reality, but to instantiate it. Penelope, however, enacts the role of *xeinodokos* while consolidating plans to abandon Odysseus's household, and thus her role of faithful wife converges also with the paradigm of Helen's betrayal, just as earlier in the poem her irresolution had suggested an association with Clytemnestra. This indeterminacy persists until the recognition speech, where the effect of Penelope's appeal to the example of Helen is to subvert the distinction between faithfulness and betrayal.

Like Shakespeare's Cressida, then, Penelope in the *Odyssey* calls into question the relation between identity and the self it represents. Cressida, constituted as such through her vows of faithfulness to Troilus, cannot but become other than what she is through her dalliance with Diomedes: "This she? No, this is Diomed's Cressida. . . . This is not she. . . . This is, and is not, Cressid!" (*Troilus and Cressida* 5.2:140, 145a, 149b; cf. Miller 1977). Similarly, the unity of Penelope's *kleos*, which is constituted through her faithfulness to Odysseus, is systematically disrupted in the *Odyssey* through its threatened displacement by another, alternate story of faithlessness and betrayal—whether Penelope's own, or that of Clytemnestra or of Helen. Troilus would "rather think this not Cressid" (5.2:136b) than generalize from her example to "womanhood," in the manner of those "stubborn critics, apt, without a theme / For depravation, to square the general sex / By Cressid's rule" (5.2:134–36). But in Agamemnon's speech, as we have seen, the "lovely song" that celebrates Penelope's *kleos* is readily displaced in the end by the paradigmatic force of Clytemnestra's ill repute, made famous in a "hateful song" (24.200–201).

Agamemnon's generalizing condemnation constitutes a gesture of narrative control—an attempt at evading the ambiguity of Troilus's despairing uncertainty. Agamemnon endeavors to stabilize the indeterminacy of the narrative around a polarity of good woman and bad, and readers throughout the centuries have responded readily to the logic of a contrast that is inscribed as canonical truth in the Western tradition. But Penelope resists conformity to the conventions of both sexual fidelity and character representation. She is constituted instead around a persistence of either/or that is drawn toward the unifying power of a monologic *kleos*, yet never comes fully under its sway. In this she is perhaps a better representative of the spirit that animates the *Odyssey* than Odysseus, even—a spirit of indeterminacy affecting both character identity and narrative form, and expressed principally as a refusal of closure, a persistence of uncertainty. For Odysseus as the master of disguises undergoes a series of refigurations of self, but he is "recognized" in the end, and thus is finally centered on a core of true being. The ambiguities of his identity are displaced onto the aftermath of his narrative history—the prophecy that consigns him to indeterminate wandering.

Penelope's *kleos* by contrast, is never fully stabilized. She remains, like the bride in Marcel Duchamp's famous work, *The Bride Stripped Bare by Her Bachelors, Even* (the *Large Glass*),[1] elusive and indecipherable, suspended in an unknowability that is only imperfectly resolved by the words to which she gives expression. The Bride transmits her desire to her suitors through a triple network of "ciphers," which are set in a nebulous cloud of "blossoming," and which sort the alphabetic units emitted by a "letter box."[2] The Bride herself is represented only as a series of intersecting metallic planes and cylinders that one critic has characterized as "a dressmaker's dummy stripped to its metal armature" (Golding 1972:43). Like Duchamp's Bride, Penelope responds to the aggressive desires of her suitors

---

[1] This work, executed by Duchamp in New York in 1915–23, is now part of an installation in the Philadelphia Museum of Art. It consists of two registers, the *Bride's Domain* in the upper portion, and the *Bachelor Apparatus* in the lower.

[2] The iconographic program of the Large Glass was first explicated by Duchamp's publication in 1924 of the *Green Box*, a collection of notes, diagrams, and sketches for this hermetic work. For further explanation and analysis, see Schwarz 1973 and Golding 1972.

with a complex mechanism of messages that occludes access to her true meaning. Constituted as she is through a *kleos* that resists the assumption of a determinate form, Penelope thus becomes the first example in a long tradition of literary figures whose representation defies the conventions that delimit the construction of the subject.

BIBLIOGRAPHY

Abou-Zeid, A. 1966. "Honour and Shame among the Bedouins of Egypt." In *Honour and Shame*, ed. J. Peristiany, pp. 243–59. Chicago: University of Chicago Press.

Alexiou, M. 1974. *The Ritual Lament in Greek Tradition*. Cambridge: Cambridge University Press.

Allen, W., Jr. 1939. "The Theme of the Suitors in the *Odyssey*." *Transactions of the American Philological Association* 70:104–24.

Allione, L. 1963. *Telemaco e Penelope nell' Odissea*. Turin: G. Giappichelli.

Ameis, K. F., and C. Hentze 1877–90. *Anhang zu Homers Odyssee*. 4 vols. Leipzig: Teubner. [Cited here as Ameis-Hentze.]

Ameis, K. F., C. Hentze and P. Cauer. [1908–20] 1964. *Homers Odyssee f. den Schulgebrauch erklärt von K. F. Ameis u. C. Hentze, bearbeitet von P. Cauer*. 2 vols. Reprint of the Teubner edition. Amsterdam: Hakkert. [Cited here as Ameis-Hentze-Cauer.]

Amory, A. 1963. "The Reunion of Odysseus and Penelope." In *Essays on the "Odyssey,"* ed. C. H. Taylor, Jr., pp. 100–121. Bloomington: Indiana University Press.

———. 1966. "The Gates of Horn and Ivory." *Yale Classical Studies* 20:3–57.

Andersen, Ø. 1977. "Odysseus and the Wooden Horse." *Symbolae Osloenses* 52:5–18.

Apthorp, M. J. 1980. "The Obstacles to Telemachus' Return." *Classical Quarterly*, n.s. 30:1–22.

Arend, W. 1975. *Die typischen Scenen bei Homer*. Problemata 7. Reprint of 1933 edition. Berlin: Weidmann.

Arthur, M. B. 1973. "Early Greece: The Origins of the Western Attitude toward Women." In *Women in Antiquity*, ed. J. P. Sullivan. *Arethusa*, special issue, 6(1):7–58. [Reprinted in *Women in the Ancient World: The "Arethusa" Papers*, ed. J. Peradotto and J. P. Sullivan, pp. 7–58. Albany: State University of New York Press, 1984.]

———. 1981. "The Divided World of *Iliad* VI." In *Women in Antiquity*, ed. H. P. Foley. *Women's Studies*, special issue, 8(1–2):21–46. [Reprinted in *Reflections on Women in Antiquity*, ed. H. P. Foley, pp. 19–44. New York: Gordon and Breach, 1981.]

———. 1982. "Women and the Family in Ancient Greece." In *Concepts of Culture*, ed. K. Erikson. *The Yale Review*, special issue, 71 (4): 532–47.

———. 1983. "The Dream of a World without Women: Poetics and the Circles of Order in the *Theogony* Proemium." In *Semiotics and Classical Studies*, ed. N. Felson-Rubin. *Arethusa*, special issue, 16:(1–2):97–116.

———. 1984. "Review of W. Thomas MacCary, *Childlike Achilles: Ontogeny and Phylogeny in the 'Iliad'*." *Psychoanalytic Quarterly* 53:621–26.

Austin, N. 1969. "*Telemachos Polymechanos*." *California Studies in Classical Antiquity* 2:45–63.

———. 1972. "Name Magic in the *Odyssey*." *California Studies in Classical Antiquity* 5:1–19.

———. 1975. *Archery at the Dark of the Moon: Poetic Problems in Homer's "Odyssey."* Berkeley: University of California Press.

Bader, F. 1976. "L'Art de la fugue dans l'*Odyssée*." *Revue des études grecques* 89:18–39.

Bassett, S. E. 1918. "The Second Necyia." *Classical Journal* 13:521–26.

Bergren, A. 1979. "Helen's Web: Time and Tableau in the *Iliad*." *Helios* 7:19–34.

———. 1981. "Helen's 'Good Drug': *Odyssey* IV 1–305." In *Contemporary Literary Hermeneutics and Interpretation of Classical Texts*, ed. S. Kresic, pp. 201–14. Ottawa: Ottawa University Press.

———. 1983. "Odyssean Temporality: Many (Re)turns." In *Approaches to Homer*, ed. C. A. Rubino and C. W. Shelmerdine, pp. 38–73. Austin: University of Texas Press.

Besslich, S. 1966. *Schweigen-Verschweigen-Übergehen. Die Darstellung des Unausgesprochenen in der Odyssee*. Heidelberg: Carl Winter.

Beye, C. R. 1974. "Male and Female in the Homeric Poems." *Ramus* 3:87–101.

Biale, R. 1984. *Women and Jewish Law: An Exploration of Women's Issues in Halakhic Sources*. New York: Schocken Books.

Block, E. 1985. "Clothing Makes the Man: A Pattern in the *Odyssey*." *Transactions of the American Philological Association* 115:1–11.

Bona, G. 1966. *Studi sull' Odissea*. Turin: G. Giappichelli.

Bourdieu, P. 1966. "The Sentiment of Honour in Kabyle Society." In *Honour and Shame*, ed. J. Peristiany, pp. 191–241. Chicago: University of Chicago Press.

Büchner, W. 1931. "Die Niptra in der Odyssee (19.308–507)." *Rheinisches Museum*, n.s. 80:129–36.

———. 1940. "Die Penelopeszenen in der Odyssee." *Hermes* 75:129–67.

Byre, C. 1988. "Penelope and the Suitors before Odysseus: *Odyssey* 18.158–303." *American Journal of Philology* 109:159–73.

Clark, M. E. 1986. "Neoanalysis: A Bibliographical Review." *Classical World* 79:379–94.

Clarke, H. W. 1967. *The Art of the "Odyssey."* Englewood Cliffs, N.J.: Prentice-Hall.

Clay, J. S. 1981–82. "Immortal and Ageless Forever." *Classical Journal* 77:112–17.

———. 1983. *The Wrath of Athena: Gods and Men in the "Odyssey."* Princeton: Princeton University Press.

Colakis, M. 1986. "The Laughter of the Suitors in *Odyssey* 20." *Classical World* 79:137–41.

Combellack, F. M. 1973. "Three Odyssean Problems." *California Studies in Classical Antiquity* 6:17–46.

Cunliffe, R. J. 1963. *A Lexicon of the Homeric Dialect*. Norman: University of Oklahoma Press.

D'Arms, E. F., and K. K. Hulley. 1946. "The Oresteia-Story in the *Odyssey*." *Transactions of the American Philological Association* 77:207–13.

Davis, N. 1983. *The Return of Martin Guerre*. Cambridge, Mass.: Harvard University Press.

Delebecque, E. 1958. *Télémaque et la structure de l'Odyssée*. Annales de la Faculté des Lettres d'Aix-en-Provence, n.s. 21. Editions Ophrys.

———. 1980. *Construction de l'Odyssée*. Paris: Les Belles Lettres.

Devereux, G. 1957. "Penelope's Character." *Psychoanalytic Quarterly* 26:378–86.

Dietz, G. 1971. "Das Bett des Odysseus." *Symbolon* 7:9–32.

Dimock, G. E. 1989. *The Unity of the Odyssey*. Amherst: The University of Massachusetts Press.

Dindorf, W. [1855] 1962. *Scholia Graeca in Homeri Odysseam ex codicibus aucta et emendata*. Amsterdam: Hakkert.

Dupont-Roc, R., A. Le Boulluec. 1976. "Le Charme du récit (*Odyssée*, IV, 219–289)." In *Écriture et théorie poétiques: Lectures d'Homère, Eschyle, Platon, Aristote*, ed. J. Lallot and A. Le Boulluec, pp. 30–39. Paris: Presses de l'École Normale Supérieure.

Edwards, A. T. 1985. *Achilles in the "Odyssey:" Ideologies of Heroism in the Homeric Epic*. Beiträge zur klassischen Philologie 171. Königstein: Anton Hain.

Edwards, M. 1975. "Type-Scenes and Homeric Hospitality." *Transactions of the American Philological Association* 105:51–72.

———. 1987. *Homer: Poet of the "Iliad."* Baltimore: The Johns Hopkins University Press.

Eisenberger, H. 1973. *Studien zur Odyssee*. Weisbaden: Franz Steiner.

Emlyn-Jones, C. 1984. "The Reunion of Penelope and Odysseus." *Greece and Rome* 31:1–18.

Erbse, H. 1972. *Beiträge zum Verständnis der Odyssee*. Untersuchungen zur antiken Literatur und Geschichte 13. Berlin: de Gruyter.

Farron, S. G. 1979–80. "The *Odyssey* as an Anti-Aristocratic Statement." *Studies in Antiquity* 1:59–101.

Felson-Rubin, N. 1988. "Penelope's Perspective: Character from Plot." In *Beyond Oral Poetry: Recent Trends in Homeric Interpretation*, ed. J. M. Bremer, I.J.F. De Jong, and J. Kalff, pp. 61–83. Amsterdam: B. R. Grüner.

Fenik, B. 1968. *Typical Battle Scenes in the "Iliad:" Studies in the Narrative Techniques of Homeric Battle Descriptions*. Hermes Einzelschrift 21. Wiesbaden: Franz Steiner.

———. 1974. *Studies in the "Odyssey."* Hermes Einzelschrift 30. Wiesbaden: Franz Steiner.

———, ed. 1978. *Homer: Tradition and Invention*. Leiden: Brill.

Fernández-Galiano, A. 1986. "Introduction and Commentary for Books 21–22." In *Omero, Odissea, vol. vi, libri xxi–xxiv: Introduzione, testo e commento*, a cura di Manuel Fernández-Galiano e A. Heubeck. Rome: Fondazione Lorenzo Valla/Milan: Mondadori.

Ferrucci, F. 1980. *The Poetics of Disguise: The Autobiography of the Work in Homer, Dante, and Shakespeare*. Trans. A. Dunnigan. Ithaca: Cornell University Press.

Finkelberg, M. 1986. "Is ΚΛΕΟΣ ΑΦΘΙΤΟΝ a Homeric Formula?" *Classical Quarterly* 36:1–5.

Finley, J. H., Jr. 1978. *Homer's "Odyssey."* Cambridge, Mass.: Harvard University Press.
Finley, M. I. 1955. "Marriage, Sale and Gift in the Homeric World." *Revue internationale des droits de l'antiquité*, ser. 3, vol. 2:167–94.
———. 1978. *The World of Odysseus*. New York: Viking Press.
Floyd, E. 1980. "*Kleos Aphthiton*: An Indo-European Perspective on Early Greek Poetry." *Glotta* 58:133–57.
Focke, F. 1943. *Die Odyssee*. Tübinger Beiträge zur Altertumswissenschaft 37. Stuttgart and Berlin: Kohlhammer.
Foley, H. 1978. " 'Reverse Similes' and Sex Roles in the *Odyssey*." *Arethusa* 11:7–26.
Forsyth, N. 1979. "The Allurement Scene: A Typical Pattern in Greek Oral Epic." *California Studies in Classical Antiquity* 12:107–20.
Frame, D. 1978. *The Myth of Return in Early Greek Epic*. New Haven: Yale University Press.
Gaisser, J. 1969. "A Structural Analysis of the Digressions in the *Iliad* and the *Odyssey*." *Harvard Studies in Classical Philology* 73:1–43.
Gernet, L. 1976. "Sur le symbolisme de politique: le foyer commun." In *Anthropologie de la Grèce antique*, pp. 382–402. Paris: Maspero. Reprint.
Goldhill, S. 1988. "Reading Differences: The *Odyssey* and Juxtaposition." *Ramus* 17:1–31.
Golding, J. 1972. *Marcel Duchamp: The Bride Stripped Bare by Her Bachelors, Even*. New York: Viking Press.
Gould, J. P. 1973. "*HIKETEIA*." *Journal of Hellenic Studies* 93:74–103.
Griffin, J. 1977. "The Epic Cycle and the Uniqueness of Homer." *Journal of Hellenic Studies* 97:39–53.
Groten, F. J. 1968. "Homer's Helen." *Greece and Rome*, n.s. 15:33–39.
Gunn, D. M. 1971. "Thematic Composition and Homeric Authorship." *Harvard Studies in Classical Philology* 75:1–31.
Hainsworth, J. B. 1988. Introduction and commentary on Books 5–8. In A. Heubeck, S. West, and J. B. Hainsworth, *A Commentary on Homer's "Odyssey,"* vol. 1, *Introduction and Books I–VIII*. Oxford: Clarendon Press.
Hansen, W. F. 1972. *The Conference Sequence: Patterned Narrative and Narrative Inconsistency in the "Odyssey."* University of California Publications in Classical Philology 8. Berkeley: University of California Press.
Harrison, A.R.W. 1968. *The Law of Athens, I: The Family and Property*. Oxford: Clarendon Press.
Harsh, P. W. 1950. "Penelope and Odysseus in *Odyssey* XIX." *American Journal of Philology* 71:1–21.
Heubeck, A. 1978. "Homeric Studies Today: Results and Prospects." In *Homer: Tradition and Invention*, ed. B. Fenik, pp. 1–17. Leiden: Brill.
———. 1986. "Introduction and Commentary for Books 23–24." *Omero, Odissea*, vol. vi, *libri xxi–xxiv: Introduzione, testo e commento*, a cura di M. Fernández-Galiano e A. Heubeck. Rome: Fondazione Lorenzo Valla/Milan: Mondadori.
———. 1988. "General Introduction." In A. Heubeck, S. West, and J. B. Hains-

worth, *A Commentary on Homer's "Odyssey,"* vol. 1, *Introduction and Books I–VIII.* Oxford: Clarendon Press.

———. 1989. "Commentary on Books 9–12." In A. Heubeck and A. Hoekstra, *A Commentary on Homer's "Odyssey,"* vol. 2, *Books IX–XVI.* Oxford: Clarendon Press.

Hoekstra, A. 1989. "Commentary on Books 13–16." In A. Heubeck and A. Hoekstra, *A Commentary on Homer's "Odyssey,"* vol. 2, *Books IX–XVI.* Oxford: Clarendon Press.

Hölscher, Uvo. 1939. *Untersuchungen zur Form der Odyssee. Szenenwechsel und gleichzeitige Handlungen.* Berlin: Wiedmann.

———. 1967a. "Die Atridensage in der Odyssee." In *Festschrift für Richard Alewyn,* ed. H. Singer and B. von Wiese, pp. 1–16. Cologne: Böhlau.

———. 1967b. "Penelope vor den Freiern." In *Lebende Antike: Symposion für Rudolf Sühnel,* ed. H. Meller and H.-J. Zimmermann, pp. 27–33. Berlin: E. Schmidt.

———. 1978. "The Transformation from Folk-tale to Epic." In *Homer: Tradition and Invention,* ed. B. Fenik, pp. 51–67. Leiden: Bill.

———. 1989. *Die Odyssee: Epos zwischen Märchen und Roman.* Munich: C. H. Beck.

Houston, G. W. 1975. Θρόνος, δίφρος and Odysseus' Change from Beggar to Avenger." *Classical Philology* 70:212-14.

Jacobson, H. 1974. *Ovid's "Heroides."* Princeton: Princeton University Press.

Jones, P. 1988. "The ΚΛΕΟΣ of Telemachus: *Odyssey* 1.95." *American Journal of Philology* 109:496–506.

Kakridis, H. 1963. *La Notion de l'amitié et de l'hospitalité chez Homère.* Thessaloniki: Ē Bibliothēkē tou Philologou.

Kakridis, J. 1971a. "Problems of the Homeric Helen." In *Homer Revisited,* pp. 25–53. Publications of the New Society of Letters at Lund 64. Lund: Gleerup.

———. 1971b. "The Recognition of Odysseus." In *Homer Revisited,* pp. 151–63. Publications of the New Society of Letters at Lund 64. Lund: Gleerup.

———. 1971c. "The Rôle of the Woman in the *Iliad.*" In *Homer Revisited,* pp. 68–75. Publications of the New Society of Letters at Lund 64. Lund: Gleerup.

Kearns, E. 1982. "The Return of Odysseus: A Homeric Theoxeny." *Classical Quarterly* 32:2–8.

Kennedy, G. 1986. "Helen's Web Unraveled." *Arethusa* 19:5–14.

Kessels, A.H.M. 1978. *Studies on the Dream in Greek Literature.* Utrecht: HES Publishers.

Kirchhoff, A. 1879. *Die Homerische Odyssee.* 2nd ed. Berlin: Wilhelm Hertz.

Kirk, G. S. 1962. *The Songs of Homer.* Cambridge: Cambridge University Press.

Klingner, F. 1964. "Über die vier ersten Bücher der Odyssee." In *Studien zur griechischen und römischen Literatur,* ed. K. Bartels, pp. 39–79. Zürich: Artemis.

Kullmann, W. 1981. "Zur Methode der Neoanalyse in der Homerforschung." *Wiener Studien,* n.s. 15:5–42.

———. 1984. "Oral Poetry Theory and Neoanalysis in Homeric Research." *Greek, Roman and Byzantine Studies* 25:307–23.

Kunst, K. 1924–25. "Die Schuld der Klytaimestra." *Wiener Studien* 44:18–32, 143–54.

Kurtz, J. G. 1989. "The Mind and Heart of Penelope." *New England Classical Newsletter and Journal* 17:22–25.
Lacey, W. K. 1966. "Homeric *HEΔNA* and Penelope's *ΚΥΡΙΟΣ*." *Journal of Hellenic Studies* 86:55–68.
Lang, H. S. 1982. "An Homeric Echo in Aristotle." *Philological Quarterly* 61:329–39.
Lattimore, R. 1969. "Nausikaa's Suitors." In *Classical Studies Presented to Ben Edwin Perry*. Illinois Studies in Language and Literature, special issue, 58:88–102.
Lesky, A. 1967. "Die Schuld der Klytaimestra." *Wiener Studien*, n.s. 1:5–21.
Levine, D. B. 1982. "*Odyssey* 18: Iros as Paradigm for the Suitors." *The Classical Journal* 77:200–204.
———. 1982–83. "Homeric Laughter and the Unsmiling Suitors." *The Classical Journal* 78:97–104.
———. 1983. "Penelope's Laugh: *Odyssey* 18.163." *American Journal of Philology* 104:172–78.
———. 1987. "*Flens Matrona et Meretrices Gaudentes*: Penelope and Her Maids." *Classical World* 81:23–27.
Levy, H. L. 1963. "The Odyssean Suitors and the Host-Guest Relationship." *Transactions of the American Philological Association* 94:145–53.
Loraux, N. 1982. "Mourir devant Troie, tomber pour Athènes: de la gloire du héros à l'idée de la cité." In *La mort, les morts dans les sociétés anciennes*, ed. G. Gnoli and J.-P. Vernant, pp. 27–43. Cambridge: Cambridge University Press.
Lord, A. B. 1951. "Composition by Theme in Homer and Southslavic Epos." *Transactions of the American Philological Assocation* 82:71–80.
———. 1960. *The Singer of Tales*. Cambridge, Mass.: Harvard University Press.
MacDowell, D. M. 1978. *The Law in Classical Athens*. Ithaca: Cornell University Press.
Mackail, J. W. 1916. "*Penelope in the* Odyssey." Occasional Publications of the Classical Association 5. Cambridge: Cambridge University Press.
Mactoux, M.-M. 1975. *Pénélope: Légende et Mythe*. Annales Littéraires de l'Université de Besançon 175. Paris: Belles Lettres.
Marquardt, P. 1985. "Penelope *Polutropos*." *American Journal of Philology* 106:32–48.
Martin, R. P. 1989. *The Language of Heroes: Speech and Performance in the "Iliad."* Ithaca: Cornell University Press.
Matsumoto, N. 1981. "Die Freier in der Odyssee." In *Gnomosyne: menschliches Denken und Handeln in der frühgriechischen Literatur. Festschrift für Walter Marg zum 70 Geburtstag*, ed. G. Kurz, D. Müller, and W. Nicolai, pp. 135–41. Munich: C. H. Beck.
Merkelbach, R. 1969. *Untersuchungen zur Odyssee*. Zetemata: Monographien zur klassischen Altertumswissenschaft 2. Rev. ed. Munich: C. H. Beck.
Miller, J. H. 1977. "Ariachne's Broken Woof." *The Georgia Review* 31:44–60.
Monro, D. B. 1901. *Homer's "Odyssey": Books XIII–XXIV*. Oxford: Clarendon Press.
Monsacré, H. 1984. *Les Larmes d'Achille. Le héros, la femme et la souffrance dans la poésie d'Homère*. Paris: Albin Michel.
Mossé, C. 1981. "La Femme dans la société homérique." *Klio* 63:149–57.

Müller, M. 1966. *Athene als göttliche Helferin in der Odyssee:* Untersuchungen zur Form der epischen Aristie. Heidelberg: Carl Winter.

Murnaghan, S. 1986. "Penelope's *Agnoia*: Knowledge, Power, and Gender in the *Odyssey*." In *Rescuing Creusa: New Methodological Approaches to Women in Antiquity*, ed. M. Skinner. *Helios*, special issue, 13(2):103–15.

———. 1987. *Disguise and Recognition in the "Odyssey."* Princeton: Princeton University Press.

Naerebout, F. G. 1987. "Male-Female Relationships in the Homeric Epics." In *Sexual Asymmetry: Studies in Ancient Society*, ed. J. Blok and P. Mason, pp. 109–46. Amsterdam: Gieben.

Nagler, M. 1974. *Spontaneity and Tradition: A Study in the Oral Art of Homer.* Berkeley: University of California Press.

Nagy, G. 1974. *Comparative Studies in Greek and Indic Meter.* Cambridge, Mass.: Harvard University Press.

———. 1979. *The Best of the Achaeans: Concepts of the Hero in Archaic Greek Poetry.* Baltimore: The Johns Hopkins University Press.

———. 1981. "Another Look at *Kleos Aphthiton.*" *Würzburger Jahrbücher für die Altertumswissenschaft*, n.s. 7:113–16.

Nortwick, T. van. 1979. "Penelope and Nausicaa." *Transactions of the American Philological Association* 109:269–76.

———. 1983. "Penelope as Double Agent: *Odyssey* 21.1–60." *Classical World* 77:24–25.

Odissea. 1981–86. [Omero, *Odissea.*] General introduction by A. Heubeck and S. West. Italian trans. G. A. Privatera. 6 vols. Vol. 1, *Libri I–IV* (1981), ed. S. West. Vol. 2, *Libri V–VIII* (1982), ed. J. B. Hainsworth. Vol. 3, *Libri IX–XII* (1983), ed. A. Heubeck. Vol. 4, *Libri XIII–XVI* (1984), ed. A. Hoekstra. Vol. 5, *Libri XVII–XX* (1985), ed. J. Russo. Vol. 6, *Libri XXI–XXIV* (1986), ed. M. Fernández-Galiano and A. Heubeck. Rome: Fondazione Lorenzo Valla/Milan: Mondadori.

Olson, S. D. 1989. "The Stories of Helen and Menelaus (*Odyssey* 4.240–89) and the Return of Odysseus." *American Journal of Philology* 110:387–94.

Onians, R. B. [1951] 1988. *The Origins of European Thought about the Body, the Mind, the Soul, the World, Time, and Fate.* Cambridge: Cambridge University Press.

Page, D. 1955. *The Homeric Odyssey.* Oxford: Clarendon Press.

Pedrick, V. 1988. "The Hospitality of Noble Women in the *Odyssey.*" *Helios* 15:85–101.

Pedrick, V., and N. Rabinowitz. 1986. "Introduction." In *Audience-Oriented Criticism and the Classics*, ed. V. Pedrick and N. Rabinowitz. *Arethusa*, special issue, 19(2):105–14.

Peradotto, J. 1985. "Prophecy Degree Zero: Tiresias and the End of the *Odyssey.*" In *Oralità: Cultura, Letteratura, Discorso*, Atti del Convegno Internazionale (Urbino, 21–25 July 1980), ed. B. Gentili and G. Paioni, pp. 429–59. Rome: Edizione dell'Ateneo.

Petersmann, H. 1981. "Homer und das Märchen." *Wiener Studien*, n.s. 15:43–68.

Pitt-Rivers, J. 1977a. "The Law of Hospitality." In *The Fate of Shechem or The Politics of Sex: Essays in the Anthropology of the Mediterranean*, pp. 94–112. Cambridge: Cambridge University Press.

Pitt-Rivers, J. 1977b. "Women and Sanctuary in the Mediterranean." In *The Fate of Shechem or The Politics of Sex: Essays in the Anthropology of the Mediterranean*, pp. 113–25. Cambridge: Cambridge University Press.

Platt, A. 1899. "Notes on the *Odyssey*." *Classical Review* 13:382–84.

Pucci, P. 1980. "The Language of the Muses." In *Classical Mythology in Twentieth-Century Thought and Literature*, ed. W. M. Aycock and T. M. Klein, pp. 163–86. Lubbock: Texas Tech Press.

———. 1982. "The Proem of the *Odyssey*." *Arethusa* 15:39–62.

———. 1986. "Les Figures de la métis dans l'*Odyssée*." *Metis: Revue d'anthropologie du monde grec ancien* 1:7–28.

———. 1987. *Odysseus Polutropos: Intertextual Readings in the "Odyssey" and the "Iliad."* Ithaca: Cornell University Press.

Qviller, B. 1981. "The Dynamics of the Homeric Society." *Symbolae Osloensis* 56:109–55.

Rankin, A. V. 1962. "Penelope's Dreams in Books XIX and XX of the *Odyssey*." *Helikon* 2:617–24.

Redfield, J. 1975. *Nature and Culture in the "Iliad:" The Tragedy of Hector*. Chicago: The University of Chicago Press.

———. 1982. "Notes on the Greek Wedding." In *Texts & Contexts: American Classical Studies in Honor of J.-P. Vernant. Arethusa*, special issue, 15:181–201.

———. 1990. "Drama and Community: Aristophanes and Some of His Rivals." In *Nothing to Do with Dionysus?* ed. J. Winkler and F. Zeitlin, pp. 314–35. Princeton: Princeton University Press.

Reinhardt, K. 1960a. "Das Parisurteil." In *Tradition und Geist*, pp. 16–36. Göttingen: Vandenhoeck und Ruprecht.

———. 1960b. "Homer und die Telemachie." In *Tradition und Geist*, pp. 37–46. Göttingen: Vandenhoeck und Ruprecht.

———. 1960c. "Die Abenteuer der Odyssee." In *Tradition und Geist*, pp. 47–124. Göttingen: Vandenhoeck und Ruprecht.

Richardson, N. J. 1983. "Recognition Scenes in the *Odyssey* and Ancient Literary Criticism." *Papers of the Liverpool Latin Seminar* 4:219–35.

Robertson, M. 1975. *A History of Greek Art*. 2 vols. Cambridge: Cambridge University Press.

Roisman, H. M. 1987. "Penelope's Indignation." *Transactions of the American Philological Association* 117:59–68.

Russo, J. 1982. "Interview and Aftermath: Dream, Fantasy, and Intuition in *Odyssey* 19 and 20." *American Journal of Philology* 103:4–18.

———. 1985. *Omero, Odissea, vol. v, libri xvii–xx: Introduzione, testo e commento*, a cura di Joseph Russo. Rome: Fondazione Lorenzo Valla/Milan: Mondadori.

Rüter, K. 1969. *Odysseeinterpretationen: Untersuchungen zum ersten Buch und zur Phaiakis*. Ed. K. Matthiessen. *Hypomnemata* 19. Göttingen: Vandenhoeck and Ruprecht.

Saïd, S. 1979. "Les Crimes des prétendants: La Maison d'Ulysse et les festins de l'Odyssée." In *Études de littérature ancienne*, pp. 9–49. Paris: Presses de l'École Normale Supérieure.

Schadewaldt, W. 1970a. "Die homerische Frage gestern und heute." In *Hellas und Hesperien: Gesammelte Schriften zur antike und zur neueren Literatur in zwei Bänden*, 1:16–21. 2nd ed. Zurich and Stuttgart: Artemis.

———. 1970b. "Der Prolog der Odyssee." In *Hellas und Hesperien: Gesammelte Schriften zur antike und zur neueren Literatur in zwei Bänden*, 1:42–58. 2nd ed. Zurich and Stuttgart: Artemis.

———. 1970c. "Neue Kriterien zur Odyssee-Analyse. Die Widererkennung des Odysseus und der Penelope." In *Hellas und Hesperien: Gesammelte Schriften zur antike und zur neueren Literatur in zwei Bänden*, 1:58–77. 2nd ed. Zurich and Stuttgart: Artemis.

———. 1970d. "Anhang: Die erste Begegnung des Odysseus und der Penelope (Odyssee 18,158ff.)." In *Hellas und Hesperien: Gesammelte Schriften zur antike und zur neueren Literatur in zwei Bänden*, 1:77–78. 2nd ed. Zurich and Stuttgart: Artemis.

———. 1970e. "Kleiderdinge: Zur Analyse der Odyssee." In *Hellas und Hesperien: Gesammelte Schriften zur antike und zur neueren Literatur in zwei Bänden*, 1:79–93. 2nd ed. Zurich and Stuttgart: Artemis.

———. 1970f. "Der Helioszorn in der Odyssee." In *Hellas und Hesperien: Gesammelte Schriften zur antike und zur neueren Literatur in zwei Bänden*, 1:93–104. 2nd ed. Zurich and Stuttgart: Artemis.

———.1970g. "Anhang: Verzeichnis der dem Dichter B angehörenden Partien der Odyssee." In *Hellas und Hesperien: Gesammelte Schriften zur antike und zur neueren Literatur in zwei Bänden*, 1:105. 2nd ed. Zurich and Stuttgart: Artemis.

Schwartz, E. 1924. *Die Odyssee*. Munich: M. Hueber.

Schwarz, A. 1973. "The Alchemist Stripped Bare in the Bachelor, Even." In A. D'Harnoncourt and K. McShine, *Marcel Duchamp*, pp. 81–98. New York: The Museum of Modern Art.

Segal, C. 1962. "The Phaeacians and the Symbolism of Odysseus' Return." *Arion* 1:17–64.

———. 1974. "Transition and Ritual in Odysseus' Return." In *Homer: The "Odyssey," A New Verse Translation*, trans. and ed. A. Cook, pp. 465–86. Norton Critical Edition. New York: W. W. Norton.

———. 1983. "*Kleos* and Its Ironies in the *Odyssey*." *L'Antiquité classique* 52:2–47.

Snell, B. [1953] 1960. *The Discovery of the Mind: The Greek Origins of European Thought*. Trans. T. G. Rosenmeyer. New York: Harper and Row.

Snodgrass, A. M. 1974. "An Historical Homeric Society?" *Journal of Hellenic Studies* 94:114–25.

Stanford, W. B., ed. 1978. *The "Odyssey" of Homer*. 2nd ed. 2 vols. London: Macmillan.

Starobinski, J. 1975. "Inside and Outside." *Hudson Review* 28:333–51.

Sternberg, M. 1985. *The Poetics of Biblical Narrative: Ideological Literature and the Drama of Reading*. Bloomington: Indiana University Press.

Stewart, D. 1976. *The Disguised Guest: Rank, Role, and Identity in the "Odyssey."* Lewisburg, Pa.: Bucknell University Press.

Suerbaum, W. 1968. "Die Ich Erzählungen des Odysseus: Überlegungen zur epischen Technik der Odyssee." *Poetica* 2:150–77.

Thalmann, W. G. 1984. *Conventions of Form and Thought in Early Greek Epic Poetry.* Baltimore: The Johns Hopkins University Press.

Thornton, A. 1970. *People and Themes in Homer's "Odyssey."* London: Methuen and Co.

———. 1984. *Homer's "Iliad": Its Composition and the Motif of Supplication.* Hypomnemata 81. Göttingen: Vandenhoeck and Ruprecht.

Tsagarakis, O. 1979. "Oral Composition, Type-Scenes and Narrative Inconsistencies in Homer." *Grazer Beiträge* 8:23–48.

Untersteiner, M. 1968. *Omero. Odissea Libro XXIV.* Florence: G. C. Sansoni.

Vallillee, G. 1955. "The Nausicaa Episode." *Phoenix* 9:175–79.

Van der Valk, M.H.A.L.H. 1966. "The Formulaic Character of Homeric Poetry and the Relation between the *Iliad* and the *Odyssey*." *L'antiquité classique* 35:5–70.

Vernant, J.-P. 1969. "Hestia-Hermes: The Religious Expression of Space and Movement among the Greeks." *Social Science Information* 8:131–68.

———. 1980a. "Marriage." In *Myth and Society in Ancient Greece,* trans. Janet Lloyd, pp. 45–70. Atlantic Highlands, N.J.: Humanities Press.

———. 1980b. "Between the Beasts and Gods." In *Myth and Society in Ancient Greece,* trans. Janet Lloyd, pp. 130–67. Atlantic Highlands, N.J.: Humanities Press.

———. 1982. "La Belle mort et le cadavre outragé." In *La Mort, les morts dans les sociétés anciennes,* ed. G. Gnoli and J.-P. Vernant, pp. 45–76. Cambridge: Cambridge University Press.

Vester, H. 1968. "Das 19. Buch der Odyssee." *Gymnasium* 75:417–34.

Walcot, P. 1970. *Greek Peasants Ancient and Modern: A Comparison of Social and Moral Values.* New York: Barnes and Noble, Inc.

———. 1977. "Odysseus and the Art of Lying." *Ancient Society* 8:1–19.

Walsh, G. 1984. *The Varieties of Enchantment: Early Greek Views of the Nature and Function of Poetry.* Chapel Hill and London: University of North Carolina Press.

Wegner, J. R. 1988. *Chattel or Person? The Status of Women in the Mishnah.* New York: Oxford University Press.

Wehrli, F. 1959. "Penelope und Telemachus." *Museum Helveticum* 16:228–37.

Wender, D. 1978. *The Last Scenes of the "Odyssey."* Mnemosyne, suppl. 52. Leiden: Brill.

West, S. 1981. "An Alternative *Nostos* for Odysseus." *Liverpool Classical Monthly* 6:169–75.

———. 1988. Introduction and commentary on Books 1–4. In A. Heubeck, S. West, and J. B. Hainsworth, *A Commentary on Homer's "Odyssey,"* vol. 1, *Introduction and Books I–VIII.* Oxford: Clarendon Press.

Wilamowitz-Moellendorff, U. von. 1884. *Homerische Untersuchungen.* In *Philologische Untersuchungen* 7, ed. A. Kiessling and U. von Wilamowitz-Moellendorf. Berlin: Weidmann.

———. 1927. *Die Heimkehr des Odysseus: Neue homerische Untersuchungen.* Berlin: Weidmann.

Winkler, J. 1990. "Penelope's Cunning and Homer's." In *The Constraints of Desire,* pp. 129–61. New York: Routledge.

Woodhouse, W. J. 1930. *The Composition of Homer's "Odyssey."* Oxford: Clarendon Press.

Zagagi, N. 1985. "Helen of Troy: Encomium and Apology." *Wiener Studien*, n.s. 19:63–88.

Zeitlin, F. I. 1981. "Travesties of Gender and Genre in Aristophanes' *Thesmophoriazusae*." In *Reflections on Women in Antiquity*, ed. H. P. Foley, pp. 169–217. New York: Gordon and Breach Science Publishers.

INDEX LOCORUM

Aristophanes, *Thesmophoriazusae*
  546–50: 5
Aristotle, *Physics*
  2.1, 193a12–14: 181
Aristotle, *Rhetoric*
  2.24,1401b35–1402a1: 39–40
Eugammon, *Telegonia*
  159
Herodotus, *Histories*
  I.32.7–8: 22n
Homer, *Iliad*,
  1.234–37: 180
  2.119: 22
  2.269: 89
  3.70: 54
  3.91: 54
  3.126–28: 188
  3.180: 40, 142
  3.282: 54
  3.285: 54
  3.351–54: 40
  3.410ff.: 40
  3.458: 54
  4.207: 68
  6.243–46: 179–80n. 33
  6.314–17: 179
  6.344: 40
  6.446: 24
  6.490–93: 36, 152
  7.87–91: 24
  9.141ff.: 174
  9.189: 7
  9.321–24: 188
  9.388ff.: 174
  9.412–16: 22
  11.762: 142
  22.304–5: 7, 22, 24
  24.426: 142
Homer, *Odyssey*
  1.4: 8
  1.28: 20
  1.34: 30, 45
  1.35–43: 29
  1.36: 29, 37
  1.39: 172
  1.41: 37
  1.88–95: 33n. 32
  1.93–95: 64
  1.206: 18
  1.213–15: 18
  1.234: 33
  1.240: 24n. 7
  1.244: 33
  1.248–50: 31
  1.249–50: 7
  1.249–50: 62
  1.249–50: 192
  1.251: 34
  1.267–70: 33
  1.269–70: 38
  1.272: 33
  1.273: 33
  1.275–78: 34
  1.275: 38
  1.276: 38
  1.279: 34
  1.279ff.: 66, 69
  1.289: 127
  1.292: 34
  1.293–305: 73
  1.294–96: 36
  1.296: 34
  1.297: 124
  1.298–300: 34, 65
  1.299–300: 42
  1.300: 24, 37
  1.311–13: 151
  1.326–27: 7, 20, 186
  1.340–41: 7, 20, 138, 186
  1.344: 20
  1.345–59: 152
  1.351: 20
  1.354–55: 20
  1.356–59: 36
  1.356–59: 152
  1.359: 157
  1.360–64: 152
  1.363–64: 140
  1.383–98: 73
  1.396: 127

1.397–98: 127
1.397–404: 37
2.7ff.: 25
2.45: 37
2.46: 37
2.49: 39
2.50: 37
2.52–53: 38
2.52–54: 37, 38
2.64: 34, 37
2.87–92: 37–38
2.91–92: 56n. 5, 62
2.92: 10, 89, 90
2.93f.: 14n. 15
2.113–14: 38
2.113: 38–39
2.117–18: 4
2.121–22: 4
2.125: 140
2.125–26: 4, 39
2.130: 39
2.132–37: 39
2.133: 39
2.195: 39
2.195–97: 38
2.212ff.: 39
2.214ff.: 69
2.220ff.: 45
2.221–23: 39
2.226: 40, 40–41n. 38
2.226–27: 45
2.227: 40–41n. 38
2.229ff.: 41
2.313: 124
2.335–36: 46
2.360: 66
3.83: 66
3.132ff.: 7
3.193–98: 42
3.194: 7, 186
3.195–248: 132
3.197–98: 42
3.198: 24
3.205–9: 65–66
3.213: 42
3.214: 42
3.214–15: 43
3.216: 42
3.225–28: 43
3.227: 43
3.232–35: 43

3.234: 44n. 44
3.241–42: 43, 72
3.250: 24
3.251–52: 68
3.266: 45
3.267–68: 45
3.269: 45
3.272: 44
3.306–10: 44
3.308: 24
3.311: 47
3.313–16: 46, 48, 59
4.91–92: 46
4.92: 24, 67
4.93: 68
4.110–12: 67
4.113: 67
4.121–22: 79
4.122: 79
4.137: 79
4.141: 133
4.145–46: 40
4.183: 67
4.200–201: 67
4.251: 78
4.260–62: 186
4.260–64: 40
4.263: 62
4.282: 79
4.282–83: 80
4.333: 171n
4.334: 171n
4.512–37: 46
4.525: 24
4.530–31: 46
4.534–37: 49
4.535: 49
4.539: 47
4.546–47: 47
4.548–49: 47
4.585–86: 47
4.611: 9
4.624–847: 73
4.625: 25
4.665: 73
4.667: 73
4.669–72: 46
4.672: 73
4.675ff.: 138
4.721: 141
4.725–26: 23

INDEX

4.758: 141
4.778: 46
4.778–86: 46
4.800: 141
4.801: 141
5.311: 24n. 7
5.365: 88
6.52: 137
6.66–67: 86
6.67: 87
6.242–43: 141
6.244: 135, 136
6.285ff.: 137
6.305: 137
7.111: 4
7.147: 137
7.153–54: 137
7.155ff.: 137
7.156–57: 137, 137n. 37
7.160: 137
7.168–69: 137
7.170–71: 135
7.226–27: 136
7.227: 136
7.295–96: 136
7.311: 136
7.312: 135, 136
7.313: 135
7.313–14: 136
7.317: 144
7.332–33: 121
8.15–16: 23
8.132ff.: 135
8.392–933: 151
8.546–47: 135
9.19–20: 23
9.435: 164
10.209: 141
10.248: 141
10.398: 141
10.457: 141
11.174–76: 41
11.177–79: 61
11.178: 9, 40–41n. 38, 70, 78
11.178–79: 62
11.179: 10, 78
11.181: 164n. 12
11.181–87: 58
11.337: 5
11.338: 137
11.342ff.: 137

11.352–53: 36
11.382–84: 52
11.405–34: 48, 49
11.409–34: 27
11.410: 49–50
11.411: 49
11.412: 50
11.412ff.: 27n. 17
11.416ff.: 50
11.418: 50n
11.421: 50n
11.421–24: 50
11.422: 24
11.422–23: 50
11.423: 7
11.423–24: 50
11.424–25: 164
11.424–26: 50
11.427: 51
11.427–28: 51
11.428: 51
11.429–30: 50
11.430–32: 50–51, 56, 185
11.432: 186
11.433–44: 51
11.434: 28, 52
11.436ff.: 80
11.436–39: 80
11.437: 54
11.438: 51
11.438–39: 8
11.439: 24, 51
11.441–43: 51
11.441–44: 54
11.441–56: 74
11.444: 51, 54
11.452–53: 51
11.453: 51
11.454–56: 51–52
11.456: 52
13.41: 151
13.70ff.: 189
13.90: 8
13.119: 189
13.298–9: 24
13.308: 58
13.332: 55
13.333–34: 55, 56, 163, 185
13.333–38: 55–58, 57, 163
13.336: 55
13.336ff.: 163

13.372–73: 56
13.376–81: 57
13.379–81: 56
13.380–81: 56n. 5, 62
13.381: 10, 89, 90
13.383ff.: 60
13.383–85: 56, 57, 58
13.393ff.: 74
13.422–23: 64
14.56–58: 171
14.90–91: 172
14.122–23: 144
14.126: 144
14.128: 144
14.151–54: 143
14.371: 24n. 7
14.391–97: 143
14.421: 45n
14.532–15.6: 59
15.10–13: 59
15.10–26: 69
15.16–17: 60
15.19: 54
15.19–26: 61
15.25: 70
15.25–26: 70
15.26: 70
15.88–91: 69
15.89: 70
15.126–27: 71
15.127–28: 71
15.174–78: 72
15.180: 72
15.268: 142
15.495–16.2: 59
15.513–17: 122, 122n
15.515—17: 138
15.518–24: 123
15.521–22: 130
15.522: 41
15.522–524: 172n. 26
15.536: 72, 116
16.33: 9
16.33–34: 10, 62
16.33–35: 71
16.37: 164n. 12
16.42: 127
16.52: 25
16.66: 121
16.67: 121
16.69–73: 122

16.71–77: 138
16.72: 25, 123n. 9
16.72–73: 125
16.73: 88, 93
16.73–77: 62
16.74: 9, 78
16.75: 169
16.76: 78
16.76–7: 10
16.95–96: 43
16.97–98: 43n
16.100–101: 44
16.121: 126
16.126–27: 7, 62, 126
16.172ff.: 160
16.186–219: 122
16.190ff.: 19
16.194–95: 161
16.205: 176
16.206: 176
16.213–14: 161
16.241–2: 23
16.269: 142
16.275: 8
16.300: 9, 157
16.300ff.: 58
16.301–5: 131
16.301–8: 163
16.322–451: 72
16.344: 25
16.358: 25
16.361–62: 25
16.376–77
16.383–92: 73–74
16.398: 45n
16.401: 74n
16.407–8: 74
16.411: 138
16.412: 138
16.431–32: 171
16.450–51: 140
17.1: 104n
17.8: 141
17.10–11: 122
17.12–15: 122
17.52–53: 122
17.150: 104
17.155–56: 116n
17.157–59: 104
17.163: 105, 116
17.170: 104n

INDEX

17.325: 154
17.342–46: 122
17.507: 138
17.508–9: 138
17.539–40: 105
17.541: 89
17.541–47: 115–16
17.542: 83
17.544: 138
17.545–47: 105
17.549: 143
17.553–88: 130
17.569–72: 137–38
17.572: 137
17.572–73: 138
17.577: 138
17.586–88: 105
18.60–65: 123
18.62: 123n. 9
18.65: 157
18.135: 164
18.157: 85n. 21
18.158–59: 106
18.158–63: 93
18.158–65: 81
18.158–303: 99n. 60
18.158ff.: 105, 116
18.160–61: 81
18.160–62: 81–83, 89
18.163: 81, 82–84, 88–89
18.164: 88, 120
18.164–65: 86
18.164ff.: 93
18.166–68: 120
18.167–68: 89n
18.204–5: 23
18.212–13: 80
18.215ff.: 89n
18.229: 124
18.248–49: 5, 139
18.251–52: 4
18.251–56: 4, 139
18.254: 139
18.255: 4
18.257–60: 91
18.265–71: 91
18.269: 91
18.269–70: 61
18.272: 92
18.279: 85
18.281–83: 78, 89, 118

18.283: 10, 89, 90
18.304: 85n. 21
18.305–6: 104n
18.313–16: 130
18.321: 130
18.325: 130
18.330–33: 131
18.390–93: 131
18.410–11: 124
19.1–475: 98
19.19: 124
19.44–45: 131
19.51–475: 96
19.53: 79
19.54: 79
19.55: 137
19.66–67: 131
19.94–95: 79
19.99: 79
19.100–507: 95
19.103–360: 132
19.107–8: 139
19.107ff.: 4
19.109: 144
19.115: 142
19.124–25: 4
19.124–29: 4, 139
19.127: 139
19.128: 4
19.134–35: 144
19.136: 138–39
19.137: 84
19.138ff.: 14n. 15
19.157–58: 84, 139
19.158: 4
19.158–60: 139
19.160–61: 124
19.203: 8
19.208–9: 141
19.209–10: 141
19.211–12: 164
19.212: 164
19.213: 141
19.249: 141
19.250: 103n. 73, 116
19.251: 141
19.253–54: 116, 141
19.253–60: 144
19.254: 141–42
19.257–59: 141
19.257–60: 144

19.262–307: 144
19.264: 141
19.268: 141
19.268–72: 115
19.269–72: 116
19.300–302: 116
19.302: 116
19.303–4: 116n
19.305: 116
19.309: 103, 103n. 71, 116, 146–47
19.309–15: 144
19.309–34: 144
19.312: 147
19.312–13: 103n. 71
19.312–14: 116–17
19.312–16: 142
19.313: 144
19.314–15: 143
19.322–23: 143
19.325–28: 143–44
19.332–34: 143–44
19.358a: 133n. 27
19.361–507: 132
19.380: 133
19.388–466: 93
19.389: 137, 137n. 38
19.389–90: 78–79
19.467ff.: 93
19.474: 176
19.476: 96
19.476–604: 96
19.480: 162
19.484: 176
19.488–90: 162
19.500–502: 134
19.506: 137
19.508–604: 95, 102
19.513: 141
19.516–17: 145
19.518: 145n
19.523: 145
19.524: 88, 146
19.524–29: 62
19.524–31: 145
19.524ff.: 92
19.525: 9, 78
19.525, 528–29: 117
19.527: 169
19.528: 78
19.528–29: 10
19.530ff.: 124

19.536–39: 71–72n. 33
19.536–50: 146
19.537: 147
19.541: 147
19.547: 146
19.550: 117
19.555–58: 146
19.560ff.: 93
19.565: 146
19.568–69: 102
19.569: 147
19.570: 147
19.570ff.: 147
19.571–72: 117
19.572: 117
19.577–81: 149–50
19.581: 147
19.582–87: 78
19.583–87: 118
19.585ff.: 103
19.603: 141
19.603–4: 140
20.6–8: 149
20.56: 141
20.58: 141
20.59: 141
20.62–90: 149
20.70–72: 5
20.78: 140n, 149
20.82: 149
20.84: 141
20.87: 149
20.88: 149
20.89: 149
20.90: 149n. 49
20.91: 104n
20.92: 141
20.146: 25
20.262–67: 123–24
20.263: 123n. 9
20.264–65: 127
20.268–69: 124
20.281–83: 143
20.290: 172n. 26
20.294–95: 171
20.308–10: 124
20.320: 124
20.333: 145
20.339–340: 145
20.341–42: 145
21.1–2: 106

INDEX

21.34: 151n
21.56: 141
21.57: 141
21.73–79: 149–50
21.75–79: 149–50
21.105: 66n. 25
21.113–17: 35–36
21.128–29: 127
21.129: 71, 157
21.131–32: 157
21.131–35: 125
21.132–33: 125
21.134: 128
21.158: 172n. 26
21.203ff.: 160
21.207: 176
21.208: 176
21.249: 41n. 40
21.281: 150
21.287: 156
21.292: 156
21.311–53: 99n. 60
21.312—13: 171
21.327: 156
21.331–33: 150
21.334–35: 156
21.336: 150
21.337: 150
21.339–42: 151
21.344–45: 152
21.344–53: 128
21.348–53: 152
21.350–53: 36, 152
21.353: 157
21.354–58: 152
21.357–58: 140
21.369–75: 128
21.369ff.: 66n. 25
21.400: 156
21.420: 156n
21.424–25: 156
21.433–34: 128
21.434: 156n
22.11: 156
22.27: 156
22.35: 156–57
22.35–40: 171–72
22.38: 172
22.63–64: 156
22.91–92: 128
23.1–24: 161

23.1–84: 160
23.21–24: 162
23.25–38: 161
23.32–33: 162
23.32–34: 161
23.39–68: 161
23.69–84: 161
23.71: 137, 174
23.83–84: 161
23.85–230: 160
23.86: 162, 175
23.87: 162
23.89: 137, 174
23.93: 175
23.95: 163
23.97: 158
23.97–98: 164
23.100: 164
23.100–103: 163
23.101–2: 176
23.103: 164
23.105: 175
23.114: 158, 178
23.117: 158
23.117–72: 167
23.122: 158
23.124–26: 168
23.133ff.: 27n. 17
23.135: 169
23.148: 169
23.148–51: 168–69
23.152: 169
23.153: 177
23.166–67: 165
23.166–72: 166
23.168: 164
23.168–70: 176
23.168–72: 164
23.169–70: 176
23.171–72: 166
23.172: 164
23.174–80: 166
23.175–76: 176
23.177: 166
23.178: 178
23.181: 178
23.183: 178
23.188–89: 178
23.189: 178
23.192: 180
23.195–96: 181

23.199: 180
23.205–6: 179
23.210–12: 190n. 49
23.213–14: 185
23.216–17: 183
23.218–24: 81, 183
23.223–24: 186
23.226: 182
23.241–88: 184
23.257ff.: 187
23.286–87: 190
23.295–96: 12
23.297–99: 184
23.302–5: 188
23.306–8: 188
23.309: 182
23.340–43: 189
23.345–46: 179
23.350: 187
23.350–53: 188
23.355: 70
24.35–97: 27
24.94: 22
24.95ff.: 69
24.96: 7, 22. 186
24.121–90: 27
24.126: 7, 31
24.127ff.: 14n. 15
24.163: 164
24.167–68: 95
24.167–69: 99n. 60
24.186ff.: 27n. 17
24.192–202: 3, 49, 52
24.194: 45
24.196: 140
24.196–97: 20–21
24.199–202: 29
24.200: 29
24.202: 28, 52
24.235–340: 163
24.321: 176

24.321ff.: 160
24.322: 176
24.331–35: 178–79
24.337–38: 179
24.386ff.: 160, 173n. 29
24.392: 160n. 7
24.392–93: 160n. 7
24.506–9: 158
24.510–12: 158
24.515: 71
24.526: 158
24.528: 158
Macrobius, *Saturnalia*
  4.6.1: 185n
Ovid, *Ars Amatoria*
  3.15ff.: 5
Pindar, fr. 100 Snell
  77n. 2
Propertius
  3.13.24: 4
Scholia in Homeri Iliadem
  9.456: 44n. 45
Scholia in Homeri Odysseam
  3.267: 44n. 43
  6.244: 136
  6.275: 136
  7.311: 136
  11.452: 52
  13.333–38: 55, 55n. 3
  13.556–57: 77
  15.19: 60
  18.160: 82, 83
  18.254: 139
  18.272: 83
  22.38: 172
  23.218: 183, 184
  23.295–96: 11–12
Seneca, *Epistuale Morales*
  88.8: 77
Servius, *In Verg. Aen. Comm*
  2.44: 77n. 3

GENERAL INDEX

Abou-Zeid, A., 174
Achilles, 7, 22–23, 27, 174. *See also* Agamemnon
achreion (18.163), 81–82, 83–84, 88–89
Aegisthus, 20, 24, 29, 30, 32, 37, 40, 42, 43, 45, 47, 49, 68, 69, 170, 172. See also *atasthalia*; House of Atreus Story
Agamemnon, 3–4, 12, 20, 22–23, 26–27, 28, 29–30, 37, 42, 43, 44, 47, 48, 49–51, 54, 56, 57, 58, 59, 68, 70, 73, 75, 164, 169, 174, 185, 186, 192, 194. *See also* House of Atreus Story; *lokhos*; *nostos*
Agelaus, 145
Alcinous, 121, 135, 144, 151, 177
Alexiou, M., 67n. 28
Allen, W. J., 101, 128
Allione, L., 30n. 23, 32, 33, 34, 36, 37, 47, 82, 83–84, 83n. 14, 89n. 34, 91n, 91–92, 93n, 107, 108, 109, 110n. 93, 111, 121, 129, 129n. 16, 139, 146, 170n. 24, 186n. 42
ambush. See *lokhos*
Ameis-Hentze, 52
Ameis-Hentze-Cauer, 21n. 2, 50, 52, 55n. 2, 56n. 4, 60, 82, 139, 142, 180, 184, 191
Amory, A., 107, 108n. 87, 108–9, 109n. 91, 110n. 93, 146, 184
Amphimedon, 3, 14n. 15, 27, 31, 95, 95n, 99n. 60, 192
Amphinomus, 74n
anagnōrismos ("recognition," "recognition-scene"), xi, 8, 97, 105, 114, 121, 126, 133, 160–64, 174; of Odysseus by Penelope, 95, 97–99, 114, 164–66, 167, 173, 175–76, 179, 181, 182, 195; of Odysseus by Telemachus, 8, 54, 114, 119, 121, 122, 126, 127, 129, 142, 160, 161–62, 174; as part of "recognition-sequence," 133; *xenia* and, 11, 162, 174, 175, 177. *See also* Dolius, Eumaeus, Eurycleia, Laertes
Andersen, Ø., 47, 79
Anticleia, 58

Antinous, 4, 6, 14n. 15, 37–38, 39, 56n. 5, 62, 73, 74, 89–90, 150, 156, 157
Apthorp, M. J., 65n. 24, 157
Arend, W., 16, 25n. 10, 88n. 32, 143n. 42, 174
Argus, 11, 154, 154n. 53
Arthur, M. B., 40, 61n, 107n. 82, 111n. 94, 112, 135, 152, 173
assemblies, on Ithaca, 4, 25, 39, 62
atasthalia ("recklessness"): moral culpability for, 23, 30, 30n, 32, 45
atē ("foolishness"), moral culpability for, 185–86
Austin, N., 11n. 11, 34, 43, 60, 66n. 25, 86n. 28, 90, 108n. 87, 109n. 89, 125, 133, 133n. 27, 136, 137, 137n. 35, 146, 148n. 47, 157, 157n, 160

Bader, F., 34, 74n, 75, 75n. 37, 170n. 23, 170n. 24, 172n. 26
basileus amumōn ("excellent king"), xi, 4, 25, 139, 144
Bassett, S. E., 40–41n. 38
Bergren, A., 11n. 11, 47, 132n. 20, 188n. 45, 189n. 48
Besslich, S., 10n. 8, 50, 51n. 55, 52n. 58, 102–3, 106–7, 166–67n. 17, 167, 167n. 18, 168, 179n. 32
Beye, C., 5–6
Biale, R., 172n. 27
Block, E., 8, 143n. 42, 174
Bona, G., 25n. 9, 89–90
Bourdieu, P., 151
bow-trial: setting of. See *toxou thesis*
"bridge-episode," 58, 59, 72–73
Büchner, W., 39n, 81–83, 83n. 14, 84, 128–29, 129n. 16, 133n. 28, 146, 169
Byre, C., 82, 83, 89n. 34, 92

Calypso, 11, 13, 98n. 58, 104
Circe, 141, 158–59
Clark, M. E., 13, 13n
Clarke, H. W., 65n. 24, 157
Clay, J., 15, 21, 26n. 13, 30n. 23, 32n. 29, 33n. 31, 55–56, 170, 170n. 24

Clytemnestra, 4, 7, 8, 21, 24, 28, 37, 43, 45, 46, 49, 51, 53, 54, 59, 61, 75, 80, 119, 127, 130, 132, 134, 160, 164, 185, 186, 192; bard as guardian of, 44, 44n. 43, 45; guilt of, 29, 43–46, 49–53, 164, 192; hateful song as *kleos* of, 6, 24, 28, 194; Helen and, 8, 51, 192; Penelope and, 4, 5, 24, 28, 45, 51, 52, 53, 58, 60, 63, 80, 119–29, 130, 132, 134, 153, 164, 166, 169, 186, 192, 193, 194; Penelope and Helen and, 54, 80, 185. *See also* House of Atreus Story
Colakis, M., 83n. 14
Combellack, F. M., 92, 94–95, 100
Ctessipus, 124, 150, 170, 171
Cunliffe, R. J., 172

D'Arms, E. F., and K. K. Hulley, 27n. 17, 30
Davis, N. Z., 156
Delebecque, E., 59, 59n. 14, 104n. *See also* "bridge-episode"
Devereux, G., 109n. 90, 146, 184
Dietz, G., 186n. 43
Dimock, G. E., 107
disguise, 8, 9, 9n. 6, 10, 74, 79, 114–15, 120, 127, 128, 129, 141, 153–54, 155–59, 176, 187, 189–90, 192–93, 194
Dolius: recognition of Odysseus by, 160, 160n. 7, 173n. 29
dolos, doloi ("trick"), xi, 10, 21, 23–24, 25, 27, 125, 164. See also *mētis*; Penelope, *dolos* and *mētis* of
Duchamp, M., *Large Glass* by, 194–95
Dupont-Roc, R. and A. Le Boulluec, 47, 79

Echeneus, 137, 137n. 37
Edwards, A. T., 6, 21, 22, 23, 26n. 13, 46, 63, 65n. 24, 66, 66n. 26, 73, 121
Edwards, M., 16–17n. 23, 69, 107, 107n. 82, 143n. 42, 174
Eisenberger, H., 14n. 14, 28, 30n. 23, 31, 32n. 27, 33n. 32, 34, 42n, 49, 59n. 14, 75n. 35, 83, 89n. 34, 90n. 39, 102, 106, 121, 129n. 16, 134, 154, 167
Emlyn-Jones, C., 17n. 25, 22, 75n. 38, 132n. 22, 133, 133n. 26, 181
epiklēros ("heiress"), 61n
Erbse, H., 8, 55, 57, 58, 75n. 35, 85, 90, 99n. 60, 106, 108, 110n. 93, 121, 129n. 16, 133n. 28, 160n. 6, n. 8, 165, 166, 167, 169, 179n. 32, 187n
erethizō ("provoke"), 131, 131n. 19, 178
Erinyes, 39, 140n, 149
ethical aspect of *Odyssey*, 14n. 17, 16, 32–33, 94, 96, 97n. 54, 98, 98n. 58, 99, 100, 170–72. See also *atasthalia*; *atē*
Eumaeus, 9n. 6, 58, 62, 71, 105, 121, 122, 125, 127, 132, 138, 143n. 41, 144, 160, 170, 171, 172, 173, 174, 176; and Philoetius, recognition of Odysseus by, 160, 173, 174
Eurycleia, 93, 124, 133–34, 138, 160–62, 164, 165–66, 167, 169, 173, 174, 176, 176n. 31, 178, 182n; recognition of Odysseus by, 174
Eurymachus, 4, 5, 37, 38, 60, 123, 130, 131, 134, 139, 150, 157
Eurynome, 81, 86, 87, 88, 93, 129, 138

Farron, S. G., 23n. 6
Felson-Rubin, N., 10, 22, 93n, 109n. 91, 111–12, 112n. 96, 119n. 4, 184
Fenik, B., 11n. 11, 13n, 17, 17n. 24, 27n. 15, 30n. 23, 32n. 29, 47–48, 59n. 14, 71, 75n. 35, 84–85, 85n. 17, 89n. 34, 102, 103–4, 105, 132n. 21, 132n. 22, 134, 157, 167, 167n. 18, 170, 170n. 24
Fernández-Galiano, A., 182n
Ferrucci, F., 10
Finkelberg, M., 26n. 13
Finley, J. H., Jr., 26, 26n. 13, 60, 85, 107, 108, 121, 146
Finley, M. I., 35, 35n, 41, 41n. 39
Floyd, E., 26n. 13
Focke, F., 57, 64, 92, 103, 133n. 28, 190–91
Foley, H., 148n. 47, 160, 173
foolishness. See *atasthalia*
Forsyth, N., 79n, 86, 137, 149n. 50
Frame, D., 27n. 16

Gaisser, J., 16–17n. 23, 17n. 24
gamos ("institution of marriage"), xi; *xenia* and, 114–15, 134–37, 154, 177
geras ("power," "privilege"), xi, 41, 41n. 40, 73, 130
Gernet, L., 61n
Goldhill, S., 68n. 30, 78n, 154n. 53
Golding, J., 194, 194n. 2
goos ("lamentation"): opposed to *thrēnos*

("public lamentation"), 67–68; Penelope's, 140–41; Telemachus's, 67–68, 140, 141
Gould, J., 135, 137, 150, 174
Griffin, J., 44n. 45, 159
Groten, F. J., 40
guardianship. See *kyrieia*
guest-friendship. See *xenia*
Gunn, D. M., 16n. 23

Hainsworth, B., 136, 151
Hansen, W. F., 17n. 24, 33n. 30, 65
Harrison, A.R.W., 35, 39
Harsh, P. W., 10, 108n. 87, 110, 110n. 93, 111, 146
Hector, 7, 22; and Andromache, 152, 173
Helen, 7, 8, 61, 62, 63, 71, 75, 76, 80, 119–20, 130, 132, 133, 160, 179, 185–86, 192; Aristotle on abduction of, 39–40; Clytemnestra and, 8, 51, 192; Clytemnestra and Penelope and, 54, 70, 185; and the *Iliad*, 40, 142, 179, 187–88; Penelope and, 12, 61, 62, 63, 75–76, 79, 80, 81, 119–20, 130, 132, 133, 134, 153, 183–87, 192, 193, 194; prophecy of, 71, 71–72n; stories of, at Troy, 46–47, 61–62, 75–76, 78–80, 132, 132n. 20, 155, 187–88, 192; *xenia* and, 54. See also Telemachus
Heubeck, A., 13, 13n, 21, 27n. 16, 29, 50, 51n. 55, 170n. 24, 179n. 32, 180n. 34, 187n
Hoekstra, A., 55n. 1, 58, 58–59n. 13, 59, 75n. 35
Hölscher, U., 15, 28, 29–30, 48, 52, 86, 87, 91, 105–6, 108, 121, 132, 155, 159–60, 163n
homecoming. See *nostos*
homilia ("conversation"): between Penelope and Odysseus in Book 19, xi, 14n. 15, 17, 25, 26, 97, 102, 103, 104, 105, 114, 115, 117, 130, 132–34, 137–38, 148; *xenia* and 134, 137–38, 144–45, 147–48, 154, 174. See also Penelope, dream of
homophrosynē ("like-mindedness"): between Odysseus and Penelope, 11, 148, 159–60, 173, 177, 182; complementarity and, 162–66, 182, 187
honor and shame, code of, 150
hospitality. See *xenia*

host. See *xeinodokos*
House of Atreus Story, 6–7, 8, 18, 20, 27, 27n. 15, 28, 29, 30, 33, 36, 41, 42–45, 46–53, 58, 61, 66–67, 68, 69, 72, 74, 78, 119, 127, 130, 155, 163, 192; summary of occurrences of, 42; variants of, 48–49
household. See *oikos*
Houston, G. W., 143n. 42, 156

ideology of exclusivity, 12, 33, 113, 160, 162, 170, 172–73, 182, 193
indeterminacy, 5, 7, 8, 11, 12, 18–19, 31, 84, 88, 93, 94, 113, 119–20, 155, 159, 165, 174, 186–87, 190–91, 192–95. See also disguise
interpretation, 12–18; aesthetic, 94, 100, 101, 105, 106, 108, 109, 113, 114; analytic, 13, 85, 87, 91, 93, 96–99, 103, 109, 110, 112, 113, 114, 166, 170, 193; audience-response, 17n. 26; feminist, 10, 109n. 91, 110, 111–12, 119; neoanalytic, 13, 13–16, 109, 166–68; neounitarian, 13, 15, 16, 86; oral-formulaic, 13, 16–17; psychological, 86, 87, 93, 94, 100, 102, 106–10, 109n. 90, 113, 114, 184–85, 187; unitarian, 10, 13, 14, 15, 17, 85, 87, 90, 93–94, 104, 106–10, 113, 114, 125, 166–68, 170, 193

Jacobson, H., 5n. 2, 77, 77n. 2, 186, 186n. 43
Jones, P., 64, 65n. 24, 125, 157

Kakridis, H., 123, 125, 148
Kakridis, J., 78, 79, 181, 181–82
Kearns, E., 11n. 11, 161n, 170n. 23
Kennedy, G., 188n. 45
Kessels, A.H.M., 146, 146n. 44, n. 45, 147n
Kirchhoff, A., 31, 60, 183
Kirk, G. S., 38, 78, 94, 95, 100
kleos ("renown"), xi, 3–6; and celebration in song, 6, 7, 20, 24–25, 28, 29, 186, 187–89, 188–89n. 47; death in battle and, 7, 64, 68, 69; *dolos* and, 23–24; etymology of, 6; grief and, 68; *mētis* and, 4, 5, 6; *nostos* and, 3, 20, 22–23, 63, 69–70, 121, 140, 188, 192; Odyssean versus Iliadic, 6–7, 21–22, 26, 27, 187–88; revenge and, 63; and *xenia* and, 121, 125, 143–

kleos (cont.)
   44. *See also* Clytemnestra; Odysseus; Penelope; Telemachus
kleos aphthiton, 26, 26n. 13
Klingner, F., 31n. 24, 33n. 32, 34, 47, 65, 80
Kullmann, W., 13, 13n, 14, 15, 25n. 9
Kunst, K., 28, 44, 44n, 45, 45n, 48
Kurtz, J. G., 146
kyrieia ("guardianship"), xi, 9, 35, 35n. 34, 35–39, 40, 40n, 45, 69, 70, 152. *See also* Clytemnestra, bard as guardian of; *kyrios*; Mentor
kyrios ("lord and master"), xi, 174. See also *kyrieia*; Odysseus; Telemachus; *xeinos*

Lacey, W. K., 35
Laertes, 9n. 6, 11, 45, 58, 71, 142, 157, 160, 163, 176, 178–80; recognition of Odysseus by, 142, 160
lamentation. See *goos*
lamentation, and song, 68, 68n. 29
Lang, H., 181, 181n
Lattimore, R., 79
Leodes, 150
Lesky, A., 28, 44, 44n. 44, 48, 49
Levine, D., 83n. 14, 84, 89, 131n. 18, 170n. 23
Levy, H., 170n. 23
lokhos ("ambush"), xi, 29, 30, 44, 46, 47, 48, 54, 73; of Telemachus, 25, 30, 46, 47, 48, 59, 72–74, 82–83, 172
Loraux, N., 22
Lord, A., 16, 16n. 23

MacDowell, D., 60n. 16
Mackail, J. W., 25–26n. 11
Mactoux, M., 5n. 2, 186n. 43
Marquardt, P., 10, 22, 111–12, 184–85
marriage: institution of. See *gamos*; fictional (= "Wedding Digression"), 166–70
marriage-system: ancient Greek, 35, 41, 60–61, 60n. 16, 61n, 87, 87–88n. 30, 136n. 34, 140n, 149, 168, 172, 174. See also *epiklēros*; *kyrieia*; Penelope, status of
Martin, R., 26n. 13
Martin Guerre, Return of, 156
Matsumoto, N., 28
Medon, 138
Melantho, 130–32, 134

Menelaus, 43, 46–48, 67–69, 75, 76, 79, 80, 104, 132n. 20
Mentor: as guardian of Penelope, 38, 40–41n, 41, 45
Merkelbach, R., 31, 57, 57n. 7, 85, 86n. 26, 90, 98–99, 99n. 59, 100, 106, 110n. 93, 159
mētis ("crafty intelligence"), xi, 4, 5, 6, 10, 21, 23–24, 25, 139, 164, 168. *See also* Penelope, *dolos* and *mētis* of
Miller, J. H., 193
Mishnah: *agunah* ("bound woman") in, 172, 172n. 27
misogyny, 28–29, 51, 58, 112, 194
mnēsterophonia ("slaughter of the suitors"), 27, 36–37, 68; and *lokhos*, 73
Monro, D. B., 39, 60n. 16, 137n. 38, 159, 172, 184
Monsacré, H., 107n. 82
Mossé, C., 35, 35n, 41n. 40
Müller, M., 26, 88n. 32, 126n. 18, 161n, 177
Murnaghan, S., 7n. 5, 9n, 10, 11n. 10, 11n. 11, 17n. 25, 22, 28–29, 58, 61n, 65, 67n. 28, 68, 68n. 29, 70, 84, 93n, 109, 110n. 93, 112, 112n. 97, n. 98, 119n. 4, 126, 133, 134, 136n. 33, 148, 155, 159, 160, 161, 173, 173n. 29, 175, 177, 182n, 185, 188–89n. 47

Naerebout, F. G., 35n
Nagler, M., 17, 79, 137, 149n. 50
Nagy, G., 4, 6, 21, 22, 24, 26n. 13, 27n. 16, 28, 29, 63, 66, 67, 67n. 28, 68, 68n. 29, 69, 86–87
Nausicaa, 11, 86n. 28, 114–15, 136–37, 137n. 35, n. 36, 174; and Penelope, 86–87, 141
nekyia ("scene in the underworld"), xi, 3, 20, 26, 27, 48–53, 54, 70, 95, 95n, 164
nēpios ("infant"), 126n. 14
Nestor, 42–45, 48, 59
niptra ("foot-bath"), 85, 95, 132–33, 145, 162, 174
Nortwick, T. van, 86n. 28, 86–87, 106n. 78, 109, 137, 137n. 36, 182n
nostos (homecoming), xi, 7, 20, 27, 34, 60, 78, 114, 192; epic tradition and, 7, 21–22, 27, 27n. 16, 46, 52, 186; *kleos* and, 3, 20, 22–23, 63, 69–70, 121, 140, 188,

INDEX   221

192; *kyrieia* and, 70; of Odysseus, 8, 20, 59, 70, 72, 75; *xenia* and, 8, 54, 74–76, 134, 155

O'Hara, J., 143n. 41
Odysseus: absence of, from first books, 20, 68; arrival on Ithaca, 55; as *kyrios*, 41, 126, 152, 156–57, 168; disguise of, 8, 79, 127, 153–54, 159; distrust of Penelope, 55–58; *kleos* of, 20, 21, 24–25, 29, 64, 192; lying-tales of, 8, 73, 131, 178; as *xeinodokos*, 142; as *xeinos*, 8, 54, 74–76, 116, 121, 137, 147–48, 150–51, 156–57, 161, 175–76, 193. See also *anagnôrismos*; *homilia*; *homophrosynê*; House of Atreus Story; *nostros*; Telemachus
oikos ("household"), xi, 135, 142, 177, 180. See also *nostos*
Olson, D., 80n. 6, 132n. 20, 133n. 29
Onians, R. B., 88n. 31
Orestes: as model for Telemachus, 27n. 15, 29, 34, 36, 37, 42–45, 47, 51, 65–66, 66n. 26, 66–67, 68–69, 127. *See also* House of Atreus Story

Page, D., 31, 38, 58, 59, 59n. 14, 60, 90, 167
Pandareus: daughters of, 145, 145n, 149
parainesis ("[Athena's] advice [to Telemachus]"). *See* Telemachus
Pedrick, V., 143n. 42, 174, 175
Pedrick, V. and N. Rabinowitz, 17n. 26
Penelope, 20; ancient traditions about, 77, 186; appearance before the suitors, 78–93, 97, 98, 99n. 60, 102–3, 105, 111, 115–18, 120, 130, 139; character of, 10, 93n, 94–112, 119, 144, 193; Clytemnestra and, 4, 5, 24, 28, 45, 51, 52, 53, 58, 60, 63, 80, 119–20, 130, 132, 134, 153, 164, 166, 169, 186, 192, 193, 194; *dolos* and *mêtis* of, 4, 6, 7, 10, 21, 24, 84, 110, 128–30, 148; dream of, 102, 109, 114, 115, 117, 132, 145–47; Helen and, 12, 61, 62, 63, 75–76, 79, 80, 81, 119–20, 130, 132, 133, 134, 153, 183–87, 192, 193, 194; Helen and Clytemnestra and, 54, 80, 185; House of Atreus Story and, 30, 48–53; indeterminacy of, 7, 12, 18–19, 88, 159, 186–87, 190; *kleos* of, 4–6, 12, 20–21, 21n. 2, 24–29, 39, 64, 139–40, 144, 159, 165, 169, 186, 187,

192, 193–95; *kyrieia* of, 9, 35n. 34, 35–39, 40, 40n, 45, 69, 70; moral autonomy of, 9, 40–41, 129, 150; narrative role of, as form of disguise, 9–10; paradigms for, 52, 54, 62, 63, 92–93, 153, 162–63, 186, 192, 193; remarriage of, as betrayal, 59–60, 61, 62, 147, 153, 162, 169, 192; status of, 7, 41, 41n. 40, 112, 150, 153, 159; weaving-trick of, 4, 5, 10, 14, 24–25, 88; as *xeinodokos*, 9, 138, 141–42, 142–45, 150–51, 177, 193; as *xeinos*, 9, 153, 175–76, 193. See also *anagnôrismos*; *goos*; *homilia*; *homophrosynê*; marriage-system; Mentor; Nausicaa; *toxou thesis*
Peradotto, J., 11, 11n. 12, 16, 29n. 20, 187, 191
Petersmann, H., 15n. 20, 16, 29n. 20
Pitt-Rivers, J., 60n. 16, 135, 151, 174
Platt, A., 185
Pucci, P., 8, 9, 10, 11n. 10, 21, 22, 23, 24n. 8, 25, 26–27, 68n. 29, 88, 88n. 31, n. 32, 155, 165n. 13, 168, 176, 188n. 46, 189, 190

Qviller, B., 35n

Rankin, A., 146
recognition, recognition-scene. *See anagnôrismos*
Redfield, J., 24, 67, 87–88n. 30, 149, 150
Reinhardt, K., 11n. 10, 14, 14n. 17, 16, 25, 26n. 12, 32, 83n. 12
renown. *See kleos*
revenge. *See tisis*
Richardson, N. J., 75n. 38, 133n. 28
Robertson, M., 87–88n. 30
Roisman, H., 124, 175–76n. 30, 184, 185
Russo, J., xi, 6, 55n. 1, 81–82, 84, 89, 108n. 87, 108–9, 109n. 90, 110n. 93, 123n. 10, 127, 129, 131n. 19, 132n. 21, 137n. 38, 145, 145n. 43, 146, 149, 150, 151
Rüter, K., 22, 23, 65

Said, S., 170n. 23
Schadewaldt, W., 14n. 14, 32, 32n. 28, 72, 87n. 29, 88n. 33, 89n. 34, 120n, 143n. 42, 160, 160n. 8, 166, 166–67n. 17, 167, 170, 170n. 24, 173, 183–84

Schwartz, E., 94, 97n. 51, n. 54, n. 55, 97–98, 98n. 58, 99n. 61, 100
Schwarz, A., 194n. 2
Segal, C., 21, 22, 23, 24, 25, 27n. 17, 137, 153n, 168, 174, 188–89n. 47
sēma, sēmata (sign[s]), xii, 103n. 73, 108–9, 115, 116, 161n. 9, 182, 182n; bed as, 164, 165–66, 176, 177, 178–82, 190; clothing as, 141; orchard-trees as, 178–79, 182, 184; scar as, 161, 178–79, 182
Shakespeare, W., *Troilus and Cressida* by, 193–94
sign. See *sēma*
Snell, B., 88n. 31
Snodgrass, A. M., 35n
Stanford, W. B., 28, 50, 56, 137n. 38, 184, 191
Starobinski, J., 155n, 176–77, 178, 180n. 36, 181
Sternberg, M., 18n. 27
Stewart, D., 110n. 93, 155n
stranger. See *xeinos*
Suerbaum, W., 7, 25
suitors: crimes of, 42, 74n, 121, 151, 170–72, 170n. 23. See also *atasthalia*; ethical aspect of *Odyssey*

Telegony, 158–59
Telemachus, 9, 13, 20, 31, 58, 59, 88, 93, 103, 104, 116, 125, 173; and Athena's *parainesis*, xi, 33–39, 58, 60, 66, 69, 70; disguise of, 9, 9n. 6, 157–59; and Helen, 71, 133; *kleos* of, 36, 37, 41, 63–72, 121, 125, 126; as *kyrios*, 9, 33–34, 35, 36–39, 61, 63, 69, 70, 71, 73–74, 114, 127, 128, 129, 145, 151–52, 154, 157, 158–59; *nostos* and *kleos* of, 70; and Odysseus, 9, 33, 54, 65–66, 71, 126, 127, 128, 131, 157–58, 174; and Orestes, 27n. 15, 29, 34, 36, 37, 42–45, 47, 51, 65–66, 66n. 26, 66–67, 68–69, 127; as *xeinodokos*, 8, 121, 122, 123–25, 126, 128, 135, 143, 153. See also *anagnōrismos; goos*; House of Atreus Story; *lokhos*, Telemachy
Telemachy, 31–32, 47, 48, 68, 91, 91n. 96
telos ("end"), xii, 7–8, 11, 12, 126, 126n. 15, 129, 152, 153, 190
Thalmann, W. G., 21n. 2, 23n. 5, 68n. 29, 187, 189, 189n. 48
Theoclymenus, 74–75, 75n. 35, 116, 116n. 117, 122

Thornton, A., 13, 16–17n. 23, 41n. 39, 41n. 40, 58, 68n. 25, 82, 85, 102, 103, 104, 106, 121, 132n. 22, 133, 134n. 30, 155, 160n. 5
thymos ("heart"), 88
tisis ("revenge"), xii, 63, 72, 98–99, 121, 126, 156
toxou thesis ("setting of bow trial"), xii, 3, 25n. 9, 35, 78, 80, 92, 93, 94–95, 99n. 60, 100, 103, 106–7, 109, 111, 112, 112n. 98, 114, 115, 116, 117, 118, 132, 141, 147, 149–50, 152
trick, trickiness. See *dolos*
Tsagarakis, O., 16–17n. 23, 143n. 42, 174

uncertainty. See indeterminacy
Underworld: scenes in. See *nekyia*
Untersteiner, M., 21

Vallillee, G., 136
Van der Valk, M. H. A. L. H., 101–2
Vernant, J.-P., 22, 35, 35n, 41n. 40, 61n, 135, 136n. 34, 180, 180n. 35
Vester, H., 11n. 9, 85, 99n. 60, 103, 106, 106n. 77, 110, 110n. 93, 119, 132–33, 132n. 21, 146, 148, 154

Walcot, P., 8, 111n. 94
Walsh, G., 68n. 29
weaving-trick. See Penelope
Wegner, J. R., 172n. 27
Wehrli, F., 62–63, 70n. 31
Wender, D., 27n. 14, 28, 164n. 11
West, S., xi, 7n. 4, 30n. 23, 35n, 38n, 41, 44n. 43, 62–63, 123n. 10, 126n. 13, 140n, 151, 170, 172
Wilamowitz-Moellendorff, U. von, 14, 15, 57, 58n. 12, 85, 85n. 21, 87n. 29, 88n. 31, 92, 94, 95, 95n. 96, 98, 99, 99n. 64, 100, 107–8, 110n. 92, 114, 125, 183
Winkler, J., 10, 22, 110, 110n. 93, 111, 111n. 94, 129, 146, 148
Woodhouse, W. J., 94, 101, 102, 108, 136

xeineion ("gift of guest-friendship"), xii, 150–51, 151n, 174
xeinodokos ("host"), xii, 8, 125, 142. See also Odysseus; Penelope; Telemachus
xeinos ("stranger"), xii, 135, 171; relation to *kyrios*, 151, 156, 174–75, 177. See also

Odysseus; Penelope
xenia (hospitality), xii, 8, 26, 134–35, 142, 151, 174–75; and *anagnōrismos*, 11, 162, 174, 175, 177; and *gamos*, 114–15, 134–37, 154, 177; and Helen, 54; and *kleos*, 121, 125, 143–44; and *nostos*, 8, 54, 74–76, 134, 155. See also *homilia*

Zagagi, N., 40
Zeitlin, F., 47, 79–80

GPSR Authorized Representative: Easy Access System Europe - Mustamäe tee 50, 10621 Tallinn, Estonia, gpsr.requests@easproject.com